Economic Valuation of the Environment

Economic Valuation of the Environment

Methods and Case Studies

Guy Garrod

Lecturer in Environmental Economics and Countryside Management, Department of Agricultural Economics and Food Marketing, University of Newcastle upon Tyne, UK

Kenneth G. Willis

Professor of Environmental Economics, Department of Town and Country Planning, University of Newcastle upon Tyne, UK

Edward Elgar
Cheltenham, UK • Northampton, MA, USA

Published by
Edward Elgar Publishing Limited
Glensanda House
Montpellier Parade
Cheltenham
Glos GL50 1UA
UK

Edward Elgar Publishing, Inc.
6 Market Street
Northampton
Massachusetts 01060
USA

A catalogue record for this book
is available from the British Library

Library of Congress Cataloguing in Publication Data

Garrod, Guy
    Economic valuation of the environment : methods and case studies /
    Guy Garrod, Kenneth G. Willis
    Includes bibliographical references.
    1. Environmental economics. 2. Environmental auditing.
  I. Willis, K. G. (Kenneth George) II. Title.
  HD75.6.G384 1999
  333.7—dc21   98–46614
                                              CIP

ISBN 1 85898 684 2

Printed and bound in Great Britain by Biddles Ltd, Guildford and King's Lynn

Contents

Figures		*vii*
Tables		*ix*
Preface		*xiii*

PART ONE: INTRODUCTION

1.	Introduction	3

PART TWO: REVEALED PREFERENCE TECHNIQUES

2.	Market Price and Cost Measures of Value	17
3.	The Travel-Cost Method	55
4.	The Hedonic Price Method	87

PART THREE: EXPRESSED PREFERENCE TECHNIQUES

5.	Contingent Valuation Methods	125
6.	Discrete Choice Methods	187

PART FOUR: CASE EXAMPLES

7.	Recreation	225
8.	Landscape	239
9.	Biodiversity	263
10.	Water Quality	289
11.	Amenity Values	311

PART FIVE: POLICY USE AND DECISION MAKING

12.	Benefit Transfer	331
13.	Policy Implications and Conclusions	359

Index		*373*

Figures

1.1	Environmental valuation methods	6
2.1	Measures of amenity value under a replacement or restoration cost scenario	42
2.2	Comparison of benefit measures when the defensive expenditure function is linear	46
4.1	Change in property value with increasing environmental quality	89
4.2	Change in marginal property value with improvement in environmental quality	90
5.1	Total value of changes in the provision of an environmental good	129
A5.2.1	Determining optimum level of environmental quality	184
A5.2.2	Determining optimum level of public goods: the free-rider case	184
8.1	Problems with the hedonic price method	244
8.2	Future landscapes in the Yorkshire Dales	between 258 & 259
9.1	Example of combinations used in the contingent ranking exercise	276
10.1	An example of a choice experiment card	294

Tables

1.1	Benefits provided by some public goods	11
2.1	Estimated change in the stocking rate due to the successful implementation of the ESA in the Somerset Levels and Moors	23
2.2	Financial (EOP), public exchequer, and social opportunity cost (SOC) of livestock output in the UK	31
2.3	Effect on production (EOP), social opportunity cost (SOC), and travel-cost model (TCM) values of nature conservation at three SSSIs in Yorkshire	31
A2.1.1	Idarado mine case: plaintiff's natural resource damage estimates	52
A2.1.2	Idarado mine case: defendant's natural resource damage estimates	53
3.1	Comparison of ZTCM and ITCM consumer surplus for six forests	63
3.2	Impact on estimated consumer surplus of alternative travel-cost specifications	71
3.3	The value of goose-hunting permits	74
3.4	Comparison of travel-cost and contingent valuation estimates of water quality improvement benefits	74
5.1	Disparities between WTP and WTA	127

5.2   Mean value estimates of welfare measures for hockey
           ticket experiment   131

5.3   Sample sizes for given levels of precision in CV surveys   139

5.4   Comparison of simulated and hypothetical market
           results: the Wisconsin Horicon goose-hunting
           experiment   145

5.5   Comparison of simulated and hypothetical market
           results: the Wisconsin Sandhill area in Wood County
           deer-hunting experiment   147

5.6   Comparison of actual and predicted decisions of
           households to connect to potable water supplies in
           Kerala, India   149

5.7   Consumer surplus estimates of recreational boating at
           four lakes using CVM and TCM   151

5.8   Bayesian representation matrix   161

5.9   Estimated price elasticity of demand for some outdoor
           recreational activities   171

5.10   Estimated income elasticities of demand for selected
           recreational goods   172

5.11   Cumulative long-run price elasticity of demand for
           outdoor recreation
                                                                          172

5.12   Contingent valuation estimates of the value of the
           Newcastle green belt   174

A5.1.1   Show card to elicit legitimate and illegitimate reason for
           not being WTP towards an environmental good   182

A5.1.2   Show card to elicit legitimate and illegitimate reason for
           being willing to pay towards an environmental good   182

7.1   Maximum likelihood estimates for Jeram Linang FRA   229

7.2	Comparison of CV and ITCM results	230
8.1	Landscape preferences for visitors and residents of the Yorkshire Dales	249
8.2	Aggregate WTP for first preference landscapes by visitors and residents and estimated public sector costs of each landscape	250
8.3	Estimated value function of ESA programme attributes in the Pennine Dales	253
8.4	Estimates of mean WTP for different landscape conservation schemes in the Pennine Dales ESA	254
8.5	Estimates of the sequential value of each programme or group of programmes in the Pennine Dales ESA when added to different combinations of programmes	256
9.1	Results of the contingent ranking experiment	278
9.2	CR model of forest biodiversity standards	279
9.3	Further specifications of the CR choice model	281
10.1	Attribute coefficients in basic choice experiment model	297
10.2	Attribute coefficients in extended choice experiment model	297
10.3	Coefficients of alternative specific variables in extended choice experiment model	298
10.4	Willingness to pay for marginal improvement in water quality	299
10.5	Median welfare estimates of CVM scenario	300
10.6	Estimated number of visitors to low flow rivers from south west	301
10.7	User and non-user populations for low flow rivers from the south west	302

10.8   Marginal WTP for unit reduction in length of low flow
         rivers in south west by user and non-user populations   302

10.9   Approximate aggregate annual benefits for improving
         low flows across the entire length of all low flow rivers
         in the south west   303

10.10   Net present value of aggregate benefits for improving
         low flows across the entire length of all low flow rivers
         in the south west   304

10.11   Recreational attributes offered in stated preference
         choice cards   306

10.12   Selected attribute coefficient values from choice
         experiment model   307

10.13   Selected attribute coefficient values from revealed
         preference model   308

11.1   Premium added to house prices by proximity to canals
         based on a hedonic price study   316

11.2   Premium added to house prices by proximity to canals
         based on a contingent valuation study of estate agents   317

11.3   Statistically significant landscape and amenity variables   321

11.4   Premium offered by proximity to landscape and other
         amenities   322

11.5   Estimated coefficient values and implicit prices from
         hedonic price model   325

13.1   Enumeration and method of evaluation of items in COBA   361

Preface

This book arose out of courses taught over many years to masters and undergraduate degree students in the Department of Agricultural Economics and Food Marketing, and the Department of Town and Country Planning, at the University of Newcastle upon Tyne. The contents of the book have also been enhanced by the authors' practical experience of investigating a range of environmental valuation issues gained through projects financed by research grants and contracts awarded by such organisations as the Economic and Social Science Research Council (ESRC), British Waterways, Department of the Environment, Transport and the Regions, Department for International Development, Environment Agency, English Nature, Forestry Commission, and the Ministry of Agriculture, Fisheries and Food.

Our insights into environmental valuation have also been enhanced over the years from our discussions with eminent environmental economists including Vic Adamowicz, Ian Bateman, Nancy Bockstael, Michael Hanemann, David Pearce, Colin Price, Ivor Strand, Kerry Turner, and Dick Walsh, amongst others. We are particularly indebted to Colin Price for permission to reproduce Figure 8.1; to Tim O'Riordan for permission to reproduce the paintings (Figure 8.2) he commissioned from Hannah Chesterman for his ESRC study of future landscapes in the Yorkshire Dales in conjunction with the Yorkshire Dales National Park Authority; and to Richard Walsh who kindly agreed to allow us to use abstracts of tabular material (Table 5.11) from his excellent book on *Recreation Economic Decisions: comparing benefits and costs* published in 1986, and to abstract material for Tables 5.9 and 5.10 from John B. Loomis and Richard G. Walsh (1997) *Recreation Economic Decisions: comparing benefits and costs*, both published by Venture Publishing Inc., State College, Pennsylvania. Excepts from the *Diary of a Church Mouse* by John Betjeman from his *Collected Poems* are produced by kind permission of John Murray (Publishers) Ltd.; *Leisure* by William Henry Davies by kind permission of Jonathan Cape, London, and Henry Holt and Company Inc., New York; *The Road Not Taken* by Robert Frost by kind permission of his Estate, editor Edward Connery Latham, and Jonathan Cape (Publishers) Ltd. *Counting* and *Money* from *Collected Poems*

Scientific insights usually start as qualitative inspirations which are subsequently reformulated into scientific theories and testable hypotheses. Similarly, insights into social phenomenon do not necessarily have their origins in the minds of economic theorists! Throughout history the work of writers and poets has encapsulated the beauty of nature and succinctly commented on social phenomenon, providing an additional reason to blend science and the arts, and serving to lighten economics as a science. Johann Wolfgang von Goethe (1749-1832) once wrote "One ought every day at least to hear a little song, read a good poem, see a fine picture . . . and if it were at all possible . . . to speak a few reasonable words". This book provides no songs, but we have included a few lines of poetry to commence each chapter and some evocative representations of Yorkshire Dales landscapes - we hope too that this book contains some reasonable words and ideas. Each poem we quote from is worth reading in its entirety both for its literary quality and for the observations it makes on the issue addressed in the respective chapters.

We believe that the rigorous application of environmental valuation techniques can make an important contribution to government policy formulation and analysis, and result in better resource allocations and outcomes in the protection and development of natural resources. To this end we trust that the application of the ideas contained in the book will help to eliminate or at least reduce our species' ability to make decisions that lead to environmental damage and degradation and that we are no longer *"reasoning but to err; Sole judge of truth in endless error hurled"* (Alexander Pope (1688-1744) *Know Then Thyself*).

Guy Garrod

Ken Willis

Newcastle upon Tyne: November 1998

PART ONE

Introduction

1. Introduction

For the Snark's a peculiar creature, that won't
Be caught in a commonplace way.
Do all that you know; and try all that you don't:
Not a chance must be wasted to-day!

Lewis Carroll (1832–1898): *The Hunting of the Snark*

1 INTRODUCTION

The protection of the environment has emerged as a one of the principal concerns of the latter half of the 20th century, and is likely to increasingly dominate the political agenda at the beginning of the third millennium. Continual growth in production, a perceived set of finite resources, the emergence of new technologies, the discovery of new pollutants, and the increasing recognition of the trans-national nature and value of some environmental resources, are just some of the factors generating concern for particular environments.[1] Advances in technology have reshaped property rights over the environment. Goods previously considered as 'public goods', such as satellite television, have become private goods as new technology has enabled broadcasting companies, to exclude viewers, thus allowing a price to

---

[1] Ecological doom has been predicted since Malthus in 1798 argued that population increased geometrically whilst food supply increased arithmetically. Subsequent predictions of ecological doom (e.g., Britain's coal reserves would be exhausted in a few years (1865); US oil reserves would run out in 13 years (1939 and again in 1951); exhaustion of minerals such as tungsten, tin, nickel, copper, and chrome (1980); desertification of land in Africa (1984); the effects of AIDS, Ebola virus, etc. on mortality rates; etc.) have all been proved to be wrong. One of the few correct predictions was that DDT would effectively eradicate birds of prey unless it was controlled. Yet people continue to peddle ecological and environmental catastrophes, on the grounds that they believe one will occur sometime, despite being wrong in the past (The Economist, 1997).

3

be charged for the consumption of the good (through consumers requiring decoders to receive signals).

In the past many environmental problems were regarded as local and straightforward. They were seen as being easily regulated by elementary command-and-control (CAC) instruments. Now, more environmental problems have come to be recognised as having greater complexity than previously thought, with wider impacts than first-round or local effects. However, evolving technology and greater willingness to experiment with more integrative, complex, and comprehensive control mechanisms, has resulted in the development of more successful systems of environmental regulation. Market-based approaches to environmental regulation have increasingly emerged in the latter part of the century, partly as a consequence of a shift from socialist to market philosophy, and also because technology has permitted the adoption and implementation of market mechanisms.

Market mechanisms will only be successful if they reflect the preferences of citizens as individuals, both nationally and internationally. In terms of environmental assessment questions arise such as: how can we identify individuals affected by an environmental issue, and how can we assess the direction and strength of their preferences over such issues? Environmental economics has made considerable progress over the last half century in devising methods that attempt to quantify the strength of preferences for various environmental amenities, and to identify and define the extent of the market (people) affected by environmental changes.

A considerable amount of work has been undertaken on evaluating the costs of various environmental policies and projects. The costs of environmental protection are quite large for some environmental programmes. However, much less is known about the economic benefits produced by environmental policies. Environmental valuation of the benefits of policy change is thus extremely important. Environmental valuation attempts to quantify the benefits of environmental projects and policies, so that they are more transparent, and can be given due and appropriate weight in any decision-making process or cost-benefit analysis.

2 ENVIRONMENTAL VALUATION TECHNIQUES

Society must choose the quantity of environmental goods it wishes to conserve or produce *vis-à-vis* other goods and services; and within this set of goods it must also select the desired quantity and quality of different environmental resources. Choices logically imply some form of valuation. A number of techniques are available to value environmental goods in economic terms. Figure 1.1 documents these techniques and illustrates how they are related. Methods to value the environment can be broadly divided, following

Turner *et al.* (1994), into two categories: those which value a commodity via a demand curve; and those which do not and hence fail to provide 'true' valuation information and welfare measures.

Non-market demand approaches have traditionally been used by governments to assess the cost of environmental impacts, and hence to determine policy responses. Environmental regulations can affect, in terms of either quantity or cost, the production of a marketed good. The cost of an environmental regulation, or the cost of preserving some environmental attribute, is the value of the lost marketed output. The *effect on production* or *opportunity cost* (OC) approach values the benefits of environmental protection in terms of what is being foregone to achieve it. This approach forms the basis of compensation payments for the compulsory purchase by government of land and property under eminent domain laws, for example to construct highways, airports, defence installations, and other public and quasi-public goods. It also forms the basis of compensation payments to farmers for loss of agricultural production by agreeing to farm in an environmentally friendly way, e.g. for management agreements under the Wildlife and Countryside Act 1981; or for the loss of rights of farmers to abstract water for irrigation purposes in the western USA.

Note that this approach assumes that the landowner or user has property rights over the use of the land or the natural resource; and that to restrict these rights government, on behalf of society, must compensate the owner.

The *dose response* approach requires information on the effect that a change in a particular chemical or pollutant has on the level of an economic activity or a consumer's utility. For example, ground levels of air pollution such as ozone (O_3) affect the growth of various plant species differentially. Where this results in a change in the output of a crop, this loss of output can be valued at market or shadow (adjusted or proxy) market prices. The situation is more complex when air pollution affects human health. Dose response relationships linking emissions of particulate matter (e.g. PM_{10}) with changes in mortality and morbidity have been established by epidemiological studies. Understanding the economic consequences of this requires some estimate of the value of human life: e.g. estimates of the values individuals attach to reducing the risk of illness and death; or their willingness to pay to avoid an increase in the risk of death or illness from exposure to PM_{10}.

The *dose response* (DR) and *effect on production* (EoP) approaches are closely linked in many instances. For example, restrictions on the application of artificial fertilisers and herbicides in the Yorkshire Dales Environmentally Sensitive Area (ESA), to conserve wild flowers and nesting birds in meadows, results in reduced grass, hay, and silage crops; which in turn reduces the livestock levels which can be sustained on these farms.

Figure 1.1: Environmental valuation methods

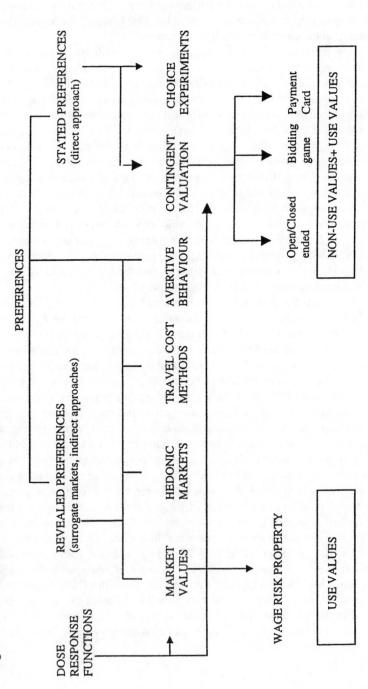

In the *preventative expenditure* (PE) approach the value of the environment is inferred from what people are prepared to spend to prevent its degradation; for example, by installing double glazing to reduce road traffic noise. The *averting or mitigating behaviour* (AB) approach infers a monetary value for an environmental externality by observing the costs people are prepared to incur in order to avoid any negative effects (e.g. by moving to an area with less air pollution at a greater distance from their place of work thus incurring additional transportation costs in terms of time and money). Both of these approaches are, again, conceptually closely linked.

The *replacement cost* (RC) approach values an environment good by the cost incurred in restoring the environment to its original state after it has been damaged. This approach forms the basis of the Comprehensive Environmental Response, Compensation and Liability Act (CERCLA) 1980 in the USA.

Demand curve approaches are broadly divided into *expressed preference* and *revealed preference* methods. The demand for environmental goods can be *revealed* by examining the purchases of related goods in the private market place. These may be complementary goods or other factor inputs in the household's production function. Alternatively the demand for environmental goods can be measured by examining individual's *expressed* or *stated preference* for these goods relative to their demand for other goods and services.

There are a number of revealed preference methods. The *travel-cost method* (TCM) is primarily employed to estimate the demand or marginal valuation curve for recreation sites. Entry to many recreation sites is free of charge. However, individuals need to purchase a private good, namely transport, to gain access to the recreation site. The demand for the recreation site can therefore be estimated by observing how the number of visits to the site varies according to the price of this private good: greater distances incur higher transport costs and hence lower numbers of visits, *ceteris paribus*. Invariably there is an inverse relationship between the cost of visiting the recreation site and the number of visits observed: people living a greater distance from the site and incurring higher transport cost make fewer visits per year than those living nearer to the site, providing the characteristic downward sloping demand curve.

The *hedonic price method* (HPM) is based on consumer theory which postulates that every good provides a bundle of characteristics or attributes (Lancaster, 1966). Again, market goods can be regarded as intermediate inputs into the production of the more basic attributes that individuals really demand. The demand for goods, say housing, can therefore be considered as a derived demand. For example, a house yields shelter, but through its location it also yields access to different quantities and qualities of public services (such as schools, centres of employment, cultural activities, etc.) and different quantities and qualities of environmental goods (such as open space, peace and quiet, woodland, etc.). HPMs extend the theory of production into consumption decisions, permitting the demand for those characteristics upon which the consumer's welfare actually depends to be assessed. The price of a house is determined by a number of factors: structural characteristics, e.g. number of rooms, garages, plot size, etc.; and the environmental characteristics of the area. Controlling for the non-environmental characteristics which affect the demand for housing permits the implicit price that individuals are willing to pay to consume the environmental characteristics associated with the house to be estimated.

Wages also vary in response to various attributes (education and training, natural dexterity, experience, demand and supply in each labour market area, occupational risks to health, probability of death, and associated living conditions including environmental ambience). *Hedonic wage models* (HWMs) have traditionally been used to measure employment attributes, principally risk of death or injury in particular labour markets. However, by observing variations in wage levels over space, and netting out the influence of other attributes, they have also been used to value the quality of life over large areas such as countries or continents. Unfortunately, wages are not generally paid as compensation for variations in environmental goods outside the work place, and do not respond to such environmental attributes as readily as house prices. Hence hedonic wages models are not usually a viable environmental valuation method.

Expressed preference techniques avoid the need to find a complementary good (travel or housing), or a substitute good (compensating wage rate), to derive a demand curve and hence estimate how much an individual *implicitly* values an environmental good or safety feature. Expressed preference methods ask individuals *explicitly* how much they value an environmental good. There are two basic types of expressed preference technique: contingent valuation methods (CVM) and *choice experiment* or *stated preference* (SP) techniques. CVM attempts to measure the value of a good holistically. CVM first defines the good to be valued in detail, listing its attributes and describing what will be protected. For example, the CVM study of lost passive use values resulting from the Exxon Valdez oil spill in Prince William Sound, Alaska in March 1989, described: (1) Prince William Sound, the birds and mammals in the area; (2) the estimated numbers of deaths in each species, the percentage of each species killed, and the number of years it would take each species to recover its original size; and (3) a feasible program which had been used successfully elsewhere to prevent such a major disaster occurring again. Respondents were then asked:

> *At present,* government officials estimate the program will cost *your* household a total of *$10.* You would pay this in a special one time charge in addition to your

regular federal taxes. This money would *only* be used for the program to prevent damage from another oil spill in Prince William Sound. If the program cost your household a total of *$10* would you vote for the program or against it? (Carson *et al.*, 1992)

This is an example of a dichotomous choice (DC) contingent valuation (CV) question. Other CV question formats, in addition to DC, are available to elicit individuals' marginal valuation: for example, open-ended, iterative bidding, and payment card formats, each of which has different merits and disadvantages. Even within these methods, there are numerous variations in the way each can be applied.

Conventional CV techniques value the good in its entirety: nothing is revealed about the value of different attributes that comprise the good. This can only be undertaken by valuing the good holistically, and then asking further questions to value individual elements of the good. Such a procedure is quite likely to give rise to an embedding effect, in which the values of the individual attributes add up to more than the value of the whole good.

Recently stated preference choice experiments, employed in transport economics and planning to value journey attributes in relation to price differences, have been used to value environmental goods. The application in environmental economics of choice experiments represents a deliberate attempt to measure the value of the individual attributes that comprise a specific environmental good. Choice experiment techniques are an explicit preference version of Lancaster's goods' characteristic theory. In choice experiments, the characteristics of the good are explicitly defined. These characteristics vary over choice cards along with a monetary metric, and individuals have to chose different combinations of characteristics of a good over other combinations at various prices.

Of course each of these environmental valuation techniques can be used to measure the value of private market goods. Indeed, environmental goods are no different in principle from the millions of private goods which are traded everyday in the market place: they exhibit the same downward sloping demand curve (as price decreases quantity demanded increases) and environmental goods within the same set are characterised by differences in attributes. However, the distinguishing feature of environmental goods is that they have 'public good' elements. A 'public good' has the characteristic that its consumption by one person in no way detracts from its availability to others (it is non-rival, i.e. has zero opportunity cost of consumption); and consumers cannot be excluded from consuming the good (it is non-excludable, i.e. producers of the good have no property rights over it). Thus, for example, whilst it is possible to charge for private good aspects of a public good, such as entry into the interior of Edinburgh Castle: visitors to

Edinburgh can enjoy the exterior views of the Castle, and its contribution to the character of the city and its skyline, free of charge.

3 CHOICE OF BENEFIT ESTIMATION TECHNIQUE

Of immediate concern in framing and designing a study is whether the total economic value (use plus non-use values) is required, or a sub-set: either use value, option value, anticipatory value, existence value, and bequest or altruistic value, or some combination of these. Different types of goods have different types of values attached to them. Table 1.1 outlines some goods with the different types of use and non-use value they might provide. For example, open access non-priced recreation in a Scottish sitka spruce forest has use value and visitors might be willing to pay for the option to visit the forest again. Sitka spruce forests have negative, rather than positive external amenity benefits on landscape values, and limited existence and bequest values: indeed individuals are often willing to pay to see sitka spruce plantations replaced by more diverse conifer and broad-leaved woodlands. Purely private goods, such as a production by an operatic society, have use value for their audience, option value, and *ex ante* anticipatory value for each production attended. By contrast, buildings of architectural and historic interest provide a variety of public good features which encompass both use and non-use values. Use values (to visitors to a town) include the external visual amenity of the building; whilst potential consumers might also derive benefit from the option to visit the interior of the building in the future and for the anticipation from such a visit. Non-use values might comprise existence value (the benefits derived from knowing the building exists, even though the individual has no intention of entering the building nor even viewing its exterior) and bequest value (from knowing that it is part of a stock of historical capital which will be passed on to future generations). Similarly, for non-visitors to the botanical gardens, benefits comprise the option to visit it in the future, plus the benefit of its existence in helping to maintain biodiversity and rare plant stocks, and in passing these on to future generations.

Although it is possible to charge for some environmental goods, whether it is optimal to do so is open to question. In the absence of congestion, it may cost no more to admit $x+1$ visitors to the Sequoia National Park in California as x visitors. The marginal cost of the additional visitor is zero, so that any non-zero price will produce an inefficiency. However, the optimal price to the US National Parks Service, as the organisation responsible for the park and the quality of facilities for visitors, is positive; whilst the optimal price to the consumer of the (undepletable) externality is zero. Obviously no price can simultaneously be zero and non-zero: thus the conventional price system is inherently incapable of producing an efficient outcome. If the price is zero (as in the case of the Royal Botanic Garden, Edinburgh, and the British Museum, London) the question then arises as to who will supply, and pay for, these public goods?

Table 1.1: Benefits provided by some public goods

	Recreation in a Scottish sitka spruce forest	Scottish Opera	Edinburgh Castle: (visitor)	Edinburgh Castle (non-visitor; but visitor to town)	Edinburgh (non-visitor)	Botanical garden (non-visitor)
Use values						
current	✓	✓	✓			
option	✓	✓	✓	✓	✓	✓
anticipatory		✓	✓			
external			✓	✓		
amenity						
Non-use values						
existence		✓	✓	✓	✓	✓
bequest		✓	✓	✓	✓	✓

Similarly, buildings of historic and architectural interest in the 18th century Georgian New Town of Edinburgh, which is a World Heritage Site, are extremely expensive to maintain, a cost which is principally borne by their occupants. However, visitors to Edinburgh can enjoy the ambience of the New Town free of charge, in an uncongested walk around the area. The fact that residents cannot charge visitors for entry to the New Town means that buildings attract a lower rate of return from their private use, compared with their total value to society, and that too little is probably spent on their maintenance.

These combinations of 'public good' 'private good' features are common, to many types of environmental good. In designing any environmental valuation study it is incumbent on the researcher to specify in detail the set(s) of benefits which the good provides, those which she intends to measure, and to apply the appropriate techniques or combination of techniques to value them.

The choice of benefit estimation technique to be adopted in any study to estimate environmental benefits depends upon a number of criteria. Such criteria comprise: the purpose of the study (e.g. whether opportunity cost estimates, or direct benefit estimates are required); the particular economic values required (use and/or non-use values, or a sub-set); the type of values required (*ex ante* or *ex post*); whether particular assumptions are deemed acceptable or not; the importance attached to particular errors (e.g. statistical errors in the technique, possible cognitive psychological biases, etc.); the conformity of the technique with theory in particular applications (e.g. whether the model proposed deals with substitution and complementary effects, or conforms to some theoretical approach, such as that suggested by Hoehn and Randall, 1989); robustness of the benefit estimates (e.g. in terms of statistical, content, criterion, and construct validity); whether the population of relevance can be identified with enough precision; and whether the benefit estimates per individual can be easily aggregated over this population.

4 APPLICABILITY OF ENVIRONMENTAL VALUES

The fact that the same environmental good, within a generic set, can have different attributes associated with it in different contexts and at different sites, poses problems for transferring values derived from one site or policy context to another. Benefit transfer has evolved out of a need to apply values derived for an environmental good in one context to another similar context, to reduce transactions costs in appraising new projects and policies.

Whilst the criteria outlined above for adopting a particular benefit estimation technique are helpful in identifying the appropriate techniques to use in a particular situation, they can give rise to problems in transferring a value derived for one environmental good to a similar good in another context. This occurs because differences in application within each method, result in values that are partly dependent upon the particular framing and design of the study. This, and the fact that any good can have different combinations of 'public good' 'private good' features in different contexts, means that the benefit transfer process is subject to error.

Hence, the penultimate chapter in this book deals with benefit or value transfer, discusses tests for the applicability of mean value and benefit function transfers, and looks at the part that meta-analysis can play in exploring how values are derived across various environmental valuation studies.

The final chapter of the book explores the use of environmental valuation techniques in decision-making. Environmental valuation is explicitly required when establishing damages to natural resources under CERCLA in the USA. However, this is the exception rather than the rule in environmental appraisal and evaluation. Environmental valuation studies under other auspices in the USA, and elsewhere in the world, have been undertaken on a more *ad hoc* basis. Where environmental valuation studies have been undertaken they have tended to provide additional information for a decision-making process in which judgement by politicians and administrators still plays a crucial role. Environmental impact assessment (EIA), which quantifies and describes the physical impact of projects and policies, plays a more dominant role in decision making, and is institutionalised in law in the European Union and the USA as the method for appraising the environmental impact of major projects. EIA documents the complexity of environmental issues, but leaves the decision maker with more discretion and power as to what to do about them than would environmental valuation.

REFERENCES

Carson, Richard T., Robert C. Mitchell, W. Michael Hanemann, Raymond J. Kopp, Stanley Presser and Paul A. Ruud (1992), *A Contingent Valuation Study of Lost Passive Use Values Resulting from the Exxon Valdez Oil Spill*, Natural Resource Damage Assessment Inc., La Jolla, California.

Hoehn, John P. and Alan Randall (1989), 'Too many proposals pass the benefit cost test', *American Economic Review* **79**, 544–51.

Lancaster, K.J. (1966), 'A new approach to consumer theory', *Journal of Political Economy* **74**, 132–57.

The Economist (1997), 'Environmental scares: plenty of gloom'. *The Economist* 20/12/97–02/01/98, Volume 345, Issue 8048, 21–3.

Turner, R. Kerry, David Pearce and Ian Bateman (1994), *Environmental Economics*, Harvester Wheatsheaf, London.

PART TWO

Revealed Preference Techniques

2. Market Price and Cost Measures of Value

If there were dreams to sell,
What would you buy?
Some cost a passing bell;
Some a light sigh,

Thomas Lovell Beddoes (1803–49): *Dream-Pedlary*

1 INTRODUCTION

Many types of good exist. A taxonomy of goods can be derived from three criteria: the opportunity cost of their consumption; property rights of the producer; and property rights of the consumer (Winch, 1971), codified as (1,1,1) where these respective attributes are present, and as (0,0,0) where they are absent.

Private goods (1,1,1) are those that have opportunity costs of consumption (if one person consumes the good it is not available for anyone else); producer rights exist which permit the owner to decide whether to sell the good and to whom; and consumer rights, which allow the consumer to decide whether or not to consume the good.

Non-congestion (0,1,1) characterises goods which have zero opportunity costs of consumption (consumption by one person in no way detracts from the good's availability to others), but which are subject to property rights: producers decide whether or not to sell, and consumers can decide whether or not to consume the good. Non-congested roads, art galleries, museums, historic houses and sites, and National Parks in the USA are typical examples of this type of good. Owners can institute a charge, but if some potential user would have derived utility from the good, at no cost to anyone (zero opportunity cost of consumption), but is prevented from doing so by a

17

marginal price, the outcome is sub-optimal from a Paretian[1] standpoint. Zero opportunity cost implies a zero marginal price.

Open access or commons (1,0,1) is the case of a good where there is an opportunity cost of consumption, but exclusion cannot be practised by the producer, although consumer rights exist. Among the various forms of market failure affecting natural and environmental resources at an international level, the problems of open access and common property resources are dominant. Typical examples of this type of good are ocean fishing, radio wavelengths, wildlife, and common oil reserves. In all of these cases, lack of ownership rights over the resource leads to excessive exploitation, and increased costs of consumption (e.g. to fishermen harvesting the resource; or in terms of more powerful radio transmitters to 'drown out' neighbouring stations). The open access problem can be solved by common agreement between all interested parties, or by governments assuming property rights over the resource. Co-operative arrangements over commons generally seek to minimise over-exploitation. However, inefficiency in common property management can still exist. In Switzerland, Stevenson (1991) has shown, through an econometric model of milk production, that Alps (mountain grazing areas) managed as dispersed operating unit commons and co-operative commons produced 11.8% and 9.8% less milk per cow per day than owner operated private property. More generally the commons are managed by governments establishing property rights over the resource and regulating its use. Thus the Endangered Species Act (1978) in the USA and the Wildlife and Countryside Act (1981) in England and Wales, seek to prevent the extinction of endangered species by making it a criminal offence to kill or destroy specified animals and plants and by protecting habitats, in which certain species are found, from commercial development.

Semi-public goods (0,0,1) are those with zero opportunity costs of consumption, no producer rights, but where consumer rights exist. Examples of this type of public good are radio and TV reception, and information. Radio signals remain as strong no matter how many people receive them: there is zero opportunity cost of consumption, the producer cannot exclude consumers[2], but a consumer can choose not to receive the signal. Provision of this type of public good either provides positive utility to the consumer or zero utility. Consumer rights ensure that it can never create a negative utility. Lighthouses are another example of this type of public good: the beam from a

---

[1] The Pareto criterion defines a welfare improvement as occuring when one person can be made better off without anyone else being made worse off.

[2] The advent of new technology has meant that some signals can now be encoded requiring the use of decoders to receive the transmission, thus giving the producer property rights over the good, permitting a charge to be levied.

lighthouse helps every ship in sight, but captains can ignore the signal. Lack of producer property rights precludes charges and hence market provision of lighthouses. There is, however, a clear private advantage to shipping in terms of lives and cargoes saved. Both John Stuart Mill and later Pigou suggested that, because of the public good nature of lighthouses, it was the proper office of government to build and maintain them for security of navigation, since it was impossible that ships which benefit from a lighthouse could be made to pay a toll on the occasion of its use. Coase (1974), however, showed that some lighthouses could be provided by private enterprise.[3] In the area of information provision, smart technology is changing the definition of some public goods, by giving producers property rights over the good thus allowing a market to be created, though zero opportunity cost consumption for the good may still exist.

Pure public goods (0,0,0) are those with zero opportunity cost of consumption, and where exclusion cannot be practised by producers or consumers. A large number of public goods occur in this category: national defence is the obvious example. Many environmental goods are also pure public goods: air quality; flood protection; noise; visual amenity benefits; conservation of buildings of historic and architectural interest, etc. Flood control benefits, for example, can be provided to residents and landowners on the flood plain by engineering works to the river bed, by raising levies or river banks, or by building a dam. The services are available to all at zero opportunity cost. Landowners cannot be forced to contribute to a private scheme of this type, and none can be excluded from the flood control services except at great cost. Moreover, the benefits of such a scheme to any one individual are likely to be much smaller than the total project costs. Not only would a single individual contemplating such a project find it impossible to charge neighbouring residents, other individuals would have an incentive to become free-riders. This position is an example of the classic prisoner's dilemma situation where the optimal course of action for society is to institute flood control, but the gains to any individual are maximised by not

---

[3] Ship owners could petition the Crown to allow a private individual to construct a lighthouse and levy tolls on ships benefiting from it when entering port. The role of government was limited to the establishment and enforcement of property rights in the lighthouse and the scale of charges which could be levied. In Britain in 1820 there were 22 lighthouses operated by private individuals; and 24 lighthouses operated by Trinity House (a government agency) and publicly funded. Only 11 of the Trinity House lighthouses had been originally built by them: 12 had been acquired by purchase or the expiry of a lease (e.g. Eddystone lighthouse in 1804), and one acquired from Chester Council in 1816. In 1836 an Act of Parliament vested all lighthouses in Trinity House which was empowered to purchase the remaining lighthouses, and this was accomplished by 1842, the three most expensive being Tynemouth (£125,000), Spurn (£330,000), and Skerries (£445,000). Such huge sums at the time presumably reflected the capitalised earning power of the lighthouse over the remainder of its lease.

participating in the scheme.[4] Thus, without collective action this type of public good will not be produced.

Public goods arise from externality effects: effects which are not priced through the market. Externalities can either be depletable or undepletable. Public goods, such as wildlife and the 'commons' are examples of depletable externalities where one person's use of the resource affects the availability and cost of the resource to other users. Depletable externalities are permitted to persist only because either (a) the cost of collecting a price exceeds the revenue generated; or (b) there are institutional restrictions inhibiting the pricing process. The common oil pool problem arises when drilling and mineral rights belong to a number of landowners. It might be more efficient to exploit the resource with a single well rather than two wells, because it costs more to drill two wells than one: similarly, the existence of one well influences the technical possibilities of the other well by lowering the common pool and reducing the pressure. Since oil in the ground belongs to an owner only when it reaches the surface each owner has an incentive to pump as much oil as possible. The assignment of rights to one owner would remove this depletable externality, but institutional impediments may prevent this occurring. Once two wells are in existence, there is an economically efficient rate of pumping for each well that will maximise the joint wealth of both owners. This is the second best outcome. However, there is an incentive for each owner to operate his well at a higher rate, to capture some of the oil that would otherwise go to the other well. This, however, reduces total profit. If owners cannot agree on an efficient rate of exploitation, if fears of moral hazard and cheating arise, or the costs of negotiation and enforcement are high, then over-exploitation of the resource will occur. Over-exploitation is likely to increase with the number of owners. Similar situations arise with respect to fish stocks in the North Sea and off the coast of Newfoundland, where many nations fish and where agreement amongst many is difficult to achieve. Institutional impediments are more likely to be resolved where the commons problem lies within national boundaries. The implementation of

---

[4] For example, if the flood control programme was instituted, individual A might see her net wealth increase by 10% if she contributed to the cost of the programme. However, if the programme was instituted and individual A engaged in free-riding, her wealth would increase by 15%. If everyone did nothing, net wealth would not change (0%); whilst if individual A undertook the flood control works, and incurred the entire cost, her wealth would decrease by 20%. Hence it is rational and probably risk averting for individual A and other property owners to do nothing.

Individual A	Participates	Does Nothing
Other property owners		
Participate	10%	15%
Do nothing	-20%	0%

normal market exclusion, assignment of property rights, and pricing procedures, might be achieved by government and licensing arrangements. At these more local levels, and in the absence of institutional impediments, either depletable externalites must be insignificant; or, if they exist, the cost of collecting the appropriate fee must be very high. If the cost of elimination is high relative to the economic significance of the resource, government intervention might be no more advantageous than other possible solutions.

Undepletable externalities emphasise one pertinent characteristic of public goods: the fact that an increase in the consumption of the good by one person does not reduce its availability to others. The fact that individual i breathes polluted city air can, to a reasonable degree of approximation, be taken to leave the quality of air available to individual j and others in society unaffected. Similarly, in the absence of congestion, it costs no more to admit $x+1$ visitors to a museum than x visitors. The marginal cost of the additional visitor is zero; so that any non-zero price will produce an inefficiency. However, the optimal price to the supplier of the external benefit is positive (just as that for the supplier of a detrimental externality is negative: the price of the social damage he inflicts) but the optimal price to the consumer of an undepletable externality is zero. Obviously no price can simultaneously be zero and non-zero: thus the conventional price system is inherently incapable of dealing with such cases.

The failure of the market to supply public goods has led to environmental regulation, public supply of these goods, taxes on pollutants, and subsidies for the provision of public goods. Where the benefits of public goods are difficult to quantify, and in a framework of budgetary constraints for specific environmental programmes (with cost minimisation a priority and where financial compensation has to be paid for rights foregone), then a cost approach to assessing priorities for environmental improvements is often appealing to regulators. Governments thus tend to value the environment by a cost approach rather than by estimating the benefits of environmental regulation through contingent valuation, hedonic price models, or through travel-cost methods. The remainder of this chapter is therefore devoted to exploring variants of the cost and dose response approaches to environmental valuation.

2 EFFECT ON PRODUCTION APPROACH

Environmental regulation may influence the profitability of producers by constraining the production process, and hence either increasing their production costs or reducing their outputs. Where such regulation has an effect on the price and supply of goods it also impinges on the welfare of consumers. If this is the case then the impact of an environmental regulation can be measured by the value of the change in output it causes: this is known as the effect on production (EOP) approach. This approach can estimate the magnitude of both negative and positive impacts, e.g. the impact on fisheries of water pollution (negative), water quality improvement (positive), or the creation of a new reservoir (which might be positive or negative).

The EOP approach is one of the most widely used of the various cost based valuation techniques, and is the typical approach to 'buying out various rights' such as rights to intensify agricultural production in the countryside and nimeral extraction rights. The approach also forms the theoretical basis of the Land Compensation Acts (1961 and 1973) for compulsory purchase and eminent domain cases; and discontinuance, purchase orders and planning blight notices served under the Town and Country Planning Acts in Britain.[5] Compensation to landowners or tenants for management agreements to conserve wildlife under the Wildlife and Countryside Act 1981 and the Agriculture Act 1986 is also based on the effect of land-use restrictions on the agricultural output of the land. For example, under the Wildlife and Countryside Act (WCA) 1981 management agreements reduce agricultural outputs or other developments by prohibiting damaging operations (e.g. ploughing, re-seeding or applying fertilisers or herbicides to traditional hay meadows) in exchange for financial compensation based on profits forgone. Thus the EOP approach has considerable practical relevance to measuring the benefits (output) forgone in attaining an environmental standard. Similarly, the EOP approach underlies payments in Environmentally Sensitive Areas (ESAs) in Britain and other European countries in which farmers are compensated for restricting agricultural output to conserve the botanical, ornithological, and historical (ancient field systems, archaeological remains, etc.) interest in the land. In Nitrogen Sensitive Areas (NSAs) compensation is paid for any decline in output through reducing the use of nitrogen-based fertilisers.

In the EOP technique, the physical effects of the environmental change are determined first,with the underlying trend or influence of exogenous factors netted out. This may be done in a number of ways, though the principal approaches involve the use of empirical estimates based on known production effects, or research-based field trials or laboratory experiments: e.g. by estimating a damage function in a dose-response (DR) model, or by using controlled experiments to observe the outcome when a given effect on a control group is deliberately induced.

---

[5]   Eminent domain is the legal right to acquire property by forced rather than voluntary exchange. In the USA and other countries, law requires that eminent domain is only used to acquire private property for 'public use' and only after payment of 'just compensation'. One of the few analyses of eminent domain has been undertaken by Munch (1976).

Table 2.1 Estimated change in the stocking rate due to the successful implementation of the ESA in the Somerset Levels and Moors

Area	Uptake hectares	Change in stocking (rate GLU/ha)	Change in stock	Compensation payments:[+] (basic)	Compensation payments:[+]* (basic plus supplementary)
Tier 1	10,500	-0.14	-1470	120	190
Tier 2	2,250	-0.34	-765	180	250
Tier 3	2,500	-0.50	-1250	-	350

[+] £ per hectare 1992 prices. * basic payment plus supplementary payment to maintain higher water tables in Tiers 1 & 2, and to create wet winter and spring conditions in Tier 3.

Source Willis et al. (1993)

The ESA scheme was designated to safeguard areas of the countryside of national importance, recognising the major influence that agriculture can have on the landscape. In the Somerset Levels and Moors, agriculturists estimated that complying with the ESA prescriptions for Tier 1, Tier 2, and Tier 3 land compared to the pre-ESA farming regime, leading to progressive reductions in inputs (such as fertilisers) and higher water tables,[6] would result in an 8% fall in the stocking rate for Tier 1 land from 1.66 grazing livestock units (GLU) per hectare to 1.52 GLU; a 20% fall in GLUs on Tier 2 land to 1.32 GLU; and a 30% decrease in output on Tier 3 land to 1.16 GLU per hectare (Table 2.1). Applying these changes to the estimated ESA uptake results in a reduction in agricultural stock output of 3,485 GLUs.

Monetary values must then be estimated for a given environmental or policy change, with market prices used to value changes in outputs. Thus the increase in the average market price of a GLU over one year can then be multiplied by the change in the number of GLUs to estimate compensation per hectare for lost production. This is theoretically valid if changes in output are too small to affect prices, and if the price is the market clearing price. Compensation to landowners or tenants for management agreements to conserve wildlife is based on the net difference between the intensive agricultural position and the position regarded as compatible with wildlife, landscape, and historical conservation.[7]

In reality, the annual value of compensation payable is based on the net annual profit foregone:

---

[6] Restrictions progressively increase for each Tier up to Tier 3 where wet winter and spring conditions (flooding) provide a habitat for wading birds.

[7] Note that agri-environmental policies are one of the few areas where compensation is paid to correct an externality. This not only fulfils the Kaldor-Hicks potential Pareto criterion of gainers being able to compensate losers, but the stronger requirement that compensation is actually paid and no-one loses.

$$FC = (c - a) - (b - d) + k \qquad (2.1)$$

where FC = financial compensation payable; c = revenue from farming more intensively; a = variable and operating costs incurred for this output level; b = agricultural revenue from the management agreement position (agricultural position compatible with wildlife or landscape conservation); d = variable and operating costs at the management agreement position; k = annuitised value of any capital (barns, machinery, etc.) made redundant by farming at the agreement position instead of the agricultural intensive position. Under the WCA compensation payable is calculated individually for each agreement; whereas for ESAs an average compensation per hectare is calculated for the farming system of the particular ESA and farmers decide whether or not to join the ESA scheme at that price.[8] At the very least, ESA payments ensure that agricultural use value plus amenity use value equals the current market value of the land, which at the margin equals the value of similar land not entered into the ESA scheme. The extent to which amenity is protected (or the extent to which an environmental attribute is valued), by offering a standard compensation payment, depends upon the production possibilities and opportunity costs facing individual farms.

The EOP approach has been applied to value a variety of environmental goods, including acid rain and Soya bean production (Adams *et al*, 1986); hydo-electric impacts (Krutilla and Fisher, 1975); nature reserves and wildlife conservation (Willis *et al*, 1988); and the value of coastal wetlands for the protection of property against hurricane damage (Farber, 1987).

Some EOP studies, such as those of air pollution, have adopted sophisticated methods to assess economic impacts to overcome certain data and theoretical problems. The problems inherent in the EOP approach can be illustrated by the example of agricultural and timber production, which is highly dependent upon environmental conditions including air pollution. Sulphur dioxide (SO_2), nitrogen oxide (NO_X) and ammonia, result, through acid rain, in economic losses in timber production in European forests (Carrier and Kripple, 1990). Low-level ozone (O_3) concentrations from transport exhaust emissions and other sources have been shown to reduce crop yields. The physical impact of ozone has been estimated through:

---

[8] Farmers will participate in ESA schemes only if the costs (including any non-pecuniary costs and/or benefits) of co-operating are at least offset by the payment received. Under a common tariff of ESA payments, set to ensure satisfactory levels of participation, many farmers may be over-compensated. Their profits from farming will be higher as a result of the ESA, where profits account for the opportunity cost of farmers' own labour and management input to the farming operation.

- foliar injury models: linking leaf deterioration with yield loss. However, yield loss to roots and tubers can occur without visible damage to leaves; whilst severe leaf damage can occur without loss of photosynthetic ability and yield loss;

- cross-sectional spatial analysis of crop yield data and ozone concentrations, although such estimates are sensitive to information on ozone concentrations which is often incomplete in continuous space, and to reliable observations on actual crop yields. In addition, it is necessary to obtain information on, and standardise for, non-air pollution variables such as soil, farm management practices, etc., which also affect crop yields;

- experimental laboratory conditions which offer more accurate estimates of changes in crop yields than foliar injury and cross-sectional analysis models, although in practice the dose-response relationship will be affected by local environmental conditions.

Once the EOP has been established, there is a need to extrapolate damage to crops across geographic areas from these DR relationships. Such projections are problematic: DR ozone relationships established in the laboratory can be affected by local meteorological, topographical, soil, and climatic conditions, as well as by farm management practices in different regions. Different crops are differentially affected by ozone concentrations, complicating estimates of potential losses where rotations of crops occur or where crop acreage is already determined by ozone levels.

The estimate of the economic cost of yield reductions has been undertaken by:

- a traditional approach similar to that outlined above in calculating compensation payments under nature conservation;

- linear and quadratic programming. Brown and Smith (1984) used a linear programming model to investigate cross crop substitution in corn, wheat, and soya bean production in response to changing ozone levels in Indiana. Quadratic programming used by Adams *et al* (1982) focused on optimal crop mix and mitigation by cross-crop substitution, due to changing ozone concentrations in four regions in southern California; with yields of ozone resistant, but relatively unprofitable, crops such as broccoli, cauliflower, carrots, and cantaloupes being reduced with reductions in ozone. Reducing ozone levels to 0.08 ppm, the state standard, and maximising the sum of producer and consumer surpluses, increased producer rents by $35.1 million and consumer surplus by $10.1 million (at 1976 prices). Production changes induced by altering ozone concentrations were assumed to leave the input mix constant. Rowe and Chestnut (1985), in an analysis of 33 crops in the San Joaquin Valley, California, of which 16 crops were judged to be affected by ozone and of which four had DR functions attached, estimated consumer surplus gains of $30.3 million and producer gains of $87.1 million (1978 prices) if the 0.08 ppm seasonal hourly maximum had been met;

- econometric methods: estimating yield losses under different ozone concentrations, and inputting these into a national econometric model of agriculture to estimate the price level and welfare effects of these crop losses.   Air pollution-induced crop damage affects the welfare of producers and consumers by changing costs, implying a supply response, and also by affecting demand: changing the attributes or quality (size, appearance, or taste) of an agricultural product affects consumers' WTP and quantity demanded of the product. Spash (1997) provides an excellent survey of the problems and issues in estimating the economic damage from ozone levels.

EOP approaches based on prohibiting a damaging environmental activity also need to explore substitution effects. Lakshminarayan *et al* (1996), for example, showed that use of atrazine, one of the most common herbicides for weed control in US corn and sorghum production and accounting for nearly 12% of US pesticide use, resulted in concentrations in Midwestern river basins exceeding the Federal drinking water standard of 3 parts per billion in 50% of sample sites. Banning all triazine would cost $240 million in lost production, but would be unlikely to improve water quality since producers would switch to other triazine-based herbicides. Banning all triazine herbicides would cost $740 million, whilst restricting their application to meet the Federal health guidelines would greatly improve water quality and cost of between $160 to $230 million.

There are clearly a number of limitations to the EOP approach. Some of the physical relationships between activities affecting the environment and the resulting effect on output changes, are not well understood. It may also be difficult to separate the physical effects of pollution from one source from those generated by other sources, especially where there are long time lags between the initial source of an environmental impact and observable effects. In addition, the interaction of multiple pollution sources, property rights, and transactions costs, in an EOP application can have important resource allocation implications. This was documented by Crocker (1971) for fluoride emissions in Polk County, Florida. Agricultural interests in the area argued that fluoride emission caused citrus damage and cattle owners reported a general enervation in their animals' health and yield losses in production. Chemical companies were unwilling to reduce emission levels because of costs: once a 95% efficiency level was attained, further increases in efficiency became relatively unresponsive to additional capital outlays. For plants at least 10 years old in 1965, it was estimated that it was unlikely that 97%

efficiency could ever be achieved; a plant less than 10 years old required an outlay of $0.5 million to move from 98% to 99% efficiency; and two 2 year old plants needed $0.25 million to increase their control efficiency from 99.1% to 99.2%. Before 1958 the options for farmers were to: (a) keep the land and accept the consequential losses in productivity; (b) sell the land and bear the capital loss; and (c) sue in court for damages under tort law. The latter option required finding expert witnesses to testify a cause-and-effect relationship and tracing a given pollutant dose to its source. The effects of fluoride on cattle and citrus were not so well understood that they could be distinguished inexpensively from a myriad of other possible causes such as frosts, water deficiencies, fertiliser misapplications, etc. In 1958, however, emitter property rights were changed: receptors no longer had to bear the costs of identifying the cause-and-effect process through to production changes, nor the responsibility of identifying individual fluoride emission perpetrators. Polluters were required to purchase the agricultural land at its value without fluoride pollutant. Land was leased back to farmers at a reduced rental depending on pollutant levels. Once land purchases had been made, the costs faced by polluters were those inherent in any joint production activity: maximising the joint value of land rental and fluoride production; and determining amongst themselves the pollution levels for which each was responsible. The net effect of the change in property rights was to reduce overall fluoride emissions.[9]

The traditional EOP approach, valuing output changes by market price, ignores consumer surplus, although this can be remedied in more sophisticated linear programming and econometric models. However, the EOP approach cannot measure the non-use benefits associated with a resource.[10]

3 OPPORTUNITY COST MEASURES

The opportunity cost (OC) approach highlights trade-offs to be made in environmental decision-making and emphasises the fact that opportunity costs are foregone benefits. The EOP and OC approaches are synonymous at the

---

[9] Joint and several liability can be applied by courts in the USA on an individual case basis, applying traditional and evolving principles of common law. Courts can also apply joint and several liability under the Comprehensive Environmental Response, Compensation and Liability Act 1980 if two or more persons violate the Act and cause a single indivisible harm. To avoid joint and several liability, the burden is on the liable party to establish that the harm is divisible and that there is a reasonable basis to apportion it (see Ward and Duffield, 1992).

[10] Preventative and mitigatory expenditures might, of course, include non-use values in assessing the value of a resource.

financial level: where environmental regulation restricts output or production to maintain some environmental attribute, then the EOP represents the opportunity cost of the environmental regulation to society. The OC approach is useful in cases where it is difficult to enumerate the benefits of an environmental change. For example, rather than compare the benefits of various alternative conservation schemes in order to choose between them, the OC approach could be used to enumerate the opportunity costs of foregone development associated with each scheme, with the preferred option, being the one with the lowest OC.

Alternatively, the opportunities of foregone development might be compared with the estimated benefits of preserving the development site: if these environmental benefits are perceived to be greater than the resulting opportunity costs, then preservation should be the preferred option. This type of model was developed by Krutilla and Fisher (1975) and extended by Porter (1982), and has been used in a number of studies such as valuing of the impacts of hydo-electricity development (Sadler *et al.*, 1980), wilderness preservation (Hanley, 1991), and green belt preservation (Willis *et al*, 1993). The Krutilla-Fisher model:

$$NPV_D = \int D_t e^{-(r+k)t} \, d_t - C_t - \int P_t e^{-(r-g)t} \, dt \tag{2.2}$$

is specified here in continuous time. NPV_D is the net present value (benefit) of the development; D_t, C_t and P_t are the development benefits, development costs, and preservation benefits without the development respectively; r is the discount rate, either an opportunity cost rate based on the marginal productivity of capital or a pure time preference rate; and k and g are rates of change for development and preservation benefits, which may be positive or negative. Technological progress or depreciation can result in D being less valuable over time, effectively generating a higher rate to discount the benefits; whilst P might be growing over time, especially if it is an income elastic good relative to the development good, effectively lowering the rate r at which preservation benefits are discounted.

If preservation benefits are difficult to quantify, development benefits and costs can be estimated, and the preservation benefits foregone can be compared against the private net present value of the development. This is a typical practice in many, smaller development decisions affecting the environment.

The decision to participate in an environmental conservation programme, where compensation is paid for enrolling, is an opportunity cost problem for the individual. For example, in the USA the Conservation Reserve Programme (CRP) provides environmental benefits by subsidising the conversion of 33.9 million acres of highly erodeable agricultural land to other uses (e.g. planting grasses and trees) at an annual rental cost of $1.7 billion.

The environmental goals of the CRP have expanded from reducing erosion to include several other objectives such as restoring wetland habitats, and sustaining open spaces. Land use choices for owners eligible for CRP payments are: (1) continue to farm intensively; (2) participate in the CRP; or (3) sell the land, possibly for some form of development depending upon planning permission. Enrolling land in CRP generates a subsidy payment depending on the land quality: the owner's problem is to choose the optimal amount of land to enrol for compensation in the programme, and to manage the rest in such a way as to maximise discounted profits including land sales. This is an OC decision problem, which was modelled by Parks and Schorr (1997) in assessing enrolment in the programme in the north-eastern states of the USA. The model aggregated land into CRP and non-CRP land by county, and employed a grouped logit method to model enrolment. The model indicated that increased discounted CRP benefits and crop production costs increased enrolment, suggesting that land with low agricultural opportunity costs was enrolled. As the proportion of high value crops increased, enrolment became less likely. When elasticities were estimated at sample means, enrolment was elastic with respect to payments, crop costs, and land quality measures. Land near metropolitan areas, and with high and increasing values, and greater proportions of recreational farms, were all associated with lower enrolment in CRP.

Market prices form the basis of individual decisions, but may be an inappropriate measure of the marginal costs and benefits to society of an environmental problem. There are a number of cases where prices are implicit rather than explicit in exchanges: where policy results in non-market changes, and where market imperfections, unemployed resources, taxes, subsidies, and constraints on use exist. In such cases market prices are not a measure of the social opportunity cost of benefits foregone to society. The social opportunity cost (SOC) approach can, therefore, extend the EOP approach to consider the social opportunity costs of environmental protection.

Agriculture is protected in many developing counties to provide income support for farmers: McInerney (1986) has argued that equity objectives remain the sole justifiable basis for agricultural support in higher income countries. Market prices for many agricultural products are above world market prices. The social value of lost agricultural output from restricting intensive agriculture in the interests of soil conservation and wildlife protection can be measured by: (1) comparing domestic and world market prices; (2) calculating producer subsidy equivalents (PSEs); and (3) assessing effective protection rates (EPRs).

Revaluing domestic prices at world prices is a simple but crude way of estimating the social value of agricultural output forgone. The method takes no account of the alternative uses of inputs nor of any protection measures (direct subsidies) on inputs. However, where subsidies on inputs (capital grants to agriculture, e.g. drainage grants, and variable inputs grants, e.g. nitrogen grants) have declined or been eliminated (e.g. in many areas of the European Union), this is no longer such a serious drawback. But depending upon the relative magnitude of the various opportunity costs of inputs, world price can either over- or under-estimate social value.

Producer subsidy equivalents measure the social value of output forgone by revaluing domestic output, minus direct subsidies and taxes, at world market prices, i.e.

$$PSE = \frac{V_m + D - V_w}{V_w} \qquad (2.3)$$

where V_m = output at domestic (UK market) prices; D = direct subsidies; and V_w = output at world prices. The comparison of domestic and world prices through PSEs only concentrates on output. Where the effect of protection on inputs to the final level of protection on outputs is significant, then measured protection needs to be assessed in terms of the value added element in production. This can be achieved through the calculation of the effective protection rate, i.e.

$$EPR = \frac{VA_m - VA_w}{VA_w} \qquad (2.4)$$

where VA_m = value added at domestic prices; VA_w = value added at world prices; $VA_w = P_j (1 - A_{ij})$; $VA_m = P_j [(1 + Tj) - A_{ij} (1 + T_i)]$; P_j = nominal price of commodity j in free trade; A_{ij} = share of input i in cost j at free trade prices; T = nominal tariff (on i or j as the case may be). The inclusion of inputs is important in estimating the social value of forgone agricultural output since it implies that the inputs would have alternative uses if not devoted to agricultural production. Variables such as fertiliser and fuel will have alternative uses; but other inputs previously used in agricultural production, such as labour, may not over the short run (e.g. because of the need to retrain) and some capital and other fixed costs such as farm buildings[11] and field drains will be immobile over the long run.

Table 2.2, for example, documents the financial (EOP), public exchequer, and social opportunity cost of livestock output in the UK at 1996 prices. The domestic market value-added ranges from £483 for dairy; £380 for suckler cows; to £98 for intensive beef. All livestock production has a negative value at world (SOC) prices with the exception of sheep. Savings to the public exchequer for this agricultural output foregone, from reductions in CAP and national government support for agricultural output, range from £770 for

---

[11] Farm buildings may have alternative uses, e.g. as weekend cottages. But planning regulations may prohibit such a change of use.

dairy; £517 for hill sheep; to £179 for lowland sheep. In the case of cereals, domestic value added is less than social value due to protection on inputs, as is the case with oilseed rape. Thus, for oilseed, beef and dairy production, there would be a social benefit from reducing acreage devoted to these products. Thus, to the extent that reductions in these agricultural outputs increases wildlife on the land, nature conservation can be secured at zero opportunity cost: indeed nature conservation provides a net benefit to society by reducing agricultural surpluses.

Table 2.2: Financial (EOP), public exchequer, and social opportunity cost (SOC) of livestock output in the UK (£s, 1996)

	Dairy	Beef, single suckler	Beef, 18 month	Beef, inten-sive	Hill Sheep	Lowland Sheep	Wheat	Barley (winter)	Oil-seed
Private financial value	483.5	206.0	380.0	98.0	213.0	230.0	298.5	184.4	-151.3
Public exchequer cost	770.0	225.0	191.0	0.0	517.0	179.0	346.0	346.0	560.0
Social opportunity cost	-164.8	-95.0	-401.0	-558.0	153.0	155.0	314.0	198.3	-136.3

Source: Saunders (1996)

Table 2.3. Effect on production (EOP), social opportunity cost (SOC), and travel-cost model (TCM) values of nature conservation at three SSSIs in Yorkshire, (£s, 1996)

Area	EOP[1]	SOC[2]	TCM[3]	TCM[4]
Derwent Ings	175	127	23	32
Skipwith Common	181	64	65	80
Upper Teesdale	165	97	32	264

Notes: [1] financial compensation payable to farmers per hectare; [2] social value of agricultural output foregone; [3] consumer surplus benefits to wildlife visitors; [4] consumer surplus benefits to all visitors.

Source: Willis and Benson (1988)

The basic assumption in all of these methods is that the social value of the agricultural output lost through wildlife conservation is the value of this output on the *free market*, since this is the price which would have to be paid to replace the lost output. The opportunity cost is this social value minus the social value of the inputs, where these inputs can be used elsewhere. The crucial question in all three methods (simple domestic minus world price; PSEs; and EPRs) is whether or not world price is the appropriate marginal social valuation. Arguments for supposing it is not, centre on governments deliberately raising prices and condoning subsidies in response to pressure groups and voters who believe that there are technological or pecuniary externality benefits, and that agricultural policy has vested landowners with property rights to agricultural output values. If prices are raised purely as a mechanism for transferring income to farmers, then the social value of agricultural output lost through conservation is the world price; even though utility attaches to income transfer, equity can be achieved at a lower resource cost by direct monetary transfer rather than by supporting agricultural production (Browning and Johnson, 1984).

Because of tariffs at the frontier and subsidies, revaluing agricultural output in SOC terms results, in a lower cost measure than financial opportunity costs or EOP value as reflected in compensation payments to farmers. Table 2.3 documents the financial opportunity cost (EOP) and social opportunity cost measures for three nature conservation areas designated as SSSIs (Sites of Special Scientific Interest), and reports travel-cost estimates of consumer surplus for comparison. The use benefits for two of the three sites were less than EOP losses. However, when the lost agricultural output was revalued in SOC terms, user benefits were less than the costs at only one site (Derwent Ings).

Harvey and Hall (1989) estimated that agricultural gross product was 22% greater in the UK under the Common Agricultural Policy (CAP) than it would have been under multilateral free trade. This provided a basis for establishing the extent to which the market price of agricultural land in the UK was higher than its SOC because of the CAP and other support policies. Agricultural land prices were estimated to be inflated by 46%, on average, because of support policy. At 1986 land prices this increase amounted to £655 per ha, or about 55% of the estimated producers' surplus gain. Thus just over half of the support provided to the agricultural sector through the 'old' CAP price support policies was capitalised into land values and rents; the remaining 45% being distributed through the factor and input markets to other resources used directly or indirectly by the industry.

The OC approach has been used to value a wide range of environmental protection measures, both in developed and developing countries (see Dixon and Sherman, 1990; Winpenny, 1991; and Abelson, 1996). As with the EOP approach, there are a number of limitations to the OC method when deriving environmental values. The OC approach often ignores consumer surplus on the consumption of goods, by valuing the displaced goods at their market price. In this respect the OC approach is likely to undervalue the benefits of an environmental improvement. However, Whittington *et al.* (1989), by analysing the trade-off between the price of potable water from vendors compared to the time spent hauling water from open wells and handpumps and the value of time to households, were able to estimate consumer surplus and annual net benefits for alternative forms of water supply investment in Kenya. The OC approach also only measures use value and the value of use foregone. It does not measure non-use values. Non-use values might form a substantial element of the economic value of some environmental goods, such as the preservation of biodiversity.

The OC approach does not include non-marketed public good values of land. The fact that land and its attributes produce externalities is explicitly recognised in regulatory land-use planning controls, which seek to minimise external bads through development control and (land) use class orders, by separating externality producing land uses spatially. Thus, planning controls seek to preserve amenity benefits by restricting the development of land. However, by imposing such restrictions, the price of land (such as green belt land) has a lower financial value than its OC value (e.g. as housing land) to society; although society is presumably willing to bear this 'cost' for the sake of the amenity benefits produced. In such circumstances, the financial opportunity cost value of the land will under-estimate the amenity benefits provided. The SACTRA report (1992) argued that the opportunity cost of land (alternative use precluded by planning control) equated with the value of amenity loss from a road development. This is erroneous: the opportunity cost of land is not an adequate measure of the benefits which society attaches to the amenity value of the land. There is no reason why the amenity benefits society loses from a particular tract of land should equal the value of that land for another marketable use, say, housing. Moreover, land use zoning is instituted through the political market place on the basis of voting or pressure group mechanisms. Public choice theory points out that preference revelation under such mechanisms is an imperfect representation of individuals' utility (Mueller, 1979) and that too much or too little land will be designated for protection depending upon whether amenity lovers or non-amenity lovers are in a majority (Willis, 1980). Because of this it is incorrect to argue that the opportunity cost of development forgone to preserve the land as green space represents the amenity value of the land. Imputing the amenity value of land through its opportunity cost as a result of zoning, can result in a gross over-estimate of the amenity value of land, or in some cases a gross under-estimate. For example, the amenity value of London's green belt has been shown to be only half of the development value of the land (Willis and Whitby, 1985); a finding supported for other areas (Cheshire and Sheppard, 1997).

4 HUMAN CAPITAL APPROACH AND DOSE RESPONSE FUNCTIONS

The human capital (HC) approach values environmental attributes through their effects on the quantity and quality of labour. Traditionally human capital theory has been used to measure health, education (Nonneman and Cortens, 1997; Knowles, 1997) and training (Wilson, 1983). The HC or loss of earnings approach focuses on the impact which adverse environmental conditions have on human health, and the resultant costs to society in terms of income lost through illness and spending on medical treatment.

DR techniques operate by (1) assessing the physical damage of a pollutant; and (2) estimating the economic value of the damage. The HC approach is only applicable in cases where there is a clear relationship between environmental degradation and illness, i.e. where the DR function has been estimated; and where the costs of lost labour supply and medical treatment are readily quantifiable in monetary terms.

The DR technique values an environmental commodity, such as air pollution, from the relationship between a specific amount of pollution (e.g. 1 tonne of SO_2/year) and the observed damage it causes (e.g. specified amount of damage to crops, buildings, individual's health, etc.). The health effects of particulate matter of less than 10 microns diameter (PM_{10}), from road transport emissions, appear to give rise to a wide range of respiratory symptoms and may also be linked to heart and lung disease since particulates may carry carcinogens into the lungs. A meta analysis of DR functions by Ostro (1994) based on DR relationships, established by Dockery *et al.* (1993), Schwartz (1994) and others over a number of different cities in the USA, indicated an average DR relationship for PM_{10} as:

$$\%dH_{MT} = 0.096.dPM_{10} \qquad\qquad (2.5)$$

where dH_{MT} is the change in mortality. This coefficient is, as far as possible, net of other factors such as smoking. Thus a 1 $\mu g/m^3$ change in PM_{10} concentrations is associated with a 0.1% change in mortality, or a 10 $\mu g/m^3$ change in PM_{10} concentrations is associated with a 1% change. However, there is considerable variation in the different DR study results, such that the upper and lower bounds of this DR estimate are given as $\%dH_{MT} = 0.130.dPM_{10}$ and $\%dH_{MT} = 0.062.dPM_{10}$, respectively.

There are many issues and problems, including econometric problems, in defining such a DR relationship. Some of these issues are reviewed by Pearce and Crowards (1995). The appropriateness of the DR relationship depends upon the functional specification: evidence from Schwartz (1994) and Dockery *et al.* (1993) suggest the mortality function is approximately linear, but more work is required to verify whether the functional relationship is linear or non-linear. In addition, there may be threshold levels which give rise to a strong attenuation effect at low exposure levels of PM_{10}, although there is no evidence of this to date. There is also the econometric question of whether the DR model has adequately controlled for all of the other variables affecting health status, such as smoking, diet, social status, income, indoor and outdoor concentrations of PM_{10}, etc. Failure to do so results in omitted variable bias, and biased estimates of the intercept and coefficients on the remaining variables in the model. Unless DR relationships between health and individual pollutants are separable, DR functions may over-estimate health impacts. There is also concern in DR studies regarding the biological pathway by which the pollutant affects health: for example, the relationship between childhood leukaemia and the location of electric power lines; and also the DR relationship between air pollution and damage to trees. Finally, there is the question of the transferability of DR functions from some American cities, to other cities, where the micro-climate and dispersion of pollutants, age, health, and other profiles for the population may be different.

The change in mortality from PM_{10} can be calculated as

$$dH_{MT} = b.dPM_{10}.\ CMR\ .\ POP\ .\ 1/100 \qquad (2.6)$$

where dH_{MT} = change in mortality; b = dose response coefficient (e.g. 0.096); CMR = crude mortality rate; POP = population; and the factor $1/100$ converts percentages to absolute numbers.

The problems in applying this DR relationship to measuring of health impacts revolve around the measurement of PM_{10}, the amount of PM_{10} from road transport compared to other sources in a locality, and the population at risk. The DR approach is further complicated by the fact that there are different ways of measuring particulate concentrations: the black smoke method draws air through a filter, and the darkness of the stain is calibrated to indicate concentration; whilst the gravimetric approach measures the weight of particulate matter on the filter paper. There is some dispute about the equivalence of these two measures. Furthermore, not all particulate matter is anthropogenic: some arises from natural background dust and only a proportion, although a major proportion, of anthropogenic dust is from road transport emissions. There is also the problem of defining the relevant population at risk. This is complicated by such factors as duration of residence in the area, commuting to work in the city, and the amount of time spent outdoors, all of which provide different amounts of exposure.

The HC approach estimates the value of a commodity as the economic costs (or losses at current market prices) associated with DR damages to that commodity. Originally, the economic value of life lost was based on an EOP approach: if wages are a measure of productivity, then earnings can be capitalised to derive the value of the future output society loses from an individual's death. Discounted future gross earnings form the 'human capital value' of the individual's life.[12] More recently the 'value of a statistical life'

---

[12] *Ex ante* (value of lives saved in the future) the human capital value of life is the loss of gross output (because the individual's life is saved, he will continue to be a member of society, hence his consumption is a benefit to society, in-as-much as, and since, he is a member of it). *Ex post* (estimate of the costs of deaths from environmental pollution last year) the relevant value of life is the individual's gross output minus his gross consumption, i.e. *net* output (or savings) lost. An implication of the human capital approach is that little old ladies have no value *ex post*: they

(VOSL) has been assessed by the 'value of a small change in risk' (VSCR) estimated through contingent valuation and standard gamble techniques (Jones-Lee, 1989).[13] Morbidity can similarly be measured as a cost of illness: loss of gross earnings plus medical expenses, to infer a lower bound value of a person's willingness-to-pay (WTP) to avoid air pollution.

The DR approach is not applicable to estimating the value of all environmental goods. For example, estimating the cost of noise using a DR function is problematic: noise can affect production, in offices and other land use classes, by reducing output (the Sturges v Bridgman case, 1879 is a classic case example of this type of tort[14] - see Coase, 1960); but for residential land uses the loss is an amenity or utility loss to consumers.[15] Thus some increases in noise will not result in any health effects by way of increased medical costs or lost output from work. Some aspects of the utility loss from noise might be better measured by an averting behaviour approach: i.e. how much people are prepared to spend to avert the consequences of an externality such as noise, e.g. by the installation of double glazing to reduce noise levels, or by moving house to a quieter area.

---

produce nothing but consume a lot! This clearly suggests that euthanasia is the best option (or more environmental pollution) since this entails a saving in consumption with no off setting loss of output: the economy will be better off! Similarly for housewives, no waged output is lost by their death! Economists of course impute a value to housewives for non-paid labour - for child care, cooking, cleaning, etc.

[13] In Britain the VOSL for road transport fatalities is £800,000 (1997); derived from a VSCR of £8 per 10^{-5} change in the probability of death. The Health and Safety Executive (HSE) (1997) values occupational asthma episodes for 'major' and 'over 3 day' industrial injuries at £18,000 and £3,000 respectively: i.e. 18 pence per 10^{-5} change in the probability of a 'major' injury, and 3 pence per 10^{-5} change in the probability of an 'over 3 day' injury.

[14] The Sturges v Bridgman (1879) case concerned a physician who moved into premises next to a confectionery manufacturer in London. The confectioner's machinery, which had been in operation for 60 years, caused the doctor no harm for 8 years until he built a new consulting room at the back of his premises adjoining the confectioner's workshop. The physician found the noise and vibration caused by the machinery made it difficult for him to use the new consulting room: the noise prevented him from examining his patients by auscultation for diseases of the chest, and made it impossible to engage in thought. The doctor sought a legal injunction to stop the confectioner using his machinery. The court found in the doctor's favour; presumably on the basis that it was the most valuable economic activity (conversely minimising the effect on production), and in recognition that the character of the area was changing and that the continued use of confectionery machinery would have a prejudicial effect upon the development of the land for residential purposes.

[15] This amenity loss can of course be valued through hedonic price models of the effect of externalities and public goods on property prices (see Chapter 4).

In some fields EOP and HC approaches are closely related in determining environmental regulations, e.g. to control pollution. Government regulations which limit or preclude some products in economic activities, because of health concerns to employees and to the general public, impact on production: substitute products may be more expensive and/or less efficient in the production process. However, there is often a failure to balance marginal costs and marginal benefits in determining environmental regulations, and this results in a large variance in the value of lives saved, accidents prevented, and environmental values. The divergence in the implicit value of a life saved has been documented by Teng *et al* (1995). The cost effectiveness of different environmental regulations varies enormously between categories. The median intervention cost is $42,000 per life year saved (over 587 different interventions), the median intervention in the transport sector costs $56,000 per life year saved, whilst some Environmental Protection Agency (EPA) measures can costs millions of dollars per life year saved.

Indeed, only two environmental laws in the USA (the Federal Insecticide, Fungicide and Rodent Act (FIFRA) and the Toxic Substances Control Act (TSCA)) require that benefits and costs are balanced in setting safety standards. Under the Clean Water Act costs are required to be considered in setting effluent standards, but benefits are not; whilst under the Clean Air Act costs are not even required to be considered in setting standards for hazardous air pollutants: standards are set to protect human health without consideration of costs. Section 112 of the 1970 Clean Air Act states:

> The Administrator shall establish any such standard at the level which in his judgement provides an ample margin of safety to protect the public health from such hazardous air pollutant.

Houtven and Cropper (1996) investigated whether the EPA balanced benefits and costs in issuing regulations, regardless of whether it was required to do so by law, across three main types of pollutants: (1) pesticides used on food crops; (2) asbestos (regulated under TSCA); and (3) air pollutants: benzene, radio nuclides, and vinyl chloride. The study was limited to the regulation of carcinogens because of the greater availability of data for these compared to other substances. For asbestos, a probit model estimated $P\ (Ban_i)$, the probability that asbestos would be banned for use in different products:

$$P(Ban_i) = P(aM_i + bC_i + u_i > 0) \tag{2.7}$$

where aM_i = value of cancer cases avoided; bC_i = cost of the ban; and u_i is an error term which captures other factors such as political considerations that influence the decision. Ignoring the error term, this is equivalent to banning asbestos in product i if the cost per life saved, C_i/M_i, falls below the threshold value $-a/b$ of the value of a cancer case avoided. From the observed regulatory decisions[16] the implied threshold value was $49 million (1989 prices) per cancer case avoided. A probit model predicting the probability of a pesticide ban estimated the value of a cancer case avoided as $51.51 million; although dietary cancer cases avoided, whilst significant in explaining a decision to ban a pesticide, had an implied value below $100,000. The model indicated that the higher the cost of a regulation the less likely was a pesticide to be banned. Hazardous air pollutants (benzene, radio nuclides, and vinyl chloride) were not regulated unless maximum individual risk exceeded 1 in 10,000, indicating that the acceptable level of risk was considerably higher for air pollutant than for pesticides. For vinyl chloride each cancer case avoided had an implicit value of $15 million.[17] Strikingly, Houtven and Cropper (1996) found that for all the regulations they examined, benefit and cost considerations alone explained 85% of all decisions issued: the EPA behaved as if it balanced benefits and costs in determining standards even when it was not required in law to do so. In environmental regulations, the EPA attached more weight to saving the lives of those occupationally exposed to asbestos and pesticides than to saving the lives of consumers. The Houtven and Cropper article raises two interesting issues. First, workers usually already receive compensating wage differentials for exposure to hazardous pollutants, so the greater weight attached to saving their lives by the EPA may be unjustified. Second, the weights implied by EPA decisions of over $45 million per cancer case avoided, under TCSA and FIFRA statutes requiring benefits and costs to be balanced, is a whole order of magnitude higher than compensating wage differentials which suggest that workers require compensation of around $5 million per statistical life[18] (Viscusi, 1993).

---

[16] EPA estimates of cancer cases made no distinction about when these would occur (most would not occur until many years in the future since there is a long latency period associated with asbestos); whilst in estimating the number of cancer cases avoided by banning asbestos it was assumed that all substitutes for asbestos were riskless.

[17] The value was the same before and after the 1987 Vinyl Chloride decision in the US Court of Appeals, District of Columbia, as long as the maximum individual risk (MIR) was less than 1 in 10,000. The 1987 court judgement ruled that the Environment Protection Agency had improperly considered costs in setting National Emissions Standards for Hazardous Air Pollutants (NESHAPS). If the MIR was greater than 1 in 10,000, then after 1987 the EPA did not consider costs at all. The value per cancer case avoided implied by regulations issued after 1987 was $194 million for risks greater than 1 in 10,000.

[18] The distinction between the voluntary and involuntary nature of the risk may explain some of this difference.

5 REPLACEMENT COST

The replacement cost (RC) approach assesses the value of a natural resource by how much it costs to replace or restore it after it has been damaged. This is the position adopted by the Comprehensive Environmental Response, Compensation, and Liability Act (CERCLA) (1980), in the USA, which requires the full restoration or replacement of natural resources damaged by pollution incidents. Liability for damages for injuries to natural resources[19] resulting from the release of hazardous substances rests with the polluter, who also has to pay for the clean-up of contaminated sites.[20] The value of natural resource damage is based upon: (1) restoration or replacement cost; (2) other use-values for which no market price is charged; and (3) any fees or other payments which would have been collected by the government. In essence, CERCLA is concerned with preserving the non-use and option values of natural resources and recovering any loss of consumer surplus (and economic rent) associated with non-market services such as open-access, non-priced recreation.

> The measure of damages is the cost of restoration, rehabilitation, replacement, and/or acquisition of the equivalent of the injured natural resources and the services those provide; plus the compensable value of the services lost to the public for the time period of the discharge or release until the attainment of the restoration, rehabilitation, replacement, and/or acquisition of equivalent of the resources and their services to the baseline. (The baseline is the without injury position.) (Federal Registrar, 1991)

Although many cases have been brought under CERCLA, details of the estimated economic damages to natural resources are rarely in the public domain, since many cases are settled out of court and with the provision that financial details remain confidential. However, to provide a flavour of the issues involved, Appendix 2.1 documents two early cases under CERCLA: New Bedford Harbour, and Idarado Mine, Colorado, further details of which, together with those from a number of other cases, can be found in Ward and Duffield (1992).

---

[19] Injuries to human resources are not covered by CERCLA. Compensation for human injuries and loss of use value of a resource (e.g. fisheries losses due to marine pollution) can be claimed through the courts under tort law.

[20] Where liability cannot be established, CERCLA, also know as 'Superfund', pays for clean-up costs with federal subsidies (see Probst *et al.*, 1995).

Clearly, restoring resources to their pre-damaged state ensures that lost consumer surplus and non-use values are recovered. Such values are omitted by some market and cost-based approaches such as the effect on production, opportunity cost, and human capital approaches. On the other hand the replacement cost approach may over-estimate society's value of a natural resource: society may value the resource at a lower value than it would cost to replace it. In recognition of this, the US Department of Interior (DOI) (1986) issued regulations which required resource trustees to 'select the lesser of restoration or replacement costs; or diminution of use values as the measure of damages' on the grounds that:

> If use value is higher than the cost of restoration or replacement, then it would be more rational for society to be compensated for the cost to restore or replace the lost resource than to be compensated for the lost use. Conversely, if restoration and replacement costs are higher than the value of uses foregone, it is rational for society to compensate individuals for their lost uses rather than the cost to restore or replace the injured natural resource.[21]

However, as replacement cost and mitigatory expenditure decisions become increasingly removed from individual preferences, then there is decreasing reason to believe that the benefits of such expenditure will reflect the costs incurred. Public choice theory explains why the benefits of public policy may be less than or exceed the costs of public provision (Mueller, 1979). Figure 2.1 illustrates why replacement cost and mitigatory expenditure approaches might result in the incorrect value being ascribed to the use and non-use values of an environmental resource.

In Figure 2.1, the horizontal axis shows the amount of restoration necessary to replace the lost environmental good or attribute; whilst the vertical axis shows the benefit of the environmental good in £/units, and also the £/unit resource cost of restoring the environmental good. Restoration costs (C) are an increasing function of the level of restoration; whilst restoration use and non-use benefits (B) decline with the cumulative increase in restoration. The environmental loss, under sustainability or the need to maintain the stock of natural capital, can be valued in terms of the monetary requirement for: (1) full restoration (100%); (2) economic efficiency (where

---

[21]   The Ohio v US DOI (1989) court case overturned the Department of Interior interpretation and restored the full restoration cost criterion: 'Congress established a distinct preference for restoration costs as the measure of recovery in natural resource damage cases', but the ruling did not completely reject the efficiency aspects of DOI's lesser-rule, vaguely stating that 'infeasibility of restoration or grossly disproportionate cost to use value, warrant a different standard'.

the difference between marginal benefits and marginal costs is maximised, i.e. at Q_E); or (3) some intermediate restoration level (e.g. where restoration costs do not exceed the use and non-use values of the environmental good, i.e. at Q_L). Position Q_L is in fact the 'lesser of' (a) the restoration or replacement costs or (b) the diminution of use values as the measure of damages. The maximum achievable level of benefits is at full restoration, where the resource is restored to 100% of its baseline quality level (which is also the 'strong condition' for defining sustainability). However, the economically efficient level of restoration of amenity damage is where the net benefit (B-C) is positive and maximised: at point Q_E. The efficient level of restoration under these conditions is well below the full restoration level. For restoration levels greater than Q_E, marginal costs are greater than marginal benefits. There is thus an allocative loss, in economic terms, associated with full restoration. Thus, it is not theoretically correct to argue that environmental losses can be valued in terms of the cost of averting, replacing, or restoring the natural resource damaged. The optimal level of restoration and replacement can only be established by determining the amenity benefits that society receives from the restoration of the natural resource or wildlife habitat.

In addition to forming the basis of CERCLA legislation in the USA, the RC method has been used to value a diverse range of environmental goods in Europe, such as the drainage function of canals (Button and Pearce, in Markandya, *et al.*, 1991) and biodiversity targets under the Rio Convention (see Department of the Environment, 1995; Willis, *et al.*, 1996). RC assumes that the existing environmental system is optimal, and that every part of a given system would need to be replaced to make those benefiting from it equally as well off as they were before the change. For example, RC values the drainage function of canals by assessing the cost necessary to replace canals to continue this drainage function. It thus assumes that the drainage function of canals (a positive externality) is optimal, without questioning whether the drainage of agricultural land by canals, in terms of the additional agricultural output with drainage compared to that without drainage, equals or exceeds the cost of replacing or restoring the canal.[22] Similarly, whilst the cost of meeting biodiversity targets is a real financial and social cost, the RC approach cannot determine whether targets for the maintenance, restoration or re-creation of reedbeds, lowland heaths, moor grass and rush pastures, native pine woodlands, sea grass beds, etc., are optimal, and whether the associated benefits exceed the costs.

---

[22] Given the social opportunity cost of agricultural output reported in Table 2.2, it is almost certain that drainage benefits are less than canal replacement costs.

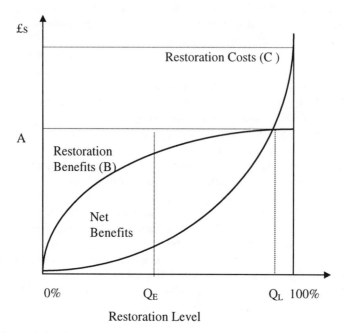

Figure 2.1: Measures of amenity value under a replacement or restoration
cost scenario

6 PREVENTATIVE, MITIGATORY EXPENDITURE AND AVERTING BEHAVIOUR APPROACHES

These approaches assess the value of non-marketed commodities such as cleaner air and water, through the amounts individuals are willing to pay for market goods and services to mitigate an environmental externality, or to prevent a utility loss from environmental degradation, or to change their behaviour to acquire greater environmental quality.

Environmental values can sometimes be inferred from mitigatory expenditure to alleviate the environmental externality. Mitigatory expenditures (such as the cost of removing turf and subsoil comprising a grassland SSSI, which would otherwise be destroyed in a quarry extension, and its removal to another suitable neighbouring location), and preventative expenditure (such as a road diversion to avoid an SSSI), create implicit prices for environmental amenities and biodiversity. People also undertake averting action to improve their environmental quality. People may purchase bottled water to avoid drinking from public water supplies or install water filtration systems in their homes. Similarly, people may spend more time indoors to avoid exposure to air pollution, and install air purifiers in their homes to improve air quality.[23] These purchases are effectively substitute goods for a cleaner environment. People may also install double glazing to reduce road traffic noise in their homes. However, this does not prevent road traffic noise from invading their gardens and backyards; thus preventative and mitigatory expenditure, in this instance, is a minimum estimate of the utility lost due to this type of noise. In extreme cases people may move to another residential location to avoid an environmental externality. However, if the general environment is improved by some policy initiative, the individual will spend less on these substitute goods. Thus changes in expenditures on substitute goods is a measure of people's values for environmental improvements.[24]

Where such preventative and mitigatory expenditure is made by individuals or private conservation groups, then there may be a reasonable expectation that the benefits derived exceed that expenditure, or at least equal it at the margin. There are many examples for such expenditure by organisations such as local Wildlife Trusts, and the Royal Society for the Protection of Birds (RSPB). In 1971 the Yorkshire Wildlife Trust undertook a fund raising campaign amongst its members and the general public to purchase 400 hectares of land at Wheldrake Ings, part of the Derwent Ings in Yorkshire, an area of alluvial grassland with ornithological and botanical interest. In summer the land provides crops of hay and grazing for cattle and sheep; but winter flooding of the land attracts wading birds. The Trust will not disclose the sum paid, but some idea of the cost can be derived from a purchase of similar land in the Derwent Ings by the Nature Conservancy Council in 1986 for £1,986 per hectare. The Yorkshire Wildlife Trust also manages Skipwith Common, incurring financial expenditure and also non-pecuniary inputs of members time (Benson and Willis, 1988). Similarly, the RSPB willingly incurs expenditure on purchasing and managing areas of agricultural land. For example, the RSPB lowland wet grassland reserve in the Nene Washes incurs expenditure of around £41,500 per year (1994/95) (£25,200 for staff; £7,500 for maintenance; £4,300 for projects; £4,200 for rent; and £300 for buildings); against a rental value received for the land of

---

[23] Whilst expenditure on air purifiers can be measured, spending more time indoors is much more difficult to value economically using market price and cost measures of value and illustrates a limitation of the averting behaviour approach to valuing some types of environmental externalities.

[24] Note that some types of policy changes may induce moral hazard. When the wearing of motor cycle crash helmets and seats belts in cars was made compulsory, it was estimated that people engaged in averting behaviour by driving faster, to maintain their preferred level of risk, so that the reduction in accidents, deaths and injuries on roads was not as great as might have been expected (see Peltzman, 1975).

£19,600. The RSPB is also prepared to spend several thousand pounds managing West Sedgemoor in Somerset, a site which attracts lapwing, Bewick's swan, widgeon and teal. The aims of managing the West Sedgemoor site are to:

- restore and maintain it as a site dominated by lowland grassland with winter flooding, holding internationally important numbers of wintering wildfowl and nationally important breeding wader populations and plant assemblages;
- alter the hydrological regime of the RSPB land to maintain the water table 10 to 20 cms below the surface from April to the end of June to provide better conditions for breeding waders and to increase the probability of greater densities of breeding waders including snipe, red shank, and black-tailed godwit;
- continue the traditional mowing and grazing regime on the Somerset Levels and Moors in order to provide suitable sward conditions for breeding waders and wintering waterfowl, and retain and restore nationally important plant communities characteristic of unimproved lowland wet grassland.

Willingness to incur these financial costs at the margin is determined by the supply of these types of sites in Britain of and also by demand for this type of site from RSPB members. Increasing the supply of such sites would reduce the amount of mitigatory expenditure per acre that the RSPB would be willing to incur at other sites. However, there is still the question of whether the RSPB would incur all this expenditure (or have a site covering such a large acreage) if ESA payments were not available to defray some of the costs.

Mitigatory activities and expenditure is undertaken in the USA and Canada by electric power companies in an attempt to avoid delays, future retrofits, and litigation. Several epidemiological studies have examined the statistical association between residential exposure to electromagnetic fields (EMFs) from electricity power lines and human health effects, including leukaemia and brain cancer. The evidence is inconclusive. The effect is difficult to disentangle: EMFs are ubiquitous and emanate from other sources such as wiring in homes, electrical appliances, and computers. Moreover, there is no consensus on the biological mechanism that might produce health effects from exposure to EMFs. Nevertheless, public concern about the association is growing and is reflected in prices consumers are willing to pay to live away from transmission lines. Various studies in North America using hedonic price models have shown a significant negative relationship between selling price and proximity to high voltage power lines for properties within 300 feet or so of the transmission line; and also for agricultural land with easements for transmission lines. Effects vary depending on distance and locality, but reductions in property values typically average 5% to 10% of market value with larger declines reported for properties bordering transmission lines. Gregory and von Winterfeldt (1996) report several examples of expensive mitigation measures to reduce EMFs, including engineering work to re-configure conductors to reduce EMFs, selecting alternative routes for lines through areas with lower population densities, and burying lines underground. Mitigation actions are particularly common as a response to school district and parents' concerns about the health effect of power lines near schools. However, avertive costs might not always be high. British Columbia (Canada) Hydro agreed to purchase houses affected by a 230kV line across a rural section of Vancouver Island. Of the 155 eligible properties, 72 home owners expressed an interest in selling, and 59 sales took place. BC Hydro spent $3.7 million on the purchases, and within one year had resold the properties for $3.5 million. The total cost of the buyout program, including transactions costs, was $1.1 million.

Where mitigatory actions and expenditures are not undertaken, litigation can ensue. Gregory and von Winterfeldt (1996) report several litigation cases in which power companies have had to compensate individuals for the adverse effects of EMFs on the value of their property. In 1982 the San Diego Gas and Electric Company (SDG&E) filed for eminent domain to acquire a 200-foot wide power line easement across land owned by Daley, a rancher in eastern San Diego County. Daley argued that EMFs, and visual degradation, would render areas of the property adjacent to the easement less desirable for buyers. The diminution in value was estimated to be 4% of the property's value before the power line, i.e. $1.26 million. The California Court of Appeals in 1988 upheld an earlier ruling in Daley's favour. In another case Klein School District in Texas was awarded $104,000 in damages and $25 million punitive damages against Houston Lighting and Power Co. for a 345kV transmission line across land housing two schools and an option for a third on the basis of EMF risks to children. The Texas Court of Appeal (1987) affirmed the judgement but dismissed the punitive damages as beyond the scope of remedies allowed in eminent domain statutes. The New York State Court of Appeals in 1993 (Criscuola v Power Authority of New York State) stated that *'there should be no requirement that the claimant...must establish the reasonableness of a fear or a perception of danger or of health risks from exposure to high voltage power lines'*; and that *'whether the danger is a scientifically genuine or verifiable fact should be irrelevant to the central issue of its market value impacts'*. In other words, what is relevant in valuation is the market response to people's subjective perception of environmental risk, not an 'objective' assessment. Subjective assessment of non-use or passive use value also forms the basis of compensation for environmental damages under CERCLA legislation, and under the Oil

Pollution Act 1990, in the USA; damages evaluated by contingent valuation methods (see Chapter 5).

7 PROXIMITY OF PREVENTATIVE AND MITIGATORY EXPENDITURE TO TRUE BENEFIT MEASURES

The degree of proximity of preventative and mitigatory expenditure measures to Marshallian and Hicksian measures of utility from a change in environmental quality is illustrated in Figure 2.2. The price of averting behaviour is $f(P_0)$ and $f(P_1)$ when pollution is at P_0 and P_1 respectively. Q_m, is the Marshallian demand curve, and Q^h_o, and Q^h_1 the Hicksian demand curves with regard to utility levels U_0 and U_1 respectively for environmental quality Q. The various utility measures of benefits from welfare change are represented by the area(s):

preventative expenditure savings with respect to Q_0	a
Hicksian compensating variation (CV)	$a + b$
Marshallian consumer surplus (CS)	$a + b + c$
Hicksian equivalent variation (EV)	$a + b + c + d$
preventative expenditure savings with respect to Q_1	$a + b + c + d + e$

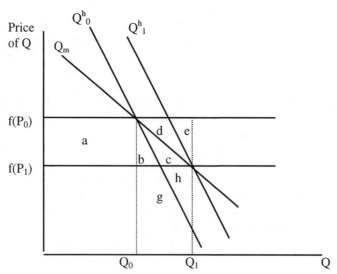

Figure 2.2: Comparison of benefit measures when the defensive expenditure function is linear

The percentage error in using preventative expenditure (PE), with respect to Q_0, instead of the CV measure of the utility change, depends on the size of area b relative to area a. Similarly, the percentage error in using PE, with respect to Q_1, instead of the EV measure of this utility change, depends on the size of area e relative to areas $a + b + c + d + e$. Bartik (1988) shows from this analysis that, for a linear function, the percentage error in PE as a measure of benefits, relative to CV, is:

$$[CV - PE\,(Q_0)]\,/\,PE\,(Q_0) = area\ b\,/\,area\ a = 1/2\ [\Delta\,price\,/\,price]\ (-\,\varepsilon)\ (2.8)$$

where ε is the Hicksian price elasticity of demand. He demonstrates that *PE* is a good approximate benefit measure if the change in *Q's* price is small or the household's demand is inelastic. For non-linear functions the analysis is more complex, but similar conclusions are reached (Bartik, 1988).

REFERENCES

Abelson, Peter (1996), *Project Appraisal and Valuation of the Environment: general principles and six case-studies in developing countries*, Macmillan, London.

Adams, R.M., T.D. Crocker and N. Thanavibulchai (1982), 'An economic assessment of air pollution damages to selected annual crops in southern California', *Journal of Environmental Economics and Management* **9**, 42–58.

Adams, R.M., J.M. Callaway and B.A. McCarl (1986), 'Pollution, agriculture and social welfare: the case of acid deposition', *Canadian Journal of Agricultural Economics* **34**, 1–19.

Bartik, Timothy J. (1988), 'Evaluating the benefits of non-marginal reductions in pollution using information on defensive expenditure', *Journal of Environmental Economics and Management* **15**, 111–27.

Benson, J.F. and K.G. Willis (1988), 'Conservation costs, agricultural intensification and the Wildlife and Countryside Act 1981', A case study and simulation on Skipwith Common, North Yorkshire, England. *Biological Conservation* **44**, 157–78.

Brown, D. and M. Smith (1984), 'Crop substitution in the estimate of economic benefits due to ozone reduction', *Journal of Environmental Economics and Management* **11**, 347–62.

Browning, E.K. and W.R. Johnson (1984), 'The trade-off between equality and efficiency', *Journal of Political Economy* **92**, 175–203.

Carrier, J.G. and J. Kripple (1990), 'Comprehensive study of European forests damage and economic losses from air pollution control', *Environmental Conservation* **17**, 365–6.

Cheshire, Paul C. and Stephen Sheppard (1997), 'Welfare economics of land use regulation', Research Papers in *Environmental and Spatial Analysis* **42**, Department of Geography, London School of Economics.

Coase, R. (1960), 'The Problem of Social Cost', *Journal of Law and Economics* **3**, 1–44.

Coase, R.H. (1974), 'The lighthouse in economics', *Journal of Law and Economics* **14**, 201–27.

Crocker T.D. (1971), 'Externalities, property rights, and transaction costs: an empirical study', *Journal of Law and Economics* **14**, 451–64.

Department of the Environment (1995), '*Biodiversity: the UK Steering Group Report', Volume 2: Actions Plans*, HMSO, London.

Dixon, J.A. and P.B. Sherman (1990), *Economics of Protected Areas: a new look at benefits and costs*, Earthscan, London.

Dockery, D.W., J. Schwartz and J. Spengler (1993), 'An association between air pollution and mortality in six U.S. cities', *New England Journal of Medicine* **329**(4), 1753–808.

Farber, Stephen (1987), 'The value of coastal wetlands for protection of property against hurricane wind damage', *Journal of Environmental Economics and Management* **14**, 143–51.

Gregory, Robin and Detlof von Winterfeldt (1996), 'The effects of electromagnetic fields from transmission lines on public fears and property values', *Journal of Environmental Management* **48**, 201–14.

Hanley, N. (1991), 'Wilderness development decisions and the Krutilla-Fisher model: the case of Scotland "flow country", *Ecological Economics* **4**, 145–64.

Harvey, David R. and J. Hall (1989) 'PSEs, Producer benefits and transfer efficiency of the CAP and alterntives', *DP 3/89*, Department of Agricultural Economics and Food Marketing, University of Newcastle upon Tyne.

Houtven, George Van and Maureen L. Cropper (1996), 'When is a life too costly to save? the evidence for U.S. government environmental regulations', *Journal of Environmental Economics and Management* **30**, 348–68.

Jones-Lee, Michael W. (1989), *The Economics of Safety and Physical Risk*, Basil Blackwell, Oxford.

Kim, S. and J.A. Dixon (1986), 'Economic valuation of environmental quality aspects of upland agriculture in Korea', in J.A. Dixon and M.M. Hufschmidt (eds), *Economics Valuation Techniques for the Environment*, John Hopkins University Press, Baltimore.

Knowles, Stephen (1997), 'Which level of schooling has the greatest economic impact on output?', *Applied Economic Letters* **4**, 177–80.

Krutilla, J. and A. Fisher (1975), *The Economics of Natural Environments: studies in the valuation of commodity and amenity resources*, John Hopkins University Press, Baltimore.

Lakshminarayan, P.G., Aziz Bouzaher and Jason F. Shogren (1996), 'Atrazine and water quality: an evaluation of alternative policy options', *Journal of Environmental Management* **48**, 111–26.

McInerney, J. (1986), 'Agricultural Policy at the Crossroads', in A. Gilg (ed.) *Countryside Planning Yearbook* (1986), Geobooks, Norwich.

Markandya, Anil, David Pearce and R. Kerry Turner (1991), 'The United Kingdom', in Jean-Philippe Barde and David W. Pearce (eds), *Valuing the Environment: six case studies*, Earthscan Publications, London.

Mendelsohn, R., D. Hellerstein, M. Huguenin, R. Unsworth and R. Brazee (1991) 'Measuring Hazardous Waste Damages with Panel Models', Report to the National Oceanic and Atmospheric Administration, Washington DC.

Mueller, D.C. (1979), *Public Choice*, Cambridge University Press, Cambridge.

Munch, Patricia (1976), 'An economic analysis of eminent domain', *Journal of Political Economy* **84**, 473–97.

Nonneman, Walter and Isabelle Cortens (1997), 'A note on the rate of return to investment in education in Belgium', *Applied Economic Letters* **4**, 167–71.

Norman, Michael and Barry Stoker (1991), *Data Envelopment Analysis: the assessment of performance*, J. Wiley, Chichester.

Ostro, B. (1994) 'Estimating Health Effects of Air Pollution: a method with an application to Jakarta', Working Paper 1301, Policy Research Department, The World Bank, Washington DC.

Parks, Peter J. and James P. Schorr (1997), 'Sustaining open space benefits in the north-east: an evaluation of the Conservation Reserve Program', *Journal of Environmental Economics and Management* **32**, 85–94.

Pearce, D.W. and T. Crowards (1995), 'Assessing health costs of particulate air pollution in the UK', CSERGE Working Paper GEC 95–27, Centre for Social and Economic Research on the Global Environment, University of East Anglia, and University College London.

Peltzman, Sam (1975), 'The effects of automobile safety regulation', *Journal of Political Economy* **83**, 677–725.

Porter, P. (1982), 'The new approach to wilderness preservation through benefit-cost analysis', *Journal of Environmental Economics and Management* **9**, 59–80.

Probst, Katherine N., Don Fullerton, Robert E. Litan and Paul R. Portney (1995), *Footing the Bill for Superfund Cleanups*, The Brookings Institution and Resources for the Future, Washington DC.

Rowe, R.D. and L.G. Chestnut (1985), 'Economic assessment of the effects of air pollution control on agricultural crops in the San Joaquin Valley', *Journal of Air Pollution Control Association* **35**, 728–34.

SACTRA (The Standing Advisory Committee on Trunk Road Assessment) (1992), *Assessing the Environmental Impact of Road Schemes,* Department of Transport, HMSO, London.

Sadler, H., J. Bennett, I. Reynolds, and B. Smith (1980), 'Public Choice in Tasmania: aspects of the lower Gordon River hydro-electric development proposal', Centre for Resource and Environmental Studies, Australian National University, Canberra.

Saunders, Caroline M. (1996), 'Financial, Public Exchequer and Social Value Changes in Agricultural Output', Working Paper 20, Centre for Rural Economy, Department of Agricultural Economics and Food Marketing, University of Newcastle upon Tyne.

Schwartz, J. (1994), 'Air pollution and daily mortality: a review and meta analysis', *Environmental Research* **64**, 36–52.

Spash, Clive L. (1997), 'Assessing the economic benefits to agriculture from air pollution control', *Journal of Economic Surveys* **11**, 47–70.

Stevenson, Glenn G. (1991), *Common Property Economics: a general theory and land use applications*, Cambridge University Press, Cambridge.

Teng, Tammy O., Miriam E. Adams, Joseph S. Pliskin, Dana Gelb Safran, Joanna E. Siegel, Milton C. Weinstein and John D. Graham (1995), 'Five hundred life saving interventions and their cost effectiveness', *Risk Analysis* **15**, 369–90.

Viscusi, W. Kip (1993), 'The value of risks to life and health', *Journal of Economic Literature* **31**, 1912–46.

Ward, Kevin M. and John W. Duffield (1992), *Natural Resource Damages: Law and Economics*, J. Wiley, New York.

Whittington, Dale, Donald T. Lauria, Daniel A. Okun and Xinming Mu (1989), 'Water vending activities in developing countries: a case study of Ukunda, Kenya', *Water Resources Development* **5** (3), 158–68.

Willis, K.G. (1980), *The Economics of Town and Country Planning*, Granada, London.

Willis, K.G. and M.C. Whitby (1985),'The value of green belt land', *Journal of Rural Studies*, **1**, 147-62.

Willis, K.G. and J.F. Benson (1988), 'A comparison between user benefits and costs of nature conservation at three nature reserves', *Regional Studies* **22**, 417–28.

Willis, K.G., G.B. Nelson, A.B. Bye, and G. Peacock (1993), 'An application of the Krutilla-Fisher model to appraising the benefits of green belt preservation versus site development', *Journal of Environmental Planning and Management* **36**, 73–90.

Willis, K.G., G.D. Garrod and P. Shepherd (1996), *Towards a Methodology for Costing Biodiversity Targets in the UK*, HMSO, London.

Wilson, R.A. (1983), 'Rates of return: some further results', *Scottish Journal of Political Economy* **30**, 114–27.

Winch, D.M. (1971), *Analytical Welfare Economics*, Penguin, Harmondsworth.

Winpenny, J.T. (1991), *Values for the Environment: a guide to economic appraisal*, HMSO, London.

APPENDIX 2.1

Natural Resource Damage Assessments under CERCLA

New Bedford Harbour

PCBs (polychlorinated biphenyls) were released into New Bedford Harbour, allegedly over many decades, and contaminated the water. Their presence was first confirmed in harbour sediments in 1976, but widespread awareness of the problem only occurred gradually: a study of beach use in 1983 found that only 50% of respondents knew of PCB pollution. Pollution was most concentrated in the inner harbour, (PCB zone 1) where swimming, fishing, and lobstering were prohibited. In zone 2, the outer harbour restrictions were imposed on lobstering and bottom fishing. Zones 3 and 4 were more remote from the harbour and contained only trace amounts of PCBs.

This resource damage was assessed using a repeat sale model (RSM) by Mendelsohn *et al.* (1991). RSMs can accurately measure pollution effects using data on property markets. RSMs are based on economic theory, but are simple to explain, and are not demanding in terms of data. However, they assume that the hedonic house price function is unchanging over time and that relevant price influencing variables which change over time have been included. Compared with hedonic price models, RSMs offer a simple solution for standardising characteristics which do not change over time.

Two variants of RSM were used:

1. differencing: the difference in sale price $V_t - V_{t+1}$
2. averaging: the difference between the house price at V_t and the average of all houses at V_{t+1}, i.e. $(V_t - V)$

However, it is necessary to correct for the effects of other influences over time: e.g. renovation expenditure, interest rates, per capita area income, and property tax changes. Data consisted of sales of single family houses in Dartmouth, Fairhaven, and New Bedford between 1969 and 1988, comprising 780 properties and 1,916 sales. Both linear and log-linear models were estimated. Environmental variables included a dummy for PCB (0 before 1982, 1 after 1982), and dummies for proximity to one of the four PCB zones of concentration.

Results for zone 1 showed that the effect of PCB was a decrease in property values of around 8% or $9,000; for zone 2 a decrease of 3% to 7%, or around $7,000. Results for the differencing and averaging models, although not identical, were similar. The results were aggregated by the number of single-family homes across census tracts in Dartmouth, Fairhaven, and New Bedford. Damages from PCBs in zone 1 were estimated at $15.3 million, and in zone 2 at $20.6 million. These estimates were conservative because of the exclusion of renters. On the basis of these estimates firms paid $20 million in CERCLA natural resource damages.

Idarado Mine: Colorado

In 1978 hexavalent chromium was discovered in two new municipal water supply wells in Telluride. The wells were located 1,600 ft. from the largest tailings pond for the Idarado complex.

The plaintiff, the State of Colorado, as trustee for the affected resources, produced estimates of natural resource damages (caused by blown tailings from tailings piles) to an aquifer, the Uncompahgre River, Ridgeway reservoir, and several properties (see Table A2.1.1).

Present value (PV) of future use and non-use damages were estimated in excess of $40 million and past use damages in excess of $100 million. PVs were derived by discounting over 10 years at 10% discount rate. The capitalisation values assumed the initial injury started in 1956 and was capitalised at 2.5% to 1975 and 10% from 1975 to 1985, the date of the study.

Table A2.1.1 Idarado mine case: plaintiff's natural resource damage estimates

Estimating Method/ Type of Damage	Unit Damage Estimate, 1985 Dollars	Discounted Present Value of Future Damage (Aggregate Estimate)
Future Damages Contingent valuation method		
Use values	$26 per household	County residents $0.22 million
	$1.80 per household	State residents $13 million
Non-use values	$42 per household	County residents $0.36 million
	$3.80 per household	State residents $28 million
Service replacement method Aquifer contamination	$2,000 per year	Town of Telluride $3–5 million
Property value appraisal Soil contamination		51 acres $2 million
Unit day method Recreational fishing	$14–22 per day	16,000 user days $0.9–1.4 million
Past Damages Contingent variation method		
Use values	$26 per household	County residents $1.9 million
	$1.80 per household	State residents $104 million

A variety of techniques were employed:

1. replacement cost was used to estimate the damage to the drinking water acquifer;
2. property value appraisal for soil contamination;
3. unit day values for lost recreational fishing.

Estimates for the replacement cost of drinking water ranged from $1,000 to $3,000 per acre foot of water lost. Multiplying this by the demand on the system, discounting over 30 years at 10%, produced estimates of $3 million and to $5 million.

Reduction in property values from soil contamination was estimated at 10% to 15% based on a similar soil contamination case in Park City, Utah.

For lost recreational fishing, the US Forest Service unit day trout fishing values of $14 to $22 per day were used, with an estimated 16,000 potential additional fishing days if the reservoir was not contaminated but was developed for fishing.

Table A2.1.2   Idarado mine case: defendant's natural resource damage estimates

Estimation Method/ Type of Damage	Unit Damage Estimate, 1985 Dollars	Discounted Present Value of Future Damage (Aggregate Estimate)
Future Damages Service replacement method		
Aquifer contamination	$205,000 per new well	Town of Telluride $205,000
Soil contamination	$0.27 per square foot	30 acres $275,400
Recreational fishing	$0.07 per day	16,000 user days $4,500

The defendant's estimates of the natural resource damages were somewhat different (Table A2.1.2). The defendant argued that because least cost alternatives were required by CERCLA:

1. damage to the aquifer corresponded to the cost of drilling new wells: $205,000;
2. soil contamination could be overcome by covering affected areas with six inches of uncontaminated soil and planting grass, at 27 cents per square foot; at a cost of $275,400;
3. it was inappropriate to seek damages for a non-existent reservoir fishery. But even if the fishery did exist, the appropriate value was not $14 to $22 per day (an average value), but the marginal value that Colorado fishermen would place on improved reservoir fishing. Using estimates for improved recreational fishing along the Uncompahgre River of only $0.07 per day — very low because of the availability of substitutes — the defendant estimated recreational fishing damages at $14,000 in aggregate.

The defendant's estimate of future damages was less than $500,000 compared with the plaintiff's estimate of $8 million to $40 million, plus an additional $100 million for past damages. Thus the plaintiff's and defendant's estimates differed by more than two orders of magnitude.

The baseline positions in both the plaintiff's and defendant's cases were the same. The differences between the two positions mainly occurred because of the estimates of past damages (the defendant assumed there weren't any); the assumption of a large number of almost perfect substitutes for recreational fishing by the defendant; the state counting non-fishing use and general non-use values and extending these to the whole state rather than just county residents; and the alternative assumptions about the cost of drinking water replacement.

The differences in the estimates between the plaintiff and the defendant arose mainly because of differences in the above assumptions, rather than being a reflection of any disagreement in the benefit estimating techniques employed.

3. The Travel-Cost Method

Two roads diverged in a wood, and I
I took the one less travelled by,
And that has made all the difference.

Robert Frost (1874–1963): *The Road Not Taken*

1 TRAVEL-COST MODELS

Conventional household-production function (HPF) models investigate changes in the consumption of commodities that are substitutes or complements for each other. This framework can be extended to derive indirect mechanisms for evaluating individual preferences for and consumption of non-market goods.

The travel-cost method (TCM) is a prominent example of an HPF-type approach and uses the cost of travelling to a non-priced recreation site as a means of inferring the recreational benefits which that site provides. Questionnaire surveys are used to collect data on the number of visits that a household or individual makes to a site and on the cost of gaining access. Such travel-cost estimates can be used to infer the demand for a recreation site because in economic terms they are weakly complementary to on-site recreation.

The logic behind this approach was first suggested by Harold Hotelling in 1947 (reported in Prewitt, 1949) and the methodology was subsequently developed in the late 1950s and 1960s by, among others: Trice and Wood (1958); Clawson (1959); and Clawson and Knetsch (1966). Since then, numerous studies have adopted a methodology based on this approach.

TCM studies have consistently shown that as the price of access (cost of travel) increases, the visit rate to the site falls. The TCM is usually estimated as a trip generating function such as the following:

$$V = f(P, S) \tag{3.1}$$

where V is the visit rate, P is the cost of travel to the site and S is a vector of travel costs to substitute sites (this may refer only to sites of a similar nature or may be extended to include other recreational attractions).

The various travel-cost models that appear in the literature are similar to the example given above, with variations arising from the manner in which the variables are defined and measured, and from the estimation procedure employed. Indeed, for many studies the approaches to structural specification, measurement, and estimation are often determined as much by the availability of data as they are by other considerations emanating from economic theory.

The task of using a TCM to measure the benefits provided by the recreational experience of visiting a given site may appear straightforward, but a range of issues arises regarding the specification and estimation of the model and the subsequent calculation of consumer surplus. All of these can have a considerable impact on the final benefit estimates. For example, even the term 'recreational experience' is problematic, suggesting that the TCM is measuring more than just the benefits generated by the recreational site (Freeman, 1979). This issue will be discussed in a later section.

Furthermore, travel-cost analysis produces estimates of public recreational benefits that are rarely verifiable. However, unlike contingent valuation methods (Chapter 5), benefit estimates derived from recreational demand models are only one step away from observable measures.

A range of methodological issues must be considered before undertaking travel-cost analysis. Estimation issues such as the form of the travel-cost model and its functional specification will be discussed first, followed by a brief analysis of a number of other issues including the separability problem and the treatment of time and travel costs.

2 THE ZONAL TRAVEL-COST METHOD

Clawson and Knetsch (1966) estimated a travel-cost model based on data relating to the zones of origin of site visitors. The zonal travel-cost model (ZTCM) approach defines the trip generating function as:

$$V_{hj}/N_h = f(P_{hj}, SOC_h, SUB_h) \tag{3.2}$$

Here, the dependent variable V_{hj}/N_h is the participation rate for zone h (visits per capita to the site j), with independent variables comprising P_{hj} the cost of travel from zone h to site j, SOC_h a vector of the socio-economic characteristics of zone h, and SUB_h a vector of substitute recreational site characteristics for individuals in zone h. The ZTCM has been applied to estimate the demand and consumer surplus for wildlife and nature conservation at specific sites since the 1960s. More recent examples are Farber (1988) investigating recreation on Louisiana wetlands, Willis (1990) and Hanley (1989) both estimating consumer surplus for forest recreation.

The Zonal Travel-Cost Method

1   *Identify site and collect data from visitors relating to their points of origin and the number of visits to the site in the specified time period (e.g. a year).*

2   *Define zones of origin and allocate visitors to the appropriate zone.*

3   *Calculate zonal visits per household to the site and average travel cost from each zone to the site.*

4   *Use census data to derive variables relating to zonal socio-economic characteristics.*

5   *Use data from (3) and (4) to estimate the trip generating function.*

6   *Derive demand curve and obtain zonal household consumer surplus estimates through integrating under the demand curve.*

7   *Calculate aggregate zonal consumer surplus.*

8   *Aggregate zonal consumer surplus estimates to obtain an estimate of total consumer surplus.*

The methodology underlying the ZTCM is relatively straightforward. Data are collected on site, recording the point of origin of visitors and the number of visits made to the site in a given period. The area surrounding the site is then divided into various zones of origin each of which has an associated average travel cost to the site. The simplest form of zonal designation is based on straight line distance away from the site, with zones defined as a series of concentric rings radiating away from the site. Using simple Geographical Information Systems (GIS) techniques, this methodology can be refined by redefining zones based on road distances or travel times (e.g. Bateman *et al.,*

1996). Alternatively zones can be defined using areas of population or other geographic units.

Once zones have been defined, household visits from any zone h to site j can be calculated by allocating sampled visitors to their zone of origin. Census data is used to estimate the number of households in each zone. These figures are used to calculate zonal visits per capita to the site (i.e. divide the number of household visits originating in zone h by the number of households in the zone). The trip generating function is then estimated, explaining per capita zonal visits by average travel cost: this, of course, assumes that all households in a given zone have similar preferences for recreation at site j and that they would react similarly to changes in the cost of access. Other explanatory variables can be generated by using census data to provide zonal socio-economic characteristics and then employing GIS techniques to calculate zonal average measures of access to any substitute recreational sites in the area.

The trip generating function is essentially a demand curve, and per household consumer surplus estimates for recreation at site j can be estimated for each zone of origin. This is achieved by integrating the demand function between the price at which visits are currently made from a given zone and the point at which the zonal visit rate per household falls to zero. Total zonal consumer surplus can then be calculated by multiplying consumer surplus per household by the number of households in each zone. Aggregate consumer surplus for the recreational experience provided by visits to site j is then calculated by summing consumer surplus estimates across all zones: to simplify this process some authors assume that consumer surplus from the most distant zones of origin is zero (e.g. Sinden and Worrell, 1979; Hufschmidt *et al.*, 1983).

Normally, travel-cost models are employed at sites where access is unrestricted and there is no admittance charge. Where a charge is made, the same methodology can be applied with the average zonal travel cost being increased by the admission charge and calculations for consumer surplus being adjusted accordingly.

Zonal definition has been an issue that has exercised the minds of a number of authors, including Smith and Kopp (1980) who demonstrated that the assumptions underlying the definition of zones can seriously impact on the resulting estimates of consumer surplus. Similarly, several authors (e.g. Bowes and Loomis, 1980; Strong, 1983) have suggested that unless zones have equal populations, a correction must be made for heteroscedasticity if ordinary least squares regression is to be used for estimation. There is no generally agreed method of defining zones and often the observed distribution of visitors will suggest an appropriate method of zoning based on spatial factors.

By contrast Pearse (1968), in a study of big-game hunting in Canada, used zones based on income bands rather than on distance from the site. Indeed, there may be some merit in future researchers re-examining zonal definition by population characteristics rather than distance: GIS tools may provide the means by which this could be achieved. GIS has already improved the data available for zonal definition, and Bateman *et al.* (1996) used GIS techniques to examine the effects of a variety of zonal definitions based on distance away from the site, again demonstrating the sensitivity of consumer surplus estimates to zonal definition.

The ZTCM is best suited to estimating consumer surplus for recreation at sites where visitor origins are relatively evenly distributed. Problems arise when visitor origins are distributed asymmetrically or where there are a few important points of origin to a single site (e.g. a ski resort which services the populations of the three nearest cities). The ZTCM is also unsuitable for estimating consumer surplus at recreational areas which are linear, rather than circular, in topology. This is principally because of the ability of visitors in the same distance zone to travel a variety of distances to gain access to different points of the same linear feature. This phenomenon makes the derivation of a single consistent travel-cost estimate for visitors from a given distance zone problematic, unless visits to each specific recreation point are analysed rather than visits to the feature as a whole.

The ZTCM is even more unsuitable where there are few visitors along the linear feature, because each access point along the feature requires visitors to be assigned to zones in relation to that point; and with few visitors, visit rates form a stochastic rather than regular pattern for each zone, undermining the underlying logic of the zonal approach. These difficulties can be overcome by employing individual data in the estimation process.

3 THE INDIVIDUAL TRAVEL-COST METHOD

The individual travel cost model (ITCM) has been successfully applied to a variety of recreational sites since the mid-1980s. The ITCM may be estimated as the following:

$$V_{ij} = f(P_{ij}, T_{ij}, Q_i, S_j, Y_i) \tag{3.3}$$

where V_{ij} is the number of visits made by individual i to site j; P_{ij} is the travel cost incurred by individual i when visiting site j; T_{ij} is the time cost incurred by individual i when visiting site j; Q is a vector of the perceived qualities of the recreation site i; S_j is a vector of the characteristics of available substitute sites (this may refer only to sites of a similar nature or may be extended to include other recreational attractions); and Y_i is the household income of individual i.

The procedure undertaken within the ITCM requires researchers to undertake an on-site questionnaire survey of visitors aimed at eliciting estimates of household or individual visit frequencies over a given time period, plus information on the cost of travel to the site, recreational preferences, use of substitute sites, and socio-economic characteristics. These data are used to derive a demand curve from which consumer surplus may be estimated. As will be seen later in this section, it may be necessary to adjust the estimation procedure for the fact that the behaviour of non-visitors is not included in the model, biasing the demand curve and over-estimating consumer surplus.

Consumer surplus for q visits may be estimated by integrating under the demand curve between zero and q. Depending on the functional form of the travel-cost model, marginal consumer surplus for subsequent visits may be different from consumer surplus for the first visit (e.g. there may be a reduction in consumer surplus as the number of visits increases over time similar to that which might be expected under conditions of decreasing marginal utility). Once per household consumer surplus has been estimated it can be aggregated across all households visiting the site.

Where per visit household consumer surplus is estimated, this must be multiplied by the average number of household visits to the site in a given time period to generate the aggregate estimate (if data on visit numbers are based on individual visits, then an adjustment must be made by dividing through by average household size, thus producing an estimate of average visits per household which avoids double counting). Average household consumer surplus may be estimated by integrating under the demand curve between zero visits and the average number of visits made by the households in the sample over the specified time period (e.g. Balkan and Kahn, 1988). Aggregate consumer surplus is calculated by multiplying this figure by estimated number of different households visiting the site in the same period (to yield this figure, estimates of total individual visits to the site would have to be adjusted by dividing through by average household size and average number of visits per household).

Any sample of visitors to a recreation site is selective, and cannot represent those people who choose not to visit the site. Hence, in an on-site sample, the observed visit rate to a site over the period of interest, say a year, starts at one visit per year and excludes values that are less than one. The dependent variable, the number of trips undertaken, cannot logically be negative, but can be zero; however, in on-site recreation surveys the sample is truncated in that only those individuals who make one or more visits are observed. This produces a dependent variable which is truncated below one visit. Similarly, some questions used to elicit information in travel-cost surveys may themselves lead to additional censoring of data (Smith and Desvousges, 1985; Shaw, 1988). Use of an ordinary-least-squares (OLS) regression model specified with a normally distributed error term implies that the number of trips can range from minus infinity to plus infinity. Thus, OLS estimation is not appropriate for the estimation of ITCM models and its use will bias consumer-surplus estimates.

The Individual Travel-Cost Method

1   Identify site and use a questionnaire survey to collect data from visitors relating to cost of travel to the site, the number of visits to the site, recreational preferences, socio-economic characteristics, etc.

2   Specify trip generating function and estimate travel-cost model taking account of truncation.

3   Derive demand curve and obtain household consumer surplus estimates through integrating under the demand curve.

4   Calculate aggregate consumer surplus for the site.

The problem of truncation can be dealt with by using a maximum-likelihood (ML) estimation approach which corrects for bias that would arise from OLS estimation (Maddala, 1983). The recognition of truncation and the application of an ML estimator alters the consumer surplus estimates for different types of recreation activity substantially, compared with OLS estimates. Smith and Desvousges (1985; 1986) compared OLS and ML estimates across 33 water recreation sites finding highly significant differences and similar results were found by Willis and Garrod (1991a, and 1991b). Balkan and Kahn (1988), in a study of deer hunting, found less pronounced differences but this does not seem to be a common result.

Several authors including Kling (1987;1988) and Smith (1988) question the efficacy of using ML techniques to combat truncation bias and suggest instead that OLS techniques can be adjusted to account for truncation effects and that this may produce more accurate estimates of consumer surplus.

While these refinements may resolve some of the problems of truncation they do not address the fundamental mis-specification of the TCM which occurs in most applications of the ITCM. This mis-specification arises from the treatment of the dependent variable as if it were a continuous rather than a discrete random variable. A number of authors have attempted to re-estimate the travel-cost model for individual data based on a non-zero discrete dependent variable (e.g. Dobbs, 1991). While this approach has some appeal from an econometric point of view, the added complexity which it brings to the estimation procedure and the consequent loss of clarity in reportage has prevented it becoming widely used.

Interpreting Travel-Cost Models

1. Linear Functional Form

$$e.g. \ V = a + \beta C + \gamma S$$

where:

V = *number of visits made to a site*
a = *constant*
β = *coefficient of C (usually negative)*
C = *cost of travel to gain access to site*
γ = *coefficient of S (probably negative)*
S = *cost of travel to gain access to respondent's preferred substitute site*

The ITCM is used to estimate a, β and γ.
Estimated consumer surplus (CS) for an individual making q visits to the site:

$$CS = -q^2 / 2\beta$$

The linear functional form implies finite visits at zero cost but has a critical cost above which the model predicts that negative visits will be demanded.

2. Log-Linear Functional Form

$$e.g. \ lnV = a + \beta C + \gamma S$$

In this case the following expression for estimated consumer surplus (CS) for an individual making q visits to the site can be derived:
$$CS = -q / \beta$$

The log-linear functional form has been widely used in travel-cost models.
It implies a finite number of visits at zero cost and never predicts negative visits, even at very high costs.

---

4 COMPARISON OF ZTCM AND ITCM

The ITCM has a distinct advantage over the zonal approach in that it takes more account of the inherent variation in the data, rather than relying on zonal aggregate data. In addition, estimation based on individual rather than zonal data should be statistically more efficient. The ZTCM assumes that the estimated demand is generated by a 'representative consumer' whose behaviour reflects the average behaviour in the population. However, Brown *et al.* (1983) pointed out that where objectively measured travel costs are only related to perceived travel costs with some measurement error, then the averaging process inherent in the ZTCM approach reduces bias in the estimates due to measurement error; similarly the ZTCM more adequately accounts for participation rate changes as distances (and price or cost) changes.

From a more practical perspective, the ITCM has the advantage that its trip generating function can be estimated using a smaller number of observations than the ZTCM. However, the former requires more information about individual visitors and the ITCM is reliant on an expensive questionnaire survey being undertaken to elicit visitor characteristics, preferences and behaviour. Nevertheless, the ITCM is generally more flexible and applicable at a wider range of sites than the ZTCM. In theory, the use of individual data means that it is possible to look at the benefits generated by site visits to individuals undertaking specific types of recreational activity. For example, for a waterside site it would be possible to estimate the consumer surplus associated with households undertaking activities such as dog walking; rambling; fishing; or boating. Given that at some sites visitors will undertake more than one type of recreational activity, then the use of an ITCM approach would be desirable so that each particular activity undertaken could be valued.

Table 3.1 Comparison of ZTCM and ITCM consumer surplus for six forests

	ZTCM Travel-Cost Coefficient	ZTCM Per Visitor Consumer Surplus	ITCM Travel-Cost Coefficient	ITCM Per Visitor Consumer Surplus	Ratio of ZTCM to ITCM Consumer Surplus
Brecon	-0.384	2.60	-0.358	1.40	1.86
Buchan	-0.444	2.26	-0.996	0.50	4.52
Cheshire	-0.525	1.91	-1.259	0.40	4.78
Lorne	-0.694	1.44	-0.327	1.53	0.94
New Forest	-0.702	1.43	-0.215	2.32	0.62
Ruthin	0.396	2.52	-0.386	1.29	1.95

Source: Willis and Garrod (1991a)

When parallel ITCM and ZTCM studies have been carried out using the same data sets considerable differences have been observed in estimated consumer surplus. Willis and Garrod (1991a) compared ITCM and ZTCM consumer surplus estimates for six UK forests and found large differences (see Table 3.1). Similar results were found by Hanley (1989).

5 FUNCTIONAL FORMS

Economic theory does not suggest any particular functional form for TCMs. The most common practice is to statistically test various functional forms such as:

(1) linear $v = a + P$
(2) log-linear $log\ v = a + p$
(3) negative exponential $v = a + log\ p$
(4) double log $log\ v = a + log\ p$
(5) hyperbolic $v = a/p$

The choice of functional form for the model is often based on a single criterion: the magnitude of the R^2 statistic. This is generally inappropriate. The functional form of the TCM should be chosen on the grounds of a number of statistical criteria, such as R^2; predicted total number of visitors compared with actual number; and the correlation between the distribution of predicted and actual visit rates across zones. Economic theory can also assist in the choice between models by comparing model results with those expected in theory, according to which variables are statistically significant in the model and their respective signs.

The assumptions underlying the functional forms also need to be considered. The linear functional form, for example, implies finite visits at zero cost but has a critical cost above which the model predicts that negative visits will be demanded. This may not always be detrimental in practice, but can cause certain problems in the statistical interpretation of the demand curve.

Logarithmic forms have the advantage that they may be more easily used to calculate demand elasticities. Less advantageously, the double-log functional form implies infinite visits per head at zero cost and generates infinite consumer surplus whenever demand for recreation is inelastic. The log linear, or semi-log dependent functional form, is widely used in TCM studies. It implies a finite number of visits at zero cost and never predicts negative visits even at very high costs. By contrast the negative exponential (or semi-log independent) functional form implies an infinite number of visits at zero cost, and like the linear form has a critical cost above which a negative number of visits are predicted.

Several studies have tried to systematically evaluate the effect of the choice of functional form on travel-cost models (e.g. Smith, 1975; Ziemer *et al.*, 1980, Adamowicz *et al.*, 1989). The most common practices, however, tend to be conventional statistical diagnosis coupled with some form of sensitivity analysis looking at the effect of functional form on consumer surplus estimates.

Conventional statistical and econometric protocols can be used to judge the fundamental suitability of any particular functional specification for a given model. Issues of multicollinearity in variables needs to addressed, while heteroscedasticity may be a problem in some cases and can be detected using, for example, a Brausch-Pagan test (see Maddala, 1977). Similarly, predicted visit rates from the travel-cost model can be compared with actual visit rates using a non-parametric pairwise comparison test such as the Wilcoxon signed rank test or a Mann-Whitney U test. Jackknife regressions (Mosteller and Tukey, 1977) can be used to examine the sensitivity of the model to changes in data, by re-estimating the model with different small subsets of data omitted at each re-estimation.

Sometimes models with different functional specifications turn out to be quite similar with respect to statistical criteria, although the implications of the results from the various models in terms of consumer surplus estimates can be very different. Economic knowledge is then important in choosing an appropriate model, in the light of results from other TCM studies, recreational studies of similar phenomenon, or known demand functions of related private goods (e.g. visit rates to privately operated properties, or to commercially run nature reserves) where prices are charged.

Consumer-surplus estimates can vary enormously depending upon the functional form chosen for the model. Hanley and Common (1987) in a study of the recreational value of the Queen Elizabeth Forest Park in Aberfoyle, Scotland, based on a survey of visitors to the Park, employed a double-log form and obtained a consumer surplus estimate of £7.50 per visitor. Willis (1990), using the same data but employing a log-linear specification and adopting a different and smaller set of zones of origin, estimated consumer surplus at £2.72 per visitor.

Divergences between the results of different functional forms in terms of consumer-surplus estimates were again demonstrated by Willis and Garrod (1991b) for the ITCM when applied to a survey of visitors to canals and inland waterways. As often happens with the ITCM, the double-log model predicted infinite consumer surplus. This situation may be alleviated by adding unity or some other positive value to the dependent variable, though as Price (1990) pointed out, this expedient is entirely arbitrary and gives different answers depending on the unit in which the rate is measured. The log linear functional form gave a consumer surplus estimate in excess of £124 per visit. Comparing this estimate with those from similar ITCM studies (e.g. Smith, 1988), and with the CVM estimates of consumer surplus on visits to waterways, suggested that the log-linear consumer surplus estimate was unreasonably high, probably due to the high concentration of single visits coupled with the asymptotic nature of the model. The linear functional form on the other hand, whilst not providing such a flexible modelling framework as the others, does not exhibit any asymptotic behaviour when used to estimate consumer surplus for a site visit, and hence in the waterways study gave a not unreasonable estimate of £3.01 or a real consumer surplus (corrected for selectivity and self-selection in the sampling frame) of £0.51 per visit.

Ultimately some measure of judgement must be used in estimating travel-cost models. A combination of statistical reliability and consistency with other similar data may provide the best evidence in support of a given specification. Failure to meet either of these criteria may place serious doubt on the usefulness of the specification.

6 RANDOM UTILITY MODELS

Random Utility Models (RUMs) are econometric models that permit the estimation of preferences for different types of recreation or recreation sites that are considered by the consumer. Their ability to deal with multiple sites with different recreational attributes within a utility maximising framework has considerable appeal to economists. Because a visitor on a day trip to a particular site considers other sites, each with a variety of characteristics, information is gained about consumer preferences regarding the site from the fact that the consumer decided not to visit the available substitutes. The RUM focuses attention on the choice among alternative sites for any given recreational trip and assumes that the individual is comparing utilities for available destinations. Thus, the RUM is especially suitable when substitution amongst quality differentiated sites characterises the problem. This substitution, and hence value, can either be appraised in a RUM for a site, by reference to other recreational activities and sites.

The RUM estimates the probability that an individual will choose to select one site out of n available sites. In practice, an individual's indirect utility function must be assumed to be stochastic, with an error terms that varies across individuals. This reflects the analyst's inability to measure or identify all possible factors that can influence a respondent's decision.

Discrete choice TCMs of recreation demand have been developed in the USA to assess whether an individual participates in the recreation activity of interest and if so, the frequency of trips the individual takes in a season and, on each choice occasion, which site she visits.

Such models have been applied to estimating the value of sites within a small geographical area, e.g. swimming at fresh and salt water beaches in the Boston-Cape Cod area. For vacation trips, the whole of England could be considered as one geographic area for visits to outdoor recreational sites. But for day trips smaller regions must be considered dependent upon visitor origins, e.g. from the conurbations of North West England recreationalists can make choices between sites in the Lake District, Peak District, Pennine Dales and North Wales.

If sufficient sites are available for analysis, then the discrete choice TCM can be used to estimate the coefficients on quality characteristics of the sites which determine choice. Site quality variables can be continuous as well as dichotomous in the model, with other variables measuring the extent to which areas are serviced by public transport, or are congested and thus deter visitors, and whether the household has access to other alternative sites. However, because of the nature of the model, variables which are present in the utility function, but do not change across alternative sites will cancel out on estimation, and hence their coefficients cannot be recovered: household income is one such variable.

Some extremely robust results have been obtained with discrete choice recreation models in the USA. Compensating variation estimates can be calculated for each household's choice event, and by the number of predicted trips the individual makes. In addition, compensating variation estimates can be calculated for changes in the quality of specific attributes and characteristics, e.g. a 30% increase in water quality at a particular beach. Thus, the discrete choice model can be used to predict how an individual's decision would change as a result of a policy which would change (some aspect of landscape or wildlife) quality at any one site or at all sites in the choice set, and can be used to value any of these changes.

The RUM approach is not without its problems. As Bockstael *et al.* (1991) pointed out, there is nothing in the underlying theory which helps to resolve the problems of non-participation or the time horizon within which the recreational choices are made. This latter is potentially crucial, as many recreational choices may be predicated by historical recreational decisions and there is no easy way of determining how different individuals make choices with regard to time. Similarly, random utility models have nothing to tell us about those individuals who choose not to participate in recreation at any of the sites included in the model.

There is also the question of how to measure site characteristics for use in the model. Sites not only possess physical attributes (e.g. water quality, landscape character, fish stocks, lavatories, visitor centres, etc.) but also service characteristics (e.g. congestion, access, etc.). These factors will enter into the decision whether or not to visit a site and will influence the utility of each visit. Their degree of influence will depend upon visitors' past experience of the site and their expectations about future visits. This has led authors such as David (1971) to suggest that all site attributes should be measured subjectively in terms of visitors' perceptions.

One important theoretical limitation of the RUM that often arises in practice, is the assumption of independence of irrelevant alternatives (IIA). This arises from the simplification of the RUM into a form that is readily estimated using the multinomial logit model. Simply put, the IIA assumption implies that an individual's choice between two sites will only depend on the attributes and costs of those sites and not on the attributes of any other site. This is clearly unrealistic but it is the price that must be paid for the simplification that is necessary if the RUM is to be useful in practice. Alternative specifications of the RUM that avoid this limitation are available (e.g. McFadden, 1981) and have been adopted in a few studies (e.g. Hanemann and Carson, 1987).

All of this suggests that for all of their theoretical superiority RUM approaches are likely to suffer from as many practical problems as conventional TCM applications.

7 SEPARABILITY ASSUMPTIONS AND MULTI-PURPOSE TRIPS

The travel-cost method assumes separability in the specification of the model. For non-priced recreation, this requires that the recreational good consumed does not depend on the quality of any other recreational good also consumed. Typically the demand equation for recreation goods does not include the demand for market goods, though there may be a subset of goods which are connected to recreation, e.g. outdoor clothing, guide books, recreational equipment, the purchase of which may predispose individuals to visit a particular site.

The utility function underlying the TCM must also be separable with respect to different recreational activities. Recreation demand equations typically estimate demand for one activity without reference to other recreation activities, mainly because of data limitations. Results will be biased if the utility function is not separable in this manner. Separability in this sense may pose some difficult questions: landscape consumption may be separable from the consumption of wildlife and historical features but the latter two are not separable from landscape consumption.

Separability of alternative recreation activities is linked to issues of joint production and cost. Time and travel cost is a classic example in TCM literature. But there is also the problem of expenditure on meals and accommodation as part of the recreational experience. Only that net proportion of expenditure incurred as a consequence of the trip should be included. However, utility might be generated as a result of, say, staying at a comfortable hotel, or taking refreshments at a hospitable diner or tea shop. In such cases, trips and accommodation/refreshments need to be considered as separate goods. Failure to do so would result in an upward bias in the cost of the trip. Alternatively, if enjoying refreshments is not separate from the enjoyment of walking in the surrounding area, because the former enhances the enjoyment of the latter, then it should be included in the demand system, but this complicates the TCM model considerably.

The TCM is usually only applied to a single site, which is perfectly legitimate if trips to that site are separable from trips to all other sites. If separability cannot be assumed (e.g. when individual sites are found within a larger area of similar landscape character) then theory requires that a system of demands for appropriate alternative sites be developed. Such recreation demand systems (Burt and Brewer, 1971 for a set of Lakes in Missouri; Cicchetti *et al.*, 1976) have been developed in the past. This would require a simultaneous study of all substitute sites. Without spatial separability, the failure to include alternative goods and/or prices of alternative areas in the demand equation of the site of interest will bias the results.

The TCM also assumes spatial separability in terms of the trip and site visit. Although TCM measures the whole recreational experience comprising: (1) anticipation of the trip; (2) actual utility from the site visit itself; and (3) reflection and recall of the experience, it assumes that the trip has the single purpose of visiting one site or undertaking one particular recreational activity. Many visitors undertake multi-purpose or multi-activity trips. Thus, visitors to a particular site may also call at other sites or attractions.

Multi-activity, joint-activity, multi-destination and joint purpose trips also raise separability problems. Lack of separability across activities is important if interest centres on one activity or outcome versus another. Cheshire and Stabler (1976) defined three categories of visitor: the site-oriented pure visitor; the multi-site transit visitors; and the meanderers who gain most utility from the journey itself rather than from individual sites. It is these last two categories that pose most problems in terms of separability effects.

It is possible to net out multi-purpose visitors from pure visitors, but this requires a larger survey of visitors to generate a sufficient sample, e.g. of site dependent recreation, as well as multi-purpose trips. Thus the importance of multi-purpose trips to a given site is again an empirical problem. One approach to this problem is to ask multi-site visitors to attempt to separate the contribution made by each site to the day's recreational experience. This can be done by asking respondents to divide up 100 points between the sites visited in order to show their relative contribution to their recreational experience (e.g. Willis and Garrod, 1991a). Similarly, the contribution of travel time and other activities may need to be accounted for in this process.

This exercise is then used to adjust the estimate of travel cost that is used in the estimation of the travel-cost model. This is clearly a rather unrealistic and mechanistic process but is one of the few ways in which multi-purpose trips can be accounted for within a conventional travel-cost framework without having to resort to more complex random utility models which may also suffer from problems of separability.

8 TIME AND TRAVEL COST

The cost or price of access to an open-access, non-priced, recreational good appears intuitively to be simple to assess and in some cases the exercise can be performed in a remarkably straightforward manner (e.g. Bojo, 1985 estimated household travel costs by multiplying household size by standard class rail fare). However, whilst the vast majority of visitors to remoter sites and areas arrive by car, others walk or arrive by bicycle, train or bus. All of these categories have different transport costs, though conventionally such costs are estimated based on round trip mileage and a constant vehicle speed. Within the group arriving by car, transport costs can vary enormously depending on the make and size of the car, and also, for the individual, its ownership. These days a substantial proportion of vehicles are company or lease cars and these will incur different marginal costs.

Consumer-surplus estimates vary depending on whether the cost of access is assumed to reflect petrol costs only or whether the full running cost, including depreciation, maintenance, insurance and other factors, are included. In a study of a number of UK Forestry Commission sites, for example, consumer surplus derived from a demand curve based on the full cost of travel was three to four times that derived from assuming that cost of travel was that of petrol cost only (Willis and Garrod, 1991a). Hanley and Common (1987) also estimated consumer surplus for forest recreation based on both petrol costs and full running costs and found that the latter yielded estimates more than twice the size of the former. A study by Willis and Benson (1988) of wildlife visitors to nature reserves in the North of England yielded similar results (see Table 3.2).

There is some validity in using a value higher than that of petrol cost alone. In the forest recreation study, respondents were asked through a contingent valuation question what they thought their journey had cost per mile. Responses ranged from zero for those arriving in vehicles for which others incurred both purchase, running and petrol costs, through to the cost of petrol alone, and to the respondent-estimated full running costs of the vehicle, which as well as petrol costs took into account variable items such as maintenance and depreciation. Overall, respondents provided estimates of the average running costs of their cars which were three times those of the estimated petrol costs, although not quite as high as the full running-costs of the vehicle as estimated later in the study.

Table 3.2 Impact on estimated consumer surplus of alternative travel-cost specifications

Travel-Cost Specification	Travel-Cost Coefficient	Model R^2	Consumer Surplus Per Visit (£1986)	Total Consumer Surplus* (£ 1986)
Petrol only	-2.67	0.83	0.59	9,001
Petrol plus other variable costs	-2.61	0.83	1.02	15,574

* Based on 15,235 visits per year.

Source: Willis and Benson (1988)

The above exercise may suggest that perceived travel costs could be used to estimate the travel-cost model as these would more accurately reflect the respondent's perceptions of the cost of access. This approach has been used by Christensen (1983) but has received relatively little interest, possibly because of the problems involved in eliciting consistent and reliable estimates of perceived travel costs.

Geographic information systems provide a means of improving the information upon which estimates of travel cost are estimated. Bateman *et al.* (1996) adopted this approach in a study of the recreational benefits of Thetford Forest in Eastern England, using GIS techniques to measure road distances from visitor origins to recreational sites with greater accuracy than had hitherto been possible.

More problematic than costs is the whole question of the value of time, a subject which has engendered considerable debate in labour economics literature. Previous research has revealed that assumptions on the value of time are an important determinant of the estimated value of recreational activities (e.g. Wilman, 1980; Smith *et al.*, 1983).

The value of leisure time in a TCM has been considered as the following:

1. zero value and therefore not included (e.g. Bojo, 1985), although this is contrary to economic theory;
2. the opportunity costs of work, and therefore leisure time is valued at the marginal fixed wage rate (e.g. Smith and Desvousges, 1986);

3.   some proportion of the wage rate based on an individual's willingness to pay to save time in a non-working situation, typically his journey to work (e.g. Willis and Garrod, 1991a).

Even accepting one of these assumptions as theoretically correct would not accurately represent reality. Any individual may value time differently on a work day compared to a weekend day or during a holiday period. Time constraints are also likely to vary across individuals. The occupation of the individual and purpose of the journey is also known to affect the value of time.

Cesario (1976) and Cesario and Knetsch (1970, 1976) conducted notable investigations of the value of travel time, examining commuters' choice of transport to and from work and the resulting opportunity costs and trade-offs. On the basis of this work Cesario (1976) concluded that the true cost of travel was somewhere between 25% and 50% of an individual's full wage rate. This analysis only reflects utility for commuting time and may not be readily applicable to the value of recreational time (Nelson, 1977). Bishop and Heberlein (1979) applied a range of different wage rates from zero to 50% in their study of maximum WTP for goose hunting permits.

A number of studies (e.g. Hellerstein and Mendelsohn, 1993; Englin and Cameron, 1996) have utilised the convention that the opportunity cost of time is 33% of the respondent's wage rate. This practice was supported by a study by Englin and Shonkwiler (1995) where factor analysis was used to investigate the contribution of the various components of travel cost. This value is similar to that found by Lockwood and Tracy (1995) when they valued travel-to-work time at 29% of the hourly wage rate.

Other studies have attempted to use statistical techniques to determine the choice of time costs (e.g. Common, 1973; McConnell and Strand, 1981; Ward, 1983; Bateman *et al.*, 1996). These approaches largely rely on identifying the value of time that optimises some form of goodness-of-fit criteria and subsequently adopting that value as the most appropriate.

Most of the studies mentioned above base their estimates of the opportunity cost of time on the assumption that individuals can make marginal substitutions between time and income. Such an assumption requires an underlying equilibrium labour market: however, this holds only where individuals are self-employed, have some discretion over how they use their time and whose incomes decline in proportion to the amount of time spent away from work. This point is underlined by authors such as McKean *et al.* (1995), who point out that few individuals will be able to trade off leisure time and work time. Bockstael *et al.* (1987) moved away from this assumption and provided an alternative model based on a disequilibrium labour market model. This type of model may be especially important at sites that attract many unwaged visitors (such as students or retired people) who do not have to forgo wages to travel.

McKean *et al.* (1995) used a disequilibrium labour market model to investigate the opportunity cost of time. In their study this assumption was empirically tested against an alternative model where time costs were based on income. Individuals were classified as being able or unable to substitute earned income for time at the margin and time costs were based on that classification. For those individuals unable to substitute time and wages at the margin, a value of time was derived from gross national product, hours worked and the composition of the labour market. Ward's (1983) method was used to calculated the opportunity cost of time based on income for those individuals who could substitute time for income. Travel-cost models were then estimated based on truncated poisson regression, a technique that takes into account the discrete, truncated nature of the dependent variable (Hellerstein and Mendelsohn, 1993). The results of this study suggested that models which assume that all respondents can substitute time for income may mis-state opportunity time costs and thus introduce a bias into consumer surplus estimates.

It is clear that the marginal utility of a visit will be influenced by travel cost and the time taken to reach the site. Omitting either of these considerations from the travel cost analysis will almost certainly bias consumer surplus estimates. The calculation of travel costs can now be relatively precise; however, there is still much controversy over the opportunity cost of time utilised in travel-cost studies. Further discussion of these issues can be found in McConnell (1975), Freeman (1979), Johannson (1987) and Shaw (1992).

9 APPLICATIONS

Travel-cost techniques have been applied to value recreation in a variety of circumstances. The most common applications relate to non-priced, open-access recreation, though on other rare occasions the methodology has been applied to estimating the benefits of access to cultural or heritage goods.

Where historical sites attract sufficient numbers of people, entry charges are usually made where these exceed transactions costs. Alternatively, moral pressure may be applied to visitors to force them to make donations through 'honesty boxes'. The latter, are often employed where visitor numbers are insufficient to cover transactions costs. An early example of a TCM study of a historical site was that of Barlaston Hall, Staffordshire, which estimated the benefits that members of society might enjoy if the building was restored and compared them with the cost of restoration (Aylen, 1978).

Table 3.3 The value of goose-hunting permits (US$1974)

Technique Used to Elicit Benefit Estimate	Valuation
1. Cash offer which varied between $1 and $200: respondents were asked to return either the cheque of their hunting permit:	$63
2. CVM hypothetical willingness to accept compensation question	$101
3. TCM, with time valued at zero	$11
4. TCM, with time valued at 25% of wage rate	$28
5. TCM, with time valued at 50% of wage rate	$45

Source: Bishop and Heberlein (1979)

Table 3.4 Comparison of travel-cost and contingent valuation estimates of water quality improvement benefits (US$1981)

	Loss of use	Boatable to fishable	Fishable to swimable
CVM – Direct question	6.57	7.06	13.61
CVM – Payment card I	6.20	9.72	15.92
CVM – Payment card II	2.16	1.38	3.12
CVM – Bidding game	12.08	6.77	13.43
TCM	82.65	7.01	14.71

Source: Desvousges *et al.* (1983)

Many more applications of TCM are encountered in respect of wildlife preservation and nature conservation, especially in the USA. In an early study Knetsch and Davis (1965) evaluated the recreational value of Pittson area woods in Northern Maine using a variety of techniques. A contingent valuation question elicited aggregate maximum WTP values of around $72,000, while a question asking individuals how much further they would drive to reach similar recreation facilities, if those in Pittson were not available to them, yielded an estimated benefit of $64,000. In comparison a zonal travel-cost model yielded an aggregate benefit estimate of $70,000.

These results were remarkably close and gave early encouragement to practitioners.

Recreational activities such as hunting are also commonly examined using a travel-cost framework. Bishop and Heberlein (1979) estimated the value of goose hunting permits via a variety of approaches, eliciting the valuation estimates shown in Table 3.3. TCM results based on a variety of time-cost assumptions were considerably lower than those generated using a contingent valuation technique. It must be noted, however, that the contingent valuation questions used in this study were quite unusual, relying on the respondent's willingness to accept compensation for the loss of their deer hunting permit within both a real and a hypothetical framework.

Desvousges *et al.* (1983) estimated the benefits of water quality improvements along the Monongahela River, Pennsylvania using both travel cost and contingent valuation techniques. Table 3.4 presents the results for user values of different changes in water quality and clearly shows how TCM results can diverge from contingent valuation results, and incidentally that contingent valuation results are very sensitive to the elicitation method employed to drive benefit estimates.

Thayer (1981) used TCM and contingent valuation to assess the loss of landscape value from the development of a geothermal power plant in the Jemez mountains in Northern New Mexico. The TCM was framed as the cost of travelling to a substitute recreational site. His results were similar for both methods, and he argued that the TCM site substitution method can be used to cross-check contingent valuation results.

Farber (1988) estimated the recreational use value of the wetlands of Terrebonne Parish, Louisiana, which cover 650,000 acres, using a ZTCM. The sampling procedure consisted of placing self-addressed, stamped questionnaires on windshields of all vehicles parked in the morning at all 27 boat launch facilities in the wetlands on various dates throughout the year including the hunting and fishing seasons. Of the 7,837 questionnaires distributed only 1,126 were returned, a response rate of 14.4 per cent. This study demonstrated the sensitivity of the results to the assumptions in the model. The annual value of the wetlands varied from $1.277 million when time cost was assumed to be 10% of the average full wage rate, to $3.898 million when time cost was assumed to equal the full wage rate. The capitalised value varied by a factor of 2.67 depending on whether a 3 per cent or 8 per cent discount rate was used, and also according to whether the population (use of the wetlands) was assumed to grow in the future. Thus the average capitalised value of the wetlands varied from $36 to $111 per acre depending on the assumptions chosen.

In a study of the Mesa Verde National Park, Winger and McKean (1991) argued that visibility (in terms of visual range) was an input into the household production function and that this implied that households and individuals adjust their behaviour to obtain optimal amounts of landscape consumption. Sightseers have some control over visual range days by staying longer at a site they believe will have optimal atmospheric conditions at a given time. Most vistas in the Mesa Verde National Park may be reached only by entering the park and driving to the top of the mesa, and vistas are affected by visibility. Visibility in the area has diminished over the past 40 years through copper mining and smelting, coal fired power plants and other urban development upwind. Winger and McKean found that tourists altered their behaviour in response to environmental quality. Not only was the relationship highly statistically significant but the variation in the visit rate from low to high levels of visibility amounted to more than half of the average visit rate. The Mesa Verde National Park attracts many more visits when visibility is high.

10 OTHER CONSIDERATIONS

10.1 The Central Assumption

The central assumption underlying all travel-cost applications is that the cost of travel to gain access to a site is a measure of recreational preference which can then be used to estimate demand. This assumption is violated when individuals or households move to an area to gain improved access to particular sites (Gibson, 1978). When this happens the cost of travel becomes endogenous and the estimated demand curve will lie under the real demand curve and consumer surplus will be under-estimated. Such behaviour may be encountered at most sites but is unlikely to be common; however, such individuals are likely to be frequent visitors and their benefits might be considerable. Where practicable these individuals should be identified and the effects of their behaviour on estimated consumer surplus noted.

Parsons (1991) argued that the adoption of an instrumental variable approach taking account of such behaviour would eliminate the endogeneity problem. An alternative approach would be to estimate the benefits of improved access to on-site recreation for these individuals using an hedonic price model (see Chapter 4). Double-counting should not be a problem as the hedonic price model will estimate the benefits of improved access to the site from moving closer to it, while the TCM will measure any additional consumer surplus gained from visiting at the reduced travel cost (See Garrod and Willis, 1992).

10.2 Treatment of Substitute Sites

While the importance of substitute sites in the estimation of trip generating functions has been acknowledged since the work of Burt and Brewer (1971) and Cicchetti *et al.* (1976), there is little agreement on how this should be achieved in practice. First, there is the problem of defining what constitutes a substitute site: should it be a close substitute or should any substitute recreational site be included? Second, there is the problem of incorporating the different attributes of the substitute sites into the model. The existence of a substitute site is in itself important, but the characteristics of this site, including how much it would cost an individual to gain access, will often determine how often an individual or household visits it.

In general, the further away an individual lives from a particular site the greater the probability that he or she will visit a substitute site. Indeed, the greater the distance between an individual and a site, the more substitutes will be available to that individual. This will have the effect of depressing the demand curve for the site of interest and reducing consumer surplus. In a similar vein, Price (1978) and Christensen and Price (1982) have shown that, depending upon the relationship between sites and population centres, changes in the supply of substitute sites can lead to either over- or under-estimates of consumer surplus.

Different specifications of the travel-cost method have different problems. For example, if the zones in a ZTCM are defined using a series of concentric distance bands then there may be widely different levels of access from that zone to any discrete substitute site. ITCMs are relatively straightforward in comparison, but there is still the problem of accounting for multiple substitutes with a variety of different recreational attributes within the TCM (e.g. Smith and Desvousges, 1986). Again, some random utility approach based on choices between different sites with different attributes (including travel cost) may offer a solution at the expense of greatly increased complexity.

Burt and Brewer (1971) identified substitute sites subjectively and calculated the distance to these sites from respondents' homes. These data were subsequently used in estimating the travel-cost model. Caulkins *et al.* (1985) used a two-site example to systematically investigate the effect of omitting substitute prices from the travel-cost model. Bojo (1985) attempted to construct a substitute availability index for use in the estimation process. This was based on individual preferences for substitute sites and the travel cost to reach them. Problems arose when Bojo found that most of his respondents were naming the same site and the index could not be operationalised. The majority of studies, however, ignore the problem of substitutes or adopt a dummy variables approach to deal with the effect of substitute sites (e.g. Willis and Garrod, 1991a).

Recent papers by Kling (1989) and Smith (1993) have made further contributions to the debate about the appropriate treatment of substitutes. The approaches reported are too detailed to be summarised here, but they further emphasise the need for researchers to collect adequate information on substitution effects. This will be especially important in cases where the treatment of substitute sites is significant from a policy context (Smith, 1993).

10.3 Congestion

A site becomes congested when the number of visitors rises to the point where subsequent visitors cannot gain access (e.g. because car parks are full) or where the utility of the marginal user is diminished because of the presence of other visitors. Congestion problems can compromise a TCM study by introducing supply constraints that invalidate the underlying assumptions of the method. Such excess demand means that the observed demand curve is an under-estimate of true demand and that the resulting travel-cost models under-estimate consumer surplus (see Fisher and Krutilla, 1972 for a well-known example of congestion effects on recreational demand).

In less extreme cases there may be a case for introducing a term into the individual's utility function that reflects congestion effects (Johannson, 1987). The effect of this term may be hard to determine as both too few or too many visitors may have a deleterious effect on an individual's recreational experience. Clearly, congestion effects will depend on the characteristics of the site and the expectations of the visitors. Congestion will be defined differently in a wilderness area and on a beach in the South of France. Stankey (1972) surveyed wilderness users in Utah, Montana, Minnesota and Wyoming, examining users' reactions to the attributes of the recreational experience. Stankey recorded that 82% of his sample felt that 'solitude — not seeing many other people except those in your own party' was a desirable attribute of a site visit.

Smith and Desvousges (1986) attempted to account for potential site congestion by eliciting the opinions of recreation site managers as to the level of site congestion. On the basis of this analysis they concluded that congestion was not an important factor at the sites studied. Freeman (1979) lists various references to the use of non-visitor samples drawn from the regional population of travel cost zones to examine how many present non-users would use the site if environmental quality were to be improved (Burt and Brewer, 1971; Brown and Nawas, 1973; Gum and Martin, 1975) and such an approach could be extended to the analysis of congestion.

10.4 Valuation of Site Attributes: The Hedonic Travel-Cost Method

Brown and Mendelsohn (1984) developed a variant of the travel-cost model based on the hedonic approach where the benefits of on-site recreation are related to the attributes of the site. In their hedonic travel-cost model the authors hoped to be able to value the attributes of a number of recreational sites rather than just the site values. This approach has certain advantages in terms of management planning in that it can suggest ways in which to maximise the benefits of investment by improving the levels of those site attributes found to make the highest contributions to recreational benefits.

This approach is data intensive and requires questionnaire surveys to be undertaken at a range of recreational sites exhibiting a variety of relevant attributes. Data are collected relating to site attributes and also from visitors at each site, and is then pooled for estimation of the hedonic travel-cost model. Rather than explain variation in visit rates by travel cost, the Brown and Mendelsohn approach attempts to explain travel cost in terms of site and visitor attributes, using the resulting equation to estimate implicit prices for attributes. These implicit prices can be used to drive the estimation of demand curves for site attributes and subsequently demand elasticities.

Problems exist with data collection and with estimation (e.g. Brown and Mendelsohn's analysis relies on an assumption of constant time on site) and Smith and Kaoru (1987) highlighted other shortcomings of the approach and stressed the importance of examining how sensitive the results of the model are to the specification and assumptions required to apply it. These reservations may explain that while this novel variation of the TCM attracted considerable interest, relatively few recent examples exist of attempts to consolidate the technique (e.g. Bowes and Krutilla, 1989; Englin and Mendelsohn, 1991; Smith *et al.,* 1991; and Hanley and Ruffell, 1993).

10.5 Sample Selection Effects

Any technique using data derived from on-site questionnaire surveys is vulnerable to sample selection effects. This is especially true of techniques that investigate site demand effects using data that does not take into account those individuals who choose not to visit a site. The truncation problem observed in the ITCM is a prominent example of such an effect.

Smith (1988) compared five different method for estimating the TCM based on data relating to individual recreation decisions. Each method dealt with selection effects differently and Smith compared the resulting parameter and consumer surplus estimates. His analysis revealed that the treatment of selection effects had relatively little effect on estimated consumer surplus and that the majority of variation resulted from the choice of estimator.

Section 4 of Chapter 7 provides a simple example of the site selection problem and suggests how an appropriate correction can be made.

11 DISCUSSION

The travel-cost method has a considerable pedigree as a means of estimating the benefits of non-priced recreation. It has been used in a wide variety of circumstances to value the recreational benefits of a range of environmental and even heritage goods. Within the hierarchy of benefit estimation techniques it has somewhat limited interest in that it can only estimate recreational use values and is not capable of examining the benefits of a full range of environmental goods and services (unlike contingent valuation methods, see Chapter 5). Furthermore, traditional TCMs measure the benefits of the total recreational experience of a trip and are not specific to the site of interest. Considerable effort must be expended to estimate benefits for one particular site.

Benefits are based on consumer surplus measures estimated from a recreational demand curve based on the trip-generating function. The specification of the trip-generating function varies widely across applications, a phenomenon which is best illustrated by the different dependent variables used in the zonal and individual travel-cost methods. Even within these variants of the basic TCM there are considerable differences in the treatment of such issues as the cost of travel and the opportunity cost of time. Similar lack of consistency is found in the choice of functional forms and the method by which the TCM is estimated.

Consumer surplus estimates have been found to be highly sensitive to the specification of the TCM and to the method of estimation. Although recent advances in GIS technology and in survey techniques can produce better data from which to estimate the models, little illumination has been shed on the most appropriate ways in which to approach these issues. Overall, there is little in the literature to convince an outside observer that a particular approach produces more reliable estimates than any other and benefit estimates derived from TCMs should be judged, and perhaps only accepted, in the light of additional evidence from other valuation methods.

Despite this, travel-cost approaches do at least have the advantage that they are based on observed behaviour and not on expressed preferences. It is generally agreed that for some individuals at least, there is a correlation between the quantity of non-priced recreation demanded and the cost of access to that recreation. This suggests that travel-cost models of recreational demand are feasible, but are difficult to estimate due to the nature of demand for non-priced recreation and to the failure of some individuals to conform to the behaviour expected under the underlying assumptions of the TCM.

A better approach would be one based on random utility models of recreational behaviour; however, this would involve considerable data collection problems and added computational complexity. If, in the absence of feasible alternatives, travel-cost approaches are still to be used to estimate the benefits of non-priced recreation, then it may be advisable to report a variety of consumer-surplus estimates based on a range of specifications. These should include estimates that can be demonstrated to represent lower bounds to consumer surplus and these should act as the baseline in any subsequent cost-benefit analysis.

REFERENCES

Adamowicz, W.L., J.L. Fletcher, and T. Graham-Tomasi (1989), 'Functional form and the statistical properties of welfare measures', *American Journal of Agricultural Economics,* **71**, 414–21.

Aylen, J. (1978), 'The social cost benefit analysis of historic building restoration: a case study of Barlaston Hall, Staffordshire', in M.J. Artis and A.R. Nobay (eds), *Contemporary Economic Analysis,* Croom Helm, London.

Balkan, E. and J.R. Kahn (1988), 'The value of changes in deer hunting quality: a travel-cost approach', *Applied Economics,* **20**, 533–9.

Bateman, I.J., G.D. Garrod, J.S. Brainard, and A.A. Lovett (1996), 'Measurement, valuation and estimation issues in the travel cost method: a geographical information systems approach', *Journal of Agricultural Economics,* **47**, 191–205.

Bishop, R. and T. Heberlein (1979), 'Measuring values of extra-market goods: are individual measures biased?', *American Journal of Agricultural Economics,* **61**, 926–30.

Bockstael, N.E., K.E. McConnell, and I. Strand (1991), 'Recreation', in J. Braden and C. Kolstad (eds), *Measuring the Demand for Environmental Commodities,* North Holland, Amsterdam.

Bockstael, N.E., I. Strand, and W.M. Hanemann (1987), 'Time and the recreational demand model', *American Journal of Agricultural Economics* **69**, 293–302.

Bojo, J. (1985), *A Cost-Benefit Analysis of Forestry in Mountainous Areas: The Case of Valadelen,* Stockholm School of Economics, Stockholm.

Bowes, M. and J. Krutilla (1989), *Multiple-Use Management: The Economics of Public Forestlands,* Resources for the Future, Washington DC.

Bowes, M. and J.B. Loomis (1980), 'A note on the use of travel cost models with unequal zonal populations', *Land Economics,* **56**, 465–70.

Brown, G. and R. Mendelsohn (1984), 'The hedonic travel-cost model', *Review of Economics and Statistics,* **66**, 427–33.

Brown, W.G. and F. Nawas (1973), 'Impact of aggregation on the estimation of outdoor recreation demand functions', *American Journal of Agricultural Economics* **55**, 246–9.

Brown, W.G., C. Sorhus, B. Chou-Yang, and J.T. Richards (1983), 'Using individual observations to estimate recreation demand functions: a caution', *American Journal of Agricultural Economics,* **65**, 154–7.

Burt, O.R. and D. Brewer (1971), 'Estimation of net social benefits from outdoor recreation', *Econometrica,* **39**, 813–27.

Caulkins, P.P., R.C. Bishop, and N. Bouwes (1985), 'Omitted cross-price variable biases in the linear travel-cost model: correcting common misinterpretations', *Land Economics,* **61**, 182–7.

Cesario, F.J. (1976), 'Value of time in recreation benefit studies', *Land Economics,* **55**, 32–41.

Cesario, F.J. and J.L. Knetsch (1970), 'Time bias in recreation benefit estimates', *Water Resources Research,* **6**, 700–4.

Cesario, F.J. and J.L. Knetsch (1976), 'A recreation site demand and benefit estimation model', *Journal of Regional Studies,* **10**, 97–104.

Cheshire, P.C. and M.J. Stabler (1976), 'Joint consumption estimates in recreational site "surplus": an empirical estimate', *Regional Studies,* **10**, 343–51.

Christensen, J.B. (1983), *An Economic Approach to Assessing the Valuation of Recreation with Special Reference to Forest Areas,* Unpublished PhD Thesis, University College of North Wales, Bangor.

Christensen, J.B. and C. Price (1982), 'A note on the use of travel cost models with unequal zonal populations: comment', *Land Economics,* **58**, 395–99.

Cicchetti, C.J., A.C. Fisher, and V.K. Smith (1976), 'An economic evaluation of a generalised consumer surplus measure: the Mineral King controversy,' *Econometrica,* **44**, 1259–76.

Clawson, M. (1959), 'Methods of measuring demand for and value of outdoor recreation', *Reprint No. 10,* Resources for the Future, Washington DC.

Clawson, M. and J.L. Knetsch (1966), *Economics of Outdoor Recreation,* Johns Hopkins University Press, Baltimore.

Common, M. (1973), 'A note on the use of the Clawson method', *Regional Studies,* **7**, 401–6.

David, E.L. (1971), 'Public perceptions of water quality', *Water Resources Research,* **7**, 453–7.

Desvousges, W.S., V.K. Smith, and M.P. McGivney (1983), *Comparison of Alternative Approaches for Estimating Recreation and Related Benefits for Water Quality Improvements,* US Environmental Protection Agency, Washington DC.

Dobbs, I.M. (1991), 'The individual travel-cost method: estimation and benefit assessment with a discrete and possibly grouped dependent variable', *Countryside Change Initiative Working Paper 17,* University of Newcastle upon Tyne, Newcastle upon Tyne.

Englin, J. and T.A. Cameron (1996), 'Augmenting travel cost models with contingent behaviour data', *Environmental and Resource economics,* **7**, 133–47.

Englin, J. and R. Mendelsohn (1991), 'A hedonic travel cost analysis for valuation of multiple components of site quality: the recreation value of forest management', *Journal of Environmental Economics and Management,* **21**, 275–90.

Englin, J. and R. Shonkwiler (1995), 'Modelling recreation demand in the presence of unobservable travel costs: towards a travel price model', *Journal of Environmental Economics and Management,* **29**, 368–77.

Farber, S. (1988), 'The value of coastal wetlands for recreation: an application of travel cost and contingent valuation methodologies', *Journal of Environmental Management,* **26**, 299–312.

Fisher, A.C. and J.V. Krutilla, (1972), 'Determination of optimal capacity of resource based recreational facilities', *Natural Resources Journal,* **12**, 417–44.

Freeman, A.M. (1979), *The Benefits of Environmental Improvement: Theory and Practice,* Resources for the Future, Washington DC.

Garrod, G.D. and K.G. Willis (1992), 'The amenity value of woodland in Great Britain: a comparison of economic estimates', *Environmental and Resource Economics,* **2**, 415–34.

Gibson, J.G. (1978), 'Recreation land use', in D.W. Pearce (ed.), *The Valuation of Social Cost,* Allen and Unwin, London.

Gum, R.L. and W.E. Martin (1975), 'Problems and solutions in estimating the demand for and value of rural outdoor recreation', *American Journal of Agricultural Economics,* **57**, 558–66.

Hanemann, W.M. and R.T. Carson (1987), *Southcentral Alaska Sport Fishing Economic Study. Report to Alaska Department of Fish and Game,* Jones and Stokes Associates, Inc, Sacramento, California.

Hanley, N. D. (1989), 'Valuing rural recreation sites: an empirical comparison of two approaches' *Journal of Agricultural Economics,* **40**, 361–74.

Hanley, N.D., and M. Common (1987), *'Estimating the recreation, wildlife and landscape benefits of forestry: preliminary results from a Scottish study',* Department of Economics, University of Stirling, Stirling.

Hanley, N.D., and R. Ruffell (1993), 'The valuation of forest characteristics', in W.L. Adamowicz, W. White and W.E. Phillips (eds), *Forestry and the Environment: Economic Perspectives,* CAB International, Wallingford.

Hellerstein, D. and R. Mendelsohn (1993), 'A theoretical foundation for count data models', *American Journal of Agricultural Economics,* **75**, 604–11.

Hufschmidt, M.M., D.E. James, A.D. Meister, B.T. Bower, and J.A. Dixon (1983), *Environment, Natural Systems and Development: An Economic Valuation Guide,* Johns Hopkins University Press, Baltimore.

Johannson, P-O. (1987), *The Economic Theory and Measurement of Environmental Benefits,* Cambridge University Press, Cambridge.

Kling, C.L. (1987), 'A simulation approach to comparing multiple site recreation demand models using Chesapeake Bay survey data', *Marine Resource Economics,* **4**, 95–109.

Kling, C.L. (1988), 'Comparing welfare estimates of environmental quality changes from recreation demand models', *Journal of Environmental Management,* **15**, 331–40.

Kling, C.L. (1989), 'A note on the welfare effects of omitting substitute prices and quantities from travel cost models', *Land Economics,* **65**, 290–6.

Knetsch, J.L. and R.K. Davis (1965), 'Comparisons of methods for recreation evaluation', in A.V. Kneese and S.C. Smith (eds), *Water Research,* Johns Hopkins University Press, Baltimore.

Lockwood, M. and K. Tracy (1995), 'Nonmarket economic valuation of an urban recreation park', *Journal of Leisure Research,* **27**, 155–67.

Maddala, G.S. (1977), *Econometrics,* McGraw-Hill, New York.

Maddala, G.S. (1983), *Limited-Dependent and Qualitative Variables in Econometrics,* Cambridge University Press , Cambridge.

McConnell, K.E. (1975), 'Some problems in estimating the demand for outdoor recreation', *American Journal of Agricultural Economics,* **57**, 330–4.

McConnell, K.E. and I. Strand (1981), 'Measuring the cost of time in recreation demand analysis: an application to sport fishing', *American Journal of Agricultural Economics,* **63,** 153–66.

McFadden, D. (1981), 'Econometric models of probabilistic choice', in C.F. Manski and D. McFadden (eds), *Structural Analysis of Discrete Data,* MIT Press, Cambridge, Ma.

McKean, J.R., D.M. Johnson, and R.G. Walsh (1995), 'Valuing time in travel-cost demand analysis: an empirical investigation', *Land Economics,* **71,** 96–105.

Mosteller, F. and J.W. Tukey (1977), *Data Analysis and Regression,* Addison-Wesley, Reading, Ma.

Nelson, J.P. (1977), 'Accessibility and the value of time in commuting', *Southern Economic Journal,* **43,** 1321–9.

Parsons, G.R. (1991), 'A note on the choice of residential location in travel-cost demand models', *Land Economics,* **67,** 360–4.

Pearse, P.H. (1968), 'A new approach to the evaluation of non-priced recreational resources', *Land Economics,* **44,** 87–99.

Prewitt, R.A. (1949), *The Economics of Public Recreation — An Economic Survey of the Monetary Evaluation of Recreation in National Parks,* US Department of the Interior, National Park Service and Recreational Planning Division, Washington DC.

Price, C. (1978), *Landscape Economics,* Macmillan, London.

Price, C. (1990), *Forest Landscape Evaluation,* Paper presented to a Forestry Commission Economics Research Group Meeting in September 1990 at University of York.

Shaw, W.D. (1988), 'On-site samples regression: problems of non-negative integers, truncation and endogenous stratification', *Journal of Econometrics,* **37,** 211–24.

Shaw, W.D. (1992), 'Searching for the opportunity cost of an individual's time', *Land Economics,* **68,** 107–15.

Sinden, J.A. and A.C. Worrell (1979), *Unpriced Values: Decisions Without Market Prices,* John Wiley, New York.

Smith, V.K. (1975), 'Travel-cost demand models for wilderness recreation: a problem of non-nested hypotheses', *Land Economics,* **51,** 103–11.

Smith, V.K. (1988), 'Selection and recreation demand', *American Journal of Agricultural Economics,* **70,** 29–36.

Smith, V.K. (1993), 'Nonmarket valuation of environmental resources: an interpretive appraisal', *Land Economics,* **68,** 1–26.

Smith, V.K. and W.H. Desvousges (1985), 'The generalised travel-cost model and water quality benefits: a reconsideration', *Southern Journal of Economics,* **52,** 371–81.

Smith, V.K. and W.H. Desvousges (1986), *Measuring Water Quality Benefits,* Kluwer and Nijhoff, Boston.

Smith, V.K., W.H. Desvousges, and M.P. McGivney (1983), 'The opportunity cost of travel time in recreational demand models', *Land Economics,* **59,** 170–89.

Smith, V.K. and R.J. Kaoru (1987), 'The hedonic travel cost model: a view from the trenches', *Land Economics,* **51,** 103–11.

Smith, V.K. and R.J. Kopp (1980), 'The spatial limits of the travel-cost recreational demand model', *Land Economics,* **56,** 234–41.

Smith, V.K., R.B. Palmquist, and P. Jakus (1991), 'Combining Farrell frontier and hedonic travel-cost models for valuing estuarine quality', *The Review of Economics and Statistics,* **73**, 228–33.

Stankey, G.H. (1972), 'A strategy for the definition and management of wilderness quality', in J.V. Krutilla (ed) *Natural Environments: Studies in Theoretical and Applied Analysis,* Johns Hopkins University Press, Baltimore.

Strong, E. (1983), 'A note on the functional form of travel cost models with zones of unequal poulations', *Land Economics,* **59**, 342–9.

Thayer, M.A. (1981), 'Contingent valuation techniques for assessing environmental impacts: further evidence', *Journal of Environmental Economics and Management,* **8**, 27–44.

Trice, A.H. and S.E. Wood (1958), 'Measurement of recreational benefits', *Land Economics,* **34**, 195–207.

Ward, F.A. (1983), 'Measuring the cost of time in recreational demand analysis: comment', *American Journal of Agricultural Economics,* **65**, 167–8.

Willis, K.G. (1990), 'The recreational value of the Forestry Commission estate in Great Britain: a Clawson-Knetsch travel-cost analysis', *Scottish Journal of Political Economy,* **38**, 58–75.

Willis, K.G. and J.F. Benson (1988), 'A comparison of user benefits and costs of nature conservation at three nature conservation reserves', *Regional Studies,* **22**, 417–28.

Willis, K.G. and G.D. Garrod (1991a), 'An individual travel-cost method of evaluating forest recreation', *Journal of Agricultural Economics,* **41**, 33–42.

Willis, K.G. and G.D. Garrod (1991b), 'Valuing open access recreation on inland waterways: on-site recreation surveys and selection effects', *Regional Studies,* **25**, 511–24.

Wilman, E.A. (1980), 'The value of time in recreational benefit studies', *Journal of Environmental Economics and Management,* **7**, 272–86.

Winger, D. and J.R. McKean (1991), 'Visibility: a determinant of park visitor behaviour', *Geoforum,* **22**, 391–9.

Ziemer, R., W.N. Musser, and R.C. Hill, (1980), 'Recreational demand equations: functional form and consumer surplus', *American Journal of Agricultural Economics,* **62**, 136–41.

4. The Hedonic Price Method

You buy a house for value with considerable care
For environmental externalities: views and quality of air;
But as you get older, these characteristics matter less,
Compared with access to a doctor and a twilight home of rest.

Patricia Hilary Willis (1936–): *House Hunting*

1 INTRODUCTION

Derived from consumer theory (Lancaster, 1966) and seen by some as the successor to the spatial equilibrium model of the city[1] (McConnell, 1990), the hedonic price method (HPM) relies on the proposition that an individual's utility for a good or service is based on the attributes which it possesses. In certain circumstances it may be possible to separate the effects of the various attributes of a good in a way which demonstrates how changes in the levels of each attribute affect the individual's utility. In hedonic pricing this is achieved by modelling individuals' willingness to pay to consume a particular good as a function of the levels of the good's characteristics (attributes).

The most common application of the HPM in environmental valuation is in relation to the public's willingness to pay for housing. In this case, each property may be assumed to constitute a distinct combination of attributes which determine the price which a potential purchaser or tenant is willing to pay. Consumer theory postulates that the purchase price which a potential buyer is willing to pay is dependent upon the existence and level of a wide range of housing attributes including:

---

[1] Here the land rent gradient represented a compromise between commuting time and space, see Alonso (1964).

(i)   structural characteristics: e.g. plot size; number of rooms; garage space; central heating; structural integrity; etc.
(ii)   local socio-economic and public sector characteristics: e.g. unemployment rate; racial composition; social conditions; wage differentials; quality of schools; local taxes; etc.
(iii)   local amenity: e.g. environmental quality; access to services; communications, etc.

By using multi-market data, household WTP for amenities may be estimated (Bartik, 1987a, 1987b). However, Bartik (1988) illustrates how in many circumstances[2] household WTP for amenity improvements at originally improved sites will underestimate true benefits and how predicted property value increases due to improvements may be used to set an upper bound to estimates.

Rather than estimate individual household WTP, a more common approach is to assume that the coefficients of the estimated hedonic price function reveal the preference structure for goods' attributes and then simply to use them to derive the implicit price (marginal WTP) for a change in the level of a given attribute. Hedonic price functions are generally reduced form equations accounting for both supply and demand influences. Rosen (1974) interpreted the hedonic price function as a price schedule for the good when the market is in equilibrium, and the partial derivatives of the price function with respect to the individual attributes as market-clearing marginal attribute prices. The latter directly measure the value of small changes in attribute levels and therefore constitute estimates of both consumers' marginal willingness to pay for attributes and the marginal returns obtained by producers from their supply. However, this approach will generally overestimate the benefits provided at the margin by the addition of a further unit of a given attribute (Harrison and Rubinfield, 1978; Freeman, 1979a). Even so, these estimates may subsequently be employed as the dependent variables in the estimation of the bid and offer functions of consumers and suppliers respectively (see Rosen, 1974; and Quigley, 1982).

Pearce and Markandya (1989) illustrate how, in general, individual social costs and benefits arising from changes in the level of an environmental resource may be inferred, using the case of pollution as an illustration. Figure 4.1 shows how an improvement in environmental quality (denoted by a decrease in pollution) raises property values at a declining, rather than at a constant rate. This is made explicit by the line AB in Figure 4.2, which represents the gradient of the curve in Figure 4.1, and by so doing illustrates the declining rate of change in property value (marginal cost). That is, in an

----

[2] i.e. for renters when the amenity improvements do not affect landlord costs and when no landlord/tenant adjustments take place.

area of high pollution a small improvement in environmental quality leads to a larger increase in house price than the same improvement in an area of relatively low pollution.

Property Value

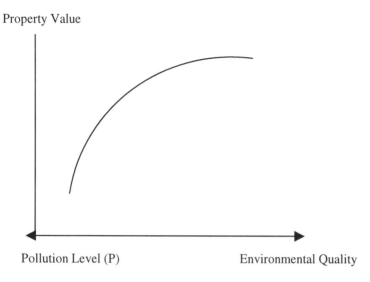

Pollution Level (P)   Environmental Quality

Figure 4.1: Change in property value with increasing environmental quality

The line CD in Figure 4.2 shows the rational consumer's negatively sloped marginal WTP curve for increased environmental quality. This indicates that the consumer will only consume additional units of environmental improvement at the margin if their price decreases. Pearce and Markandya describe how the point E^0 represents the unique equilibrium point where the consumer's WTP for pollution level P^0 is identical to the change in house price which that particular level induces. Thus, if the consumer were to move from an area with a higher pollution level than P^0 (i.e. from a point to the left of P^0), this would mean that the consumer's WTP for an extra unit of environmental quality is greater than the associated increase in the value of the property. The reverse would be true if the consumer were to move from an area with a lower pollution level than P^0.

Pearce and Markandya point out that the hedonic price model identifies one point on the line CD, the 'consumer's marginal WTP for environmental quality curve'. To see how the hedonic relationship reacts to change, they consider the environmental improvement which occurs when there is a reduction in pollution from P^0 to P^1 in Figure 4.2. This brings about a change in WTP from W^0 to W^1, and means that consumer surplus has increased by an amount equal to the area $E^0E^1W^0W^1$. Summing the changes in consumer surplus for all households affected by the particular environmental improvement would give an estimate of its overall value. However, as Pearce and Markandya note, the curve CD is not in practice observable, and most empirical studies merely approximate the increase in consumer surplus from the area under the curve AB.

Change in property
values WTP

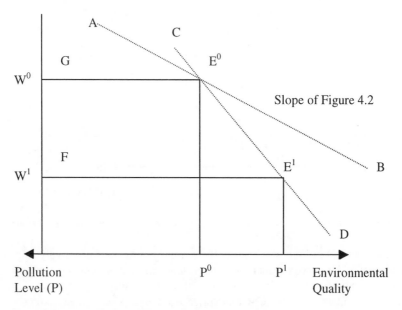

Source: Pearce and Markandya (1989)

*Figure 4.2: Change in marginal property value with improvement in
environmental quality*

There are certain problems with this interpretation as Pearce and Markandya point out: two papers by Freeman (1979a and b) illustrate some of these. First, hedonic price studies may ignore the problems of mobility restrictions, particularly in urban areas, thus biasing estimates of implicit price. Second there is the question of so-called 'averting behaviour,' where money is spent on measures to prevent or cut down negative environmental effects, e.g. double glazing or air filters. If data are unavailable on these measures, hedonic price estimates may be seriously biased.

Further, the assumption of equilibrium implicit in the theoretical model and illustrated by point E^0, is not always valid (MacLennan, 1977). This may occur when supply problems or rationing of property in the public sector (e.g. shortage of council houses) mean that a household cannot satisfy its demand for an environmental improvement because there are no properties available to them in areas of higher environmental quality. Alternatively, because sellers have no foreknowledge of the size of the maximum bid their property might yield, they may sell before that figure is reached, thus upsetting the market equilibrium (Horowitz, 1985).

There remains the question of the role of the premium paid by housebuyers for an improvement in environmental quality. This premium provides not only an immediate environmental benefit to the consumer but a future stream of benefits for as long as the level of environmental quality is maintained. Abelson and Markandya (1985) investigated this phenomenon, and looked at the relationship in the hedonic price between the present capitalised value and the discounted expected future benefits of the environmental improvement. Clearly, to set the current value of an environmental improvement by using the unadjusted hedonic price would be to over-estimate that value considerably.

2 THE THEORETICAL MODEL

2.1 The First-Stage Model

Rosen (1974) provided a theoretical model for the hedonic regressions which were already commonly used at that time (see Griliches, 1971). Rosen modelled goods as single commodities differentiated by the amounts of the various characteristics which they possess. Consumers derive utility from these characteristics and producers incur costs that are dependent upon the variety of goods which they provide. The interactions of consumers and producers in a competitive market for a differentiated product determine the equilibrium hedonic price schedule.

Rosen's model assumes:

(a) that the price of product is a function of its characteristics;

(b) that the range of product choices is continuous (where it is not, discrete choice modelling is required);

(c) that the amount of a particular characteristic can be varied independently — permitting a linear price function: if this is not possible then the price function will be non-linear.

The hedonic technique may be used to estimate the implicit prices of the set of characteristics which differentiate between similar products in a product class (Freeman, 1979a). To apply this technique to the housing market requires the identification of the set of structural and locational characteristics which describe a house and which may influence its selling price. This being done, a house may be described by the vector of its characteristics:

$$HC = (hc_1, hc_2, hc_3,...,hc_n) \qquad (4.1)$$

where hc_j is the jth characteristic of the house.

Now, assume that all individual households participating in the market behave identically and maximise the following well-behaved utility function:

$$U = U (H, G, A) \qquad (4.2)$$

where H is the housing commodity described by HC, G is a vector of goods available locally and A is a vector of local amenities. The utility function is constrained by the following relationship:

$$I = P_g \cdot G + P_h \cdot H \qquad (4.3)$$

where I equals household monetary income, P_g is a vector of the prices of local goods and P_h is the price of housing. Treating (4.2) and (4.3) as simultaneous equations, and solving for the chosen specification of H and G, yields an indirect utility function relating utility to income, house price, house characteristics, local goods and amenities:

$$W = W(I, A, P_g, P_h) \qquad (4.4)$$

Assuming that utility is constant[3] at W^*, a house price acceptance function may be derived as:

$$P_{ha} = P_{ha} (W^*, I, A, P_g) \qquad (4.5)$$

where P_{ha} is the price at which the house will be purchased by its purchasers. Differentiating (4.5) with respect to a specific amenity A, while holding W^*,

---

[3] This assumes that all individuals are able to move freely in the market.

I, and P_g constant (i.e. $dW* = dI = dP_g = 0$) allows the following relationship to be derived:

$$\Delta = dP_{ha} / dA = - (\partial W / \partial A) / (\partial W / \partial H)$$ (4.6)

This is interpreted as the marginal utility of an improvement in amenity A with respect to house price, and gives the equilibrium willingness to pay, Δ, for that improvement.

Equilibrium is reached at the point of tangency between the house price acceptance function (4.5) and another function, the house price opportunity locus, which incorporates the existence of the housing market. This function is specified as:

$$P_{ho} = P_{ho} (I, B, HC, A)$$ (4.7)

where P_{ho} is the price at which vendors are willing to sell their property. The partial derivative of (4.7) with respect to the level of a particular amenity or housing characteristic is interpreted as its marginal implicit price. Because of its properties this function is often used to estimate the hedonic house price model.

2.2 The Second-Stage Model

Under certain conditions and assuming that the house price opportunity locus is continuous, the first-stage model yields estimates of the implicit price which may be used in the second stage to derive demand functions for particular amenities or characteristics of interest. These demand functions may be specified for the nth amenity I as:

$$A_n = A_n (\Omega_n, SOC, SUB, COM)$$ (4.8)

where Ω_n is the marginal implicit price of the nth amenity, *SOC* is a vector of local socio-economic characteristics, including age, income, number of children and marital status, while *SUB* and *COM* are vectors of substitute and complementary amenities, respectively.

The usual two-stage approach to hedonic pricing is based on Rosen's (1974) work on implicit markets, and requires the estimation of the compensated demand curve for the factor of interest. This is usually accomplished by utilising the appropriate system of demand-supply equations, which are simultaneously estimated to yield the parameters of the structural system (e.g. Nelson, 1978a, Jud and Watts, 1981).

Simultaneous estimation is only required when the hedonic price function is dependent upon the observed units of demand. This is the identification problem noted by, among others, Brown and Rosen (1982), Mendelsohn

(1985) and Epple (1987), and arises due to the fact that the marginal price of an attribute and the inverse marginal demand curve are simultaneously determined by the level of consumption of the attribute. When this occurs, the price function may be influenced by the random error terms in either the demand or the supply equations, and so, consequently, may the marginal implicit price. In order to compensate for this effect, the estimation of the demand parameters in (4.8) must be carried out using the simultaneous demand-supply system equations.

According to Follain and Jimenez (1985), however, for studies which deal with micro data in a single market, such simultaneous estimation should not be necessary. This derives from the observation that for a particular good, an individual household's demand would not normally affect the price function which clears the market. Because of this, the hedonic price function and its parameters, including marginal implicit price, are independent of the error terms in both supply and demand equations. This means that the incorporation of the supply-side variables into a simultaneous estimation system to estimate the demand parameters is unnecessary. Similarly, as Follain and Jimenez (1985) point out, the assumption of fixed supply as a means of avoiding the simultaneity issue in micro data sets is also inappropriate.

There remains however, a further simultaneity problem which arises from the probable non-linear nature of the hedonic price function. Because any non-linear price function is dependent on the precise bundle of characteristics being consumed by each household, the implicit price for a particular attribute is affected by the choices which that household makes. Follain and Jimenez (1985) describe the situation as one where the consumer is presented with a fixed price function, points along which he, or she, is free to choose. This being so, and because implicit price varies along the range of the price function, the choice of the marginal implicit price paid for an attribute is simultaneously determined by how much of that attribute is consumed.

The non-linearity of the hedonic price function and the resultant simultaneous determination of price and quantity, imply that any attempts at estimation using OLS regression techniques will give biased results. The traditional approach to this simultaneity problem is to apply an instrumental variable to the marginal implicit price (see Linneman, 1981; Quigley, 1982 and Follain and Jimenez, 1983). The instrumental variable is derived by regressing the marginal implicit price against a set of variables which are thought to be correlated with marginal implicit price but not with the residual error of the individual consumer's demand equation (Follain and Jimenez, 1985). The instrumental variable on price is then incorporated into the demand equation using an appropriate regression technique, e.g. two or three-stage ordinary least squares.

Cropper *et al.* (1993) used simulation techniques to compare the performance of hedonic models and discrete choice multinomial logit models in valuing goods attributes. The discrete choice approach estimates the consumer's utility function for a good and can be used to directly estimate the prices of goods' attributes in much the same way as in the choice experiments described in Chapter 6. Cropper *et al.* found that the two approaches worked equally well in estimating marginal attribute prices (i.e. for the hedonic approach, those based on the first-stage model) but that the discrete choice approach outperformed the two-stage hedonic approach when it came to valuing non-marginal attribute changes.

3 APPLICATIONS OF THE HEDONIC HOUSE PRICE METHOD

The application of the hedonic method to examine the impact of environmental factors on house prices has been widespread. The one linking factor in most of these studies, however, is that their analysis has been *ex post,* and has examined the effects of developments and policy changes only after their implementation. This is a logical consequence of the hedonic approach, where a normal good is more likely to be valued for the attributes it already possesses than for those it will possess at some time in the future.

Even so, this implies that each attribute is not only valued with respect to the benefits it currently provides, but for the stream of future benefits which it will subsequently generate. Thus, it is possible that the purchase price of a house may well include some premium for benefits which will only accrue in the future and not in the present; furthermore, those benefits may not even be certain and may only be inferred.

The long-term nature of many schemes designed to alter or preserve landscape characteristics means that the landscape in these areas will evolve over a number of years. These changes will alter the level of the environmental amenity which the scheme provides, and will have the effect of shifting the hedonic price function (Freeman, 1971; Polinsky and Shavell, 1976). This effect implies that the price function would not be able to correctly predict the benefits which the environmental improvements should provide over coming decades.

The following sub-sections briefly describe how hedonic pricing has been used to examine a variety of issues ranging from environmental risk to landscape, noise and social factors.

3.1 Environmental Risk

Brookshire *et al.* (1985) examined the effect on property values of information on different levels of earthquake damage in residential areas of Los Angeles and San Francisco. This information was provided by the designation of special study zones (SSZs): these were areas of elevated relative risk of earthquake damage. The location of a house outside an SSZ, with the consequent lower risk of earthquake damage, could be expected to increase the value of a property, without providing any tangible benefits until the time when an earthquake does affect the region.

At the time of the study, the probability of a large earthquake in Los Angeles was roughly twice that of one occurring in San Francisco. Brookshire *et al.* predicted that the property value differential for houses outside SSZs in San Francisco's Bay Area should be about half that observed in Los Angeles. The observed differentials of $2,940 in San Francisco and $4,650 in Los Angeles largely confirmed these predictions, suggesting that individuals in both areas were processing the unusually high levels of information available to them in an accurate and rational fashion, and that their judgements of the potential benefits were being reflected in the institutional mechanisms of the housing market.

3.2 Landscape and Water Quality

Changes in landscape due to development or to changes in environmental or agricultural policy may increase or reduce amenity benefits for local residents, and hedonic pricing is frequently called on to estimate the magnitude of these changes.

Several studies have used the hedonic method to analyse the impact of well-established trees within individual housing plots on house prices. Morales (1980) for example, sampled houses in Amherst, Massachusetts both with a substantial amount of tree cover on the plot, and with no tree cover at all. Trees were estimated to add $2,686, or 6 per cent of the total, to the value of the houses observed. A rather more comprehensive study by Anderson and Cordell (1988) of 844 single family residential property sales in Athens, Georgia, indicated that landscaping with trees was associated with a 3.5 to 4.5 per cent increase in sales prices.

A study by Garrod and Willis (1992a) of the area surrounding the Forest of Dean concluded that the presence of at least 20 per cent woodland cover in the one kilometre grid square encompassing a property would increase the purchase price by as much as 7.1 per cent (see Chapter 10). This result was refined in a similar study looking at the effects of the relative concentrations of Forestry Commission (FC) woodland on house prices in Great Britain (Garrod and Willis, 1992b). A 1 per cent increase in the relative proportion of broadleaved woodland was found to increase the value of a property by about £42, whereas a similar increase in the relative proportion of mature conifers such as sitka spruce was found to depress house prices by around £141. The premium for broadleaves was common for all ages and species, and was considered to reflect not only the current benefits of more mature stands, but the future benefits as younger trees approach maturity.

The value of property is also known to differ according to differences in water quality. The implicit marginal price of proximity to water was estimated by Kirshner and Moore (1989) using a HPM on two residential areas adjacent to San Francisco Bay which have different water conditions. The circulation of water in the North Bay ranges from one day, during peak winter river flows, to two months during low summer flows, whereas water in the semi-enclosed South Bay has a turnover period of several months. Differences in water quality between the North and South Bays were confirmed by professional water sanitary engineers, and reflected in water quality measurements. The average sales price of properties in the North Bay area sample was $358,000 compared with an average South Bay sample price of $231,000. Waterside location was indicated by a dummy variable in the HPM: with a value of one if the property was within a hundred feet of water and zero otherwise. View was also included as a variable: houses fringing water were considered to have a view, except houses on narrow canals with a width of less than fifty feet. Houses across the street from water, or on a hillside, were also considered to have a view. The implicit marginal price of proximity to water was estimated from each area compared to equivalent properties not near water in each area. The implicit marginal price of proximity to water was estimated to be $65,000 (1985 prices) or 20 per cent of the property's value in the area of better water condition, and $24,000 or 9 per cent of property value in the area of poorer water condition. Thus the marginal implicit price of the change in the water condition was estimated to be approximately $41,000 per waterfront property in absolute terms, or approximately 11 per cent of the value of a waterfront property in relative terms.

The impact of water quality on waterfront property values was comparatively large in this study, but there were relatively few properties of this sort, and no values were estimated for properties further from the water. Even though the benefits were likely to be smaller for properties further away, since there were many more properties of this type, the bulk of economic benefits from water improvement may in fact have accrued to these properties.

Although concentrating on the effects of water quality, the Kirschner and Moore study indirectly focused on the effects on property values of the proximity of water. Several hedonic price studies have focused directly on the effects of proximity to water on property values, including Brown and

Pollakowski (1977) who found that location near to water or water-related open space was significant in determining prices. A study by Willis and Garrod (1993) of the effects on property values of location near to inland waterways in the UK which reached similar conclusions is reported in Chapter 10.

3.3 Environmental Protection

The economic effects of a policy which has the power to veto development was investigated by Frech and Lafferty (1984) in their investigation of the California Coastal Commission's effect on housing prices between 1966 and 1975. The Commission's influence on house prices was studied in four towns to the west of Los Angeles, both with respect to its protection of the positive externality provided by the coastal zone, and its ability to limit the amount of land available for housing. The study revealed that the activities of the Commission raised the price of homes in the area by amounts ranging from $990 to $5,043 (1975 dollars), and concluded that their activities 'caused significant economic harm.'

3.4 Urban Amenity

A number of hedonic price studies have attempted to estimate the benefits of urban amenity areas. These include Darling (1973) who used HPMs and an iterative bidding contingent valuation method to estimate the value of urban water parks in Oakland, San Diego, and Santee in the USA.

The HPM revealed that distance from water was negatively related to property value, although this varied somewhat according to the type of property. This result held whether the results were obtained from actual housing sales prices using HPMs, or through plotting CVM estimates of the value of the water by willingness to pay for access to it by distance from the water. Darling found that the value of the urban water resource was large. Of course the CVM benefits were an alternative and not an addition to the HPM estimated benefits: if fees were charged for the use of the parks, prospective home buyers would capitalise them and would be willing to pay less for property surrounding the park. A decrease in property value would result. Unless the price of property used in the HPM study reflects uncertainty about future access or charges for the park, there is no justification for adding CVM and HPM measures together.

The establishment of green belts are also known to have a positive impact on neighbouring house prices. Wabe (1970) in an analysis of house prices to establish the value of journey time, the rate of time preference, and the valuation of some aspect of the environment in the London region, estimated, on the basis of 1,800 house purchase transactions, that proximity (indicated by a dummy variable in the HPM) to a given belt added £276 per house at 1968 prices:[4] this represented about 4.9 per cent of the value of the house.

A study in the USA by Correll *et al.* (1978) sampled residences within one kilometre of a green belt and measured the actual distance of the property from three green belts in Boulder, Colorado. Results revealed that distance from the green belt had a statistically significant negative impact on the price of residential property. Specifically, *ceteris paribus,* there was a $13.78 decrease in the price of residential property for every 1 metre one moved away from the green belt, and holding other variables constant the average value of properties adjacent to the green belt would be 32 per cent higher than those a kilometre away. This was a very high value and implied that value fell rapidly with increasing distance from a green belt.

3.5 Agricultural Land Values

As well as valuing environmental improvements, hedonic pricing has been used in the past to value the effects of improving agricultural land. Both Miranowski and Hammes (1984) and Ervin and Mill (1985) used an hedonic technique to examine the effects of soil quality and erosion on land values. The earlier of these two studies concluded that topsoil quality had the expected positive effect on land values, though the results of the latter were less conclusive.

A study by Palmquist and Danielson (1989) used the hedonic approach to investigate the effects of erosion control and drainage on agricultural land in North Carolina. Land that was wet enough to require drainage caused an estimated 25 per cent reduction in land values (about $374 per acre), while susceptibility to soil erosion also depressed land values by about $3.06 per unit increase in erosive potential. The study also found that arable land was worth $488 per acre more than forested land. Palmquist and Danielson's estimates were found to perform quite well when compared to other estimates of the costs and benefits of drainage and erosion

3.6 Pollution

The impact of air pollution on property values is often difficult to estimate through HPMs, because multicollinearity between air pollution attributes means that one pollution measure inevitably picks up the effects of all forms of air pollution. In a review of a number of air pollution HPM studies, Pearce and Markandya (1989) demonstrated that a 1 per cent increase in sulphation levels resulted in a fall in property values between 0.06 and 0.12 per cent; a 1 per cent increase in particulates lowers property values by 0.05 to 0.14 per

---

[4] This applied to houses within two miles of the green belt.

cent; while a 1 per cent increase in a variable which picked up a number of measures of air pollution was associated with a 0.09 to 0.50 per cent depreciation in property prices.

Harrison and Rubinfield (1978) measured the marginal WTP as a percentage of income for an improvement in air quality at designated high levels of nitrogen oxides. They concluded that homebuyers would be willing to pay up to 19 per cent of their yearly income (about $5,500) for a given improvement in air quality.

3.7 Noise

While small reductions in noise levels are unlikely to have a significant impact on house prices, it is feasible to investigate the effects of larger reductions in cases where noise pollution is a problem. Studies of the effects of noise pollution are relatively common in the literature, and usually relate to aircraft or traffic noise. Few such studies have, however, been carried out in the UK, the most notable being the Roskill Commission's (1971) investigation into the proposed third London airport.

Nelson (1980) reviewed a number of empirical studies of the effects of aircraft noise on property values using cross-sectional HPMs. The most commonly used noise measure in the USA, the Noise Exposure Forecast (NEF) indicates the sum of noise produced by different aircraft flying different flight paths weighted by the number of day and night flights. NEF values range from 15 to 55, with little or no annoyance to individuals between 15 and 25 and considerable annoyance above 40. NEF 20 approximates to 55–60 dBA. Results suggested a unit reduction in NEF would result in a 0.51 per cent appreciation in property values, although results varied between airports from 0.29 percent at Cleveland to 0.74 per cent at San Diego. Evidence from 13 studies suggested that noise discounts ranged from 0.4 to 1.1 per cent per decibel. Thus, an £80,000 house would sell for £64,000 if located in a noisy zone: a total discount of 10 to 20 per cent. Noise discounts are commonly 0.5 to 0.6 per cent, though higher values occur in some high income areas e.g., Boston, Washington DC, and London (Nelson, 1980).

In another study of the relationship between highway noise and property values covering nine different empirical studies in the USA and Canada, Nelson (1982) concluded that noise discounts lie in the range 0.16 to 0.63 per cent per decibel, with a mean of 0.40 per cent. Noise can be characterised in numerical terms in an HPM, and this is a distinct advantage over qualitative characteristics such as landscape. Psychological perception of noise is known to be logarithmic in nature: thus the sensation of noise roughly doubles with each 10 dB increase in the intensity level.

Similar results have been found in other studies which have investigated the effects of noise. Larsen (1985) reported a reduction of 0.8 per cent to property values in Oslo for every thousand vehicles per day on the nearest road, while in another Norwegian study, Hoffman (1984) found a 60db threshold for aircraft noise above which a 1db increase deflated house prices by about 1 per cent. In a study of airport noise in Toronto, Canada, Mieszkowski and Saper (1978) estimated a discount of up to 15 per cent on the price of properties located in areas with a NEF rating of 35.

3.8 Social Factors

Hedonic pricing has also been used to investigate a variety of other issues. These include the impact of racial discrimination in the Boston housing market (Schafer, 1979), the effect of schools on house prices (Jud and Watts, 1981), and the impact of urban railways (Forrest *et al.*, 1992).

4 HEDONIC WAGE MODELS

The hedonic technique can also be applied to wage rates. An individual's choice of job may be influenced by the location of that job if it improves access to desirable services, such as good schools, recreational and leisure amenities. Clark and Kahn (1989) applied the hedonic wage model to investigate recreational fishing benefits in the United States by linking wage rates with a number of variables including several related to the quality of local water, fish and game stocks.

There are particular problems in applying this technique to value environmental goods. Most important, in this era of high unemployment, are the assumptions underlying the hedonic model of a fixed supply of jobs and a freely functioning job market where individuals choose jobs based on perfect information and with no mobility restrictions. These assumptions may not be valid when a shortage of jobs means that individuals cannot satisfy their demands for environmental improvement because there are no suitable jobs available for them in areas of higher environmental quality.

In Clark and Kahn's study public data sets detailing house sales and wage rates were utilised along with data on environmental quality. A two-stage approach was adopted where in the first stage the marginal prices of amenity characteristics were estimated using a simple hedonic-wage model, while in the second a willingness-to-pay function was derived by regressing estimated marginal price against a range of socio-economic and climatic variables. According to the authors, this approach produced robust results and was subsequently used to estimate recreational fishing benefits under a variety of water quality improvement scenarios.

The hedonic technique has also been used in wage-risk analysis to determine the value of life and limb in relation to the hazards faced at work. This is achieved by modelling respondent's willingness to accept a given wage level as a function of the skills required for the job, the attributes of the job and the risk of death that the job entails. The general hedonic wage equation is:

$$P = P(J, R, S) \qquad (4.9)$$

where P is the payment rate for a given job, S is a vector of skills required to do the job, J is a vector of other job-related attributes (e.g. working hours, holiday, sickness benefits, etc.) and R is the risk of death. The partial differential of this function with respect to R gives an estimate of the additional payment required by individuals to accept a marginal increase in the chance of death.

In practice the technique is complicated by the difficulty in assessing an objective measurement of the risk of death, particularly when most occupations carry a tiny risk of death. Generally some measure such as accidental deaths per thousand workers is used as a measure of risk, but these empirically-based probabilities may bear little relation to an employee's perception of risk, e.g. the average office worker is not likely to consider the risk of death when making a decision as to accept a particular job offer. Cropper and Freeman (1990) list a number of wage-risk studies conducted in the developed world; by contrast, the composition of labour markets in developing countries make it unlikely that this approach would be of great importance in that context.

5 DATA REQUIREMENTS

The data requirements for a hedonic price study may be divided into two broad categories: the specific and the local. The specific data category relates only to observed property transactions, and must include details of the property being sold or rented, including structural and locational information, and details of the purchase or tenancy, such as price, date, and the personal and financial particulars of the purchasers. The local data category is far broader, and should contain details of neighbourhood, amenity, environmental and socio-economic factors in the area where the property transaction occurs.

The sources of specific data differ depending on the country or state involved. For instance in the United States most property sales are recorded in some detail at a local, state or national level and may be obtained either from the appropriate authorities or from local estate agents and valuers, e.g.

the Tax Supervisor of Mecklenburg County, North Carolina (Jud and Watts, 1981); the Board of Realtors Knoxville, Tennessee (Johnson and Kasserman, 1983), the Bureau of Census and the Bureau of Labor Statistics (Cobb, 1984) and the Society of Real Estate Appraisers (Michaels and Smith, 1990).

In the United Kingdom the fund of data sources is not so rich, with the main supplier of details of house purchases being mortgage granting institutions such as building societies or banks. The wide variety of such bodies means that only the largest, or most regionally concentrated, are able to provide data sets which are large enough, and sufficiently broad geographically, to be used in hedonic price studies. To facilitate the use of data in hedonic price studies it is important that individual house purchase records have some form of spatial reference, such as a postcode or map reference, allowing comparison between building society data and records kept on the same basis by other organisations, including those dealing with environmental data.

Many of the variables included by a building society for its own accounting purposes may not be required for a hedonic house price study, while others which are relevant and important factors in determining house price are omitted. The lack of such information may result in less satisfactory explanation of variation in house prices by the HPM.

Such problems of omitted data are likely to occur with most data sets, and it is always useful to check alternative sources of data before engaging in a study in order to compare their coverage in terms both of observations and variables. If it becomes clear that there are missing variables in the data set being used to estimate the hedonic price function, then this will have specific consequences for the choice of functional form.

Another source of information on owner-occupiers in the UK which has been used in hedonic house price studies (e.g. Rosenthal, 1989) is the 5 per cent Sample Survey of Building Society Mortgages (see Evans, 1975). This is a large data set compiled by the building societies and used by the UK Department of the Environment, Transport and the Regions to compile statistics on new housing purchases. It comprises personal details of the buyer, purchase price and some physical details of the property involved. Certain limitations do exist in the data set and these are summarised by Rosenthal (1989).

Some studies rely on collecting raw data from estate agents and realtors (e.g. Dodgeson and Topham, 1990). The latter approach has the advantage of frequently providing a photograph of the properties involved, but this is often outweighed by the magnitude of data collection problems.

Once data have been collected on the structure of the property and the socio-economic profile of the purchasers/renters, the next step is to obtain data relating to its immediate neighbourhood. The measurement of neighbourhood quality is in itself an important subject and this is discussed later in this chapter. In the UK there are two useful postcode-based broad classifications of neighbourhood type which may be used in an hedonic study (e.g. Forrest *et al.,* 1992). The ACORN (A Classification Of Residential Neighbourhoods) classification provides 39 different residential categories, such as council estate, or multi-occupier property, into which every residence in the country has been placed on the basis of its postcode. Similarly, the parliamentary constituency (PC) classification identifies each postcode with its parliamentary constituency, and classifies those on a scale of 1 to 9: e.g. PC7: solid middle class; PC3: deprived inner city.

Classifications, such as the above, are reflected in disaggregated local socio-economic data, relating to wealth, employment, education and social class. The sources and availability of these data vary from region to region, and access may prove expensive or difficult to obtain. Some data will be carried in national archives, while much will be in the hands of local authorities, educational institutions and pressure groups such as Shelter. Access may be easier to census data, which though usually somewhat out of date, will still provide useful information at a district level on socio-economic indicators such as population density, car ownership, employment in various classes and home ownership.

Details of local employment by industrial and occupational classifications can be obtained in the UK by accessing the National Online Manpower Information System (NOMIS), which also carries small area census statistics. Information on unemployment rates is also available from this facility, which also includes various analytical tools, such as shiftshare analysis, which can be useful in generating comparative data. Information is accessed by specific geographical area rather than by postcode or grid reference. Area categories include: job centre office areas; travel to work areas; local authority districts; counties; and national regions. Not all information is, however, available for each area type, which may mean that statistics cannot be as regionally disaggregated as might be desirable.

Data on access to local amenities and services may be harder to find. National Data Protection Acts may prevent records being kept which can be easily identified as relating to particular individuals. Thus, in the UK while a building society database may be used to identify a property by its postcode as being in a particular street, there is no information as to exactly which house or flat in the street the record relates to. This means that only approximate measurements may be made of the location of a property with respect to shops, schools, recreational areas and workplaces. This is more significant in rural areas than in urban ones, though in rural areas the same postcode usually relates to fewer properties than it would in an urban area.

Geographical information systems (GISs) are a useful source of neighbourhood amenity data and may provide some environmental data as well, particularly with regard to the location of environmental goods such as woodland, rivers and open water. An alternative to the GIS approach is to use annotated maps as the data source; this is particularly useful when a discrete area such as a city or rural district is involved. For urban areas detailed town plans are usually available, sometimes with postcodes appended to them, while for rural areas Ordinance Survey (OS) maps provide useful data, though they may have to be updated by hand to provide full information on local schools, leisure amenities and so on (see Garrod and Willis, 1992a for an example of the OS approach).

Cobb (1984) reviewed several papers which have investigated the effect which omitting neighbourhood characteristics in HPMs has on included variable coefficient estimates. Some studies, including Butler (1982) and Follain *et al.* (1979), found evidence to suggest that the errors induced into individual coefficient estimates by the omission of neighbourhood variables were sufficiently small that such variables could be safely ignored. Conflicting advice is to be found in Gillingham (1973), Linneman (1980) and McDonald (1980) who each show that the omission of neighbourhood characteristics may significantly change variable coefficients. Cobb's own work suggested that this latter viewpoint is more likely to be correct.

Environmental data may be derived from various sources, depending on the nature of the data required. Several institutions have their own databases relating to their own areas of interest, e.g. the UK Forestry Commission's sub-compartmented database gives details on a 1km OS grid square basis of the species and age compositions of their holdings, while the UK Environment Agency holds data on water quality from the waterways they monitor. For a package of environmental goods provided or enhanced by a particular policy instrument, such as the designation of an area as a National Park, the extent of the designation itself can be used to define a dummy variable, indicating the policy on/policy off position. If the policy designation provided the composite environmental benefit to be valued, then the single dummy variable would be sufficient to estimate the implicit price through the hedonic price model. This approach might be adopted simply because the wide range of interacting benefits both ecological and environmental being generated by the policy would be impossible to value individually within the hedonic framework.

6 DATA PROBLEMS

The two main concerns with utilising the data obtained in the previous section are the problems with measurement error and with multicollinearity. While the former relates to errors in the observed values of the dependent and explanatory variables being used in the model, the latter concerns the difficulty in the interpretation of hedonic estimates when the effects of several variables are closely linked. An additional consideration in some cases is whether the data can be treated as if they correspond to a single market, or whether they need to be divided into separate sub-markets, each of which is described by its own distinct hedonic price function.

6.1 Measurement Error

The first measurement problem comes with the choice of dependent variable: that is the decision whether to use purchase or rental data. In the UK, as in many other western countries, there is a larger owner-occupier than rental sector, making it more convenient to use price data. Furthermore as Pearce and Markandya (1989) point out purchase price is often found to outperform rental data in this type of study. In the developing world different housing structures exist, and rental prices may be used as the dependent variable. Nelson (1978b) used professional valuers' data and found that not to contain any highly significant or systematic errors.

Once the choice of dependent variable has been resolved, there remains the measurement of the environmental variable to be studied. In the case of air pollution for instance, even without the problems of multicollinearity, which will be discussed later, there is still the problem of what measure to use. Is a seasonally weighted mean appropriate, or will a simple arithmetic or geometric mean be sufficient? These sorts of questions usually require expert guidance to solve, and may also arise in studies of water and noise pollution.

Things may be even more complicated when the good being valued produces a wide variety of effects across several environmental categories. This is the case when examining the benefits of an environmental policy. To measure the differences in individual environmental attributes would be almost impossible, due to the large number being affected and the difficulty of assessing the magnitude of some of these changes. Even if this could be achieved, multicollinearity problems would be so great as to render the exercise pointless. Instead the usual approach is simply to measure the impact of the policy as merely being on or off: that is, to use a single indicator variable which takes the value of 1 in an area with a given designation and the value 0 otherwise. Thus, while the impact of individual environmental improvements cannot be measured, the broader set of environmental benefits brought about by the policy can.

In some cases individual environmental attributes must actually be measured, e.g. woodland access in Powe *et al.* (1997) and various forms of pollution in other studies. This is one of the easier tasks in an hedonic price study, and though it may prove time-consuming and sometimes expensive, it is generally straightforward.

One element in the hedonic price model which may be difficult to measure is neighbourhood quality, mainly because there is little agreement in the literature as to which variables to use either as direct measures or proxies.

Even if important quality determinants are identified, there may be problems with intercorrelations between them. Dubin and Sung (1990) point out that most hedonic regressions include neighbourhood variables, but few actually discuss the issue of the measurement of neighbourhood quality. They list the few honourable exceptions to this rule, including Li and Brown (1980) who use income as a proxy for neighbourhood quality, and Jud and Watts (1981) who find that the racial composition of schools is insignificant in determining housing prices when compared with school quality.

Dubin and Sung hypothesised that neighbourhood characteristics could be grouped into three categories: socio-economic status (SES), municipal services and racial composition. In a survey of 25 studies they found that 13 used some measure of SES, 14 some measure of public services and 18 a measure of racial composition: 21 of the studies used at least one of the above to control for neighbourhood quality. They went on to estimate their own models using various quality measures, and found that both the racial and socio-economic status of neighbours were important determinants of neighbourhood quality. Further, they rejected the notion that race was only important because of its links with SES. In comparison with race and SES, public services were found to be relatively unimportant.

6.2 Multicollinearity

Multicollinearity may be a serious problem in hedonic price models. It is difficult to list all of the attributes of a particular good, especially a house, and some of these attributes will certainly be correlated with one another.

This problem is frequently associated with structural characteristics: for instance the number of rooms is often highly correlated with the plot size or with the possession of a garage. In most environmental studies these structural features are not of direct interest and, provided that they are not correlated with the environmental attributes being studied, intercorrelations between them can usually be ignored: this will mean that the effects of some structural characteristics on house price may be impossible to interpret individually, but that the overall effect of groups of characteristics will be apparent. It is when measures of environmental quality are significantly correlated that the most problems arise. If the correlation is ignored and the affected variables are all included in the model then it will be difficult to estimate what their individual effects are.

The possibility of multicollinearity may be initially investigated by looking at the sensitivity of the coefficients of environmental quality variables to the omission of other significant explanatory variables. This should provide some indication of the likely effects of any omitted explanatory variables. Problems of multicollinearity can be investigated further by estimating the Variance Inflationary Factor (see Maddala, 1992). This shows the extent to which a given explanatory variable is correlated with the environmental quality variables and also measures the extent to which the model deviates from the ideal situation of no multicollinearity.

It may be possible to avoid multicollinearity in the model by careful data selection. Principal component analysis may be used to identify the independent sources of variation within the data (e.g. Powe *et al.,* 1997). Identification of principal components enables more careful variable selection to be undertaken, with one variable from each important explanatory component initially included in the model. Thus, the chosen variables act as proxies for groups of collinear variables, reducing the likelihood of multicollinearity within the hedonic price model. This does not help with the problem of interpretation, as there is no way of separating out the effects on house price of each element of the collinear group. All that can be estimated is the marginal effect of a given set of characteristics proxied by the level of the principal variable.

An interesting example of multicollinearity in measures of environmental quality is that of airborne pollution, where the levels of one form of pollution, say suspended particulate matter, may be closely correlated with the levels of another such as nitrogen dioxide. Lack of information may thus cause a single variable to be used as a proxy for all forms of air pollution, an approach which as in the principal components example implicitly includes multicollinearity. Freeman (1979b) adopted this approach in an air pollution study, attempting to identify the major pollutant and use that as the proxy.

Other more sophisticated approaches than principal components analysis may be used to combat this problem. Firstly, rather than using a single proxy variable a composite variable may be used instead: thus, in the case of air pollution one variable relating to all pollutants might be used thus cutting out the possibility of multicollinearity between different pollution measures. This approach may be extended to the case where a single major change occurs over a relatively short time period, possibly a proposed new road or a nature reserve. In these situations there is often no multicollinearity to be found within the variables of interest.

Alternatively, the individual effects of each correlated variable may be separated out using some form of statistical approach similar to that developed by Klepper and Leamer (1984). This may prove difficult, with a complicated statistical technique made even more so by the need to take account of the often complex physical relationships between the effects being measured.

In an attempt to overcome the problem of multicollinearity, Feitelson (1992) randomly assigned short narratives or vignettes to housing in a survey of respondents living in different urban and rural communities around Chesapeake Bay. Because the vignettes were generated in a random orthogonal design, their characteristics were independent of each other, i.e.

the orthogonal nature of the vignettes therefore overcame the multicollinearity problems of HPMs. Respondents evaluated vignettes both as complete packages, and in terms of the contribution of each characteristic to their overall judgement and WTP was assessed using OLS regression techniques. For each vignette, the respondent was asked:

(1) how desirable is this (vignette) for you as a place to live?
(2) how much would you have been WTP for this residence?
(3) suppose this residence is for sale today, for how much do you think it would sell?

A large mail survey was conducted in various counties in Maryland around Chesapeake Bay, (excluding Baltimore), generating 992 usable questionnaires. Average perceived mean market house prices amounted to $99,710. Households were willing to pay a premium for water frontage of between $10,000 to $13,000. Waterfront buyers in commuting belts and in rural areas were willing to pay $6,000 to $8,400 more than the average for the Bay as a whole and these differences were found to be statistically significant. Consumers also differentiated between types of water relationship in their willingness to pay, e.g. water frontage, assured access to water, water view, and proximity to water.

It is important for development to identify the market segment attracted to water frontage residences. In the Chesapeake Bay area water front residences tended to be associated with upper income groups and those looking for a retirement home, and also those with an affinity for water related leisure activities. Areas differed in their ability to attract water related development. For example, a water front town house development may be suitable for commuting areas, but not attractive enough in rural areas where waterfront buyers typically seek single detached family type housing. Feitelson argued that such considerations explained the relative lack of success of waterfront townhouse development in rural counties around Chesapeake Bay.

6.3 Use of Submarkets

For some applications the specification of a single hedonic price function to cover a whole area may be inappropriate. This may apply whether data relate to a single metropolitan area or to a more diverse rural or suburban area. Michaels and Smith (1990) identified two situations where the assumption of a single, continuous housing market may be questioned. First there is the case where exogenous factors such as race, income or political boundaries constrain individual households to participate only in certain segments of a larger housing market (e.g. Schnare and Struyk, 1976). Then there is the second reason, the information available to participants in a housing market.

The theoretical model discussed earlier relies on the assumption that there are no information constraints in the particular housing market being examined: this implies that households in the market for property should have sufficient information upon which to base their housing choice. In most cases much of this information would be provided by estate agents or valuers (Michaels and Smith state that in the United States in 1981, 82 per cent of private house sales involved realtors). It is the expert local knowledge of these individuals which is often crucial in the definition of housing submarkets. Such expert judgement is difficult to approximate in an HPM, because it stems from knowledge of a variety of factors which are weighted according to the local context. and to the realtor's judgement To try and model this process econometrically across housing submarkets would be futile, and to ignore it would introduce a bias into the results.

Michaels and Smith (1990) used the judgement of realtors to define four distinct housing submarkets in the city of Boston. The submarkets they defined[5] were 'remarkably consistent' and were shown to be distinct by statistical testing, suggesting that a single hedonic price function was not sufficient to describe the determinants of the Boston housing market. In response to this finding Michaels and Smith set up four separate hedonic price functions each relating to one of the four housing submarkets. This approach was then used to test their main objective, the determination of household WTP for the removal of hazardous waste sites.

7 THE CHOICE OF FUNCTIONAL FORM

Estimation of the hedonic price function requires the choice of a specific functional form for the statistical model. Economic theory is of no help in this matter since it imposes no restrictions on the form of the hedonic price function (Rosen, 1974).[6] The choice of a particular functional form for use in empirical analysis is therefore essentially arbitrary and, whatever function is chosen, it should properly be interpreted as an approximation of the true but unknown hedonic price function.

It can be shown that an inappropriate choice of functional form may lead to mis-specification errors in the hedonic price function, which may in turn lead

---

[5] The submarkets were classified as: premier, above average, average and below average: greater segmentation was found to provide insufficient information with which to rank the submarkets.

[6] The sole theoretical restriction on the hedonic price function is that the price elasticities with respect to the attributes should lie between the corresponding price elasticities of supply and demand. This implies no particular restriction on the form of the function and since the supply and demand curves are not in general observable is of little empirical consequence.

to errors in the estimation of the implicit price of a given attribute. Some practitioners may trade off between convenience and precision, and tolerate the introduction of bias through the mis-specification of some simpler functional form, rather than adopt a more rigorous but more time-consuming approach. Others may not, and will examine a variety of functional forms, selecting the one which performs best for some specified criteria.

The choice of functional form will depend on whether the principal objective of the study is to derive estimates of the marginal prices of the attributes or to generate conditional predictions of house prices or rents. The former objective requires careful consideration of the structure and parameterisation of the hedonic price model whereas the latter demands close attention to the robustness of the model and its extrapolative plausibility. It follows that there will be no single 'best' parametric hedonic price function for all purposes. In particular, the functional form which provides the best overall fit to the sample data may not necessarily yield the most satisfactory estimates of marginal attribute prices.

In practice, the range of functional forms that have been employed in hedonic price studies of the housing sector may all be classified as either 'restrictive' or 'flexible'. The restrictive functional forms include the linear, semi-log, log-linear and linear Box-Cox, which are special cases respectively of the quadratic, quadratic semi-log, translog and quadratic Box-Cox flexible functional forms.

The use of the linear, semi-log and log-linear functional forms in the early hedonic price studies was dictated by limited computational resources, though these forms are still popular. The main advantage of these traditional functional forms is the simplicity and transparency of the relationships between the marginal attribute prices and the parameters of the function. Less apparent are the restrictive implications which follow from the lack of generality in the characterisation of the hedonic price function. These are frequently unrealistic, and may call into question the validity of the analysis and any conclusions drawn from it.

The simplest of the restrictive forms is the linear function, for which the marginal attribute prices are constants. Thus, all houses are assumed to have the same vector of marginal attribute prices irrespective of either the composition of the attribute bundle of a house or its price. For example, Johnson and Kasserman (1983) utilised the linear functional form to study the relationship between energy efficiency and house prices, but in so doing they assumed, *a priori,* that the same level of efficiency improvement would be valued identically whatever the initial efficiency level of a house, its other attributes, such as the number of bedrooms, or its selling price. This assumption was intuitively implausible and its imposition as a maintained hypothesis was inappropriate in the absence of corroborative evidence.

In fact, as Rosen (1974) pointed out, non-linearity in the hedonic price function is to be expected since house buyers cannot treat individual housing attributes as discrete items from which they can pick and mix until their desired combination of characteristics is found. On the contrary, most properties embody a set of attributes which are not readily adjustable and homebuyers are limited in their choice to those properties available on the market. This argument may also be applied to the rental market though renters will have more opportunity than buyers to obtain their optimal mix of attributes if landlords are more likely than house owners to combine, divide or otherwise alter housing units. Goodman and Kawai (1984) and Goodman (1988) found that renter-occupier housing functions were regularly more linear than those for owner-occupiers.

The specification of a non-linear function implies that the marginal attribute prices will not be identical for all houses but this does not necessarily mean that the representation of the hedonic price function will be more general. The utilisation of a semi-log function, for example, implies that marginal attribute prices are proportional to the price of housing. Any pair of houses with the same market price will have the same vector of marginal attribute prices, even if those houses have very different attribute bundles (Rasmussen and Zuehlke, 1990).

In the case of the log-linear function, each marginal attribute price is proportional to the ratio of the level of the given attribute to the price of housing. Thus, any pair of houses will have the same vector of implicit attribute cost shares, even if those houses have very different prices and mixes of attributes. These restrictions may prove more appropriate than the imposition of a constant vector of marginal attribute prices but are no less severe.

The statistical methodology developed by Box and Cox (1964) and used by Cassel and Mendelsohn (1985) and Dinan and Miranowski (1989), among others, may be used to discriminate between the traditional functional forms on the basis of goodness of fit. The unrestricted linear Box-Cox (ULBC) function facilitates a search over a variety of alternative forms, and under certain restrictions subsumes the various functional forms of interest as special cases, e.g. the linear, semi-log and log-linear forms.

Tests by Cassel and Mendelsohn (1985) and Dinan and Miranowski (1989) rejected all three sets of restrictions and suggest that the ULBC function itself is to be preferred as the best fitting restrictive functional form. However, the ULBC has various disadvantages as a functional form for empirical use. First, the estimation procedure is computationally expensive since the global maximum of the likelihood function is located using a grid search over the values of the non-linear parameters. Second, the Box-Cox transformations result in complex estimates of the economic effects of interest which are cumbersome to manipulate and lack any clear economic interpretation (see

Cassel and Mendelsohn, 1985). Finally, the ULBC is not suitable for the investigation of certain issues such as the relationships between marginal attribute prices and individual attribute levels. This is because the function, in common with all other restrictive functional forms, is strongly separable in attributes which implies that the ratio of the marginal prices of any two attributes will be independent of the level of all other attributes.

The main appeal of flexible functional forms is that they impose little structure on the data with marginal attribute prices being determined explicitly as functions of the individual levels of all attributes. This generality is desirable *per se* and may be required for the investigation of such issues as the nature of the relationships between attributes. Yet the estimation of distinct interaction effects between all the attributes places heavy demands on the data. The various flexible functional forms result from the direct expansion of particular restrictive functional forms by the inclusion of quadratic 'interaction' terms between the attributes.

Empirical studies have uniformly found that the interaction or quadratic terms are jointly significant as a group, irrespective of the particular functional specification under review. However, it does not necessarily follow that flexible functions will also provide 'better' measures of marginal attribute prices than their restrictive counterparts in terms of some mean square error criterion. This is because the inclusion of the additional interaction terms will result not only in a reduction in mis-specification bias but also in an offsetting increase in the variance around each parameter (Rao and Miller, 1971). Graves *et al.* (1988) suggest that if estimated marginal prices are found to be relatively insensitive to functional form then the use of a restrictive form may be preferable to obtain relatively precise estimates.

In most cases even the best fitting functional form will be only an approximation to the real-life relationship between house price and the factors which influence it. With this in mind, some trade-off must be achieved between the aims of a particular study and the underlying statistical considerations. It is not possible, therefore, to recommend one single functional form for use in hedonic studies irrespective of the purpose of the analysis. Rather we should be asking whether the empirical conclusions drawn from hedonic price studies are sufficiently insensitive to the choice of functional form to be considered reliable. This issue has been addressed by Cropper *et al.* (1988) and Graves *et al.* (1988).

Cropper *et al.* generated an artificial data set from observations on actual housing stock in order to test the ability of alternative functional forms to yield unbiased estimates of the (known) marginal attribute prices. Two main points of interest emerge from their study. First, the marginal prices of important attributes which account for a high percentage of total utility from housing are measured with greater accuracy than those of unimportant attributes. Second, when attribute variables are omitted or measured with error then the restrictive functional forms yield more accurate measures of marginal prices than the flexible functional forms.

In particular, the latter functions tended to produce the largest average biases and it may be expected that estimates of marginal attribute prices will be especially unreliable for extreme values of the attribute bundle due to the effect of the quadratic terms. This finding is of empirical importance since attributes in hedonic studies commonly have to be measured by proxies: data on neighbourhood attributes in particular may be omitted due to lack of data and other variables may also be dropped due to multicollinearity. Cropper *et al.* found that overall the ULBC performed best in the tests that they conducted, though this result was clearly dependent on the design of the experiment and should not be interpreted as a general endorsement for the ULBC.

In the absence of extraneous information or the demonstration of empirical robustness, misgivings on the part of practitioners should warn against the literal acceptance of quantitative results drawn from hedonic studies. Nor should the apparent emergence from a number of studies of a consensus as to the impact of a particular factor on property prices be taken as a guarantee of convergence upon the true impact given the selective reporting of results and the understandable tendency to claim support for results on the basis of conformity to past studies.

The emphasis in future studies should be placed less on the comparison of goodness-of-fit measures of a number of functional forms and more on the sensitivity of those forms to changes in model specification. This approach was demonstrated well by Graves *et al.* (1988), whose study of urban air quality specifically examined the robustness of hedonic-based estimates of marginal environmental values, investigating the empirical consequences of a range of econometric issues, including variable selection, measurement error and choice of functional form.

In their study, Graves *et al.* found that the treatment of these issues affected not only the quantitative but also the qualitative estimates of the impact of air quality on property prices. While the importance of avoiding errors in the measures of environmental quality which are of direct policy interest was stressed, the choice of model specification was also shown to have a major influence on results. The wide range of benefit estimates which can be derived under a variety of model specifications suggests that the issue of sensitivity analysis has wide-ranging policy implications. Therefore it is suggested that, for the purposes of policy appraisal, empirical studies should report the consequences of changing model specification in terms of changes in welfare estimates and discuss any implications this would have for cost-benefit ratios or other decision rules.

8 OTHER CONSIDERATIONS

8.1 Estimation Procedures

The selection of an appropriate functional form in an empirical situation must take place in the context of model estimation. The usual estimation method is that of maximum likelihood (ML), though some studies, particularly those using more restrictive functional forms, may use ordinary least squares. If a form such as the ULBC is used, then a two-dimensional grid search is required in order to maximise log-likelihood with respect to the ULBC parameters.

8.2 Robustness and Reliability of Estimates

Once the hedonic regression has been estimated there remains the question of the robustness and reliability of the results. This is particularly important when there is some question of multicollinearity in the data. There are several techniques which may be applied to investigate this issue. One technique is that of repeat sales analysis which is described by Palmquist (1982). This approach uses repeat sales of the same property to test whether environmental changes have affected the relative prices of houses over time. Consequently, the method relies on several rather restrictive assumptions, notably that the hedonic price function does not shift over time for those housing characteristics not being investigated.

The general reasoning behind the technique is to estimate the change in valuation of an environmental amenity or disamenity over time, using repeat sales-pairs which are equally distant from the site being investigated. This requires an equation of the form:

$$ln(PRICE2/PRICE1) = f \text{ (initial sale date, final sale date, DIST)} + e \quad (4.10)$$

where *PRICE1* is the initial sale price, *PRICE2* is the sale price at the end of the repeat sales period, *DIST* is the distance of the property from the site of the amenity/disamenity and *e* is an error term. If the coefficient on *DIST* is positive, then there is evidence that properties farther from the particular site are worth more at the end of the repeat sales period relative to the beginning. Conversely, if the coefficient is negative then properties are worth relatively less for a marginal increase in distance from the site.

Kohlhase (1991) used this technique in a study of the impacts of toxic waste sites on housing values in the US, using the announcements of the US Environmental Protection Agency (EPA) as an indicator of public awareness of the dangers associated with waste sites. In all, 45 repeat sales were observed over a five-year period, and subsequent analysis reinforced the basic findings of the study, which were that EPA announcements on waste sites were seminal in creating a market for safer housing away from the sites.

Kohlhase also employed a validation technique which compared the estimates from her study area with estimates from a control group, which consisted of a version of the original data set, greatly expanded by increasing the radius of the study area from 7 miles to 31 miles. The results of the control again supported the original findings of the study, providing further evidence that the estimates were robust and reliable. Such expansion of the data set is not feasible in all applications of HPMs, particularly those looking at localised effects, but the technique is usable provided that data are available in investigations of the amenity value of particular sites or areas.

Another approach used to assess the reliability of hedonic price estimates is to perform Jackknife regressions, (see Mosteller and Tukey, 1977) which re-estimate the model when randomly chosen groups of observations have been removed. The logic behind this procedure is that under conditions of serious multicollinearity the removal of a few observations might be expected to cause coefficient estimates to change by a large magnitude.

In the study of the amenity value of woodland by Garrod and Willis (1992b) briefly described in Section 3.2, Jackknife regressions were performed using 189 groups of five observations, each of which were removed sequentially from the data set and the regression coefficients re-estimated. On average, the re-estimated coefficient values showed only small differences from those estimated with a full data set.

In the same study another technique was used to investigate the possible effects of coefficient bias being introduced through the omission of potentially important explanatory variables. This approach simulates the effects of omitted variable bias by omitting variables from the model which are known to have a statistically significant effect on house price. If the omission of these variables is shown to have potentially large effects on the coefficient values of the environmental effects being examined, and if any important variables are known to be missing from the data set then there is cause for concern about the existing coefficient estimates. In their study Garrod and Willis re-estimated their model with each significant variable being omitted in turn. The coefficient values of the environmental amenity variables were examined at each stage, and were shown on average to deviate by 5 per cent from the values estimated in the full model, indicating that the omission of variables was not likely to have a profound effect on the estimates of environmental benefits.

Michaels and Smith (1990) adapted a time-series test for the stability of parameters in a regression equation in order to test the stability of an hedonic price function based on a full data set (the authors also defined separate models for each of four housing submarkets within that data set: see Section 6.3) The test they used was the Brown-Durbin-Evans (Brown *et al.*, 1975) cusum of squares test. Briefly, the test involves recursive fitting of the model using a base data sample, progressively adding individual observations to the sample and examining the residuals. A test statistic was derived, based on a scaled set of these residuals.[7] If the constant parameter model described house sale adequately then the test statistic should follow a linear path; if it fails to this to the extent that it falls outside a given confidence interval then the null hypothesis of stable (constant) coefficients should be rejected. The test performed by Michaels and Smith indicated functional instability in their full model.

9 DISCUSSION

Despite its apparent complexity, the hedonic price technique has become a well-established method for estimating the disaggregated benefits of various goods attributes. In the case of housing these attributes include not only basic structural and amenity characteristics, but also environmental characteristics such as clean air, landscape and local ecological diversity. Thus, when a particular policy is implemented which will have a profound effect on the local environment, the hedonic approach may offer a useful way of estimating the change in amenity benefits.

In *ex post* policy evaluation it is important to measure the change in benefits arising from any environmental changes rather than the total costs or benefits resulting from a given level of environmental quality. The assumptions underlying the hedonic technique means that it is better suited to the estimation of the *ex post* benefits generated by an established environmental policy, than to the prediction of the *ex ante* benefits which may accrue from a proposed change in environmental policy. The environmental effects resulting from various policy designations are only likely to become fully apparent over a number of decades. Thus, while an hedonic price function may be used to estimate the environmental benefits provided to local residents by an area as it exists today, it cannot reliably predict the benefits which will be generated by future improvements because those improvements will have the effect of shifting the existing function.

Some discounted future benefits will, of course, form part of the implicit price of location within a given area, and these will represent the households' future stream of expected benefits from the current landscape and the amenity which it offers. These cannot, however, fully encompass any future unforeseen increase in amenity benefits which may evolve in the future.

---

[7] See Michaels and Smith, 1990: Equations (2) and (3).

Hedonic pricing has little history of use in the developing world. In theory, the methodology could be used to model the price of housing or the cost of land in a developing country, e.g. as a function of area, fertility, irrigation, fuelwood, etc. Many developing countries (e.g. Ghana) have little tradition of buying and selling houses, with most dwellings either built by the owner or inherited from family members. In these instances estimation of an hedonic rent model would be a more practical methodology to adopt. Problems arise from the underlying assumptions required by hedonic pricing. In some instances housing supply is a problem, while in others rents are kept at artificial levels by rent control or other regulatory mechanisms. Similarly land pricing may be influenced by cultural factors which are hard to incorporate into an economic model and again supply may be a problem. Even if the underlying assumptions are met, there may still be data problems to overcome. Records of house transactions may be incomplete or fail to include much relevant information. Often individual properties may be hard to locate due to idiosyncrasies in numbering.

REFERENCES

Abelson, P.W. and A. Markandya (1985), 'The interpretation of capitalized hedonic prices in a dynamic environment', *Journal of Environmental Economics and Management*, **12**, 195–206.

Alonso, W. (1964), *Location and Land Use*, Harvard University Press, Cambridge, MA.

Anderson, L. M. and H. K. Cordell (1988), 'Influence of trees on residential property values in Athens, Georgia (U.S.A.): A survey based on actual sales prices', *Landscape and Urban Planning*, **15**, 153–64.

Bartik, T. (1987a), 'The estimation of demand parameters in hedonic price models', *Journal of Political Economy*, **95**, 81–8.

Bartik, T. (1987b), 'Estimating hedonic demand parameters using single market data: the problems caused by unobserved tastes', *Review of Economics and Statistics*, **69**, 178–80.

Bartik, T. (1988), 'Measuring the benefits of amenity improvements in hedonic price models, *Land Economics*, **64**, 172–183.

Blomquist, G. C., M.C. Berger, and J.P. Hoehn (1988), 'New estimates of quality of life in urban areas', *American Economic Review*, **78**, 89–107.

Box, G. and C. Cox (1964), 'An analysis of transformations', *Journal of the Royal Statistical Society, Series B*, **26**, 211–52.

Brookshire, D. S., M.A. Thayer, J. Tschirhart, and W. D. Schulze (1985), 'A test of the expected utility model: evidence from earthquake risks', *Journal of Political Economy*, **93**, 369–89.

Brown, G.M. Jr. and H.O. Pollakowski (1977), 'Economic valuation of shoreline', *The Review of Economics and Statistics*, **59**, 272–8.

Brown, J.N. and H. Rosen (1982), 'On the estimation of structural hedonic pricing models', *Econometrica*, **50**, 765–8.

Brown, R.L., J. Durbin, and J.M. Evans (1975), 'Techniques for testing the constancy of regression relationships over time', *Journal of the Royal Statistical Society, Series A, 7702*, 149–63.

Butler, R. (1982), 'The specification of hedonic indexes for urban housing', *Land Economics,* **58**, 96–108.

Cassel, E. and R. Mendelsohn, (1985), 'The choice of functional forms for hedonic price equations: comment', *Journal of Urban Economics,* **18**, 135–42.

Clark, D.E. and J.R. Kahn (1989), 'The two-stage hedonic wage approach: A methodology for the valuation of environmental attributes', *Journal of Environmental Economics and Management,* **16**, 106–20.

Cobb, S. (1984), 'The impact of site characteristics on housing cost estimates', *Journal of Urban Economics,* **15**, 26–45.

Correll, M.R., J.H. Lillydahl, and L.D. Singell, (1978), 'The effects of green belts on residential property values: some findings on the political economy of open space', *Land Economics,* **54**, 207–17.

Cropper, M.L., L.B. Deck, and K.E. McConnell, (1988), 'On the choice of functional forms for hedonic price functions', *Review of Economics and Statistics,* **70**, 668–75.

Cropper, M.L., L.B. Deck, N. Kishor, and K.E. McConnell (1993), ' Valuing product attributes using single market data: a comparison of hedonic and discrete choice approaches', *Review of Economics and Statistics,* **75**, 225–32.

Cropper, M.L. and A.M. Freeman (1990), ' Environmental health effects', in J.B. Braden and C.D. Kolstad (eds) *Measuring the Demand for Environmental Quality,* North Holland , Amsterdam.

Darling, A.H. (1973), 'Measuring benefits generated by urban water parks', *Land Economics,* **49**, 22–34.

Dinan, T.M. and J.A. Miranowski (1989), 'Estimating the implicit price of energy efficiency improvements in the residential housing market: a hedonic approach', *Journal of Urban Economics,* **25**, 52–67.

Dodgeson, J. S. and N. Topham (1990), 'Valuing residential properties with the hedonic method: a comparison with results of professional valuations', *Housing Studies,* **5**, 209–13.

Dubin, R.A. and C-H. Sung (1990), 'Specification of hedonic regressions: non-nested tests on measures of neighborhood quality', *Journal of Urban Economics,* **27**, 97–110.

Epple, D. (1987), 'Hedonic prices and implicit markets: estimating demand and supply functions for differentiated products', *Journal of Political Economy,* **95**, 59–80.

Ervin, D.E. and J.W. Mill (1985), 'Agricultural land markets and soil erosion: policy relevance and conceptual issues', *American Journal of Agricultural Economics,* **67**, 938–42.

Evans, A. (1975), *Studies for Official Statistics, 26: The Five Per Cent Sample Survey of Building Society Mortgages,* Central Statistical Office, London.

Feitelson, E. (1992), 'Consumer preferences and willingness-to-pay for water related residences in non-urban settings', *Regional Studies,* **26**, 49–68.

Follain, J.R. and E. Jimenez, (1983), 'Demand for housing characteristics in developing countries', World Bank Discussion Paper WUDD 43, Washington DC.

Follain, J.R. and E. Jimenez (1985), 'Estimating the demand for housing characteristics', *Regional Science and Urban Economics,* **15**, 77–107.

Follain, J., L. Ozanne, and V. Alburger (1979*), Place to Place Indexes of the Price of Housing,* Urban Institute Paper on Housing.

Forrest, D., J. Glen, and R. Ward, (1992), 'Both sides of the track are wrong: a study of the effect of an urban railway system on the pattern of housing prices', ESRC Urban and Regional Economics Seminar Group Meeting, Glasgow, April 6th–8th, 1992.

Frech, H.E. and R.N. Lafferty, (1984), 'The effect of the California Coastal Commission on housing prices, *Journal of Urban Economics,* **16**, 105–23.

Freeman, A. M. (1971), 'Air pollution and property values: a methodological comment', *Review of Economics and Statistics,* **53**, 415–6.

Freeman, A. M. (1979a), 'Hedonic prices, property values and measuring environmental benefits', *Scandinavian Journal of Economics,* **81**, 154–73.

Freeman, A. M. (1979b), *The Benefits of Environmental Improvement Theory and Practice,* John Hopkins University Press, Baltimore.

Garrod, G.D. and K.G. Willis (1992a), 'Valuing goods' characteristics: an application of the hedonic price method to environmental attributes', *Journal of Environmental Management,* **34**, 59–76.

Garrod, G.D. and K.G. Willis (1992b), 'The environmental economic impact of woodland: a two stage hedonic price model of the amenity value of forestry in Britain', *Applied Economics,* **24**, 715–28.

Gillingham, R. (1973), 'Place to place rent comparisons using hedonic quality adjustment techniques', BLS Research Discussion Paper No. 7.

Goodman, A.C. (1988), 'An econometric model of housing price, permanent income, tenure choice and hedonic prices', *Journal of Urban Economics,* **23**, 327–54.

Goodman, A.C. and M. Kawai (1984), 'Replicative evidence on the demand for owner-occupied and rental housing', *Southern Economic Journal,* **50**, 1036–57.

Graves, P., D.C. Murdoch, M.A. Thayer, and D. Waldman (1988), 'The robustness of hedonic price estimation: urban air quality', *Land Economics,* **64**, 220–33.

Griliches, Z. (1971), 'Introduction: hedonic price indexes revisited', in Z. Griliches, (ed.), *Price Indexes and Quality Change,* Harvard University Press, Cambridge, MA.

Halvorsen, R. and H.O. Pollakowski (1981), 'Choice of functional form for hedonic price equations', *Journal of Urban Economics,* **10**, 37–49.

Harrison, D. and D.L. Rubinfeld (1978), 'Hedonic housing prices and the demand for clean air', *Journal of Environmental Economics and Management,* **5**, 81–102.

Hoffman, J.V. (1985), 'Air traffic noise and the value of housing properties', *Working Paper,* Institute of Transport Economics, Oslo.

Horowitz, J.L. (1985), 'Inferring Willingness to Pay for Housing Amenities from Residential Property Values', Report EPA 600/7-85-034.

Johnson, R. and D.L. Kasserman (1983), 'Housing market capitalization of energy saving durable good investments', *Economic Inquiry* , **21**, 374–86.

Jud, G.D. and J.M. Watts (1981), 'Schools and housing values,' *Land Economics,* **57**, 459–70.

Kirschner, D. and D. Moore (1989), 'The effect of San Francisco Bay water quality on adjacent property values', *Journal of Environmental Management,* **27**, 263–74.

Klepper, S. and E.E. Leamer (1984), 'Consistent sets of estimates for regression and errors in all variables', *Econometrica*, **52**, 163–83.

Kohlhase, J.E. (1991), 'The impact of toxic waste sites on housing values', *Journal of Urban Economics*, **30**, 1–26.

Lancaster, K. J. (1966), 'A new approach to consumer theory', *Journal of Political Economy*, **74**, 132–57.

Larsen, O.I. (1985), 'Road traffic and the value of housing properties', *Project Report*, Institute of Transport Economics, Oslo.

Li, M. and H. Brown (1980), 'Micro-neighbourhood externalities and hedonic prices', *Land Economics*, **56**, 125–41.

Linneman, P. (1980), 'Some empirical results on the nature of the hedonic price function for the urban housing market', *Journal of Urban Economics*, **8**, 47–68.

Linneman, P. (1981), 'The demand for residence site characteristics', *Journal of Urban Economics*, **9**, 129–48.

McConnell, K.E. (1990), 'Double counting in hedonic and travel cost models', *Land Economics* , **66**, 121–7.

McDonald, J. (1980), 'The use of proxy variables in housing market analysis', *Journal of Urban Economics*, **7**, 75–83.

MacLennan, D. (1977), 'Some thoughts on the nature and purpose of house price studies', *Urban Studies*, **14**, 59–71.

Maddala, G.S. (1992), *Introduction to Econometrics: Second Edition*, Macmillan Publishing Company, New York.

Mendelsohn, R. (1985), 'Identifying structural equations with single market data', *The Review of Economics and Statistics*, **67**, 525–8.

Michaels, R.G. and V.K. Smith (1990), 'Market segmentation and valuing amenities with hedonic models: the case of hazardous waste sites', *Journal of Urban Economics*, **28**, 231–42.

Mieszkowski, P. and A.M. Saper (1978), 'An estimate of the effect of airport noise and property values', *Journal of Urban Economics*, **5**, 425–40.

Miranowski, J.A. and B.D. Hammes (1984), 'Implicit prices of soil characteristics for farmland in Iowa', *American Journal of Agricultural Economics*, **66**, 745–9.

Morales, D.J. (1980), 'The contribution of trees to residential property value', *Journal of Arboriculture*, **6**, 305–8.

Mosteller, F. and J.W. Tukey (1977), *Data Analysis and Regression*, Addison-Wesley, Reading, MA.

Nelson, J.P. (1978a), 'Residential choice, hedonic prices, and the demand for urban air quality', *Journal of Urban Economics*, **5**, 357–69.

Nelson, J.P. (1978b), *Economic Analysis of Transportation Noise Abatement*, Ballinger, Cambridge, MA.

Nelson, J.P. (1980), 'Airports and property values: a survey of recent evidence', *Journal of Transport Economics and Policy*, **14**, 37–52.

Nelson, J.P. (1982), 'Highway noise and property values: a survey of recent evidence', *Journal of Transport Economics and Policy*, **16**, 117–30.

Palmquist, R.B. (1982), 'Measuring environmental effects on property values without hedonic regressions', *Journal of Urban Economics*, **11**, 333–47.

Palmquist, R.B. and L.E. Danielson (1989), 'A hedonic study of the effects of erosion control and drainage on farmland values', *American Journal of Agricultural Economics,* **71**, 55–62.

Pearce, D.W. and A. Markandya (1989), *Environmental Policy Benefits: Monetary Valuation,* OECD, Paris.

Polinsky, A.M. and S. Shavell (1976), 'Amenities and property values in a model of an urban area', *Journal of Public Economics,* **5**, 119–29.

Powe, N.A., G.D. Garrod, and K.G. Willis (1995), 'Valuation of urban amenities using an hedonic price model', *Journal of Property Research,* **12**, 137–47.

Powe, N.A., G.D. Garrod, C. F. Brunsdon, and K.G. Willis (1997), 'Using a geographic information system to estimate an hedonic price model of the benefits of woodland access', *Forestry,* **70**, 139–49.

Quigley, J.M. (1982), 'Nonlinear budget constraints and consumer demand: an application to public programs for residential housing', *Journal of Urban Economics,* **12**, 177–201.

Rao, P. and R. Miller, (1971), *Applied Econometrics,* Wadsworth, Belmont, California.

Rasmussen, D.W. and T.W. Zuehlke (1990), 'On the choice of functional form for hedonic price functions', *Applied Economics,* **22**, 431–8.

Rosen, S. (1974), 'Hedonic prices and implicit markets: product differentiation in pure competition', *Journal of Political Economy* , **82**, 34–55.

Rosenthal, L. (1989), 'Income and price elasticities of demand for owner-occupied housing in the UK: evidence from pooled cross-sectional and time-series data', *Applied Economics,* **21**, 761–77.

Roskill Commission (1971), *Report of the Commission on the Third London Airport,* HMSO, London.

Schafer, R. (1979), 'Racial discrimination in the Boston housing market', *Journal of Urban Economics,* **6**, 176–96.

Schnare, A.B. and R.J. Struyk (1976), 'Segmentation in urban housing markets', *Journal of Urban Economics,* **3**, 146–66.

Wabe, J.S. (1970), 'A study of house prices as a means of establishing the value of journey time, the rate of time preference and the valuation of some aspects of the environment in the London Metropolitan region', *Research Paper 11,* Department of Economics, University of Warwick, Coventry.

Willis, K.G. and G.D. Garrod (1993), 'Not from experience: a comparison of experts' opinions and hedonic price estimates of the incremental value of property attributable to an environmental feature,' *Journal of Property Research,* **10**, 193–216.

PART THREE

Expressed Preference Techniques

5. Contingent Valuation Methods

Quarterly, is it, money reproaches me:
'Why do you let me lie here wastefully?
I am all you never had of goods and sex.
You could get them still by writing a few cheques'.

So I look at others, what they do with theirs:
They certainly don't keep it upstairs.
By now they've a second house and car and wife:
Clearly money has something to do with life.

Philip Larkin (1926–85): *Money*

1 INTRODUCTION

The term contingent valuation is derived from the nature of the method: responses are sought from individuals as to their actions *contingent* on the occurrence of a particular hypothetical situation. For example, individuals might be asked their maximum willingness-to-pay (WTP) to enter a National Park contingent upon a charge being introduced or a park being created. Alternatively they may be asked to state the minimum amount of compensation required to maintain their original utility level, if the park was closed to the public.

Contingent valuation is an important tool in environmental valuation because revealed preference, or behaviour in the market place, cannot value all environmental goods. Revealed preference estimates the value of a National Park by assessing the demand for a related market good, e.g. how much people are prepared to spend on travel to gain access to the park (the travel-cost method); or by assessing the house price premium people are prepared to pay to live in a National Park (the hedonic price method). However, travel-cost and hedonic price methods cannot estimate non-use values, since there is, by definition, no related market good for the mere existence, as distinct from use, of the park. Thus, for example, contingent valuation (CV) is required to value public goods such as wilderness and landscape preservation; biodiversity; the existence value of national book collections such as the Library of Congress or the British Library; the value of preserving historical artefacts, monuments, and the character of old towns and villages.

Individuals and businesses are faced with similar questions for some private market goods. For example, firms have to think about how much to bid for a television operator's licence when these are periodically auctioned. Individuals have to think, *ex ante*, about the maximum they are prepared to pay for a work of art at an auction, or how much they are prepared to pay to improve their housing[1]. *Ex post,* individuals also have to think about the minimum they would be willing to accept as compensation, for injury (under tort law), slander, libel, or the non-provision of a service (under contract law), to settle out of court rather than go to trial.

The ultimate use of CV depends upon whether contingent valuation methods (CVMs) produce accurate, reliable, and consistent estimates of the value which individuals place upon environmental and other goods.

2 PROPERTY RIGHTS

Underlying the use of CV is the question of property rights. If the individual does not own the right to a good, then the relevant measure of the utility of the good to the individual is the maximum he or she would be willing to pay to acquire it. Conversely if the individual owns the good, then the minimum the individual would be willing to accept as just compensation for its loss is the relevant utility measure, since this is the amount that would restore the individual to his utility level before being deprived of the good.

WTP and WTA should be similar in magnitude for most goods which are close substitutes and for which the income effect is small. However, numerous experiments have revealed that WTP is typically 2 to 5 times the magnitude of WTA values for the same good (Table 5.1). There are a number of reasons that could explain this divergence.

First, the theory may be correct, so that the observed difference is a function of the inadequate empirical procedures used to elicit WTP and WTA, such as questionnaire design, interviewing technique, etc.

---

[1] Indeed an early example of contingent valuation in Britain was Flowerdew and Rodriguez (1978) value to tenants of local authority housing renovation.

Table 5.1 Disparities between WTP and WTA

Study		WTPA/WPA ratio
Hammack and Brown (1974)		4.2
Banford *et al.* (1977)	(i)	2.8
	(ii)	4.2
Bishop and Heberlein (1979)		4.8
Brookshire *et al.* (1980)	(i)	1.6
	(ii)	2.6
	(iii)	6.5
Shaw and Willis (1982)		2.9
Coursey *et al.* (1983)	(i)	3.8
	(ii)	1.6
Knetsch and Sinden (1984)		4.0
Adamowicz *et al.* (1993)	(i) video	1.95
	(ii) hockey ticket	1.70

Source: adapted from Pearce and Markandya (1989).

Second, the WTA measure might be faulty. Respondents may reject the property right implied by WTA questions; that they have to sell their 'right' to some environmental attribute. In addition, psychologists argue that ownership itself makes a commodity more valuable resulting in a higher selling price. Kahneman *et al.* (1991) note the 'endowment effect' in a number of markets, from investment, and insurance,[2] to experimental laboratory markets.

Third, respondents might behave strategically. Consumers may act rationally in formulating their WTP bids, conscious of their income and budget constraints; and preferences for other goods. However, a CV framework might not give respondents enough motivational incentives to give truthful answers, especially about the *minimum* they would be willing to accept as compensation for their loss to restore them to their original utility level. Respondents have a greater incentive to act strategically in demanding compensation for the loss of a good. This is a factor implicit in the compulsory purchase or eminent domain powers that governments assign

---

[2] For example, for automobile insurance residents in New Jersey and Pennsylvania are offered a choice between two types of insurance: a cheaper policy which restricts the right to sue and a more expensive one that does not. In New Jersey, where the cheaper policy is the default option, 83% chose this policy. Under Pennsylvania law, the default option is the expensive policy, and 53% of respondents opted for this policy.

themselves to acquire land for roads, and other goods. Eminent domain permits the acquisition of land and property at 'market value', which is taken to be the amount which the land or property, if sold on the open market by a willing seller, might be expected to realise. Loss of consumer surplus (utility over and above market price) is ignored on the basis that it is extremely difficult to establish the scale of this loss if people behave strategically and over-estimate their loss. However, the WTA/WTP difference has been observed for minor goods, and in simulated markets (e.g. classroom experiments), where strategic behaviour and income effects should be inconsequential, as well as in hypothetical markets valuing major environmental damage.

Fourth, the observed difference between WTA and WTP might be real. Psychological factors might explain the disparity. Kahneman and Tversky (1979) argue that individuals have different values for losses and gains of the same magnitude (Figure 5.1). The fact that people often demand much more to give up an object than they would be willing to pay to acquire it, creates asymmetry of value: i.e. loss aversion. People's values and willingness to trade goods are conditioned by their initial endowment of goods. In a laboratory experiment Kahneman *et al.* (1991) gave pens and mugs to participants. Since the mugs and pens were randomly assigned, on average only half those who preferred a mug received one. This implies that in the subsequent experimental markets half of the mugs should be traded, given zero transactions costs and income effects. However, the volume traded was less than half of that expected, and the ratio of selling to buying prices was about two to one. Samuelson and Zeckhauser (1988) also noted that in both experimental markets and in real market selections, individuals disproportionately prefer the *status quo*.

Fourth, Hanemann *et al.* (1991) argued that the difference between WTA and WTP can be explained in theory where there is an absence of substitutes for the good being valued. Willig (1976) showed that Hicksian compensating and equivalent variations and Marshallian measures of consumer surplus are close approximations of each other; i.e. WTA should closely approximate WTP. Thus, if the product of income elasticity and the ratio of surplus change to total income divided by two is less than 0.05 in absolute value, no more than about a 5 per cent error is made by using consumer surplus as a measure of either Hicksian compensating or equivalent variation. This condition holds for many environmental goods where there are no strong income effects and where the environmental good has substitutes (i.e. is not unique). Randall and Stoll (1980) argued that for environmental goods income elasticity (η) should be replaced by 'price flexibility of income' (ε) and reformulated Willig's limits as:

$$(M - WTP) / M \cong (\varepsilon * M) / 2Y \tag{5.1}$$

and

$$WTA - WTP \cong (\varepsilon * M) / Y \qquad (5.2)$$

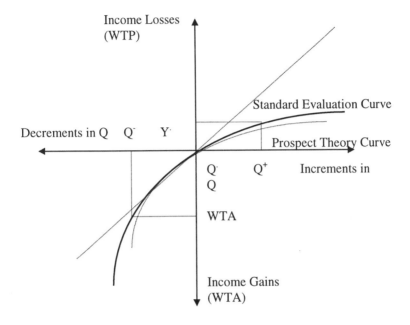

Source: Adapted from Brookshire et al. (1980); Kahneman and Tversky (1979)

Figure 5.1 Total value of changes in the provision of an environmental good

where M = Marshallian consumer surplus; Y = respondent's mean income; ε = price flexibility of income. Randall and Stoll estimate ε in a similar manner to ordinary income elasticity by regressing WTP on the quantity of the good, income and other explanatory variables. Hanemann (1986, 1991) demonstrated that ε should really be $\varepsilon = (\eta/\sigma)$ where η = income elasticity of demand for the environmental good, σ = elasticity of substitution between the environmental good and all other goods. To illustrate the impact of this Mitchell and Carson (1989) found that households with an average income of $18,000 were willing to pay an average of $250 to improve water quality from non-boatable to swimmable, with $\varepsilon = 0.70$.

Using Randall and Stoll's equations: WTA and M (the Marshallian consumer surplus) can be derived. WTP is the compensating surplus (CS) and WTA the equivalent surplus (ES). Thus, CS ($250), < M ($251.22) < ES ($252.45). The difference between WTP and WTA is about 1%, or $2.50.

However, if the income elasticity of an environmental attribute is 2 ($\eta = 2$), and the elasticity of substitution between the environmental good and all other goods is 0.1 ($\sigma = 0.1$), both of which are not reasonable estimates, then the price flexibility of income = 20. This gives a difference between WTA and WTP of $70 based on the above estimates of M and Y. Hence WTA is some 28% (70/250) greater than WTP.

In a test of Hanemann's substitution effect, Adamowicz *et al.* (1993) estimated WTP for a ticket to a hockey game, and the WTA amount for giving up the same ticket. One group of respondents was informed that the particular hockey game would be broadcast live on radio and television (the usual practice in reality, and hence a substitute for the hockey ticket); whilst the other group was informed that they could watch the game only at the stadium (no substitutes available). Respondents were asked a dichotomous choice (DC) question: if they would be either (a) willing to pay $X to purchase a ticket for the game; or (b) willing to accept $X to sell a ticket; where $X was a randomly generated amount between $5 and $100. The mean results are reported in Table 5.2, which reveals the gap between WTA and WTP was considerably reduced (30% smaller) in the presence of a substitute, compared with the no substitute situation, lending some credence to Hanemann's substitution hypothesis. However, the presence of substitutes did not eliminate the difference between WTA and WTP.

Finally, Coursey *et al.* (1987) demonstrated convergence between WTA and WTP in an experiment in which respondents had to state how much they would be either:

(a) WTP to avoid tasting for 20 seconds an unpleasant but harmless liquid (sucrose octa-actuate). To avoid strategic behaviour an auction was conducted amongst the eight subjects who submitted bids on the understanding that the top four bidders would avoid the tasting;[3]

(b) WTA to avoid the obligation to taste the liquid, again on the understanding that the four lowest bidders would be able to sell their obligation for a compensation amount equal to the lowest rejected bid[4] (here 5th lowest bid).

---

[3] The actual auction was a Vickrey auction in which the individual(s) who acquire the good pay only the amount equal to the highest rejected (here 5th) bid. The dominant strategy of this type of auction is to bid one's true WTP because the respondent's bid does not affect the price, only whether or not the individual acquires the good (in this case avoiding tasting the unpleasant substance). A bid below the individual's true WTP creates the possibility of not obtaining the good (avoiding the unpleasant taste) when there is a price she would be willing to pay to acquire it. Conversely, a strategic bid above her true WTP creates the possibility of acquiring the good at a price that exceeds her utility for it.

[4] Again the optimal bid in this Vickrey auction is the individuals' true WTA value.

Table 5.2: Mean value estimates of welfare measures for hockey ticket experiment

Sub-sample	WTA	WTP	WTA-WTP
Substitute	$48.5	$28.5	$20.0
No-substitute	$70.0	$36.6	$33.4

Source: Adamowicz *et al.* (1993).

Whilst in the early rounds of this auction elicitation experiment, WTA was higher than WTP; in later rounds WTA fell to only slightly above WTP, such that the difference was not statistically significant. Financial incentives and experience appeared to reduce the difference between WTA and WTP to an insignificant amount.

The increasing willingness to accept compensation over time is illustrated in an empirical analysis of the Swiss proposals for siting a nuclear waste repository which were initially rejected by local residents at Wolfenschiessen. Initial attitudes are the net outcome of the perceived negative externalities of the repository and public spiritedness to accept a nationally necessary but locally unwanted land use (LULU). If there is insufficient public support for the repository, monetary compensation might be introduced to off set the negative externality. When such compensation is perceived as a 'bribe', moral indignation at this reduces public support further. However, Frey *et al.* (1996) observed that whilst 75% of residents initially rejected financial 'bribes' [varying from $2,175 (N=117), to $4350 (N=102), to $6,525 (N=86)] when first offered in a CV survey, two thirds of voters in a town hall meeting approved the siting of the repository one year later when the developer offered $4,687 per family. Thus an amount that was initially rejected in a CV survey was accepted one year later as an actual payment, by which time moral principles had been substituted.

3 UNDERTAKING A CONTINGENT VALUATION STUDY

Once the property rights issue has been resolved for the particular good under investigation, the actual CV study can be split into a number of stages (Hanley and Spash, 1993):

1. setting up the contingent valuation or hypothetical market
2. obtaining WTP or WTA amounts
3. estimating mean and median WTP and/or WTA amounts
4. aggregating the WTP or WTA amounts
5. assessing the validity of the CV exercise.

3.1 The hypothetical market

The process of devising a convincing CV scenario consists of a number of elements. The first step is to devise a hypothetical market for the environmental good that is the subject of the study. For example, Dillman and Bergstrom (1991) attempted to measure WTP values for the environmental amenity benefits of agricultural land. The environmental amenity value of agricultural land was specified as: (1) scenic value (such as quaint barns, and rustic fences and hedges); and (2) nostalgic value (rural heritage, and myths that farm life produces good and morally strong citizens). Both scenic and nostalgic values are largely non-rival in consumption. The study presented respondents with sets of photographs: (A) depicting prime agricultural land in Greenville County, South Carolina; and (B) depicting how (A) might look if developed for commercial or residential purposes. Respondents were asked their WTP to preserve prime agricultural land if:

- only a quarter of the existing prime land in the county was protected (18,000 acres);
- half of the existing prime land in the county was protected (36,000 acres);
- three quarters of the existing prime land in the county was protected (54,000 acres);
- all of the existing prime land in the county was protected (72,000 acres).

3.2 Bid vehicle

After the reason for the payment (hypothetical CV scenario) has been detailed, respondents must also be presented with a believable vehicle by which the funds will be raised. There are many different bid vehicles through which WTP bids can be collected: income tax, value added or sales tax, trust fund payments, entry charges, property taxes, and changes in utility bills. Not all bid vehicles are viable options for collecting WTP bids in a given situation. The chosen bid vehicle should have a plausible connection with the amenity it is being used to value, and also be perceived to be 'fair' and 'equitable' in its incidence and in relation to those deriving benefits for the proposed good. Different types of bid vehicle provide different opportunities for free riders. People have different views on the acceptability of different types of taxes: e.g. poll, property, income, and sales taxes. A survey of local residents on WTP additional local water or sewerage charges to fund improved water quality, might result in protests against the bid vehicle if the principal beneficiaries of the improved water quality are tourists in the area who do not share any of the costs. A survey of tourists would probably reveal large WTP values for an increase in a local tax (water charge) which they do not have to pay. In the latter case a hotel room tax might be a more appropriate payment vehicle.

Countries such as Kenya charge foreign tourists for entry into their National Parks and wildlife sanctuaries and the revenue provided helps to cover the costs of conservation. Such a payment vehicle might elicit user values for the parks, but it is not capable of measuring non-use or preservation values for wildlife. Moreover, where people are familiar with an entry charge to an existing park comparable to the new park being valued, their maximum WTP for the new park may be anchored to the entry charge of the old park.

3.3 Focus groups

CV surveys may be preceded by focus groups which are designed to provide insights into the respondents' likely understanding of and attitude towards the environmental good or issue being investigated. Focus groups are drawn from a cross-section of the population to be surveyed, although the actual composition of any one focus group may be stratified by social class to aid communication and interpretation of results. Participants, around 8 to 10 in any one focus group, discuss their understanding of the context of the good, the good itself, its 'value', who should provide it, how it should be paid for, whether they would contribute, and how much they might be willing to pay. Focus groups, typically last between one and two hours, and can provide valuable information in framing and designing a CV study and questionnaire survey. Although practical guidance to focus group work has been published (see Advertising Research Foundation, 1985), there are few pointers to its appropriate use in CV surveys.

However, responses in focus groups may not be value-free nor unbiased, but may be anchored to the approach and suggestions of the person conducting the focus group. For issues difficult to comprehend, the organiser often has to lead participants through the subject, creating perspectives for them to comment on which they may not otherwise have thought about. The incorporation of these perspectives into the framing and design of a CV study will obviously lead to a set of WTP responses which might differ from those derived in an alternative design. In a focus group people also have longer to discuss and think about the issue than in a typical CV survey. Moreover, individuals are known to behave differently in group situations, compared to situations where they decide alone, as is typical in WTP surveys. There are a few instances where focus groups have not only been used to aid CV survey design, but have also been used to deconstruct and discuss CV participants' responses (Garrod and Willis, 1997a). The usefulness of focus groups is questionable: in both pre-and post-focus group meetings participants have more information (about the good and about other individuals' responses) than occurs with individual responses in a CV survey. Different amounts of information should not be expected to produce identical responses in and outside focus group situations.

3.4 Eliciting WTP or WTA Bids

Bids are obtained through some form of questionnaire survey and elicitation format, in which individuals are asked to state their maximum WTP for the environmental good (either to increase the quantity of the good, or to prevent a decrease in the quantity of the good); or their minimum WTA compensation for the environmental good (either to forgo an increase in the quantity of the good, or to accept less of the good). The principle elicitation methods are:

an open-ended question in which no value is specified and individuals are asked a simple question on their maximum WTP for the good; e.g.

'Suppose the National Park authority charged a fee to enter this recreation site. What is the most you would be willing to pay to use it per person per day?'

Where respondents have experience of purchasing similar goods (e.g. access to other private recreation sites) then open-ended questions offer a relatively easy method of eliciting bids. However, where respondents have no prior experience of purchasing the environmental good (e.g. biodiversity, or protection of a particular species) then respondents may experience considerable difficulty with this format. For this reason the National Oceanic and Atmospheric Administration (NOAA) report by Arrow *et al.* (1993) advocated that open-ended formats should not be used to elicit non-use or passive use values for environmental goods: those very situations for which there is no market in the good or a similar good.

a closed-ended question in which a range of values are specified and the respondent chooses one of the values; e.g.

'Suppose the National Park authority charged a fee to enter this recreation site. What is the most you would be willing to pay to use it per person per day?' (please circle **one** value)

$1 $2 $3 $4 $5 $6 $7 $8 $9 $10'

Such a format anchors the respondent's answer to the range of values presented, although they can be offered an 'other' category in which they specify a value. This type of format might be applicable to non-priced open access recreational areas, where values in the range presented have already been determined for other comparable sites.

a dichotomous choice question in which a single payment amount is presented to the respondent who either agrees or disagrees with the amount; e.g.

'Suppose the National Park authority charged a fee of $5 per person per day to enter this recreation site. Would you be willing to pay this fee?
YES / NO'

The payment amount is randomly varied in the sample questionnaire survey across a pre determined range. This is the elicitation method which is advocated by NOAA. The irony is, of course, that the price range must be determined in some way, and this is invariably established in a pre-survey through an open-ended elicitation method! A large-scale pilot survey is essential for a dichotomous choice or referendum type format, to establish that responses are well calibrated. If a substantial percentage, say 20% or 30%, of respondents are willing to pay the highest amount offered in the survey, then a proportion of these might have be willing to pay more, and hence no information is obtained on the shape of the demand curve or function at higher prices. Conversely, if 99% of respondents were only willing to pay a $5 price out of a range of values up to $10, then questionnaires with values of $6 to $10 provide no useful information, and if these cover half of the questionnaires then survey costs have simply been doubled for no purpose. The referendum or dichotomous choice elicitation format establishes binary responses (agree/disagree), and hence must be analysed using a binary response technique such as logit analysis to estimate mean and median WTP values. This is discussed in more detail in Chapter 6.

an iterative bidding format or series of dichotomous choice questions. The iterative bidding approach begins as a dichotomous choice question: is the respondent willing to pay $X for the environmental good. Depending upon the response, the respondent is then asked if she would be willing to pay $X +/- 1 and if the answer is affirmative, then $X +/- 2, and so on. This type of iterative bidding game has been employed by Whittington *et al.* (1989, 1990) to estimate WTP for water services in Nigeria and Haiti; and to estimate WTP for coastal protection in Britain (Bateman *et al.*, 1995). To avoid tedious repetition the iteration might double or halve the previous dollar bid presented to the respondent. However, this can lead to a wide monetary range within which the exact WTP amount of the respondent is unknown. The bidding process must then iterate between the sum the respondent is willing to pay and that which she is not, to determine a more precise WTP amount. Herriges and Shogren (1996) report that dichotomous choice and any subsequent bidding game can be subject to starting point bias but that once this bias has been eliminated the efficiency gains from follow-up WTP questions (iterative bids) were small.

a payment card: an approach in which respondents are presented with a card with potential contributions to the public good being valued from $0 to some upper payment limit. The advantage of a payment card is that it can present visual information to respondents, for their respective income/taxation group, on the amount which they contribute in tax or other charges to various 'public good' programmes. Respondents are asked: 'What amount on this card is the most you would be willing to pay for X?' where X is the quantity/quality public good amount being proposed. Revealing to respondents the amount they contribute to other substitute and complementary goods, and other public goods independent of the one being valued, provides a frame of reference to help them value the good. It can, however, give rise to problems of anchoring, which are discussed later in this chapter.

3.5 Questionnaire survey

After the hypothetical scenario has been set up and the elicitation method decided, WTP or WTA bids are obtained through a questionnaire survey. CV questionnaires typically obtain three sets of information from respondents: (a) attitudes to environmental goods in general and preferences for the particular good under investigation *vis-à-vis* others; awareness of substitute goods; use of the good, perhaps in relation to uses of other goods; and any perceived non-use benefits of the good; (b) WTP and/or WTA bids for the good using one or more of the elicitation methods outlined above, with questions to respondents exploring their reasons for their bids, which can be used to eliminate illegitimate responses (strategic bidding, etc.) later in the analysis; and questions to gauge the respondents' ambivalence[5]; and (c) socio-economic information on the respondent and his or her household.

Socio-economic data is gathered to assess: (1) whether the sample is representative of the general population when eliciting non-use values, and representative of visitors if profiles of visitors are available; and (2) the theoretical validity of the WTP or WTA bids, using a regression model

---

[5] A clearer picture of the respondents' true WTP towards an environmental good, can be determined by asking how likely they would be to pay their stated bid. Ready *et al.* (1995) permitted respondents to express intensity of preferences through polychotomous choice valuation questions which revealed wide ambivalence between money and environmental amenity trade-offs. Whitehead *et al.* (1995) found that WTP was less valid for respondents who had no information about the natural resource before they participated in the survey, compared with those who had on-site use of the resource. All of these studies reveal that a substantial proportion of CVM estimates of non-use values might be neither very robust nor reliable and are subject to considerable ambivalence and variance.

relating bids to price, quantity demanded, income, preferences, and other variables which theory suggests should explain the inverse demand curve. Data on use, preferences, and substitutes, can be collected at the beginning of the questionnaire to get the respondent to think about her preferences, use of the good, use in relation to other goods, and non-use benefits of the good, before attempting to elicit a WTA or WTA compensation amount.

The survey can be administered in a number of ways: by face-to-face interviews; self-fill questionnaires; telephone interviews; and mail shots. Face-to-face interviews are the usual method adopted, and the procedure recommended by Arrow *et al.* (1993) for NOAA. The good can be defined and explained more thoroughly in a face-to-face interview and non-response is minimised. However, face-to-face interviews are expensive to conduct, especially if repeat calls have to be made to ensure a high response rate.

Self-fill questionnaires can be left at recreation sites for visitors to complete; or in public places like shopping centres to obtain the views of the general public. Response rates tend to be low compared with face-to-face interviews, but data collection is cheap. Different elicitation methods are also not identical with respect to incentive compatibility in responses. Posted-offer auctions have, for example, been observed to result in different bids and slower convergence than oral bid auctions (Davis and Holt, 1993). Hence, different elicitation methods can themselves result in different expressed WTP values.

Where the hypothetical market is easily explained to respondents, mail shots become feasible. Response rates are lower than those for face-to-face interviews. However, where respondents are widely scattered over space (which makes house calls expensive); and where respondents have expert knowledge, an interest in the good, and already something pay towards the good (e.g. assessing additional WTP for wildlife conservation by members of a wildlife trust, see Garrod and Willis (1994)), then mail shots may become the most appropriate survey method. Mail shots have been used by authors such as Walsh, *et al.* (1984), amongst others. Both self-fill questionnaires and mail shots limit the questions used to those which can be easily comprehended. It is difficult to use 'skip' or 'go to' patterns, where the choice of the next question depends upon the respondent's answer to the current question; bidding patterns; or WTP formats more advanced than simple OE and DC questions.

The absence of visual cues in conventional telephone surveys is a major problem for CVM when conveying the WTP scenario, as is maintaining the attention of the respondent. However, for some goods a combined telephone and mail shot can be cost-effective and achieve higher response rates than a mail shot alone. A telephone survey can initially secure the respondent's interest and consent to participate in a survey, whilst the mail follow-up provides visual and questionnaire material. A subsequent telephone call guides the respondent through the questionnaire and obtains answers to the questions. Such an approach was successfully used by Lewington *et al.* (1996) and Willis and Garrod (1997) in studies of the value, to businesses and households, of avoiding electricity supply outages.

3.6 Sample size

The choice of sample size in a CV survey determines the precision of the sample statistics used as estimates of population parameters such as mean WTP or WTA. In general, the larger the sample the smaller the variation in mean WTP as measured by the standard error, and described in confidence intervals.

Mitchell and Carson (1989) devised a system to determine an appropriate sample size for OE CV questions which relies on the researcher's choice of an acceptable deviation between 'true' WTP and estimated WTP. For a given level of precision, a sample size can be chosen which ensures that estimated WTP will be within X per cent of 'true' WTP, either 90% or 95% of the time. The smaller the value of X, the larger the sample size required to achieve it (see Table 5.3). Mitchell and Carson state that for most applications an initial estimate of overall precision given by a coefficient of determination of 2 is advisable. For this level of precision a sample of over 6,000 would be required to ensure that estimated WTP deviated from 'true' WTP by within 5 per cent 95 per cent of the time. Alternatively, if it was acceptable that estimated WTP could deviate up to 20% of 'true' WTP 90% of the time, then a usable sample of only 286 is required. Mitchell and Carson argue that, for applications which seek to evaluate policy, the sample size should be at least 600. At the given level of accuracy this would ensure an estimate of WTP within 15% of the 'true' WTP 95% of the time.

It is not possible to state *a priori* the optimal sample size for other question formats.

CVMs applied to users may be subject to site selection bias in sampling. The survey might disproportionately sample frequent visitors (a common problem in TCM visitor surveys).[6] 'On-site' selection bias might well result in CV values under-estimating total consumer value. This will arise where a CV

---

[6] Sampling 'on-site' samples visits not visitors, hence the problem. Assume a site has two types of visitor (a) 120 visitors who visit 5 times per year (b) 120 visitors who visit once per year. Assume visits are evenly distributed over the year: January has 50 visits from type (a) visitors and 10 visits from type (b) visitors, as has February to December. If a 10% sample of visits were randomly selected in any month, the sample would consist of five type (a) visitors and one type (b) visitor. However, the true proportion of type (a) and type (b) visitors is 1:1. Site selection bias can be corrected by weighting the number in the visit sample by its reciprocal to derive the true proportion of visitors: in this case $[(50\ (1/5)) + (10\ (1/1))]$.

question asks 'what is the maximum entrance fee you would be willing to pay for your current visit to this site?'.[7] If frequent visitors are disproportionately sampled there will be a disproportionate number of observations with a low WTP reflecting the individual's nth visit, i.e. marginal visit, compared with intra-marginal or single visit observations. Too little attention has been devoted in CV to tracing out a WTP demand curve for an individual over his frequency of visits schedule; although the 'scope' test is now more widely and regularly applied in environmental economics (see Carson *et al.*, 1996).

Table 5.3: Sample sizes for given levels of precision in CV surveys

	$\Delta = 0.05$	$\Delta = 0.10$	$\Delta = 0.15$	$\Delta = 0.20$
V = 1.5, a = 0.10	2,571	643	286	161
V = 1.5, a = 0.05	3,458	865	385	217
V = 2.0, a = 0.10	4,570	1,143	508	286
V = 2.0, a = 0.05	6,147	1,537	683	385
V = 2.5, a = 0.10	7,141	1,786	794	447
V = 2.5, a = 0.05	9,604	2,401	1,608	601

Δ = difference between x_1 and x_2 (of the two CV samples) expressed as a percentage of x_1. V = relative error (or coefficient of variation: standard deviation / mean). a = 0.10 indicates that 90% of the time estimated mean will be within Δ of true mean WTP. a = 0.05 indicates that 95% of the time estimated mean will be within Δ of true mean WTP.

Source: Mitchell and Carson (1989)

3.7 Estimating Mean and Median WTP and WTA Amounts

Mean WTP or WTA amounts are easily derived from a survey by averaging the observed bid responses. However, a CV survey permits many different statistical values for a good to be calculated: means; medians; modes; trimmed estimators; modified estimators (with biased and ineligible responses omitted); standard deviations and other measures of dispersion. Mean WTP values, or trimmed or modified estimators based on mean WTP values, are the most appropriate, since in economic theory they are a cardinal measure of the utility individuals derive from the good.

However, the median bid has much to recommend it: it is unaffected by large bids in the upper tail of the distribution (unlike the mean); and is the amount of money which a one person one vote system would allocate to the policy or public good. Median bids are almost always less than mean bids.

---

[7] The same problem arises if a dichotomous choice question is asked about WTP for the current visit.

But, unless mean and median bids coincide — i.e. in a normal distribution — the median bid will underestimate the utility individuals derive from an environmental good. Nevertheless, the median bid reflects the value of the median voter who, in public choice theory, decides on a issue in a simple majority voting system (Mueller, 1979).

Perhaps the most appropriate measures of value are the trimmed and modified estimators. Trimmed estimators can be employed if outliers exist, which are believed to reflect, for whatever reason, erroneous WTP responses by some individuals. One or two such outliers can increase average WTP dramatically, and provide a false indication of the worth of a public good. Some zero WTP responses to the CV question may also be erroneous values. The problem with trimmed estimators is to decide what observations are actually erroneous, and hence those which should be excluded from the calculation of average WTP values and subsequent analysis. To avoid making decisions on the truthfulness or falsity of individual observations in a data set, a common practice is to simply trim the top and bottom 5% or 10% of the distribution of WTP observations. Clearly this is not strictly legitimate: some of these observations may be true WTP estimates.

Modified estimators provide the 'truest' estimate of WTP values. Modified estimators are mean WTP values with biased and illegitimate responses removed. Biased and illegitimate responses are identified by a series of questions designed to find out why respondents gave that particular WTP response. Illegitimate responses occur where strategic bidding, free-riding, protest behaviour and so on, mean that the observed bid is not an accurate reflection of actual WTP.

Whilst a simple averaging of OE responses provides an estimate of mean WTP, bid curves can also be estimated from OE CV data, i.e.

$$WTP_i = f(Y, V, P, S) + e \tag{5.3}$$

where Y = income, V = visits, P = preferences, and S = substitutes. Differentiating bid curves ($dWTP/dV$) provides the Hicksian compensated demand curve for the good, and permits the average Hicksian consumer surplus per visitor to be estimated, as the area under the demand curve for the average visitor who is assumed to make the mean number of visits in a given time period. This approach was adopted by Seller *et al.* (1985) but produced quite different results from a simple OE WTP average, probably due to the poor fit of their models which had R^2 values varying from 0.06 to 0.14.

The calculation of WTP values for dichotomous choice CVMs is outlined in Chapter 6.

3.8 Aggregating WTP or WTA Amounts

Mean WTP or WTA estimates from the CV sample survey must be aggregated across the total population to derive a total value figure. The reliability of population information varies. National Parks in the USA may charge an entrance fee and undertake a visitor count. In Europe, entry to National Parks is often free. Since National Parks embrace local rural communities, or straddle rural trunk roads, an entrance charge is generally unfeasible and visitor counts extremely difficult. Where access is open and non-priced a variety of visitors are attracted, from those on vacation, or enjoying day outings to the area, to meanderers visiting a variety of areas, and those merely passing through or briefly stopping to admire the view. The profile mix of these visitors is usually unknown, although each type may have very different mean WTP values.

Resident populations can be relatively easily determined from population census data. But as in all benefit-cost studies there is the conundrum of the community or population of relevance: e.g. the local community, the state population, federal population, or international population. This is particularly problematic in the case of the non-use value of goods. Measures to save whales, Giant Pandas, and other species may cross national boundaries. But many 'public goods' are small, relatively unknown, and local in extent, and non-use values many not extend over a great distance.

Although WTP estimates are often modest for non-use benefits, the populations over which they are aggregated can be quite large, producing enormous aggregate WTP amounts. This occurred in the Exxon Valdez case where non-use values were a whole magnitude higher than WTP to avoid loss of use-value, and two orders of magnitude higher than actual damages to fishing and recreational industries in Alaska. Such large aggregate values are of major concern to companies being sued for environmental damages under the Comprehensive Environmental Response, Compensation and Liability Act (CERCLA) 1980, in the USA.

3.9 Assessing the Validity of CV Studies

The ultimate test of the accuracy of contingent valuation methods and their use in measuring benefits in a cost-benefit analysis (CBA), is whether subjects will *actually* pay the amounts that they *say* they would be willing to pay in a CV study.[8] This validity of CV estimates has been judged in a

---

[8] This methodological position is consistent with Friedman's (1953) proposition that hypotheses should be chosen because they are successful in yielding true predictions. Thus a theoretical model is deemed to be valid if behaviour predicted by the model reasonably approximates actual behaviour, even if one or more assumptions underlying the model (in this case CVM) are not true.

number of ways following the taxonomy suggested by Mitchell and Carson (1989) in terms of:

1. content validity: the appropriate framing of the study, and questions asked in relation to the good being valued;

2. criterion validity: the comparison of CV estimates with actual market or simulated market experiments;

3. construct validity: the correspondence or *convergence* between a CV measure and other (e.g. travel-cost or hedonic price) measures of the value of the same good; and the extent to which the findings of the CV study are consistent with *theoretical* expectations.

3.10 Content validity

Content validity is difficult to assess, since it depends upon the intuitive judgement and experience of any person reviewing the study. Obvious criteria within content validity are lised below.

1. Is the description of the good being valued unambiguous? Is it defined in enough detail? Is it a good which respondents can comprehend?[9]

2. Is the payment vehicle realistic? Do respondents accept the WTP format? Are there large numbers of protest bids?[10] Have respondents been given enough time to think in answering the WTP question and assess the implications of their answer in the light of all other commitments on their budget and the availability of substitute goods to the one being valued?[11]

---

[9] For example, asking respondents their WTP to preserve biodiversity is meaningless. Biodiversity *per se* is difficult to define, even experts disagree over its definition and people have very different ideas what it means in terms of species threatened, protected, conserved, or in terms of probabilities of extinction, genetic diversity in organisms, and similarity in the taxonomic hierarchy.

[10] For example, people refusing to answer because they object to the payment vehicle, WTP/WTA perspective, or simply because they 'don't know' and are unable to put a monetary value on the good. A large number of zero bids may be quite legitimate. Indeed, a majority of zero bids might be expected, given that there are many worthy environmental causes in the world today, but any individual is only likely to contribute to a small minority of them.

[11] Whittington *et al.* (1992) for example, showed that giving people time overnight to think and to assess their response to the situation posed, reduced their WTP values significantly compared with initial intuitive WTP judgements.

3. Are embedding and substitution possibilities in the study adequately addressed? If the good is part of a multi-good or attribute programme, are these issues dealt with?

3.11 Criterion validity

Hypothetical questions can produce hypothetical answers. This might arise because CV markets lack incentives to induce individuals to put as much time and effort into thinking about the value of a good and the price they are prepared to pay for it, compared to actual markets. Hypothetical markets do not penalise respondents for 'getting it wrong'; whereas in actual markets people learn from their spending mistakes in subsequent purchasing decisions. Thus, Bishop *et al.*, (1983, p.627) argued that no CV market could replicate the process of value formulation that takes place in actual markets:

> *conversion of utility into monetary terms in the real world may involve repeated market transactions over time, consultation with peer groups, assessment of markets for complements and substitutes, consultations within the household, and references to consumer information. It is questionable whether the interviewer or questionnaire designer can fully compensate for the lack of such experience and information in the limited time available.*

One way of testing whether CVMs are subject to hypothetical bias is to assess whether behaviour and values in experimental markets are consistent with or parallel to behaviour and prices in actual markets. Early work by Brookshire *et al.*, (1986) suggested parallelism did not hold when actual and experimental markets for privately traded goods were compared. However, the results of such comparative studies are crucially dependent upon how the study was designed and the incentives offered in the experimental market. Nevertheless, comparisons between CV and actual markets offer another test of CVMs, termed criterion validity.

Criterion validity has the greatest potential for offering a definitive test of CV WTP estimates (Mitchell and Carson, 1989). Unfortunately, market prices are rarely available for public goods; but they are available for private goods. Private goods also meet the Fishbein-Ajzen (1975) conditions for the accuracy and reliability of WTP estimates, which are that accuracy will be greatest where there is:

1. correspondence between the question asked and the inference drawn in answer;
2. proximity between the survey stage and the behavioural intention stage;

3. familiarity with the consequence of the change in the quantity, and quality, of the good in question.

If CV values for private goods do not closely approximate their real values to people, then it is unlikely that CVM will provide accurate and reliable values for public goods: goods which are further from satisfying the Fishbein-Ajzen criteria. Thus, reviews of private good experiments are just as meaningful as those involving public goods in assessing whether CV values represent real economic commitments.[12]

A number of CV studies involving goods familiar to respondents demonstrate that there are significant differences between CV values and market values. The earliest simulated market experiment was Bohm's (1972) study of WTP to watch a prominent programme on closed-circuit TV, a programme which was not scheduled to be shown on regular TV for two or three months. The study sought to assess the effects of different payment incentives on non-hypothetical WTP statements. The experiment compared five approaches[13] for estimating average WTP. Each approach had different payment consequences with one incentive being to overstate WTP; another incentive to understate WTP; and a group of mixed incentives. For comparison, approach VI(I) was a standard hypothetical CV WTP question, with nothing being said to the subject about being offered the opportunity to watch the programme.[14] The study did not reveal any significant differences in WTP amounts under the five different incentive approaches, despite a clear incentive to under report WTP in approach I, and a clear incentive to over-report WTP in approach V. Thus misrepresentation of preferences (e.g. free-riding) was not revealed. When observations from the first five approaches were pooled and compared to approach VI(I), the hypothetical CV scenario produced upwardly biased estimates compared with the non-hypothetical

---

[12] A point also made by Bateman *et al.* (1997) who use an incentive compatible procedure in experimental economics to investigate whether embedding problems also characterise the valuation of private goods. The value of parts consistently exceeded that of the whole for a private good, suggesting further refinement of CVM will not lead to the eradication of part-whole bias in public goods.

[13] These were: (I) subject paid according to his stated WTP; (II) subject paid according to some fraction of stated WTP, with the fraction determined equally for all in the group such that total costs were just covered; (III) subjects did not know the specific payment scheme at the time of their bid, but did know it was a lottery with equal probability attached to the payment schemes of procedures I, II, IV and V; (IV) each subject paid a fixed amount; (V) subject paid nothing.

[14] Approach VI(I) involved the subject bidding for the right to see the programmeme against what they thought was a group of 100: an auction with the highest bidders actually paying their bid and being able to see the programmeme.

auction approaches (Bohm, 1994), suggesting that hypothetical questions tend to give unreliable estimates of WTP.

In another experiment, Bishop *et al.*, (1983) compared the results of a simulated market and a hypothetical market. In the simulated market, hunters, who had obtained free early season permits to bag a maximum of one goose in the Horicon zone in central Wisconsin, were sent dollar cheques of varying amounts which they could keep if they surrendered their hunting permit. Separate samples were asked whether they would be willing to pay a specified amount for such a goose-hunting permit, and whether they would be willing to accept a specified amount for such a permit, in a hypothetical market situation. A logit regression was used to calculate consumer surplus. Table 5.4 outlines the results. It shows that both hypothetical measures were biased, with WTA over-estimating consumer surplus and WTP under-estimating consumer surplus as compared with that determined by a simulated market. These results show that contingent values could easily be in error by + or - 50% or more (Bishop *et al.*, 1983: p.620).

Table 5.4: Comparison of simulated and hypothetical market results: the Wisconsin Horicon zone goose-hunting experiment (US$, 1981 prices)

	WTP	WTA
Cash offer	-	63
Hypothetical market: no cash	21	101

Source: Bishop *et al.* (1983)

In a subsequent study Bishop and Heberlein again compared the results of a simulated and hypothetical market. In 1983, 6,000 hunters applied for 150 permits to hunt deer in the Sandhill area of Wood County, Wisconsin. Bishop and Heberlein were granted four permits to sell in 1983 and 75 to sell in 1984. The results of the Sandhill experiments suggested that hypothetical markets can in some circumstances value goods, such as hunting permits, which are well defined and familiar to respondents, with reasonable accuracy using simulated market prices as the 'gold standard' criterion. They compared WTP amounts from sales of permits under different auction formats with hypothetical estimates of WTP from a sample of 600 hunters who failed to obtain a deer hunting permit under the lottery system which allocates the annual free Sandhill deer-hunting permits. However, some statistically significant differences between the simulated and hypothetical WTP estimates left the issue of the accuracy and reliability of CV estimates unresolved (see Table 5.5).

Dickie *et al.* (1987) conducted a field experiment to compare the results of hypothetical and simulated markets for a private, non-durable, familiar good: strawberries. One hundred and forty four households were randomly selected in Laramie, Wisconsin, and interviewers identified the household member who regularly shopped for groceries. In the hypothetical CV market respondents were asked 'Suppose that a pint of strawberries could be purchased at $X per pint. How many pints would you buy?' The price was randomly varied from $0.60 to $1.60 per pint between households. In the simulated market strawberries were actually sold for money if the respondent desired to make a purchase at the price offered. Dickie *et al.* concluded that a comparison of the demand curves failed to disprove the null hypothesis of structurally identical demand equations estimated from actual sales and CV data. However, Cummings and Harrison (1994) argued that these results were equivocal if subject to greater scrutiny. They pointed out that:

1. there were large differences in actual and hypothetical demand schedules using the predicted demand equations based on regression results. Depending on the price used, the hypothetical demand curve can overstate the quantity demanded from 351% to 69%, if all observations are included; and by 100% to 4% if errant observations are excluded;

2. the results were heavily dependent on the deletion of one outlier.[15] However, if this case is not regarded as an outlier, and included, then the hypothetical and real expenditures per household differed by 58%.

In 1988, the World Bank surveyed 1,150 families in Kerala State, India, to ascertain their willingness to pay for household connections to a proposed piped water supply system. A probit model was used to control for individual, household, and community characteristics, that could affect responses on the three policy variables (monthly tariff, connection cost, and reliability) on the choice to connect. In 1991 these families were surveyed again, and their actual decisions recorded. The accuracy and validity of the 1988 CV study was judged by whether:

---

[15] A consumer who said he would buy 10 pints at $0.60 per pint and freeze or can half of them.

Table 5.5: Comparison of simulated and hypothetical market results: the Wisconsin Sandhill area in Wood County deer-hunting experiment (US$, 1983 prices)

	Estimated bid: Cash (N)	Estimated bid: Hypothetical (N)	Difference significant at 0.10
1983 experiments			
A. Sealed bid auction	$24 (68)	$32 (71)	No
B. *Bidding game 1*: initial sealed bid solicited by mail; allowed to change bid in subsequent telephone interview	$19 (65)	$43 (62)	Yes
C. *Bidding game 2*: initial response to mail offer of fixed amount chosen at random between $1 and $500; this amount was used as a starting point in a subsequent telephone interview	$24 (68)	$43 (69)	No
D. *Fifth price*: sealed bid solicited under condition that four highest bids would receive a permit by paying the amount offered by the fifth highest bidder	$25 (69)	$42 (70)	Yes
1984 experiments			
E. *Single price offer*: asked if willing to pay specified amount randomly chosen from $18 to $512 range	$31 (70)	$25 (62)	No
F. *Single price offer plus bidding game*: same procedure as in E; this amount was used as a starting point in a subsequent telephone interview	No data	$35	No

Source: Bishop and Heberlein (1986); and Mitchell and Carson (1989)

1. the correct proportion of connectors had been predicted, irrespective of whether the actual behaviour of each household was predicted correctly;[16]

2. households behaved as they said they would, judged by the sensitivity and specificity of the CVM test, and the predictive value positive and predictive value negative of the CVM.

There are two issues related to the accuracy of CVMs: how accurately CVMs predict WTP values, and how accurately CVMs predict the numbers of consumers actually prepared to 'buy the good' at these different WTP values. The World Bank study essentially investigated the proportion of consumers willing to pay more than a specified (connection charge) amount. Table 5.6 reveals the gross accuracy of the World Bank 1988 CV study to be high: 91.2% [(15+120)/148] of consumers were correctedly identified as connecting, or not connecting, at the price charged. However, the true positive rate (TPR) of the CVM test was only 68.2%;[17] whilst the predictive value positive (PVP) was only 71.4%.[18] Of course the true negative rate (TNR), and predictive value negative (PVN) rate, were much higher: 95.2% and 94.5% respectively; but this is not unusual where the majority of actual cases are negative. It is much more difficult to predict proportionally a small number of positive cases amongst a large group of negative cases. Table 5.6 also reveals that the gross accuracy of the probit model of households' decision behaviour to connect, or not to connect, was 81.6%, which was less than the accuracy of the simple CV analysis. The lower accuracy of the behavioural model is reflected in the TPR of 35.7%; the PVP 43.5%; the TNR 90.7% and the PVN 87.7%.

Neill *et al.* (1994) conducted two experiments to compare hypothetical and actual WTP for a small framed painting of a south-western USA rural scene by an unknown Navajo Indian artist. The first experiment compared CV maximum WTP estimates with those of a Vickrey auction in which subjects were actually required to pay for the painting out of their own pocket if their bid was successful. The average valuations were $37.04 (n=41) for the CVM, and $9.49 (n=16) for the Vickrey auction; with medians of $30 and $6 respectively. The null hypothesis of no significant difference between the two

---

[16] In appraising a future commercial venture it is important that the estimated number of consumers is as close as possible to the actual number of consumers.

[17] The TPR indicates, *given* that the household actually connected, what the chance was of the household being positive on the CVM test too.

[18] The PVP indicates, *given* that the household was positive (would connect) on the CVM test, the chance that the household would actually connect.

distributions was rejected. Because the CV question did not specify rules of provision for the good, and hence altering these to match those in the Vickrey auction could alter the elicited CV WTP, a second experiment was conducted. The second experiment compared the results of a hypothetical Vickrey and an actual Vickrey auction in which the bid involved a financial commitment. In the second experiment, the average and median bids in the hypothetical Vickrey auction were $301 and $60 respectively (n=51); and in the real auction $12 and $5 (n=60). The null hypothesis of no significant difference between the two bid distributions was also rejected in this experiment.

Table 5.6: Comparison of actual and predicted decisions of households to connect to potable water supplies in Kerala, India

	Actual	*behaviour*	
Predicted behaviour	Did connect	Did not connect	Total
Will connect	15 (10)	6 (13)	21 (23)
Will not connect	7 (18)	120 (128)	127 (146)
Total	22 (28)	126 (141)	148 (169)

Note: actual numbers based on the 1988 CV survey, compared to 1991 re-survey of households. Numbers in brackets are predictions based on a probit model of the 1988 households.
Source: Griffin *et al.*, 1995

An experiment was conducted of visitors to Warkworth Castle by Willis and Powe (1998), in which the maximum WTP elicited in a CV survey of potential visitors[19] to the medieval castle was compared against the acceptance of an entrance ticket at their stated CV price, to provide a real monetary test of behaviour intention. Only 40% of potential visitors at the castle gate were willing to make a real economic commitment following their CVM WTP response. This study revealed that even when the CV survey stage is juxtaposed to the behavioural intention stage, a substantial proportion of stated CV WTP values are not translated into real economic commitments and purchases. Perhaps this should not be so surprising from knowledge of the actual market place. Individuals often make purposeful trips to towns to purchase a good (new clothes, furniture, or whatever), only to inspect the good closely and decide not to buy. The problem is that CV surveys treat such individuals as valid respondents and count their WTP as an element of the total utility of the environmental good. As a consequence environmental

---

[19] Those who had parked their car and walked to the castle entrance, but who had not entered after seeing the entrance charge.

goods are frequently overvalued in aggregate.[20] CV studies must adopt more stringent criteria in deciding the 'truthfulness' and legitimacy of WTP responses and actual decisions to purchase, especially for environmental goods where the legitimacy of WTP responses cannot be judged against real economic commitments.

3.12 Construct validity

Construct validity involves the degree to which the WTP measure relates to other measures predicted by theory. Theory suggests that, under certain circumstances, CV estimates should be similar to those predicted by other techniques such as TCM and HPM (convergent validity); and that WTP measures for changes in the quantity of a good should be predictable by explanatory variables, i.e. WTP should decline for additional marginal units of the good, whilst WTP should increase with income if the good is income elastic.

3.13 Convergent validity

TCM, HPM, and CVM are constructs of the same use value measure of the benefits conferred by a specific good. Clearly, TCM and HPM cannot measure non-use values of environmental goods, so convergent validity should not be expected in situations where use and non-use measures are amalgamated. However, Willig (1976) outlined conditions under which compensating and equivalent variations and Marshallian consumer surplus measures approximate each other.[21] Where these hold, TCM, HPM, and CVM measures of a good should produce similar estimates. Comparisons may still be problematic. For example, TCM measures the total recreational experience of the trip, so unless some method is employed to net out any benefit from travelling to the site, and any utility attached to visits to other sites made *en-route*, TCM is not measuring the exact same construct as a

---

[20] Respondents' maximum WTP is their point of indifference between obtaining or not obtaining the good at that price. It is the point where a respondent should be indifferent between tossing a coin and buying the good if it's heads, and not bothering to acquire it if it's tails. Obviously at such a point of indifference only half of the respondents will actually really purchase the good. This provides a justification for the unsupported recommendation in the report to NOAA by Arrow *et al* (1993), that DC WTP values should divided by 2. Note that the 40% acceptance of a ticket at the respondent's stated maximum WTP amount in the Warkworth Castle experiment by Willis and Powe (1998) was not statistically different from the 50% indifference acceptance rate.

[21] Where the income effect is small (income elasticities are not significantly different from zero), and substitute sites and activities are available.

CVM which concentrates on the utility of a particular site. This is partly what Seller *et al.* (1985) observed in comparing CVM and TCM values of boating at four lakes in the United States (see Table 5.7). Open-ended CVM provided significantly lower estimates of average consumer surplus at each lake, compared with TCM. However, simple dichotomous choice CVM produced similar values to TCM.

Table 5.7: Consumer surplus estimates of recreational boating at four lakes using CVM and TCM (US$ 1980 prices, mean values)

		Contingent	valuation
Lake	TCM	Open-ended	Dichotomous choice
Conroe	32.06	*-0.87	39.38
Livingston	102.09	*6.21	35.21
Somerville	24.42	*11.17	-
Houston	13.01	5.40	13.81

Note: * Null hypothesis that the estimated value was the same as other estimates rejected at 95% level. The negative value at Conroe indicated a WTP value less than the annual boat launch ramp fee they already paid when this was divided on a per visit basis.

Source: Seller, Stoll and Chavas (1985)

A meta analysis comparison between revealed preference (RP) and CV values from 83 studies that provided 616 comparisons of CV to RP estimates, revealed a mean CV/RP ratio of 0.89 with a 95% confidence interval [0.81–0.96], and a median of 0.75. (Carson *et al.*, 1996). The correlation coefficient between CV and RP vales was 0.83. Clearly, the CV/RP ratio is less than 1.0. Some individual CV estimates exceeded their RP counterparts, although only 5% of the sample had CV/RP ratios in excess of 2.0.

Many empirical CV and RP estimates diverge by more than the margin of error suggested by Willig. This may be partly explained by variations in the framing of valuation studies, inadequate design of individual TCM and CVM studies, sampling errors in surveys of respondents, and fitting models to the data.[22]

---

[22] Variations in functional forms of models can produce very different consumer surplus and attribute values in CVM, TCM, and HPM.

3.14 Theoretical validity

Theoretical validity involves assessing the degree to which the results of a CV study are consistent with theoretical expectations. Almost all studies assess theoretical validity, since it is relatively easy to regress the respondents' WTP or WTA bids against independent variables believed to be theoretical determinants of these values. Theoretical validity is judged by whether the sign and size of the estimated coefficients are consistent with theoretical expectations. This means that only those variables expected by theory to determine the inverse demand function should be included in the regression equation, precluding a data mining approach to obtain the highest R^2 value. Low R^2 values are not necessarily evidence of theoretical inconsistency: they could merely be indicative of less tightly clustered observations around the regression line and stochastic variation in the data which overshadows the systematic influence of variables. Indeed, given respondents' uncertainty and ambivalence in valuing non-marketed environmental goods, especially non-use values, considerable dispersion around the regression line is likely to be the norm rather than the exception. Nevertheless, high R^2 values do provide evidence of reliability.

Mitchell and Carson (1989: 213) suggest that a CV study which has an R^2 of less than 0.15 might be deemed unreliable. R^2 values, based on regressing WTP against consumption of the good, availability of substitutes, preferences, and socio-economic characteristics of the respondent such as income, can vary tremendously. In some studies regression models only manage to explain 3% or 4% of variance in WTP responses (e.g. Bateman *et al*, 1995); whilst in others 60% or more of the variance is explained. Low R^2 values, and statistically insignificant coefficients on predictor variables, are often associated with environmental goods which attract very small bids. Since these goods are such a minor part of real income, income itself does not explain varation in WTP: the consumption (use or passive use) of such goods may depend purely upon preferences which are more difficult to incorporate in a regression model, or consumption may be purely stochastic. R^2 values, and the statistical significance of explanatory variables, might be expected to be higher for: (1) goods which form a more significant element of income; (2) for a generic set of goods, compared to a single good which is part of the generic set (see Willis and Garrod, 1995); and (3) for goods which are consumed in an active sense,[23] compared to passive consumption.

Referendum WTP models usually fit the data well with the model sometimes being able to predict 90% or more of cases in which a respondent answered 'yes' or 'no' to the random dollar bid amount in the questionnaire.

---

[23] Garrod and Willis (1997b) explained 60.8% of the variance in an open-ended CV survey of WTP for entry to Telok Bahang Forest Recreation Area in Penang, Malaysia.

However, these logit or probit models explain the response in terms of the bid amount or price of the good; few other variables, including income, are usually statistically significant. It is generally much easier to predict quantity in relation to price, as referendum models do, than it is to predict respondents' maximum WTP for a given quantity in relation to income.

4 MINIMISING BIASES

4.1 Design Biases

CVMs may be subject to a number of biases that can be conveniently categorised as either psychological or statistical. Psychological biases are discussed here. Statistical biases in CVMs are those traditionally encountered in sample surveys, and documented by authors such as Deming (1950).

Strategic bias is a traditional concern of economists. If respondents believe that their WTP bids will actually be collected, they may understate their 'true' WTP for environmental goods which are non-excludable. This is the classic 'free-rider' problem. On the other hand, if respondents believe bids are purely hypothetical and will not be collected, they may over-estimate their WTP for an environmental good or policy, as this increases the probability that it will be implemented and that someone else will have to pay for it. Strategic bias is extremely difficult to detect and to test for in CV surveys; however, laboratory experiments suggest that strategic bias may not as strong as generally imagined (Smith, 1980). Indeed, people provide public goods out of a sense of pride (e.g. maintaining their own front gardens), altruism, and for bequest motives (e.g. providing seats in public parks, donating art and book collections for public use, etc.).

A bi-modal distribution of WTP bids (a large number of low bids and a larger number of high bids) may be evidence of strategic bias, but it is not a sufficient condition and may merely reflect reality. Practical steps within the CV process itself to minimise strategic bias include the following.

1.   Removing outliers (either individual observations, or by trimming the top and bottom 5% or 10% of all observations to produce a trimmed estimate). However, there is no theoretical justification for removing any observations in this way, unless a bid is subject to bias, and this is generally unknown.

2.   Inserting questions in the CV questionnaire, after WTP or WTA responses, to ascertain why respondents gave that bid. Typical questions are provided in Appendix 5.1. Responses to these types of question are then used to judge whether respondents' bids are legitimate or illegitimate.

3.   Stressing in the questionnaire that respondents should answer honestly (to prevent free-riding state that if bids are insufficient the environmental good will not be provided); and that payment by others is guaranteed (to prevent strategic overbidding to ensure that the good is provided).

4.   Making the environmental change dependent upon the bid to prevent respondents anticipating that the change will be automatically forthcoming irrespective of their bid.

5.   Concealing the bids of others. This is the usual practice in CV surveys because they are administered to individuals or households. However, focus group responses are open to strategic manipulation.

6.   Adopting a referendum format, rather than an open-ended WTP format. Respondents can then only answer 'yes' or 'no' to the bid offered instead of choosing a high or low bid for strategic or free-riding motives.

Hypothetical CV studies can be designed to minimise strategic bias. Concentrating on the median WTP value ensures that low free-rider and high strategic bids do not unduly weight the WTP estimate that will be used in decision making. Unfortunately, median values do not measure society's true utility for the environmental good, and could lead to too little or too much of the environmental good or protection being provided. The optimal provision and efficient allocation of a public good is determined by a Lindahl equilibrium; where individuals pay for the provision of a public good in proportion to the benefit they derive from it (see Nicholson, 1985). The Lindahl equilibrium is a conceptual solution: a technical procedure is still required to implement a Lindahl equilibrium which will permit tax shares to be computed in accordance with intensity of preferences, and strategic bias and the free-rider problems to be avoided. One such scheme to devise a perfect market to arrive at a Lindhal equilibrium has been proposed by Barnett and Yandle (1973). It allows an individual, within a community of individuals, to express his preferences in terms of monetary votes, and thereby determine the desired level of environmental quality and simultaneously allocate cost shares to attain that level of quality amongst competing bidders (see Appendix 5.2). However, these types of bidding games involving real monetary payments for an environmental good (such as water quality in a river) compared with an alternative good foregone (such as household waste discharged into a river) are difficult to construct in practice and fail to capture broader environmental concerns such as existence values for water quality in non-local rivers where the household does not have to trade-off an alternative use (waste disposal).

The design of CV surveys can have a large impact on the magnitude of the WTP or WTA responses obtained. Anchoring or starting point bias, framing effects, and scale and context effects, can all affect the monetary measurement of an environmental good.

Starting point bias can affect closed-ended and iterative bidding games. The starting point commencing the range of WTP amounts offered to respondents influences the final WTP value for the good.[24] People tend to believe that the starting point suggested is the norm: i.e. it is what other people pay, and therefore that which is expected of them.[25] Starting point bias has been found in many CV studies. Boyle *et al.* (1985) found the final bid to be significantly correlated with the starting bid in a number of studies, and that it was possible to influence a respondent's final bid over a substantial range by the choice of the initial bid.[26] Unfortunately, the researcher rarely knows what values to choose as appropriate starting bids for most environmental commodities; and no single starting bid will be appropriate for all respondents.

Contingent valuation is sometimes used to estimate the 'value of a small change in risk' (VSCR). In assessing the benefits of health and safety measures, individuals are asked their WTP for small changes (decreases) in the risk of death or injury.[27] People's preferences for the same good can vary depending upon the context in which it is framed. An essential condition of von Neumann and Morganstern's theory of choice under uncertainty

---

[24] This has been confirmed in many psychological experiments. Tversky and Kahneman (1974) asked a group of college students to estimate within 5 seconds the product of the numerical expression 1 x 2 x 3 x 4 x 5 x 6 x 7 x 8; whilst another group estimated 8 x 7 x 6 x 5 x 4 x 3 x 2 x1. The median estimate for the ascending sequence was 512, and for the descending sequence 2,250; whilst the correct answer is 40,320. To rapidly answer such questions people typically perform a few steps of the calculation then estimate the product by extrapolation or adjustment. Because the result of the first few steps of the multiplication performed, from left to right, is higher in the descending sequence than in the ascending sequence, it is judged to be larger. The result is thus anchored on the initial starting point.

[25] This also includes private market goods, which are unfamiliar to the individual or for which he is uncertain about the price. Hawkers in developing countries sometimes start at four to 10 times the market price of a good. Potential buyers often believe the norm is for the seller to initially only double the price, and are quite happy to purchase the good when bargaining has halved its price. This type of anchoring by buyers generates handsome profits for sellers!

[26] Rowe *et al.* (1980) in a study of the value of visibility, found that an increase of $1 in the starting bid resulted in a $0.60 increase in the final bid.

[27] Contingent valuation and standard gamble approaches have been used by Jones-Lee (1989) to estimate the value of a small change in the reduction of the risk of death. Indexed to 1997 prices, this amounts to a VSCR of £8 per 10^{-5} change in the individual probability of death, which is used by the Department of Transport in the UK to value lives saved in road accidents.

(expected utility theory) is the principle of invariance: different representations of the same choice problem should yield the same preference. However, Tversky and Kahneman (1981) demonstrate invariance in a number of choice experiments. One experiment asked respondents to:

> *Imagine that the US is preparing for the outbreak of an unusual Asian disease, which is expected to kill 600 people. Two alternative programmes to combat the disease have been proposed...the consequences of the programmes are:*

> *If programme A is adopted, 200 people will be saved.*   *[72%]*

> *If programme B is adopted, there is a 1/3 probability that 600 people will be saved, and 2/3 probability that no people will be saved. [28%]*

Another experiment presented respondents with the same scenario, but with different descriptions of the alternative programmes:

> *If programme C is adopted 400 people will die.*   *[22%]*

> *If programme D is adopted there is a 1/3 probability that nobody will die, and 2/3 probability that 600 people will die.*   *[78%]*

The percentage of respondents who chose each option in the two experiments are indicated in brackets. Clearly programmes A and C, and programmes B and D, are identical. The only difference is that programmes A and B are framed in terms of lives saved (relative to an expected loss of 600 if no action is taken); whilst programmes C and D are framed in terms of lives lost. Different preferences are evoked by the two frames: many respondents expressed a wish to remain risk averse in the lives saved version, and risk seeking in the lives lost version, although they also expressed a wish for their answers to be consistent. Such *framing effects* have also been noted in other contexts such as lotteries, business decisions, insurance, credit card charges and road accidents (Poulton, 1994). Framing effects are not inevitable: they can be avoided by creating a neutral frame to enable unbiased judgements to be made. For example, a neutral frame could be created for the above case, if respondents were presented with all the information in one package (i.e. programme A+C; and programme B+D). Which option respondents choose, depends upon their attitude to risk, rather than the frame with which they are presented. However, framing effects can still be important in CVM. In an econometric investigation of framing effects on the value of old growth Douglas fir forests in Oregon and Washington States, Bergland (1993) adopted two frames:

- What percentage of this 1.83 million acres would you like to see *preserved and made exempt from* logging?
- What percentage of this 1.83 million acres would you like to see *made available for* logging?

Framing effects were found to be less pronounced for those with more articulated preferences and more prevalent amongst those with less extreme positions on the issue: the position of convinced individuals was not easily biased by framing effects (Bergland, 1993).

The choice of the payment or bid vehicle can also affect the WTP results. Some people have an aversion to certain types of taxes: a poll tax is often regarded as unfair, creating *payment vehicle bias*. There are also, often quite logical, preferences for some forms of payment mechanisms over others and these preferences can vary, depending upon the good being valued, and the actors and agents involved in the process. Rowe, *et al.* (1980) found that respondents were willing to pay more to preserve visibility and landscape views when the payment vehicle was income tax rather than an entrance fee to the recreation site. People are probably willing to pay more for a public good when they think everyone who is benefiting from the good is contributing, rather than just a few. Some studies (Bateman *et al.*, 1995; Jakobsson and Dragun, 1996) have found that people are willing to pay more when the payment vehicle is income tax rather than a contribution to a conservation trust fund to provide or maintain the good. Often people don't trust trust funds, especially if they are regarded as ineffectual and only a small proportion of the money raised is devoted to the environmental good, with the majority of funds being spent on management costs. The payment vehicle chosen in a CV study should be that which most closely resembles how the money would be actually raised. However, such an approach can create problems. For example, low flow alleviation in British rivers requires water companies to abstract less water from these rivers and underlying aquifers, and to obtain more water from river catchments further afield, thus necessitating increased water charges to pay for the increased investment involved. Asking respondents their WTP increased water charges to pay for low flow alleviation invoked protest bids by those who thought water companies were making excess profits and that funding ought to come from these profits[28] (Willis and Garrod, 1995). Nevertheless, increasing the number of objections and refusals to answer, and the number of zero bids because of payment vehicle bias, does not necessarily lead to biased WTP results as long

---

[28] In Britain water companies are local private monopolies, albeit regulated. Compared to state ownership, privatisation in the early 1990s resulted in dramatic increases in water charges and remuneration to directors whose salaries increased up to 10 fold leading to public criticism.

as protest bids can be identified and dropped from the analysis and computation of mean and median WTP values.

The *scale and context* of an event can also affect WTP values. Psychological research has revealed that people's concerns are influenced by the magnitude of events, amongst other criteria (such as availability or information, voluntariness of risk, immediacy of effect, dread, control over the risk, chronic or catastrophic nature, and newness) (Slovic *et al.*, 1980). This can influence WTP to avoid environmental risks and events. Thus for example, Jones-Lee and Loomes (1994) found that people's WTP to avoid a fatality on the London Underground was 69% greater than their WTP to avoid a road fatality. A small part of this difference (11%) was due to scale: WTP to avoid multiple (25 to 30) deaths in a single event compared with the same number of single accident deaths over the same period. However, the context effect accounted for most of the additional WTP: holding scale constant, WTP to reduce the risk of an accident on London Underground was 58% greater compared with such accidents on roads. People abhor the notion of dying underground in a train crash or fire, a catastrophic event, over which they have no control.

Scale or scope effects exist when respondents do not distinguish differences in the quantity or scale of a good: for example, valuing three wetland areas the same as only one wetland area. The scope effect has generated considerable controversy in environmental economics since Desvousges *et al* (1993) undertook a CV study of WTP to save migratory waterfowl on the central flyway (from Montana and North Dakota to Texas) from dying by landing in waste-oil holding ponds. The waterfowl could be saved by a programme to cover the ponds with wire mesh. The Desvousges study found that WTP for a programme that saved 2% of the birds was not significantly different from WTP for a programme that saved less than 1% of the birds. The percentages referred to programmes to restore the bird population back to the 100% level; i.e. what it would have been in the absence of the waste-oil ponds, namely from 98% to 100%, and from 99% to 100% respectively. The Desvousges result appears to be at variance with consumer theory. Theory implies that, because of diminishing marginal utility, WTP to go from 98% to 100% should be more than twice as great as WTP to go from 99% to 100%. Fisher (1996) argued that such a result could be explained if respondents believed that once the protection of a viable ecosystem of a certain kind has been assured, preservation of additional acreage, or areas, or species, adds little or nothing to utility. Hanemann (1996) questioned the validity of the survey results, suggesting that the survey was biased.[29] Respondents might also see little difference between the 'much

---

[29] Because the sample was unrepresentative of the general population; was self administered; and took only 10 minutes to complete (whereas 30 minutes might have been a more reasonable time); and because 2% of respondents were willing to pay more than a quarter of their income.

less than 1%', 'less than 1%', and 'about 2%' of the bird population, in the WTP scenarios presented, especially out of a total of 8.5 million birds. Hanemann also argues that neo-classical economics provides no theoretical basis for specifying the shape and content of a utility function; and hence Desvousges' finding is not inconsistent with theory. WTP need not increase with income; nor, for all goods, with the scope or scale of the item being valued.

4.2 Information effects

There is no exogenous criterion to specify how much information or what context to provide to respondents in valuing an environmental good. For example, WTP to preserve a particular animal is tied to the individual's marginal rate of substitution between income and utility for preservation, and the perceived marginal efficiency of investment in the preservation fund. Information provided to the individual that changes either the marginal rate of substitution or the marginal efficiency of investment will affect WTP bids. Thus, Samples *et al.* (1986) showed that information disclosed about physical characteristics, behaviour, and endangered status, affected respondents' WTP to preserve humpback whales. Hanley and Munro (1992) also found that WTP for heathland preservation depended upon the level of information. Increasing the level of information on both the characteristics of heathland (names and pictures of flora and fauna), and its relative scarcity (such as extent and rate of depletion over time), significantly increased mean bids. In another study, by Hoevenagel and van der Linden (1993), the effect of different descriptions of the same ecological good, in terms of the number of attributes mentioned as being associated with the good, were found to produce significantly different WTP values, as predicted by economic theory.

CV responses cannot be context free. Indeed Randall (1991) has argued that market prices are conditional: they depend on institutions, information, supply and demand conditions, and expectations about these. The rational markets hypothesis posits that the market price at any moment in time reflects all the available information at that moment.[30] Thus Randall argues that price is conditional, generated by conditions unique to that moment in time: a natural experiment which can never exactly be replicated. Both observed market prices and contingent values are conditional: CV responses are sensitive to information provided, the wording of questions, the inclusiveness of the choice set, etc. By deliberate experimentation in providing information

---

[30] Randall cites the notorious sunflowers painting by Van Gogh, valued at $10 million in the early 1980s, purchased by Alan Bond for $50 million in the late 1980s, and sold for less than $30 million two years later.

and systematically reporting variations in valuations, it should be possible to map the relationship between the various conditions which influence value.

It should not be expected that CVM will estimate similar WTP values in the presence of different amounts of information. The same information effects are present in the sale of private goods: respondents' value or utility for a good changes when a salesman or brochure informs them that good X has some feature which is absent in an otherwise identical good Y. The manner in which goods are presented and described (contextual information) impacts on sales, and price differences. Indeed, if such effects were absent, they would violate Lancaster's (1966) theory of consumer behaviour.

4.3 Representativeness

Representativeness covers a number of biases from insensitivity to prior probability of outcomes (people don't think in Bayesian terms!); to insensitivity to sample size; misconceptions of chance; insensitivity to predictability; illusions of validity; and misconceptions of regression (Tversky and Kahneman, 1974). Such biases affect judgement under uncertainty, and hence influence individuals' perceptions of issues such as the value of biodiversity, WTP to increase the probability of survival of a species, and option values.

Insensitivity to prior probability is aptly demonstrated in a note by Salop (1987) in which a town has two taxi companies: Green Cabs and Blue Cabs. 85% of taxis are green cabs and 15% are blue cabs. A pedestrian is injured by a taxi speeding the wrong the way down a one-way street one night. An eye-witness stated the taxi was blue. The witness is 80% reliable at distinguishing the colour of taxis at night. The pedestrian sues the Blue Cab Co. for compensation for injuries and medical expenses in a tort claim. When asked to act as 'judge' most people believe there is a 'preponderance of evidence' (i.e. >50% chance) (the criterion in a civil case) that the taxi was blue. Indeed, most people believe the probability is >75%, because they base their judgement on the last piece of information available, i.e. the eye-witness; discounting the fact that the additional evidence (eye-witness) is imperfect and subject to error and ignoring the prior probability of the cab being blue. Table 5.8 provides a Bayesian representation of the problem. A true assessment of the probability the taxi was blue can be derived from Bayes' theorem, which weights prior evidence (proportion of blue taxis) by the reliability of additional evidence (eye-witness):

$$[P(E_i) . P(F|E_i)] / [\Sigma^r_{i=1} P(E_i) . P(F|E_i)] = P(E_i|F) \qquad (5.4)$$

where $P(E_i)$ is the prior probability of event E_i; $P(F|E_i)$ is the conditional probability that the test F is positive, given that E_i has occurred; and $P(E_i|F)$ is the posterior probability of event E_i given that test F is positive; and r are mutually exclusive occurrences. Thus $[0.15(0.80)] / [0.15(0.80) + 0.85(0.20)]$ $= 0.41$.

Table 5.8: Bayesian representation matrix

| | | Colour in fact | | |
		Blue	Green	Total
Colour perceived	Blue	12	17	29
by eye-witness	Green	3	68	71
	Total	15	85	100

The predictive value positive (PVP) of the eye-witness as a test is 12/29, or 41%. The PVP is the same as the posterior probability for a positive result. Bayes theorem expressed in an odds formulation is: *OE (TPR/FRP) = PP*, where *PP* is the posterior odds; *OE* is the prior odds (in the above case 15/85), TPR = true positive rate and FPR = false positive rate.[31] The TPR = 12/15; and the FPR = 17/85. Hence, even with the eye-witness, the preponderance of evidence is that the taxi was not a blue cab.[32] In fact, if the government's taxi registration officer testified, she would state that the taxi was probably green! Her testimony only has an error rate of 15%, i.e. a lower error rate than that of the eye-witness!

The inability to think in Bayesian terms has been widely documented in clinical medicine (Arkes, 1981; Eddy and Clanton, 1982), and other areas of decision-making such as college admissions (Dawes, 1980); as has over-confidence in judgement in general (Einhorn, 1980), and an inability to accept

---

[31] The true positive rate (TPR) of a test is the proportion of all those (taxis) who actually have that condition (blue colour), according to some gold standard, who are positive on a test (the eye-witness). The false positive rate (FPR) of a test is the proportion of all those (taxis) who actually don't have that condition (are not blue in colour), according to some gold standard, but who return a positive result on a test (the eye-witness). A gold standard is a 24 carat test used to evaluate all other tests. The TPR states that given the cab is blue (by some gold standard), there is an 80% chance that the test (eye-witness) will indicate that it's blue. The FPR reports the error in diagnosing green cabs as blue cabs: given that the cab is green, there is a 20% chance that the test (eye-witness) will report that it is blue.

[32] This raises an interesting ethical question: a tort case would fail against the blue cab company, and the registrar's statement of *a priori* probability without corroborating evidence would be deemed insufficient to secure judgement against the green cab company. Yet it is undisputed that the pedestrian was injured by a taxi. Joint and several liability, based on the proportion of market share would overcome the problem; but this could lead to moral hazard by reducing the incentive for blue cab drives to drive carefully.

error to make less error (Einhorn, 1986). Arkes (1981) argues that the first impediment to diagnostic accuracy is the inability to assess covariation accurately: people (including clinicians, see for example Wolf *et al.*, 1985) base their assessment on whether a symptom is present and the outcome is positive.[33] Yet no research has been undertaken in environmental economics to assess the importance of various forms of representativeness bias in people's perception of the chance of environmental events occurring; how WTP is influenced by such biases at the time of the interview; and the extent to which subsequent thought and experience results in less emphasis being placed on the last piece of available information (the brochure or interview information) and more weight given to prior beliefs and other commitments on the household's budget in subsequent expenditure decisions.

4.4 Availability bias

Availability bias refers to situations in which people access the frequency of a class or the probability of an event by the ease with which instances or occurrences are brought to mind.[34] Lichtenstein *et al.* (1978) show that some types of death are grossly over-estimated (e.g. deaths from accidents, childbirth, tornadoes, floods, cancer, fire, venomous bites, and homicide); whilst others are grossly under-estimated (e.g. deaths from diabetes, stomach cancer, lightening, stroke, tuberculosis, asthma, and emphysema). Biases in

---

[33] Thus they base their judgement largely on instances in Cell A, augmenting these on occasion with the salience of instances in Cell B. Information in Cell C is perceived to irrelevant to contingency estimates, as is Cell D, even though mathematically information in Cell C lowers true contingency as much as information in Cell B does. Typically, CV studies ascertain WTP based on asking respondents to compare two cells (A and B) or (A and C). But to test hypotheses accurately, and to accurately determine true WTP, information is required on all cells.

		Outcome	
		X	Not X
Symptom	Present	A	B
	Absent	C	D

[34] A simple example is consider a group of 10 people who form committees. How many different two person committees can be formed? How many different eight person committees can be formed? The availability of 10 people to form different two person committees suggests that more two person, committees can be formed compared to eight person committees. The typical median estimate for two person committees is 70, and for eight person committees 20. The correct answer is 45 in both cases since a two person committee automatically forms an eight person committee out of the remaining members of the group. This can be checked from the combinatorial equation $^{n}C_{r} = n! / [(n - r)! \, r!]$, where $^{n}C_{r}$ = number of combinations of r objects taken from n different objects. The reason for the bias is that two person committees are much more available: they come to mind more readily.

perceived risk compared to actual risk can be explained by a number of psychological factors (Slovic *et al.*, 1980). People dislike risks which are involuntarily imposed upon them (e.g. homicide) compared to voluntary risks (e.g. death from skiing); catastrophic (risks which kill a large number in one event, e.g. airline accidents) compared to chronic risk (that kills one person at a time in independent events, e.g. asthma); over which they have no control (e.g. floods and tornadoes); for which they have a common dread (e.g. terrorism and crime); which have severe consequences (e.g. nuclear accidents); and which are new (e.g. genetic engineering). The availability of information in determining people's perception of environmental risks is instrumental in understanding their WTP to avert such risks. The difference between perceived and actual risks, and hence between what people are actually WTP and what society should be WTP to avert environmental risks deserves much greater research attention.

5 EMBEDDING AND SUBSTITUTION EFFECTS

Embedding arises when the same good is assigned a lower value if WTP for it is inferred from WTP for a more inclusive good, compared with when the particular good is evaluated on its own. Embedding is also implied when WTP values for different quantities of the same good are approximately the same, although this should perhaps be more properly described as a scope or scale effect.

An observed embedding effect can be interpreted in two ways, as either resulting from:

1.   flaws in the design of studies which use CVM (as suggested by Smith, 1992);
2.   flaws in the CVM itself, and inconsistencies in the axioms of consumer theory (as suggested by Kahneman and Knetsch, 1992).

Embedding effects were reported by Kahneman and Knetsch in 1984 (see Cummings *et al.* 1986) when similar WTP estimates were obtained for cleaning up lakes in the Muskoka region of Ontario and for cleaning up all of the lakes in Ontario. The article by Kahneman and Knetsch (1992) focused the attention of environmental economists on the issue[35], and the controversy was further fuelled by the Kemp and Maxwell (1993) experiment in which a top-down disaggregation method resulted in estimates of WTP for a particular

---

[35] Kahneman and Knetsch report many examples of supposed embedding effects; where WTP for the specific good appears to be a larger percentage of the generic good of which it is part, than might be supposed *ex ante*.

commodity that were approximately 300 times smaller than those obtained for the same commodity from a comparable single-focus question.   Further controversy arose when Desvousges *et al.* (1993) reported invariance of WTP with respect to scale and scope of protection for ducks and geese on the central flyway in the USA (see section 4.1).

The NOAA Report by Arrow *et al.* (1993) largely accepted that embedding effects were produced by careless questionnaire design, and that embedding also reflected the fact that different levels of provision of the good had not been clearly specified to respondents. The NOAA Panel suggested that increasing information and more carefully specifying context would reduce embedding effects. This perspective was also suggested by Smith (1992). CVM design might be flawed at the theoretical stage prior to the design of the questionnaire, by failing to adequately address issues of substitution and budget constraints.

Indeed, an earlier well designed study by Majid *et al.* (1983) showed, through a series of refutable hypotheses (H) derived from theory, including:

1. H_1: as the number of parks increases, WTP for any specific park as an increment to the system becomes smaller;
2. H_2: WTP for any park considered alone, having common and unique features, exceeds that for any park with only common features;
3. H_3: as the number of parks increases, WTP for an additional park with only common features diminishes more rapidly than WTP for adding a park with common and unique features.

that the benefits of any park in isolation are substantially greater than the benefits of the same park considered as an increment to the existing park system. The value of additional increments can either be determined by:

(a)   asking respondents their WTP for the first X number of parks; and then their WTP for (X + 1) parks (i.e. all parks);
(b)   asking respondents their WTP for X number of parks, and their added WTP for one more park additional to the original set of X.

In further work, Randall and Hoehn (1996) demonstrate that

(1)   As the number of prospects (goods and policies) increases, the impact on a budget becomes more pronounced, and hence WTP for the package becomes smaller than the sum of WTP for the component prospects each valued independently.
(2)   Where the package is built up sequentially the incremental contribution of a particular component to the total value of the package will be smaller the later its place in the sequence: i.e. component values are sequence dependent.

(3)   For WTA compensation for reductions in goods, (1) and (2) hold
        with their signs reversed: as the number of prospects becomes large,
        WTA for the package becomes larger than the sum of WTA for the
        components valued separately. WTA for the loss of any good
        increases as substitute goods deteriorate in quantity and quality.

(4)   Where the discretionary budget is small relative to total wealth (e.g.
        because of committed expenditure on housing, food, and other
        'necessities') the relationships under (1) to (3) are exacerbated, and
        the incremental contribution of a component to total WTP for the
        package declines even more rapidly as the component is placed later
        in the sequence.

(5)   Total compensating variation for all goods in an environmental
        programme is path-independent: i.e. it is independent of the valuation
        sequence chosen. However, a valid measure of value of all goods
        requires that price changes be sequenced and not valued
        independently. Conversely, an independent valuation of each good
        provides an invalid measure of total valuation.

Thus Randall and Hoehn argue that embedding, where WTP for a good is
larger when valued alone than when included in a larger set of goods, is
precisely what theory predicts. They also argue that the order, scope, or scale
effect [(2) above] is also predicted by economic theory and that reliable
measures should exhibit this effect. What economic theory does not predict,
however, is the magnitude of the embedding effect that should be expected.
Hence, there is no way of judging whether observed embedding effects are
approximately correct, or whether the design of the CV study (e.g. in the
process of partitioning the goods, or evolving a multi-stage budgeting
framework) has exacerbated the predicted effects by depressing WTP to a
greater degree for the more inclusive set of goods.

   Clearly, the presence or perceived presence of substitutes is also important:
as more substitute goods are added to the choice set, the value of any one
individual component decreases. Thus it can be argued that the valuation
results derived from embedding studies are precisely what would be predicted
from consumer theory: as the number of substitutes increases, so the
consumer surplus on any one particular good declines.[36]

---

[36] The substitute problem of course does not explain other Kahneman and Knetsch results where
mean WTP for the specific good was greater than the generic environmental good which
encompassed it. For example, WTP for research on dengue fever, a tropical disease $52.42, for
research on all tropical diseases $17.83; for protection for the peregrine falcon, an endangered
bird $125.00, for all endangered birds $59.07; improve sports facilities in small communities in
British Columbia (BC) $209.75, improve sports facilities in small communities in Canada
$55.96; rehabilitate recently released young offenders $233.16, rehabilitate all recently released
criminals $25.04; improve literacy for recent adult BC immigrants $190.53, improve literacy of
adults in BC $56.61; replant trees in cutover areas in BC $151.70, replant trees in cutover areas

Embedding effects predicted by economic theory apply to both market and non-market goods. Randall and Hoehn (1996) examined embedding effects in market goods by calculating both total valuation and independent valuation of a series of price changes for all food items in the Dominican Republic. The results conformed to economic theory: total valuation in terms of Hicksian compensating variation was always less than independent valuation (for a price decrease), and the difference increased with the magnitude of the price change. In addition, the welfare effects of a change in the price of rice were reduced as rice was evaluated later in the sequence: the welfare effect of a 95% reduction in the price of rice was reduced by more than 50% when evaluated after similar price reduction for the other nine food items. Thus the valuation of any particular good is path-dependent.

6 MULTI-ENVIRONMENTAL PROGRAMMES

Evaluating an environmental policy which simultaneously alters several related resource services, which households view as either substitutes or complements for one another, creates particular problems for CVM, and embedding effects typically arise in valuing these environmental programmes.

The Hicksian compensating (CS) measure for an environmental change is the maximum (minimum) amount of money that can be taken from (or given to) an individual in order to leave her indifferent between her *ex ante* and *ex post* programme situations. Conventional CVM procedures value each policy element (q) of a programme as if it was a single independent element, maintaining all other elements at their initial level. This independent valuation and summation (IVS) measures is

$$CS(q^1, q^0, u^0) = y\text{-}e(p, q_1^1, q_2^0, q_3^0, ...q^{k0}, u^0) + y\text{-}e(p, q_1^0, q_2^1, q_3^0, ...q_k^0, u^0) + y\text{-}e(p, q_1^1, q_2^0, q_3^1, ...q_k^0, u^0) + y\text{-}e(p, q_1^0, q_2^0, q_3^0, ...q_k^1, u^0)$$ (5.5)

Randall and Hoehn have shown that such independently valued elements of a programme cannot be aggregated directly without biased results. The IVS

---

in western Canada $54.74; increase research on toxic waste disposal $234.12, increase research on environmental protection $98.77; famine relief in Ethiopia $157.67, famine relief in Africa $72.68; research on breast cancer $243.14, research on all forms of cancer $162.09. WTP more for the specific good than for the generic good of which it is part: is probably explained by context and theatre effects. But the absence of substitutes in the choice set can explain their other embedding results, where WTP for one specific good was only three to four times less than its generic good area which contained literally hundreds of other substitute goods; including: WTP to reduce acid rain damage in Muskoka, Ontario $40.91, WTP to reduce acid rain damage in eastern Canada $214.55; restore rural BC museums $32.78, restore rural Canada and heritage museums $113.47; improve sport fishing stocks in BC fresh water $41.89, improve sport fishing stocks in Canada fresh water $147.16; protection for marmot, a small animal in BC $33.27, protection for small animals in BC $141.75.

measure is equal to CS only if the K programme elements are independent, which is unlikely to be the case for many environmental programmes. In the Yorkshire Dales Environmentally Sensitive Area (ESA), for example, visitors perceive the elements of the ESA programme (maintaining and enhancing dry- stone walls and barns, flower-rich hay meadows, and farm woodland) as substitutes at the margin. IVS over-estimates the true valuation of environmental benefits if programme elements are substitutes; and under-estimates their value when they are complements.

As the number of environmental programmes or policies increases, substitution effects increase, and IVS will over-estimate CS, and misidentify detrimental policies as potentially beneficial (Hoehn and Randall, 1989).

Alternative measures are to value programme elements sequentially or simultaneously. When elements of a programme are measured sequentially the order in which the subcategory benefits are valued influences the values ascribed to these elements. Goods that are valued first are valued more highly than goods valued later. The value ascribed to each element is not unique, but depends on the sequence selected. This path dependency has been revealed by Santos (1996) in the valuation of environmentally sensitive area (ESA) programmes.

Hoehn (1990) shows that a holistic valuation measure can be disaggregated into separate valuations for the K components of a programme by a valuation path beginning at $q_0 = (q_1^0, q_2^0, ... q_k^0)$ and ending at $q_0 = (q_1^1, q_2^1, ... q_k^1)$. A sequential path shifts programme components one at a time from their initial *ex ante* position to their *ex post* programme prescription, in a sequence of valuation changes, q_1^0 to q_1^1, then q_2^0 to q_2^1, and so on until all the sub-programme elements effects are complete with q_k^0 to q_k^1.

$$CS(q^1, q^0, u^0) = y - e(p, q_1^1, q_2^0, q_3^0, ..., q_k^0, u^0) + e(p, q_1^1, q_2^0, q_3^0, ..., q_k^0, u^0) - e(p, q_1^1, q_2^1, q_3^0, ..., q_k^0, u^0) + e(p, q_1^1, q_2^1, q_3^0, ..., q_k^0, u^0) - e(p, q_1^1, q_2^1, q_3^1, ..., q_k^0, u^0) + ... + e(p, q_1^1, q_2^1, q_3^1, ..., q_k^0, u^0) - e(p, q_1^1, q_2^1, q_3^1, ..., q_k^1, u^0)$$
(5.6)

where y is the initial income level, p is a vector of market prices and u^0 is initial utility. Each line of the equation expresses the value of a change in the level of a specific component of the programme, and the sequential nature of the expression means that all but the first and final terms cancel out.

This reduces to a quantity identical to the aggregate valuation for the overall policy:

$$CS(q^1, q^0, u^0) = y - e(p, q_1^1, q_2^1, q_3^1, ... q_k^1, u^0)$$
(5.7)

The sequential approach was used by Majid *et al.* (1983) to value the benefits of increments to national park numbers and facilities in Australia; and by Santos (1997) to value increments to agri-environmental programmes in England and Portugal. Note that a sequential rather than a simultaneous disaggregation strategy is required to estimate benefits if these are to be used in a cost-benefit analysis to choose the optimal attribute programme mix for a multi-attribute conservation scheme. This is the only approach which will value incremental additions to an environmental programme.

In the simultaneous path approach, which evaluates a derivative of the expenditure function between the *ex ante* and *ex post* environmental programme,

$$CS((q^1, q^0, u^0) = \delta[de(q_1, q_2,...q_k, u^0)/d_{q1}]d_{q1} +$$
$$\delta[de(q_1, q_2,...q_k, u^0)/d_{q2}]d_{q2} + ...+ \delta[de(q_1, q_2,...q_k, u^0)/d_{qk}]d_{qk} \qquad (5.8)$$

the aggregate and component valuations are unique. In this approach, respondents value the environmental programme as a whole, and asked to subdivide this value to individual elements of the programme using monetary apportionment, or through points and tokens. This approach has been used to value the conservation of Swedish agricultural landscapes (Drake, 1992); environmentally sensitive areas in Britain (Willis *et al.*, 1995); and low flow alleviation in rivers (Willis and Garrod, 1997).

In a study of the benefit of reductions in nutrient leaching into the North Sea from 3 Norwegian rivers [the Halden (H), Glomma (G), and Vansjø-Hobøl (V)] Magnussen (1996) confirmed these effects predicted by theory, in terms of mean WTP per respondent:

(1) IVS (HGV) (independent valuation summation of the benefits of nutrient reductions in each river H, G, and V), was 1,836 Norwegian Kronor (NOK).
(2) SEQ (HGV) (WTP for the sequence H, G, V) was NOK 1,653 (although the difference between (1) and (2) was not significant).
(3) SIM (HGV) (WTP for the simultaneous valuation of rivers H, G, and V, was NOK 1,344-statistically significantly different from IVS at the 10% level). The simultaneous valuation was derived by determining WTP for HGV in total, and then asking respondents to allocate total WTP between each river.

Goods valued as an element of a larger entity produce a smaller WTP than when goods are valued alone. Hence, there is no price for a good independent of its setting, so that setting must be recognised in using the results (Magnussen, 1996). It is clearly important to recognise this when searching for benefit transfer methods, and attempting to apply environmental values in a benefit transfer situation.

7 INCOME ELASTICITIES FOR ENVIRONMENTAL GOODS[37]

It is frequently observed that conventionally estimated income elasticities for environmental goods appear to be less than 1.0. This seems counter-intuitive, and at odds with causal observation and introspection. Thus, it may be argued that the income elasticity of demand for environmental preservation measures such as the conservation of agricultural landscapes, wildlife amenity benefits, and the separation of towns by green belts, etc. might be much higher than commonly thought. This has obvious implications for conservation. The argument can be developed using a simple linear demand function for an environmental good expressed as:

$$Q = a + bP + cY \qquad (5.9)$$

where Q = quantity demanded; P = price; and Y = income. The respective price and income elasticities for this linear demand function are:

$$\varepsilon = b*(P/Q) \qquad \text{and} \qquad \eta = c*(Y/Q)$$

The value of an environmental good is typically estimated through a CVM in terms of the willingness-to-pay for the good, so the relationship of interest is the price-dependent demand function:

$$P = (Q - a - cY)/b \qquad (5.10)$$

From this price-dependent equation, the 'income flexibility', as a proportionate change in the price (willingness to pay) per proportionate change in income is defined as:

$$f(y) = (-c/b)*Y/P \qquad (5.11)$$

This is the measure that is intuitively grasped when considering the effect of income on the demand for an environmental good. It is this measure that should be considered in the case of a public good, since for any individual the

---

[37] We are indebted to David Harvey for these observations, which draw upon the work of Flores and Carson (1995).

quantity of a public good is not a control variable: it is fixed by public or collective action. Furthermore, in the case of many environmental goods, the total supply is frequently strictly limited.

In this linear case, therefore, the relationship between income flexibility for an environmental good and the conventional income elasticity is as follows:

$$f(y) = (-c/b)*Y/P = [c*(Y/Q)] / [-b*(P/Q)] = \eta / -\varepsilon \qquad (5.12)$$

Thus, although income elasticities for public goods are often measured as less than 1.0, so long as the corresponding price elasticity is less in absolute terms than this income elasticity, the income flexibility for the public good is greater than 1.0. Since price elasticity of demand for environmental public goods may typically be quite inelastic, this condition is quite likely to be met in many cases.

Price elasticities of demand for various recreational and environmental goods are presented in Table 5.9. Price elasticity for amenity and recreational activities is generally low when the good is considered a necessity, when substitutes are not available to satisfy perceived need, when the proportion of income spent on the good is low, or when the good is purchased frequently.

A relatively constant quantity of necessities such as access to recreational resources for walking, viewing nature, etc. will be purchased almost irrespective of price, within the price ranges normally encountered. For these general experiences there are no close substitutes. However, for specific recreation sites and areas of environmental amenity, the greater the competition, and the more substitutes that are available, the more the demand for these goods is dependent upon price. Furthermore, the demand for high priced goods and services, which account for a large proportion of consumers' incomes, is also relatively sensitive to price. The price elasticity of demand for boats is much higher than those for camping, walking, and viewing nature. The small percentage of income spent on the latter goods and services means that it is simply not worthwhile spending time and energy worrying about their prices (Loomis and Walsh, 1997).

The low price elasticity for generic recreational activities such as walking and nature observation, and goods such as landscape preservation, etc., arise because:

- most are unique: having few substitutes their demand is relatively inelastic;
- they are general activities: the price elasticity for specific recreational activities and sites is higher. Thus the observed price elasticity for trout fishing is -0.4, compared with fishing in general which has a price elasticity of -0.2;

- of the quality of the resource. Price elasticities are lower where the quality of the environmental resource, or recreational experience, is higher;
- they have a low impact on the consumers' budget. Thus, price elasticity is lower for viewing nature on a day outing than on vacation trips.

Table 5.9: Estimated price elasticity of demand for some outdoor recreational activities

Activity	Occasion	Price elasticity of demand
Walking	vacation	-0.22
	weekend	-0.19
	day outing	-0.20
Viewing nature	vacation	-0.22
	weekend	-0.18
	day outing	-0.07
Sailing	vacation	-0.25
	weekend	-0.11
	day outing	-0.40
Golf		-0.70
Camping		-0.40
Pleasure boats		-1.30

Source: Loomis and Walsh (1997)

The estimated income elasticities of demand for most recreational goods and services is positive. Table 5.10 documents some income elasticities for selected recreational goods. Luxury recreational goods have higher income elasticities (indeed this is how they are categorised!) Income levels have historically doubled every 20 to 30 years in western economies. Hence, the demand for recreation and amenity goods should increase, not only for urban recreational goods such as theatre trips, restaurant meals, etc., but also for countryside recreational goods such as walks, nature observation, and landscape preservation. As the recreational good becomes more specific and the number of substitutes increases, income elasticity declines. Thus, estimates of the income elasticity for particular recreational activities and sites are inelastic, i.e. less than 1.0.

However, simple price elasticities are much lower than simple income elasticities for environmental goods. Thus the income flexibility for public goods in the environment is much greater than 1.0. The demand for such goods will increase substantially necessitating environmental control, regulation, and planning to ensure their long-term supply where they are a joint product with agricultural production, and to guard against their short-term consumption to the detriment of future demands.

Table 5.10: Estimated income elasticities of demand for selected recreational goods

Good or service	Income elasticity
Swimming trips	0.31
Boating trips	0.34
Camping trips	0.42
Fishing trips	0.47
Theatre	1.98
Restaurant meals	1.48
All food	0.20
Automobiles	3.00
Liquor	1.00
Wine	1.40
Housing	0.60 – 0.80
Preservation of Scottish 'flow country'	0.73
Amenity from broad-leaved woodland	0.82
Recreation expenditure	1.40

Source: Loomis and Walsh (1997) and others

Table 5.11: Cumulative long-run price elasticity of demand for outdoor recreation

Year	Cumulative price elasticity of demand in the long run	Percentage of total long-run demand effect
1	-0.20	15.7
2	-0.45	19.3
3	-0.69	19.3
4	-0.90	16.4
5	-1.06	12.9
6	-1.17	8.6
7	-1.24	5.0
8	-1.27	2.9
9	-1.27	0
Total	-1.27	100.0

Source: Walsh (1986)

The only caveat to this argument is that long-run elasticities may differ from the short-run elasticities outlined in Table 5.9. Short-run demand for recreation and environmental goods is relatively inelastic. However, over the long run, consumers will adjust their purchases of the environmental or recreational good whose price has risen. Table 5.11 illustrates the sensitivity of the long-run quantity demanded to a change in the direct costs or price compared with Year 1. Whilst empirical studies reveal price elasticity of demand for recreational experiences to be inelastic (<1.0) in the short run, it is expected to be elastic (>1.0) in the long run, especially for specific recreational sites and activities with substitutes. Thus, whilst a 10% increase in the price of consuming a particular type of outdoor recreation would result in a 2% decrease in demand in the first year when price is inelastic (-0.2); in the long run a 10% increase in price would reduce recreational demand by 12.7% (Table 5.11).

Any loss in the quantity of agricultural land which resulted in reduced recreational use or experience in the quality of walks, wildlife experiences, and views might have a dramatic long-term effect on the demand for these experiences, *ceteris paribus.*[38]

Thus, for example, the price elasticity of demand for walking is -0.20 (day outing). A recent study by Willis and Garrod (1997) estimated, from a random samples of 932 visitors, that people would be willing to pay £0.23 to avoid a 1% increase in the number of pipe bridges, pylons, and cable crossings, encountered in walking along canals in the countryside. Assuming that the direct cost per individual of visiting a canal for a walk is £1.50, then the visual effect of a 1% increase in utility service crossings over canals is 15.3% (= £0.23/£1.50). Thus if the visual effect of an increase in utility services across canals continued for a decade, recreational walks along canal towpaths would be expected to decrease by 3.1% (= 15.3 * 0.20) in the first year; by 6.9% in the second year; and so on until it reached a level of about 19.4% of what it was originally. Thus the long-term visual impact of utility service networks could be to substantially reduce recreational walks in the countryside, assuming other factors such as population do not change. Of course this estimate should be treated as a first approximation, to be verified by future studies of the long-run demand for specific recreation activities and environmental resource attributes. It is also entirely possible to imagine that the amenity value of agricultural land would increase if more walkers were attracted to agricultural landscapes by reductions in agricultural intensity and the re-creation of a more traditional agricultural landscape, with more intimate fields, hedgerows, and coppice woodlands.

The amenity value of agricultural land also depends upon the property rights perspective adopted. Amenity values estimated by travel-cost models and hedonic price models are based on a WTP framework. Contingent valuation methods invariably also adopt a WTP framework to estimate the

---

[38] Recreational demand could, however, still increase if housing development resulted in more people living near these recreational facilities and visiting them, despite a deterioration in their quality.

value of environmental goods. However, if individuals or society have a right to an environmental good, then the correct monetary measure of utility change for the loss of the good is the level of compensation necessary to restore the individual or society to her or its original utility level.

An early CV study of the amenity benefits of Tyneside's green belt agricultural land, revealed the difference between WTP and WTA to preserve the green belt, and the importance of the assignment of amenity property rights. Table 5.12 shows the mean WTP and WTA values for two areas adjacent to the green belt to the north of Newcastle. WTP and WTA were in terms of changes in local authority taxes (rates) on houses. No respondent indicated that a 100% reduction in tax would be required to compensate for his loss: the maximum reduction specified was 60%; and 26% of respondents said they would not require any compensation for the loss of the green belt. Except in two cases, WTA > WTP for respondents, indicating rationality and conformity to (economic and psychological) theory.

The Tyneside green belt study demonstrated that the preservation of the greenbelt in terms of the amenity value of the land was highly dependent upon the property rights perspective and whether WTA or WTP measures were used in the evaluation. WTP to avert the loss of the green belt was only one third of WTA compensation for its loss. If the WTP measure had been used to value the amenity benefits of the green belt then this would have justified, compared with the alternative value of the land to housing (£56,600 per ha in 1980), a smaller greenbelt area than that designated at the time (7,700 ha). Adopting WTA as the appropriate framework to value amenity change (£2386 per ha per year in 1980) for the loss of agricultural land in the green belt justified the area designated, assuming that the annual amenity benefits were capitalised at 6% and that the amenity value of the agricultural land grew at 1.8% per year in real terms relative to the value of land in housing. Not an unreasonable assumption given contemporary levels of concern over the loss of land to various forms of economic development in Britain.

Table 5.12: Contingent valuation estimates of the value of the Newcastle green belt (£, 1981)

| | Average per household per year (£) | | |
	Brunton Park	Melton Park	Both areas
WTA (compensation for loss of green belt land)	65	127	104
WTP (to avert loss of green belt land)	23	42	35

Source: Willis and Whitby (1985).

The example illustrates the importance of the property rights perspective to the valuation of an asset. It might be argued that in Britain amenity rights to greenbelt land are vested with the local community. Unfortunately, local authorities are all too willing to grant planning permission for urban development on green belt land without compensating local residents in any way for the amenity loss. Governments too in many countries are quite willing on occasions to abrogate the environmental rights of citizens, and countenance the diminution of some public goods to satisfy the myopic greed of business interest groups.

REFERENCES

Adamowicz, W.L., V. Bharadwai and B. Macnab (1993), 'Experiments on the difference between willingness to pay and willingness to accept', *Land Economics* **69**, 416-27.

Adamowicz, Wiktor L., V. Bhardwai and B. Nacnab (1993), 'Experiments on the difference between willingness to pay and willingness to accept', *Land Economics* **69**, 416–27.

Advertising Research Foundation (1985), *Focus Groups: issues and approaches*, Prepared by the Qualitative Research Council of the Advertising Research Foundation, New York.

Arkes, Hal R. (1981), 'Impediments to accurate clinical judgement and possible ways to minimise their impact', *Journal of Consulting and Clinical Psychology* **49**, 323–30.

Arrow, Kenneth J., R. Solow, P.R. Portney, E.E. Leamer, R. Radner and H. Schuman (1993), 'Report of the National Oceanic and Atmospheric Administration (NOAA) Panel on Contingent Valuation', *Federal Register* **58** (10), 4016–614.

Banford, N., J. Knetsch and G. Mauser (1977), 'Compensating and equivalent measures of consumer's surplus: further survey results', Department of Economics, Simon Fraser University, Vancouver.

Barnett, A.H. and B. Yandle (1973), 'Allocating environmental resources', *Public Finance* **28**, 11–19.

Bateman, I., A. Munro, B. Rhodes, C. Starmer and R. Sugden (1997) 'Does part-whole bias exist? An experimental investigation' *Economic Journal* **107**, 322-32.

Bateman, Ian J., Ian H. Langford, K.G. Willis, R.K. Turner and G.D. Garrod (1995), 'Elicitation and truncation effects in contingent valuation studies', *Ecological Economics* **12**, 161–79.

Bergland, Olvar (1993), 'Framing effects in CVM experiments: old-growth forests preservation in the Pacific north-west', *Discussion Paper*, Department of Economics and Social Sciences, Agricultural University of Norway, Ås, Norway.

Bishop, R.C. and T.A. Heberlein (1986), 'Does contingent valuation work?', in R.G. Cummings, D.S. Brookshire and W.D. Schulze (eds) *Valuing Environmental Goods: A State of the Arts Assessment of the Contingent Valuation Method*, Rowman and Allanheld, Totowa, New Jersey, 123–47.

Bishop, R.C., T.A. Heberlein, and M.J. Kealy (1983), 'Hypothetical bias in contingent valuation: results from a simulated market', *Natural Resources Journal* **23**, 619–33.

Bishop, Richard C and T.A. Heberlein (1979), 'Measuring values of extra market goods: are indirect measures biased?', *American Journal of Agricultural Economics* **61**, 926–30.

Bohm, P. (1972), 'Estimating demand for public goods: an experiment', *European Economic Review* **3**, 111–30.

Bohm, P. (1994), 'CVM spells responses to hypothetical questions', *Natural Resources Journal* **34** (1), 37–50.

Boyle, K.J., Bishop and M.P. Welsh (1985), 'Starting point bias in contingent valuation bidding games', *Land Economics* **61**, 188-94.

Brookshire, David S., A. Randall and J.R. Stoll (1980), 'Valuing increments and decrements in natural resource service flows', *American Journal of Agricultural Economics* **62**, 478–88.

Brookshire, David S., Don L. Coursey, and William D. Schulze (1986), 'Experiments in the solicitation of public and private values: an overview', in L. Green and J. Kasel (eds) *Advances in Behavioural Economics*, JAI Press, Greenwich, Connecticut.

Carson, Richard T., Nicholas E. Flores, Kerry M. Martin and Jennifer L. Wright (1996), 'Contingent valuation and revealed preference methodologies: comparing the estimates for quasi-public goods', *Land Economics* **72**, 80–99.

Coursey, D.L., J. Hovis and W.D. Schulze (1987), 'The disparity between willingness to accept and willingess to pay measures of value', *Quarterly Journal of Economics*, **102**, 679-90.

Coursey, Don L., John L. Hovis, and W.D. Schulze (1987), 'On the supposed disparity between willingness to accept and willingness to pay measures of value', *Quarterly Journal of Economics* **102**, 679–90.

Cummings R.G., D.S. Brookshire and W.D. Schulze (eds) (1986), *Valuing Environmental Goods: an assessment of the contingent valuation method*, Rowman and Allenheld, Towowa, New Jersey.

Cummings, R.G. and G.W. Harrison (1994), 'Was the Ohio Court case well informed in its assessment of the contingent valuation method?', *Natural Resources Journal* **34** (1), 1–36.

Davis, Douglas D. and Charles A. Holt (1993), *Experimental Economics*, Princeton University Press, Princeton, New Jersey.

Dawes, Robyn M. (1980), 'You can't systematise human judgement: dyslexia', *New Directions for Methodology of Social and Behavioural Science* **4**, 67–87.

Deming, William E. (1950), *Some Theory of Sampling*, J. Wiley, New York.

Desvousges, William H., F. Reed Johnson, Richard W. Dunford, Sara P. Hudson, K. Nicole Wilson and Kevin J. Boyle (1993), 'Measuring natural resource damages with contingent valuation: tests of validity and reliability', in J.A. Hausman (ed.) *Contingent Valuation: a critical assessment*, North Holland, Amsterdam.

Dickie, M., A. Fisher, and S. Gerking (1987), 'Market transactions and hypothetical demand data: a comparative study', *Journal of the American Statistical Association* **82**, 69–75.

Dillman, B.L. and J.C. Bergstrom (1991), 'Measuring environmental amenity benefits in agricultural land', in N. Hanley (ed) *Farming and the Countryside: an economic analysis of external costs and benefits*, CAB International, Wallingford.

Drake, Lars (1992), 'The non-market value of the Swedish agricultural landscape', *European Review of Agricultural Economics* **19**, 351–64.

Eddy, D.M. and C.H. Clanton (1982), 'The art of diagnosis: solving the clinicopathological exercise', *The New England Journal of Medicine* **306**, 1263-8.

Einhorn, Hillel J. (1980), 'Overconfidence in Judgement', *New Directions for Methodology of Social and Behavioural Science* **4**, 1– 16.

Einhorn, Hillel J. (1986), 'Accepting error to make less error', *Journal of Personality Assessment* **50**, 387–95.

Fishbein, M. and I. Ajzen (1975), *Belief, Attitude, Intention and Behaviour: An Introduction to Theory and Research,* Addison-Wesley, Reading, Massachusetts.

Fisher, Anthony C. (1996), 'The conceptual underpinnings of the contingent valuation method', in David J. Bjornstad and James R. Kahn (eds) *The Contingent Valuation of Environmental Resources*, Edward Elgar, Cheltenham.

Flores, Nicholas E. and Richard T. Carson (1995), 'The relationship between the income elasticities of demand and willingness to pay', paper presented at the World Congress of Agricultural Economics, Melbourne.

Flowerdew, A.D.J. and F. Rodriguez (1978), 'Benefits to residents from urban renewal: measurement, estimation and results', *Scottish Journal of Political Economy* **25**, 285–300.

Frey, Bruno S., Felix Oberholzer-Gee, and Reiner Eichenberger (1996), 'The old lady visits your backyard: a tale of morals and markets', *Journal of Political Economy* **104**, 1297–1313.

Friedman, Milton (1953), 'The methodology of positive economics', in M. Friedman (ed.) *Essays in Positive Economics*, University of Chicago Press, Chicago.

Garrod, G.D. and K.G. Willis (1994), 'Valuing biodiversity and nature conservation at a local level', *Biodiversity and Conservation* **3**, 555–65.

Garrod, G.D. and K.G. Willis (1997a), 'The non-use benefits of enhancing forest biodiversity: a contingent ranking study', *Ecological Economics* **21**, 45–61.

Garrod, G.D. and K.G. Willis (1997b), 'The recreational value of tropical forests in Malaysia', *Journal of World Forest Resource Management* **8**, 183-201.

Griffin, Charles C., John Brisco, Bhanwar Singh, Radhika Ramasubban and Ramesh Bhatia (1995), 'Contingent valuation and actual behavior: predicting connections to new water systems in the state of Kerala, India', *World Bank Economic Review* **9** (3), 373–95.

Hammack, J. and G. Brown (1974*) Waterfowl and Wetlands: towards bioeconomic analysis*, John Hopkins University Press, Baltimore.

Hanemann, W. Michael (1996), 'Theory versus data in the contingent valuation debate', in David J. Bjornstad and James R. Kahn (eds) *The Contingent Valuation of Environmental Resources*, Edward Elgar, Cheltenham.

Hanemann, W. Michael, J. Loomis and B. Kanninen (1991), 'Statistical efficiency of double bounded dichotomous choice contingent valuation', *American Journal of Agricultural Economics* **73**, 1255–63.

Hanemann, W.M. (1986), 'Willingness to pay and willingness to accept: how much can they differ?', Draft manuscript, Department of Agricultural and Resource Economics, University of California, Berkeley.

Hanley, N. and C.L.Spash (1993), *Cost Benefit Analysis and the Environment*, Edward Elgar, Cheltenham.

Hanley, Nick and Alistair Munro (1992), 'The effect of information in contingent markets for environmental goods: a survey and some new evidence', Working Paper 848, Institute for Economic Research, Queen's University, Kingston, Ontario, Canada.

Herriges, Joseph A. and Jason F. Shogren (1996), 'Starting point bias in dichotomous choice valuation with follow-up questioning', *Journal of Environmental Economics and Management* **30**, 112–31.

Hoehn, John P. (1990), 'Valuing the multi-dimensional impacts of environmental policy', *Staff Paper No. 90-03*, Department of Agricultural Economics, Michigan State University.

Hoehn, John P. and Alan Randall (1989), 'Too many proposals pass the benefit cost test', *American Economic Review* **79**, 544–51.

Hoevenagel R. and J.W. van der Linden (1993), 'Effects of different descriptions of the ecological good on willingness to pay values', *Ecological Economics* **7**, 223–38.

Jakobsson, Kristin M. and Andrew K. Dragun (1996), *Contingent Valuation and Endangered Species: methodological issues and applications*, Edward Elgar, Cheltenham.

Jones-Lee, Michael W. (1989), *The Economics of Safety and Physical Risk*, Basil Blackwell, Oxford.

Jones-Lee, Michael W. and Graham Loomes (1994), 'Towards a willingness-to-pay value of underground safety', *Journal of Transport Economics and Policy* **28**, 83–98.

Kahneman, D. and J.L. Knetsch (1992), 'Valuing public goods: the purchase of moral satisfaction', *Journal of Environmental Economics and Management* **22**, 57–70.

Kahneman, Daniel and Amos Tversky (1979), 'Prospect Theory: an analysis of decisions under risk', *Econometrica* **47**, 263–91.

Kahneman, Daniel, Jack L. Knetsch and Richard H. Thaler (1991), 'Anomalies: the endowment effect, loss aversion, and status quo bias', *Journal of Economic Perspectives* **5**, 193–206.

Kemp, M.A. and C. Maxwell (1993), 'Exploring a budget context for contingent valuation estimates', in J.A. Hausman (ed.) *Contingent Valuation: a critical assessment*, North Holland, Amsterdam.

Knetsch, J. and J. Sinden (1984), 'Willingness to pay and compensation demanded: experimental evidence of an unexpected disparity in measures of value', *Quarterly Journal of Economics* **99**, 507-21.

Lancaster K. (1966), 'A new approach to consumer theory', *Journal of Political Economy* **74**, 132–57.

Lewington, P., K.G. Willis, G.D. Garrod and R. Frazer (1996) 'London Electricity Supply Study', Report to London Electricity and the National Grid Company, ERM, London.

Lichtenstein, S., P. Slovic, B. Fischhoff, M. Layman and B. Combs (1978), 'Judged frequency of lethal events', *Journal of Experimental Psychology: Human Learning and Memory* **4**, 551–78.

Loomis, J., M. Lockwood and T. DeLacy (1993), 'Some empirical evidence on embedding effects in contingent valuation of forest protection', *Journal of Environmental Economics and Management* **24**, 45–55.

Loomis, John B. and Richard G. Walsh (1997), *Recreation Economic Decisions: comparing benefits and costs*, Venture Publishing Inc., State College, Pennsylvania.

Magnussen, Kristin (1996), 'Substitution or embedding? Valuation and aggregation of policy components of environmental goods by the contingent valuation method', *Working paper*, Østfold Research Foundation, Fredrikstad, Norway.

Majid, I., J.A. Sinden and A. Randall (1983), 'Benefit evaluation of increments to existing systems of public facilities', *Land Economics* **59**, 377–92.

Mitchell R.C. and R.T. Carson (1989), *Using Surveys to Value Public Goods: The Contingent Valuation Method*, Resources for the Future, Washington D.C..

Mueller, Dennis C. (1979), *Public Choice*, Cambridge University Press, Cambridge.

Navrud, S., P.E. Pedersen and J. Strand (1992), *Valuing our cultural heritage: a contingent valuation survey*, Centre for Research Economics and Business Administration, Oslo.

Neill, H.R., R.G. Cummings, P.T. Ganderton, G.W. Harrison and T. McGuckin (1994), 'Hypothetical surveys and real economic commitments', *Land Economics* **70**, 145–54.

Nicholson, Walter (1985), *Microeconomic Theory: basic principles and extensions*, Dryden Press, Chicago.

Pearce, David W. and A. Markandya (1989), *The Benefits of Environmental Policies*, OECD, Paris.

Poulton, E.C. (1994), *Behavioural Decision Theory*, Cambridge University Press, Cambridge.

Powe, Neil A. and Kenneth G. Willis (1996), 'The value of heritage sites: a case study of visitors to Warkworth Castle', Working Paper, Department of Town and Country Planning, University of Newcastle upon Tyne.

Randall, A. (1991), 'Self-reported values and observable transactions: is there a trump in the deck?', *Invited Paper, W-133*. Western Regional Science Association Meeting, Monterey, CA. 27/2/91.

Randall, Alan and John P. Hoehn (1996), 'Embedding and market demand systems', *Journal of Environmental Economics and Management* **30**, 369–80.

Randall, Alan and John R. Stoll (1980), 'Consumer surplus in commodity space', *American Economic Review* **70**, 449–55.

Ready, Richard C., John C. Whitehead and Glenn C. Blomquist (1995), 'Contingent valuation when respondents are ambivalent', *Journal of Environmental Economics and Management* **29**, 181–96.

Rowe, Robert D., Ralph C. d'Arge and David S. Brookshire (1980), 'An experiment in the value of visibility', *Journal of Environmental Economics and Management* **7**, 1–19.

Salop, Steven C. (1987), 'Evaluating uncertain evidence with Sir Thomas Bayes: a note for teachers', *Journal of Economic Perspectives* **1**, 155–60.

Samples, Karl C., John A. Dixon, and Marcia M. Gowan (1986), 'Information disclosure and endangered species valuation', *Land Economics* **62**, 306–12.

Samuelson, William and Richard Zeckhauser (1988), 'Status quo bias in decision making', *Journal of Risk and Uncertainty* **1**, 7–59.

Santos, José (1996), 'Valuing alternative bundles of landscape attributes: cost-benefit analysis and the selection of optimal attribute bundles for agricultural landscapes', paper presented to the annual meeting of the European Association of Environmental and Resource Economists, Lisbon, June 1996.

Santos, José Manuel L. (1997), *Valuation and Cost Benefit Analysis of Multi-Attribute Environmental Changes: upland landscapes in England and Portugal.* PhD thesis, University of Newcastle upon Tyne.

Seip, K and J. Strand (1992), 'Willingness to pay for environmental goods in Norway: a contingent valuation study with real payment', *Environmental and Resource Economics* **2**, 91–106.

Seller, Christine, John R. Stoll and Jean-Paul Chavas (1985), 'Validation of empirical measures of welfare change: a comparison of non-market techniques', *Land Economics* **61**, 156–75.

Shaw, Tim and K.G. Willis (1982), 'Green Belts: evaluating their impact, effectiveness and efficiency: the case of the Tyne and Wear Green Belt', *Planning & Transport Research and Computation, Proceedings of the Summer Annual Meeting 1982: Structure and Regional Planning Practice Seminar.* PTRC, London. pp 11–25.

Slovic, Paul. B., Fischhoff, and Sarah Lichtenstein (1980), 'Facts and fears: understanding perceived risk', in R.C. Schwing and W.A. Albers (eds), *Societal Risk Assessment: how safe is safe enough?* Plenum Press, New York.

Smith, V. Kerry (1992), 'Arbitrary values, good causes, and premature verdicts: comment', *Journal of Environmental Economics and Management* **22**, 71–89.

Smith, Vernon L. (1980), 'Experiments with a decentralised mechanism for public good decisions', *American Economic Review* **70**, 584–99.

Tversky, A. and D. Kahneman (1974), 'Judgement under uncertainty: heuristics and biases', *Science* **185**, 1124–31.

Tversky, A. and D. Kahneman (1981), 'The framing of decisions and the psychology of choice', *Science* **211**, 453–58.

Von Neumann, J. and O. Morganstern (1947), *Theory of Games and Economic Behaviour*, Princeton University Press.

Walsh, Richard G. (1986), *Recreation Economic Decisions: comparing benefits and costs*, Venture Publishing Inc., State College, Pennsylvania.

Walsh, Richard G., John B. Loomis and Richard A. Gillman (1984), 'Valuing option, existence, and bequest demands for wilderness', *Land Economics* **60**, 14–29.

Whitehead, John C., Glenn C. Blomquist, Thomas J. Hoban and William B. Clifford (1995), 'Assessing the validity and reliability of contingent values: a comparison of on-site users, off-site users, and non-users', *Journal of Environmental Economics and Management* **29**, 238–51.

Whittington, D., V.K. Smith, A. Okorafor, A. Okore, J.L. Liu and A. McPhail (1992), 'Giving respondents time to think in contingent valuation studies: a developing country application', *Journal of Environmental Economics and Management* **22**, 205–25.

Whittington, Dale, Donald T. Lauria and Xinming Mu (1989), 'Paying for Urban Services: a study of water vending and willingness to pay in Onitsha, Nigeria', *Report INU 40*, Infrastructure and Urban Development Department, The World Bank, Washington DC.

Whittington, Dale, John Briscoe, Xinming Mu and William Barron (1990), 'Estimating willingness to pay for water services in developing countries: a case study of the use of contingent valuation surveys in southern Haiti', *Economic Development and Cultural Change* **38**, 293–312.

Whittington, D., V. Kerry Smith, A. Okorafor, A. Pkore, J.L. Liu, and A. McPhail (1992), 'Giving repondents time to think in contingent valuation studies: a developing country application', *Journal of Environmental Economics and Management* **22**, 205-25.

Willig, R.G. (1976), 'Consumer's surplus without apology', *American Economic Review* **66**, 589–97.

Willis, K.G. and G.D. Garrod (1993), 'Valuation of the South Downs and Somerset Levels and Moors Environmentally Sensitive Area Landscapes by the General Public', *Appendices Report of the Ministry of Agriculture, Fisheries and Food*, Centre for Rural Economy, Department of Agricultural Economics and Food Marketing, University of Newcastle upon Tyne.

Willis, K.G. and G.D. Garrod (1995), 'The benefits of alleviating low flows in rivers', *Water Resources Development* **11**, 243–60.

Willis, K.G. and G.D. Garrod (1997), 'Disamenity externalities from utility networks', *Utlities Policy* **6**, 35-41.

Willis, K.G. and G.D. Garrod (1997), 'Electricity supply reliability: estimating the value of lost load', *Energy Policy* **25**, 97-103.

Willis, K.G. and G.D. Garrod (1998), 'Water companies and river environments: the externality costs of water abstraction', *Utilities Policy*, 7, 35-45.

Willis, K.G. and M.C. Whitby (1985), 'The value of green belt land', *Journal of Rural Studies* **1**, 147–162.

Willis, K.G. and N.A. Powe (1998), 'Contingent valuation and real economic commitments: a private good experiement' *Journal of Environmental Planning and Management* **41**, 611-9.

Willis, K.G., G.D. Garrod, and C.M. Saunders (1993), 'Valuation of the South Downs and Somerset Levels and Moors Environmentally Sensitive Area Landscapes by the General Public', *Report of the Ministry of Agriculture, Fisheries and Food*, Centre for Rural Economy, Department of Agricultural Economics and Food Marketing, University of Newcastle upon Tyne.

Willis, K.G., G.D. Garrod, and C.M. Saunders (1995), 'Benefits of Environmentally Sensitive Area Policy in England: a contingent valuation assessment', *Journal of Environmental Management* **44**, 105–25.

Wolf, Fredric M., Larry D. Gruppen and John E. Billi (1985), 'Differential diagnosis and the competing-hypotheses heuristic: a practical approach to judgement under uncertainty and Bayesian probability', *Journal of the American Medical Association* **253**, 2858–62.

APPENDIX 5.1

A5.1.1: Show card to elicit legitimate and illegitimate reason for not being WTP towards an environmental good (here low flow alleviation in rivers).

a	I cannot afford to pay more water charges at present	
b	I have no interest in having different flow levels in rivers	
c	I would not pay any more in water charges but I would be prepared to pay by some other means of payment	
d	Someone else should pay rather than me	
e	The water company should pay, not customers	
f	Low levels in rivers are not a problem	
g	I require more information to answer this question	
h	Other reason. Please specify:	
i	Don't know	
j	Refused to answer	

Illegitimate answers are (c) [payment vehicle bias]; (d) [strategic bias]; (e) [bid vehicle bias]

A5.1.2: Show card to elicit legitimate and illegitimate reason for being willing to pay towards an environmental good (here water quality).

a	It was the most I could afford to pay	
b	Rivers and beaches are important for recreation and I am happy to pay to ensure that they are well looked after.	
c	I would pay this much each year to ensure that rivers and beaches are protected for future generations.	
d	Rivers and beaches are important for wildlife and ecology and I am happy to pay to ensure that they are well looked after.	
e	I wanted to show my support for environmental improvements in general	
f	It's an important issue and by saying I'd pay such a large sum each year I hope to get something done about it.	
g	I'm very concerned about this issue and although I'm not sure I could afford to pay this much each year I wish I could	
h	Rivers and beaches are important for a number of reasons and I am happy to pay to ensure that they are well looked after.	
i	Other reason. Please specify:	
j	Don't know	
k	Refused to answer	

Illegitimate answers are (e) [strategic bias]; (f) [strategic bias]; (g) [hypothetical bias]

APPENDIX 5.2

A Lindahl solution was proposed by Barnett and Yandle (1973). It allows an individual, within a community of individuals to express her preferences in terms of dollar votes, and thereby determine the desired level of environmental quality and simultaneously allocate shares in that level of quality amongst competing bidders. Faced with the problem, for example, of making the most efficient use of a watercourse: that is, determining the optimal level of water quality and allocating the resultant units of stream quality amongst competing uses, Barnet and Yandle envisage the controlling agency providing technical information to all interested parties on natural colour, odour, discharge levels, discharge charges to consumers (which will increase if more treatment before discharge is required), fishing and swimming consequences. This would be linked with detailed explanations of the damage to ecology of the area, the effects on employment, income, etc. of the various alternative compromises. Participants would then be allowed to bid dollar amounts for and against discharge privileges in some categories and for purity in others. In essence, positive and negative votes would be cast by the same individual. The bids would be tabulated to determine the equilibrium quality level.

In Figure A5.2.1, DCE is the summation of bids by purity lovers for withholding of waste. ACB represents the schedule of bids for waste discharge. W would be the optimal level of purity. Polluters would pay an amount equal to the area $OACW$ for their discharge rights, and would receive an amount equal to $WCBQ$ for their quasi rights foregone. Purity lovers would pay an amount $WCEQ$ and receive damages payments of $ODCW$. Thus some individuals would pay or receive a net amount after benefits had been accounted for, but, if an individual bids for and receives certain units of purity, she will pay for them. One of the advantages of an allocation model of this form is that each individual has something to gain by bidding as long as corner solutions do not result.

It is easy to see what would happen to a free-rider in this bidding process (Figure A5.2.2). Assume there are three individuals involved in the bidding process: A is interested in discharging waste; and B and C are purity lovers. Let A and B bid honestly, and let C be a free-rider, i.e. she plans not to bid at all. In Figure A5.2.2, XY represents the value of pollution rights as viewed by A; and HA the true value that B places on clean water. Since C has refused to bid, the level of purity outcome is W_I. At this level A pays $WXDW_I$ and receives W_IDYW_2 in damage payments. B pays an amount W_IDAW_2 and receives $WHDW_I$ in damage payments. C has avoided the payment $DGEA$ for the benefits she has received, but she has also incurred damages of $HFGD$ for which she has received no compensation. She has suffered a net loss by not bidding, and in the future she will be encouraged by the system to express her preferences honestly.

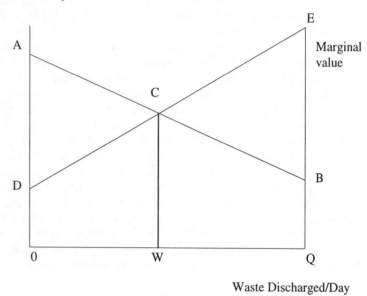

Figure A5.2.1   Determining optimum level of environmental quality

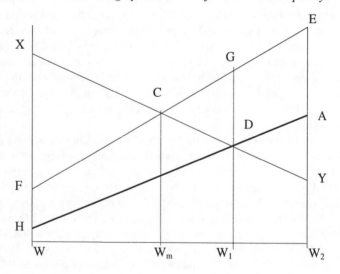

Figure A5.2.2 Determining optimum level of public goods: the free-rider case

Under this system, those individuals who underbid run the risk of receiving compensation payments that are less than the damage they expect to experience. If an individual overbids, she may pay more than the true valuation of the benefits received, should she be successful in receiving the items for which she bid. Of course, it is possible to overbid and receive larger payments than by bidding honestly, or to underbid and pay smaller amounts. To be successful in this strategy it is necessary to predict the final outcome of the system. Like any other market speculator she may win or lose, but the honest bidder will be assured of paying for value received and being paid for the value of rights foregone.

The question of transactions costs remains to be considered. In order to justify the organisation involved, all expenses must be covered by an amount left over to the authority after all payments are made and all charges received. In Figure A5.2.2 this amount would be *FXC* plus *YCE*. If this amount is not sufficient the process should either be abandoned or some other approach adopted.

6. Discrete Choice Methods

Thinking in terms of one
Is easily done -
One room, one bed, one chair,
One person there, makes perfect sense; one set
Of wishes can be met,
...
But counting up to two
Is harder to do;
For one must be denied
Before it's tried.

Philip Larkin (1926-85): *Counting*.

1 INTRODUCTION

Until the mid-1980s contingent valuation studies had been conducted using elicitation formats based on open-ended questions and iterative bidding games, either with or without the use of payment cards. Problems associated with these techniques led a number of researchers to investigate alternative elicitation formats that did not require respondents to construct their maximum WTP for a particular environmental good but instead asked them to choose between discrete alternatives relating to the specification of that good and its cost.

Discrete choice expressed preference questions generally require individuals to make decisions involving a trade-off between a sum of money and a specified change in environmental quality. The simplest examples involve the respondent accepting or rejecting a single option, while more complex applications may require respondents to rank a number of alternative options that are distinguished by the levels of the various attributes that they possess. Given the appropriate experimental design these choices can then be used to impute some measure of willingness to pay for the change in quality.

Discrete choice contingent valuation methods were the first to be utilised in an environmental economics context, followed by contingent ranking and stated preference choice experiments. To some extent, each of these approaches has benefited from the work carried out in the fields of psychology, economics, and marketing research, where practitioners have sought to understand how people process information, form preferences and subsequently make decisions that reflect these processes. In particular, random utility theory (Thurstone, 1927; McFadden, 1974) has proved to be important in modelling the decisions that individuals make when choosing between alternatives that offer different levels of environmental quality at different costs.

2 DISCRETE CHOICE CONTINGENT VALUATION METHODS

2.1 Description

One of the recommendations made by the US Department of Commerce's National Oceanic and Atmospheric Administration's (NOAA) Blue-Ribbon Panel on the use of contingent valuation in natural resource damage assessment for oil spills, was for the use of a discrete choice question format with a sample size of at least 1,000 respondents (Arrow *et al.*, 1993). The discrete choice question format, often referred to as referendum CVM, was introduced by Bishop and Heberlein (1979) and popularised in the mid 1980s in studies such as those by Sellar *et al.* (1985) and Bowker and Stoll (1988). By the mid-1990s this format had become the pre-eminent approach to contingent valuation in the US and elsewhere.

In referendum CVM the respondent is typically asked a question that attempts to elicit whether or not she is willing to pay a particular bid amount $X for a specified environmental improvement. This is analogous to the first round of an iterative bidding game but instead of continuing with further bids, the process typically stops here with the respondent's answer of 'Yes' or 'No' recorded along with the bid amount. The existence of only two possible choices has led to these questions being referred to as 'dichotomous' choice questions. Respondents may be given the opportunity to select a 'don't know' option or can refuse to answer but such responses are generally ignored in any subsequent analysis of the choice decisions.

On first inspection this procedure seems too limited to enable the researcher to say anything useful about maximum WTP. The only information that the researcher gains is, for example, that individual A is willing to pay

$10 for the environmental improvement, individual B is not willing to pay $20 for the same improvement, and so on. However, provided that the bid amounts are varied systematically across a large enough sample, the set of 'Yes'/'No' responses can subsequently be used to estimate a welfare measure such as mean or median WTP for the environmental improvement.

This is achieved by estimating the probabilities that respondents will say 'Yes' to the various bid amounts offered. As we shall see, measures of maximum WTP consistent with economic theory can be derived by modelling these probabilities using an appropriate statistical model.

Several advantages of referendum CVM are cited by its proponents. Firstly, it is argued that simple dichotomous choice questions are easier for respondents to answer than open-ended questions because they mimic the consumer-choice decisions that most of us make in our everyday lives. In addition, individuals answering dichotomous choice questions may never be fully aware of the purpose of the survey and are thus less able to identify and act on self-interested responses (although this property has been questioned as shall be shown subsequently).

Referendum Contingent Valuation

1   Identify the good or service to be investigated.

2   Develop a suitable experimental design for bid amounts

3   Design questionnaire survey and incorporate referendum CVM question.

4   Validate bids

5   Develop an appropriate model of willingness to pay

6   Estimate welfare measures based on willingness to pay

2.2 Bid Design in Referendum CVM

An important issue in the design of referendum CVM studies is the choice of monetary amounts used as bids. Cooper and Loomis (1992) demonstrated how sensitive welfare estimates were to the specification of bid amounts in referendum CVM, showing that in some cases WTP estimates varied by as much as 60 per cent across different specifications. Some authors (e.g. Mitchell and Carson, 1989; Holmes and Kramer, 1995) have contested that anchoring or starting-point bias due to bid selection may effect welfare estimates based on dichotomous choice questions, in much the same way as these effects have been observed to influence estimates based on bidding games. Similarly, selection of the highest amounts in the bid set may strongly influence WTP estimates (McFadden and Leonard, 1993).

Other authors (e.g. Schuman, 1996) have argued that the choice of bid amounts in referendum CVM is often made in an arbitrary way, or at the very best on the basis of a limited pilot survey. This may be the case in some applications, but in others considerable work is put into the appropriate selection of bid amounts. A variety of methods have been put forward to facilitate the choice of bids for referendum CVM. The majority of these methods are complex and involve considerable computational effort.

Boyle *et al.*, (1988), Cooper (1993), Elnagheeb and Jordan (1995) and Alberini (1995) have each provided approaches to the selection of bid amounts. Boyle *et al.*'s (1988) approach is relatively straightforward and relies on data from a pilot survey based on an open-ended question. The responses to the pilot survey are used to construct a WTP distribution from which bid amounts are generated. To yield an even number, n, of bid amounts, $n/2$ random numbers $(P_1, P_2, ..., P_{n/2})$ are generated from a uniform distribution on the interval $[0, 1]$ and these are used along with the additional $n/2$ numbers $(1 - P_1, 1 - P_2, ... , 1 - P_{n/2})$ to identify n quantiles along the bid distribution which after rounding form the bid amounts.

Cooper (1993) also utilised a distribution of WTP amounts based on a pilot open-ended survey to allocate bid amounts for referendum CVM. His approach was more sophisticated than Boyle *et al.*'s and required a considerably greater investment of computational effort to achieve increased statistical efficiency.

Alberini (1995) used a simulation approach to examine a number of optimal designs to estimate WTP based on referendum CVM surveys. Based on the assumption of a log-normally distributed WTP, Alberini derived designs for both conventional dichotomous choice questions and for those cases where follow-up questions are utilised after the initial round of bids. She found that the traditional format, coupled with an assumption of a log-normal distribution for WTP, performed well in terms of providing robust estimates of median WTP, though yielding somewhat less encouraging results in terms of estimating mean WTP. Designs based on the use of a follow-up question (termed double-bounded CVM) performed equally well for both mean and median WTP. Alberini's approach is relatively complex and requires knowledge of the distribution of WTP and some prior information about the parameters of the distribution; however, it does suggest how optimal designs could be devised for various assumptions about the distribution of WTP or for different elicitation formats.

Elnagheeb and Jordan (1995) used Monte-Carlo models of WTP to compare Boyle *et al.*'s estimates with Coopers' and an *ad-hoc* approach of their own. On comparison, the bids generated by each of the three methods were found to be highly correlated. Following this initial comparison, the next step was to simulate referendum CVM data by comparing each set of bid amounts with a set of WTP values generated by the Monte-Carlo analysis: if a particular bid amount was smaller than the WTP value a 'Yes' response was recorded, and if it was higher a 'No' response was specified. These simulated responses were used to estimate the mean and standard deviation of expected WTP and these estimates were then compared with the 'true' WTP values based on the Monte-Carlo simulation.

Elnagheeb and Jordan found that Boyle *et al.*'s method generally performed better than the two others, particularly when variation in WTP amounts was small. As variability and sample size increased, WTP estimates became more similar for each of the three approaches. Overall, both Cooper's and Boyle *et al.*'s approaches out-performed the *ad-hoc* approach when the latter was not based on pre-test data: this suggested that using bid amounts based on systematic analysis of pilot data may be preferable to using those generated on a more *ad hoc* basis.

This argument is developed by Hanemann and Kanninen (1998) in their discussion of the optimal experimental design for referendum CVM studies. They defined the objective of optimal experimental design in referendum CVM, as the provision of bid values that, for a given sample size, maximise the information about the parameters of the WTP distribution. Hanemann and Kanninen compared the performance of five simple bid designs in generating estimates of median WTP. They found that the design that performed best in terms of minimising bias and variance for individual parameter values and welfare measures was one where the bid values were specified fairly close to the true value of median WTP, and the design that performed worst was the one that placed the bids in the tails of the WTP distributions. They also found that increasing sample sizes had a considerable impact in reducing biases both in parameter estimates and estimated welfare measures.

Overall, they concluded that, provided the responses probability model was correctly specified, bid design had little impact on the point estimation of welfare measures but a substantial impact on the variance of these measures, especially in small samples. They recommended using sample sizes of between 500 and 1,000 where possible and not specifying bids in the tails of the estimated WTP distribution (e.g. the outer 12% of each tail for normal and logistic distributions). Thus, following a pilot survey using an open-ended CV question, the distribution of WTP values should be used to generate bid amounts that stay within the main body of the distribution and avoid the tails.

Another of Hanemann and Kanninen's findings was that optimal bid designs often required very few bids, a notion that may prove unattractive in practice, where an experimental design based only on, say, two bids may be seen to provide less flexibility and more scope for error in terms of estimating parameter values than one based on a larger number of bids. Hanemann and Kanninen sought to alleviate these concerns by recommending the sequential design of referendum CVM surveys as set out by Kanninen (1993).

Kanninen (1993) demonstrated that statistical efficiency improves if bid amounts are updated on a sequential basis within the survey. Thus, within this classification, the practice outlined above, where a pre-test is used to inform the experimental design of the referendum CV study, can be viewed as a two-stage procedure. Kanninen recommended that a number of iterations be performed, with the results at each stage being used to update the bid design. She found that efficiency gains diminished after three iterations. If several different bid values are used at each iteration then the overall number of bids used increases. Furthermore, the researcher retains the ability to change the shape and position of the WTP distribution across iterations by changing the functional specification of the model.

In cases of uncertainty about the true WTP distribution, Hanemann and Kanninen suggested using multiple bids based on the optimal designs for its most likely forms. Even then, they caution against using more than six bid amounts because increasing the number of bid points reduces the number of observations at each point and this practice may mean that bids from within the tails of the distribution are used.

2.3 Modelling Referendum CVM Data

Once the dichotomous choice question has been applied across the sample, the responses to the various bid amounts must be analysed. Responses can be validated by the inclusion of follow-up questions which investigate why respondents said 'Yes' or 'No' to the bid amount. Sometimes answers to follow-up questions may reveal that the response does not reflect 'true' WTP but was made under a misapprehension or for protest or strategic reasons. Follow-up questions may require respondents to choose reasons from a closed-ended set shown to them on a card: certain of these reasons would suggest that the response was not a genuine reflection of WTP. Follow-up questions can also be open-ended but this requires that the researcher analyse responses to determine whether or not the response to the dichotomous choice question was valid. Responses not deemed to be valid can be omitted from the analysis to avoid bias (of course, this itself could lead to a response bias if illegitimate bids were correlated with particular sections of the sample).

In addition to illegitimate responses, there will be a class of respondents who cannot, or will not, answer the dichotomous choice question and these must be considered separately. The remaining responses will correspond respectively to acceptance or rejection of the bid amount. From a modelling perspective this response set can be viewed as defining a discrete binary dependent variable with a 'No' response corresponding to 0 and a 'Yes' response corresponding to 1.

Models with discrete dependent variables are non-linear and cannot be estimated reliably using linear probability models such as those derived using ordinary least squares regression techniques. A number of statistical models are, however, capable of analysing data with discrete dependent variables. These models have been derived for a number of purposes, notably for the analysis of bioassay data. Only some of these models are consistent with the economic theory underlying contingent valuation and it is upon these that most attention has been focused.

Typically, the respondent to a referendum CVM question has to choose between two alternatives. The utility function for alternative i can be specified as:

$$U_i = V_i + e_i \qquad (6.1)$$

where U_I is the unobservable overall utility, V_i is the observable objective or deterministic component of utility and e_i is the stochastic or random component.

Assuming that the individual is a utility maximiser the probability that she will choose alternative i over alternative j is:

$$P_i = Prob[\ U_i > U_1 > U_2 > ... > U_{i-1} > U_{i+1} > ... > U_j\ ] \qquad (6.2)$$

Therefore:

$$P_i = Prob[\ (V_i + e_i) > (V_1 + e_1) > (V_2 + e_2) > ... > (V_{i-1} + e_{i-1}) >$$
$$(V_{i+1} + e_{i+1}) > ... > (V_j + e_j)\ ] \qquad (6.3)$$

So:

$$P_i = Prob[\ (e_1 - e_i) < (V_i - V_1),\ ...,\ (e_j - e_i) < (V_i - V_j)\ ] \qquad (6.4)$$

If the random terms are assumed to be independently, identically distributed with Weibull density functions, then the above probability can be expressed as a variant of McFadden's Mother Logit (MOL) model (McFadden, 1974):

$$P_i = exp\ [V_i]/\textstyle\sum exp\ [V_j] \tag{6.5}$$

Alternatively, if the error terms are thought to be normally distributed , the probability can be expressed in terms of a probit model. Dividing both numerator and denominator by $exp\ (V_i)$ yields the expanded form of the probability shown below:

$$P_i = 1 / \{\ 1 + exp\ [V_1 - V_i\ ] + exp\ [V_2 - V_i] + ... + exp\ [V_{i-1} - V_i\ ] +$$
$$exp\ [V_{i+1} - V_i] + ... + exp\ [V_j - V_i\ ]\ \} \tag{6.6}$$

In the bivariate case this compresses to an expression of the utility difference between choice i and choice j:

$$P_i = 1 / \{\ 1 + exp\ [V_j - V_i\ ]\ \} \tag{6.7}$$

The utility difference $[V_j - V_i\ ]$ can be expressed as a function of the characteristics of each choice and the associated price.

Now if we assume that choice i is a 'Yes' response to a referendum CVM question with bid amount X and choice j is a no response to the same question then:

$$P('Yes'\ response) = 1 / \{\ 1 + exp\ [f(X)]\} \tag{6.8}$$

where $f(X)$ is the functional specification of the utility difference (Hanemann, 1984).

The economic foundations of the statistical models used in the analysis of referendum CVM data, and in particular the underlying random utility framework, are far more complex than portrayed here and for a much fuller discussion of these issues readers are directed to Hanemann and Kanninen's (1998) extremely thorough exposition.

The logit model often used in the analysis of referendum data is a re-arranged version of equation (6.8) above:

$$log[\ P('Yes'\ response) / \{1 - P('Yes'\ response)\ \}\ ] = f(X) \tag{6.9}$$

The simplest case is where $f(X)$ is a simple linear function based only on the bid amount X. This can be extended by introducing a number of other explanatory variables based on the behaviour and preferences of the respondent. The choice of functional form may lead to widely different welfare estimates, as shown in a number of studies (e.g. Bowker and Stoll, 1988; Boyle, 1990). Where there are no clear statistical or theoretical grounds for preferring one specification over another, reliability requires that the resulting welfare estimates should be similar (Desvouges *et al.*, 1996): this criterion is often conveniently ignored by researchers.

A number of studies have claimed that conventional techniques for modelling referendum CVM responses do not adequately explain the variation in the observed data. For example, Langford (1994) detected over-dispersion in data generated by referendum CVM and suggested that this problem should be dealt with by including an over-dispersion factor in the model being estimated.

Additionally, Ozuna *et al.* (1993) provided misspecification tests for omitted explanatory variables, heteroscedastisity and for the incorrect specification of the underlying probability distribution. Using data from other referendum CVM studies (e.g. Bowker and Stoll, 1988; Bishop and Heberlein, 1979) they demonstrated that misspecification can lead to biases in maximum likelihood estimates and consequently to inconsistent parameter estimates and incorrectly estimated welfare measures. As there is little in the underlying economic theory to guide the choice of distribution, such problems may be relatively common.

The estimation procedures outlined in this section rely on the restrictive assumption of certain parametric specifications of the underlying probability distribution of the 'Yes' bids. These assumptions about the shape of the probability curve are quite strong and not readily testable and, as shown above, can lead to misspecification error.

The popularity of parametric estimation techniques such as logit and nested logit probably rests on the ease with which they can be applied using conventional econometric software packages, rather than on any advantages they have to offer from the point of view of estimation. A number of more robust estimators for the parameters of the indirect utility function relating to discrete choices have been developed by authors including Cosslett (1983; 1987) and Horowitz (1992; 1993), but have been utilised only infrequently by CVM practitioners, exceptions including studies by McFadden, (1994) and Li (1996).

The use of such estimators has been suggested on the basis that less restrictive probability estimates should be utilised in preference to more restrictive parametric specifications to derive welfare measures (Kriström, 1990; Hanemann and Kanninen, 1998). This has led to semi-parametric (e.g. Li, 1996; Creel and Loomis, 1997) and non-parametric approaches (e.g. Kriström, 1990; Scarpa *et al.*, 1998) to estimation, which impose fewer restrictions on the analysis.

Because non-parametric estimators rely on much weaker assumptions than their parametric counterparts, they are less prone to introduce bias through misspecification errors. Thus, appropriate maximum likelihood non-parametric estimators can be used to model the survival curves associated with the probability of accepting a given bid level. Such estimators can also deal with the censored or grouped data that might result from various referendum CVM applications. The disadvantage of such estimators is that they are relatively statistically inefficient and depend heavily on sample size and the specification of bid amounts.

2.4 Estimating Willingness to Pay from Referendum CVM Data

When an appropriate model of the set of referendum CVM bid decisions has been formulated, it is then necessary to calculate some measure of WTP. The logit model described above expresses the probability that a respondent agrees to pay a given bid amount. The probability surface associated with the logit model can be reduced to a simple two-dimensional form by substituting values for all explanatory variables apart from the bid amount. This leaves a logit curve with bid amounts on the horizontal axis and the probability of acceptance on the vertical axis.

If the values of the explanatory variables relate to a specific individual, then the resulting bid curve reflects the likelihood of that individual accepting each of the various bid amounts. It is more usual, however, to substitute values based on the whole sample (e.g. sample means) rather than on individuals, and the resulting bid curve can then be viewed as reflecting the probabilities that a randomly chosen individual from the sample will accept the given bid amounts.

The logit model can be used to calculate mean WTP. The method utilised by Duffield and Patterson (1991) requires the evaluation of equation (6.10) which is shown below:

$$E(WTP) = X_{max} - \int_0^{X_{max}} P(X)dX \qquad (6.10)$$

where $E(WTP)$ is mean WTP, X_{max} is the maximum bid amount and $P(X) = 1 - G(X)$, where $G(X)$ is the cumulative distribution function corresponding to $g(X)$, the probability distribution for a 'Yes' response.

This welfare measure is, in fact, the truncated mean WTP value, with the point of truncation taken to be the maximum bid (X_{max}), and is the measure preferred by Duffield and Patterson over both the median and the overall mean (where the truncation point is infinity), because of the desirable properties it possesses. These properties are its consistency with theoretical constraints, its statistical efficiency and its ability to be aggregated in a meaningful way. Duffield and Patterson argued that the choice of truncation point/maximum bid should be made with care in order that 'the welfare measure is based on the observed distribution and is not based on an extrapolation beyond that data.'

Haab and McConnell (1996) noted that welfare estimates could be inflated due to the use of parametric specifications of the cumulative probability function of affirmative bids. This is a result of the 'thick tails' problem where there is a high probability of obtaining a 'Yes' response to high bid values (Desvouges *et al.*, 1996). If the observed probability of making a high bid does not approach zero, then this has serious implications for setting the upper bound of the integral and hence for the derivation of the welfare estimate.

Evaluating the integral term in equation 6.10 is equivalent to integrating over the same limits for the curve defined by equation 6.8. To do this all of the explanatory variables used in the specification of equation 6.8, except bid amount, must be set to their mean values and the resulting function integrated. Integration may be carried out numerically using Simpson's rule (see most basic calculus texts, e.g. Kleppner and Ramsey, 1985). Mean WTP can then be obtained by subtracting the resulting figure from the maximum bid amount.

Median WTP can also be derived from the logit model by setting the probability of saying 'No' equal to 0.5, and solving for bid amount, with all other independent variables set at their mean values. The figure can be interpreted as the maximum amount that at least half of the population would be willing to pay for the environmental improvement. The process of evaluating median WTP is also described by Hanemann (1984), and is equivalent to finding Cameron's (1988) estimate of net WTP. Some authors (e.g. Duffield and Patterson, 1991) do not consider median WTP to be a suitable welfare measure in referendum CVM applications, because unlike the truncated mean, it cannot be aggregated over a population; however, other authors such as Hanemann (1984), have argued strongly regarding the merits of the median as the most suitable welfare measure.

2.5 Referendum CVM and Preference Uncertainty

It has been argued that one particular advantage that referendum CVM has over other elicitation formats is that respondents have no incentive to behave strategically (e.g. Arrow *et al.*, 1993). Thus, when a respondent is asked whether or not she is willing to pay $50 for a specific environmental improvement she has no reason to say 'Yes' unless her 'true' WTP for that improvement is at least $50. As Fisher (1996) pointed out, this assertion has little substance in situations where respondents feel that there is no credible mechanism to extract the payment. Thus, in the same way that a respondent who is only willing to pay up to $30 per year could strategically overstate this in an open-ended format and claim to be willing to pay a greater annual sum, so too could the same respondent state, through the medium of a dichotomous choice referendum CVM question, that she would be willing to pay an offered bid of $50 per year.

Indeed, in the referendum format this phenomenon may not necessarily be the result of strategic behaviour. The referendum format only allows the respondent one means of stating a positive preference for environmental improvement, and that is an affirmative response to the referendum CVM question. If a respondent's 'true' WTP $A is non-zero, but less than the referendum CVM amount $B, it is feasible that some respondents could still say they would pay $B, especially in cases where the two amounts were quite close. While such a response is illogical from a strictly economic viewpoint, it is consistent with the behaviour of respondents in other CV formats. This phenomenon is referred to explicitly in a number of papers as a manifestation of respondents' uncertainty about the true magnitude of their WTP for the non-market good in question (e.g. Li and Mattsson, 1995).

A related issue concerns the frequency of implausible responses in referendum CVM applications. Typically, the maximum bid amount used in the application is expected to have a probability of being accepted that is close to zero. This expectation is based either on the results of pilot open-ended questions about the same good or on other CV studies relating to similar goods. In a number of studies it has been observed that significant numbers of respondents vote to pay these relatively high bids. These responses may be due to the framing of the questionnaire or may be due to the respondent. For example, Schuman (1996) suggested that the inclusion of a 'don't know' option may reduce this problem as respondents can avoid the problem of ambivalence that may arise when respondents would otherwise have to refuse to pay for something that they may be strongly in favour of.

The field of experimental economics has also contributed evidence that may cast doubt on the usefulness of referendum CVM. This evidence is based on the investigation of posted-offer markets, where over a number of trials respondents decide whether or not to purchase a good at the prices specified. Such markets are found to perform poorly in early rounds, when respondents are inexperienced, but to improve as practice and familiarity lead respondents to make better decisions. Generally, the poor performance is reflected in respondents agreeing in early rounds to purchase goods at too high a price (Davis and Holt, 1993).

Referendum CVM is essentially offering respondents the same choice as a posted-offer market: accept or reject a good at the given price. Unlike the trials of the posted offer market this choice is not repeated and respondents are only exposed to the first-round bid where in posted-offer markets respondents are found to perform worst. If responses to referendum CVM applications are formulated in a similar manner to those of posted-offer markets, then this could suggest that referendum CVM responses may systematically over-estimate WTP (Schulze *et al.*, 1996). Similarly, it may also suggest that over repeated experiments responses should become more realistic.

Preference uncertainty may also be the result of ambivalence on the part of the respondent. Ready *et al.* (1995) discussed the problems that arise when respondents to referendum CVM surveys are ambivalent about the choices they are asked to make regarding trade-offs between monetary amounts and levels of environmental quality. This arose from an examination of the results of two separate studies where split-sample comparisons were made of the results of referendum CVM questions using two different elicitation formats. These studies permitted the authors to examine the width of the region of ambivalence in terms of responding to referendum CVM questions, that is, the region where respondents are unsure whether to accept or reject the price quality trade-off they are offered. It was hypothesised that conventional referendum questions requiring 'Yes'/'No' answers may force respondents to make choices when they feel ambivalent and that this may have an impact on estimated WTP.

The first format used in each study was a conventional dichotomous choice question, while the second format allowed respondents to demonstrate ambivalence by offering them six different responses within a polychotomous choice (PC) framework, which expressed intensity of preference for the amenity/cost trade-off offered to them in place of the baseline level of environmental amenity (e.g. 'definitely yes', 'probably yes', 'maybe yes', 'maybe no', 'probably no', 'definitely no').

The authors found that levels of respondent ambivalence, based on the PC approach, were relatively high; however, this approach generated a higher proportion of 'Yes' responses than the conventional approach. The higher level of 'Yes' responses in the PC approach in turn generated higher estimates of value than the conventional dichotomous choice question. It was argued that this resulted from the fact that the PC approach allowed 'Yes' responses to be made less strongly than in the conventional approach and encouraged more of the ambivalent respondents to vote in favour of the offer. Balanced against this, was the suggestion that the greater ease and reduced commitment of a 'Yes' answer in the PC approach might provoke more poorly-considered responses. Furthermore, the PC approach may provide too much opportunity for 'fence sitting' behaviour. This lack of care in answering questions was highlighted by greater variability in estimated WTP for the PC approaches compared with the conventional approach.

The study led Ready *et al.* to conclude that referendum-type CVM questions tended to induce ambivalent respondents to adopt a conservative strategy where they reject any move away from current levels of environmental quality. This is reflected in ambivalent respondents answering 'No' to a referendum bid, when in reality they may actually be willing to accept the trade-off being offered. This type of induced behaviour may have the effect of lowering estimated WTP. Even so, the conventional approach led to more carefully considered responses and should be preferred to the PC approach, especially if ambivalence can be reduced by improved information, more practice or inducements to take more time and trouble responding.

2.6 Comparison of Open-ended and Referendum CVM Formats

A number of studies have compared open-ended and referendum CVM responses (e.g. Bishop *et al.*, 1983; Sellar *et al.*, 1985; Kealy and Turner, 1993; Garrod and Willis 1995; etc.) Most of these have shown that mean WTP estimates based on referendum CVM responses are between 1.5 and 4 times as large as those based on open-ended questions. Of course, mean WTP can vary for a number of reasons apart from question format (e.g. payment vehicle and other aspects of the context of the questionnaire) but in most comparisons the only substantive difference between the samples was the format of the WTP question.

Kealy and Turner (1993) devised a parametric test to investigate the null hypothesis that both open-ended and referendum CVM generate identical estimates of sample mean WTP. They found that the differences in mean WTP between these two formats was statistically significant. Schulze *et al.* (1996) looked at six studies that elicited both open-ended and referendum CVM responses and found that in five of the six referendum CVM estimates were higher than open-ended estimates. They went on to suggest that this result was consistent with the evidence from experimental economics, where Vickrey, or English, Auctions, which like open-ended CVM questions require respondents to state their maximum WTP for a good, perform more efficiently in early rounds than posted-offer markets. On average, referendum CVM estimates of WTP were found to be seven times higher than the open-ended equivalents, though the median difference was closer to two times higher. This compared with UK comparisons (e.g. Garrod and Willis, 1995) where referendum estimates were between three and four times higher than open-ended ones.

In another development, Neill *et al.* (1994) designed a set of experiments (using Vickrey auctions) to investigate whether or not respondents' 'true' WTP is reflected in the bids made to open-ended CVM questions. They found that WTP based on hypothetical WTP questions was consistently higher than WTP reflecting real economic commitments and concluded that these variations were due to differences between the real and hypothetical payment mechanisms used. Coupled with the observation that WTP estimates based on referendum CVM questions tend to be higher than those based on open-ended questions, this result provides further food for thought for those practitioners using referendum CVM to generate welfare measures.

2.7 Referendum CVM with Follow-up Questions: Multiple Bounded CVM

In order to improve the statistical efficiency of traditional referendum CVM, some authors (e.g. Cameron and James, 1987) have proposed that a further round of bids follow the first round, with the level of the second bid dependent upon the response to the first, i.e. an affirmative response to the first bid amount would lead to the respondent being asked about a higher amount, while a rejection of the first bid would lead to the second bid amount being lower. The assumption underlying the resulting analysis is that identical value distributions are elicited by both the initial and the follow-up questions (Cameron and Quiggin, 1994). Some studies (e.g. Langford *et al.*, 1996) have even investigated the effects of including a second follow-up question.

Kanninen (1992 and 1993) investigated the optimal design of such multiple-bounded experiments and sought to address issues such as the specification of the values that should be used in the follow-up questions and the use of sequential estimation techniques as outlined earlier in this chapter to improve the efficiency of WTP estimation. Alberini (1995) investigated optimal bid design for double-bounded CVM and found that though this approach reduced statistical efficiency for the estimation of median WTP this was compensated by the improved information that the approach provided regarding the shape of the WTP distribution. Adding further rounds of bids after the second was found to reduce statistical efficiency but not dramatically.

The follow-up question approach may compound the problems of referendum CVM and a number of authors have shown responses to double-bounded CVM questions to be inconsistent (e.g. Cameron and Quiggin, 1994). If the first response is more likely to over-estimate true WTP than under-estimate it (as evidence would suggest) then following up an affirmative response with a question based on a higher bid amount can only compound the initial error. Indeed, as Schulze *et al.* (1996) point out, experience with posted-offer markets suggests that bids subsequent to the first should, on average, be rationalised downwards, a contingency not allowed for in this approach.

In acknowledging this problem, Cameron and Quiggin (1994) argued that, in the analysis of referendum CVM questions with a follow-up, it is crucial to acknowledge the imperfect correlation between the responses to the two valuation questions. They demonstrate that the assumption that the same implicit value underpins the response to both questions (i.e. assuming that the underlying value distributions are the same), can introduce potentially serious distortions into valuation estimates. The authors go on to suggest that the respondent's underlying 'true' value may not be fixed and rather than having some point valuation, respondents have some form of distribution of WTP values that they draw upon to answer these types of question. The follow-up question may thus draw upon a different value to that used to answer the initial question.

Such an argument allows for respondent uncertainty about their 'true' WTP value. A study reported in Li and Mattsson (1995), proposed a model that accommodates respondent uncertainty about their true values for an environmental good. In their paper, Li and Mattsson attempted to extend the theoretical framework of previous studies by introducing preference uncertainty in individuals' responses. They assumed that respondents had incomplete knowledge about their 'true' valuation of the good in question and were, thus, capable of giving wrong answers to referendum-type questions about their WTP. To characterise preference uncertainty, Li and Mattsson attempted to elicit a post-decisional confidence measure on each 'Yes/No' answer. Their model allowed them to identify the degree of preference uncertainty for each respondent, and thus adjust the conventional standard deviation estimates in order to re-estimate mean WTP. Using data on the valuation of forests in Northern Sweden for recreational purposes, the authors found that incorporating preference uncertainty into their models reduced overall estimates of mean WTP by about six times. This suggests that ignoring preference uncertainty in dichotomous choice CVM questions with a follow-up can lead to serious over-estimation of welfare estimates.

Herriges and Shogrun (1996), in a further study of the effect of following up traditional dichotomous choice CVM questions, generated results that suggested that some form of starting-point bias could be present in this format. This would result from respondents anchoring subsequent bids to the initial bid presented to them. Herriges and Shogrun demonstrated that even if the analysis corrected for this effect, the resulting losses in statistical efficiency were almost as great as those gained from the follow-up questions.

Alberini *et al.* (1997) also examined the use of referendum-format questions with follow-ups. Like Li and Mattsson (1995), they derived a structural adaptation to the double-bounded model, but this time the adaptation is made in order to reflect response incentive effects such as starting-point bias, yea-saying (see Holmes and Kramer, 1995) and ambivalence (see Ready *et al.*, 1995). Their paper makes the valuable point that it is important to develop a comprehensive theoretical framework that allows CVM researchers to fully understand how respondents deal with the valuation task and how incentives faced by respondents and the information available to them may influence their responses. All too often, as Alberini *et al.* point out, researchers are tempted to impose econometric solutions on CVM data that are not guided by an understanding of how the underlying preferences and values are constructed.

The studies reported here suggest that the use of follow-up questions to referendum WTP produces data that must be treated with some caution. The conventional assumption that responses result from the same underlying 'true' value may introduce serious upward biases in estimates of mean WTP. The possibility of preference uncertainty, and its effects on the reliability of responses in referendum format questions, may be combated through improving the models used to estimate mean WTP. It remains to be seen whether or not these models produce estimates that are sufficiently reliable to justify the continued widespread use of this approach.

3 CHOICE EXPERIMENTS

3.1 Description

Contingent valuation exercises concentrate on the valuation of a particular scenario, like the return of river flows to a given level, or a particular environmental quality change. This requires researchers to concentrate on providing adequate information about the scenario for the respondent to judge the quality change. The results of these exercises tend to provide information on preferences for the whole scenario rather than for a specific aspect of it.

In contrast to this, choice experiments can be used to examine the response of the individual to changes in the attributes of the scenario, as well as to the scenario as a whole. Thus, rather than examining the entire scenario as a package, the choice experiment approach allows researchers to break down the relevant attributes of the situation and determine preferences over attributes. While this task is more abstract than that in contingent valuation, it allows for increased flexibility in the analysis because the attributes themselves can be valued, as well as the overall scenario. This valuation of attributes can be a significant advantage of choice experiments over traditional contingent valuation methods. Indeed, if there is some uncertainty about the final attribute levels, the results of choice experiments can be used to determine the values for each possible outcome. Contingent valuation methods, on the other hand, tend to provide a single value for an expected quality change.

While they have only recently been used in environmental valuation exercises (for example, Adamowicz *et al.,* 1994; Roe *et al.,* 1996), choice experiments and similar techniques have been utilised by psychologists since the 1960s, and in transportation and marketing research since the early 1970s (Louviere, 1988a; 1996). Choice experiments may be found in the literature under a variety of guises, and confusion may arise from the different terms which are used to describe the various techniques which fall into this category.

Stated preference and stated choice are terms found in transportation literature to describe some of the discrete choice experiments used in that field (e.g. Kroes and Sheldon, 1988; Wardman, 1988; Ouwersloot and Rietveld, 1996) and these terms have also been used by some environmental economists (e.g. Adamowicz *et al.*, 1994). In marketing, the discipline of conjoint analysis (e.g. Green and Srinivasan, 1978; Cattin and Wittink, 1982) has been used in commercial and academic contexts to determine consumer preferences for product attributes and embraces a number of choice-based techniques including: trade-off matrices; card sorts; hierarchical choice; the transfer price method; and various forms of preference-based analysis.

While the various terms attempt to describe some of the particular nuances of the choice-based techniques available to practitioners, these approaches all share common goals, among the most of important of which is the determination of how consumers construct preferences for goods and services. Broadly speaking, these techniques attempt to identify the utility that individuals have for the attributes of these goods or services by examining the trade-offs that they make between them when making choice decisions.

Underlying all of these techniques is microeconomic theory and the notion that utility or value is derived from attributes of a particular good or situation (e.g. Lancaster, 1966). Thus, most choice experiments are predicated on the assumption that preferences are not based on single attributes but are based jointly on several attributes (hence the derivation of the term 'conjoint' analysis). Random utility theory, originally proposed by Thurstone (1927) to model dominance judgements in paired comparisons, may be used to model choice decisions, as may decision-theoretic techniques based on psychological paradigms (Louviere, 1996).

Despite this common ground, choice experiments continue to be conducted in a variety of ways. One frequently used approach is the use of 'profiles' to describe the good or service being researched. Profiles are defined by the levels of the individual attributes which are used to define the good and the specification and choice of these attributes forms an important part of the research process. A study may be designed to identify the profile which offers the greatest utility for consumers or to determine the contribution made by individual attribute levels to the overall utility provided by the good.

Profiles may be used in a number of different ways but most applications involve some form of survey where respondents are asked to study a series of profiles and then make choices based on their preferences for them: these choices are often similar to those that they would make in a real-world context. The set of profiles shown to respondents is generally determined by some form of experimental design. This is necessary to limit the task facing respondents. For example, a good could be defined using five attributes, three with three levels and two with four levels. The number of possible profiles resulting from this specification is 432 (i.e. 3 x 3 x 3 x 4 x 4) and respondents could not be expected to evaluate more than a small fraction of these. Appropriate experimental designs will reduce the number of profiles shown to respondents while at the same time permitting useful results to be obtained.

The task that respondents are set may be to rank a given set of profiles, or to rate them, perhaps using some form of semantic difference scale. Alternatively, respondents may be asked to make choices based on pairwise comparisons of profiles, or to select their most preferred profile from a small set (with or without the option not to select any of the profiles offered). Often respondents are asked to perform these tasks a number of times; this is often the case when smaller sets of profiles are involved.

3.2 Choice Experiments for Environmental Valuation

In environmental valuation studies, the profiles used in choice experiments define the key attributes of an environmental good or service in question, and individual profiles offer varying levels of these attributes and thus provide different levels of utility to individuals. The random utility framework adopted by economists to explain choice decisions suggests that, when given the choice between several alternatives, consumers attempt to select the one that they like best (i.e. that offers them the most utility) subject to various constraints (e.g. income, information).

Choice Experiments

1   *Identify the good or service to be investigated.*

2   *Identify key attributes and determine the attribute levels to be used.*

3   *Develop an appropriate experimental design for profiles.*

4   *Design questionnaire survey and incorporate choice experiments.*

5   *Perform pre-tests and undertake survey.*

6   *Analyse choices made and determine trade-offs made by respondents.*

7   *Calculate welfare measures.*

8   *Aggregate over population of relevance.*

The commonest approach to choice experiments is to present individuals with several profiles (or alternatives) and ask them to choose which one, if any, they most prefer. Single or repeated choices from various sets of alternatives reveals the trade-offs that an individual will make between attributes.

The research process involves: (1) initial screening of the attribute and levels of attributes for the situation at hand, (2) development of an experimental design that constructs the combinations of attributes that will be presented to the respondents, (3) analysis of the choices made (see Batsell and Louviere, 1991).

3.3 Initial Screening of the Attributes

The definition of attributes and attribute levels for use in a choice experiment is a crucial stage in the study design. Generally, environmental goods or services can be characterised by a number of component attributes and the choice among these is a key issue for the researcher. For example, water quality could be characterised by the levels of various pollutants, by flow levels, or by the numbers of various types of organism that it supports. Often experience and common sense will identify the most important attributes. Attributes should be familiar and relevant to respondents and their levels should be measurable in a meaningful way using quantitative or qualitative scales.

The way in which attributes are portrayed may also be important. In marketing applications, product attributes can be described using words, pictures or even a mock-up of the product in question. Similarly, in environmental valuation, verbal or pictorial representations may be used to portray attributes and attribute levels. Some further explanation may be required to enable respondents to fully grasp the implications of the descriptions offered. For example, an attribute may be given three levels described on the profiles as low, medium or high, and some additional detail in a factsheet or brochure may be needed to ensure that respondents have a clear and consistent understanding of what these levels mean in relation to one another. In this respect, choice experiments may be subject to problems of framing and information provision similar to those encountered in contingent valuation studies. Pre-testing and focus groups should prove useful in helping researchers to define attributes in an optimal way.

Defining attributes is only part of the task facing researchers. It is also important to define an appropriate number of attributes. For example, including too many attributes in the profile may place too great a burden on respondents, while too few will cause problems with estimation and reliability. Often there will be a number of key attributes that are responsible for the majority of the utility provided by a good or service. It is upon these that the study should concentrate. If necessary, these can also be determined in pre-tests and through focus group research. It is also necessary to specify attributes that are independent of each other to avoid problems of multicollinearity which will prevent the meaningful derivation of attribute utilities.

Considerable thought must be given to the attribute levels to be used in constructing the profiles. Too few levels may impede the analysis while too many would make commonly used experimental designs infeasible. A balance must be drawn between realism and experimental necessity and a number of levels must be chosen within a realistic range based on *a priori* experience with the environmental good in question.

3.4 Experimental Design

In order to reduce the magnitude of the task facing respondents and to reduce the computational complexity of estimation, the desired set of attributes and attribute levels can be used to define the profiles through the specification of a factorial or fractional factorial experimental design to estimate the utility function for the good in question. Complete factorial designs typically offer a huge number of combinations of profiles and the design problem condenses down into the question of how to sample from the complete factorial design in such a way that all parameters of interest can be estimated with reasonable statistical efficiency (Adamowicz *et al.*, 1994).

A common approach to this is to use an orthogonal main-effects plan, sampled from the complete factorial design, to select the profiles to be used in the choice experiment (Louviere and Woodworth, 1988; Louviere, 1988a). The main effects are defined as the responses generated when moving from one level of a given attribute to the next, whilst holding the level of all of the other attributes constant.

Use of strictly additive main-effects designs means that the utility function must be estimated based on the assumption that any higher order and interaction terms are insignificant and that consumer preferences depend upon individual attribute levels alone and are not influenced by the combination of levels offered across different attributes (Louviere, 1988b). Of course, if this is not the case and the data is not strictly additive, the main-effects design may produce biased welfare estimates. Furthermore, use of this design means that this eventuality cannot be tested for and that there will be no way of measuring the magnitude of any resultant bias (Louviere, 1996). More encouragingly, Louviere (1988b) suggested that the main effects element of the utility function explains around 80% of observed variation in choices, with second and third-order interaction terms tending to explain less than

10% of the remaining variation, with higher order terms accounting for little or no variation.

To facilitate the use of main effects designs, procedures in computer packages, such as SAS or SPSS, may be used to create an orthogonal matrix based on the attribute levels specified by the researcher. This design eliminates collinearity between attributes and implies that only strictly additive main effects utilities can be evaluated on the basis of the choice experiment.

3.5 Analysis of the Choices

Since individuals are asked to choose one alternative from each set of profiles shown to them, random utility theory may be used to model the choices as a function of attribute levels. Random utility theory is based on the hypothesis that individuals make choices based on the attributes of the alternatives (an objective component) along with some degree of randomness (a random component). This random component arises either because of randomness in the preferences of the individual or the fact that the researcher does not have the complete set of information available to the individual. The utility function for alternative i can be specified as:

$$U_i = V_i + e_i \tag{6.11}$$

where U_i is the unobservable overall utility, V_i is the observable objective component of utility and e_i is the random component.

V_i is a conditional indirect utility function which is generally assumed to be linear in form:

$$V_i = \beta_1 + \beta_2 x_{i2} + \beta_3 x_{i3} + \beta_3 x_{i3} + \dots + \beta_m x_{im} \tag{6.12}$$

where x_{im} are the attributes of the alternative including price.

If an individual chooses alternative i over j, then U_i must be greater than U_j. Based on repeated observations of choices, one can examine how the levels of various attributes affect the probability of choice. A number of different assumptions can be made about the distribution of the random term. An assumption of normality (e.g. Thurstone, 1927) leads to the binary probit model, while the assumption of a Gumbel distribution (e.g. McFadden, 1974) means that the multinomial or Mother Logit can be employed to examine the factors explaining the choice of one alternative over another.

Indeed, most choice experiments are designed under the assumption that the decision process can be modelled using an MOL approach. The MOL approach is based on the estimation of likelihoods and odds and is thus highly suitable for examining questions of choice. Typically, choices are predicted based on the premise that respondents attempt to maximise their utility.

Unlike some of the simpler models commonly used in regression analysis, Logit models are neither linear nor additive, rather they assume an S-shaped or sigmoidal response curve. When used to model utilities logit models may be seen to provide a realistic framework within which to investigate consumer choices. Where utilities are near zero the curve is flat suggesting that large increases in utility are necessary before consumers are stimulated into thinking about a particular choice. The steeper middle section illustrates how smaller increases in utility can lead to strong interest in a choice that individuals are already interested in. The flattening off of the curve towards the end equates diminishing marginal utility to a levelling off in interest.

A key assumption of the MOL model is the independence of irrelevant alternatives (IIA). In practice this means that the researcher assumes that the probability of choosing one alternative in preference to another is not influenced by other available alternatives that are not being considered. Thus, in a pairwise comparison the choice between the two profiles on offer is assumed not to be influenced by the possibility that other profiles could be chosen. Some critics regard this assumption as a flaw in choice experiment methodology, arguing that consumers consider all available choices before making a decision. Conversely, it can be argued that when individuals are asked to choose only one of a given set of alternatives they will make that choice without reference to other alternatives that they could have been offered.

Fortunately, the MOL approach based on a fractional factorial orthogonal main effects design provides the means of testing the validity of the IIA assumption for a given choice experiment (Adamowicz *et al.*, 1994). Econometric packages, such as LIMDEP (Greene, 1995), provide simple tests of this assumption.

The assumption of a linear utility function in 6.12 may be argued to be a matter of convenience rather than of economic theory. The assumption of a non-linear utility function (generally expressed in an additive linear form) would require an experimental design that allows for interaction and higher order terms, not just main effects. This increases the costs of the design stage and has implications for data collection and analysis. Exclusion of interaction and higher-order terms from the model may, in many circumstances, have only a limited effect; however, if these terms are significant, then errors may be introduced into the estimated coefficient values. Thus, while incorporating these forms in the model will increase the complexity of the experimental design considerably and complicate the analytical process, in a minority of cases this could lead to significantly more robust welfare estimates.

Ouwersloot and Rietveld (1996) explored the influence of autocorrelation effects in choice experiment data caused by individual respondents making multiple choices. This approach is frequently used in choice experiments as a means of providing additional data without having to undertake more interviews; however, it has the unwanted side-effect of introducing interdependency problems in the error structure of the model (autocorrelation) which are ignored in conventional logit and probit analysis. Using an estimation procedure derived from the literature on the analysis of panel data, Ouwersloot and Rietveld demonstrated that it was possible to account for autocorrelation effects in data based on repeated choices. Analysis of their case, however, showed that the effects of autocorrelation in their discrete choice model were statistically insignificant, though this may not necessarily be the case in other applications.

3.6 Welfare Measurements from Choice Experiments

Since choice experiments are based on random utility theory, welfare economic principles developed for random utility models can be employed (Hanemann, 1984) to analyse the welfare impacts of a change. To demonstrate how welfare measurements can be calculated from random utility models based on choice experiments, consider the most simple choice experiment where respondents are asked to choose between a base case and an alternative. In this case individuals must choose between one profile which does not require any payment and another profile which does. The latter profile also includes enhanced environmental attributes. By choosing between these two profiles, respondents provide data from which the value of the enhanced environmental conditions can be determined.

Following Hanemann (1984) let the utility of the situation without the enhancement (at no additional cost) be represented by:

$$V(Y, 0) \tag{6.13}$$

where V is utility, Y is income and 0 indicates no environmental enhancement. Let the improved situation be represented by:

$$V(Y\text{-}C, 1) \tag{6.14}$$

where C is cost and 1 indicates the enhanced environmental condition. In the random utility context, the individual must choose between:

$$V(Y,0) \text{ and } V(Y\text{-}C,1) \tag{6.15}$$

If the individual chooses the second option, then she is willing to pay at least $C for the environmental improvement. Analysis of such comparisons over various specifications of the amount $C reveals the probability of supporting the environmental improvement, as a function of the payment required. A welfare measure proposed by Hanemann (1984) is the median, that is the payment $C_m that would result in at least half of the sample choosing the profile offering an environmental improvement.

As Adamowicz *et al.* (1995) show, extending this simple choice to multiple attributes is relatively easy. Rather than representing the environmental improvement by a single value (1 or 0) the improvement is defined across two attributes, i.e. two arguments in the utility function. Now the utility function without any improvements can be written as $V(Y,0,0)$ and this situation can be compared to $V(Y-C,1,0)$, $V(Y-C,0,1)$ and $V(Y-C,1,1)$. Each improvement can then be compared to the base situation and the marginal value of improvements can be analysed.

Where MOL is used to specify a linear in parameters model describing the decision process underlying the choice experiment the coefficient values on attributes can be used directly to determine at the relative utilities across attributes. Where cost is included, a monetary value can be placed on the utility resulting from a change in attribute levels.

4 THE CONTINGENT RANKING METHOD

4.1 Description

The contingent ranking method offers an alternative approach to choice experiments by asking respondents to rank their choices rather than just choose the one that they most prefer. The technique has been used relatively infrequently for the valuation of environmental goods and has not received the same level of scrutiny as contingent valuation and conventional choice experiments. Nevertheless, the underlying model is of some interest and we shall report it here along with some of the criticisms commonly levelled at the technique.

4.2 The Underlying Model

In contingent ranking (CR) a sample of individuals is required to rank a discrete set of alternatives from their most to their least preferred. Each alternative in the choice set differs from the others in the levels of its component attributes. The attribute values of each alternative are subsequently used along with the observed rankings to estimate a discrete choice, utility maximising model for the sample data. The estimated parameters of this model are then used to estimate the trade-off which respondents make between disposable income and an improvement in the provision of the commodity (e.g. environmental quality) described in the choice sets. The model can be used to generate an income compensated measure of WTP for a specified environmental improvement.

Most applications in the literature follow the methodology developed by Beggs *et al.* (1981) to assess the demand for the attributes of electric cars. An alternative exposition can be found in Chapman and Staelin (1982), who analysed rank order data on college choices in an MOL framework based on the ranking theorem of Luce and Suppes (1965). A number of studies subsequently adopted the methodology of Beggs *et al.* including: Rae *et al.* (1986) for estimating WTP for improved visibility in US National Parks; Desvouges *et al.* (1983) in their comprehensive study of water quality issues; Garrod and Willis (1997) for valuing forest biodiversity; and Foster and Mourato (1997) for valuing multiple environmental impacts from pesticide use.

Beggs *et al.* used a purpose built discrete-choice model to analyse the data from a CR exercise. Their model made full use of the ranked data and in so doing represented an extension of the approaches typically used to model data where the dependent variable represents an ordered response. Traditional ordered-response models are used in cases where each respondent falls into one of a given number of categories each of which can be ordered relative to the others (e.g. educational attainment categories: did not complete secondary education; completed secondary education; went on to further education; went on to higher education; educated to postgraduate level). These categories are used as the basis of an ordinal dependent variable (e.g. the five educational attainment categories listed above would be coded respectively as 0, 1, 2, 3 and 4). Ordinal-level probit models (e.g. McKelvey and Zavoina, 1975) and logit models (e.g. Gurland *et al.*, 1960) have been applied in the analysis of such data for many years.

The CR case with *j* alternatives in the choice set does not generate a single response for each respondent but rather *j* responses where each response is differentiated by the rank of a given alternative and by the levels of the attributes of that alternative. Thus, the data from a CR exercise is akin to the panel data used in time-series analysis and requires a different form of analysis from simple ordered-response data.

The discrete-choice model used to estimate the parameters of the CR model takes advantage of the greater set of information provided by a full set of ranked choices. Information on the first choice of respondent i, say alternative k, merely indicates that respondent i's utility for that alternative, i.e. U_{ik}, exceeds her utility for any other alternative in the choice set. Thus, for any given alternative a probability model based on this level of data merely gives the probability that a respondent's utility for that alternative exceeds that for all other alternatives. With a full set of rankings, information is provided on the respondent's relative utilities for each of the j alternatives, and a probability model based on this ordered data will yield the probability of a complete ordering:

$$i.e. \; pr \, [\; U_{i1} > U_{i2} > ... > U_{iJ}] \tag{6.16}$$

Beggs *et al.* specify the following random utility model:

$$U_{ij} = V \, (s_i, \, x_{ij}) + \varepsilon_{tj} = V_{ij} + \varepsilon_{tj} \tag{6.17}$$

where s_i is a vector of the attributes of respondent i; x_{ij} is a vector of the attributes of the choice set (for $j = 1, ,..., J$); V_{ij} is the utility for the representative respondent; and ε_{ij} is a stochastic component which is assumed to follow some distribution function. When this distribution function is assumed to be logistic Beggs *et al.* derived the following expression for 6.16 (note that for generality the subscript for individuals is dropped):

$$pr \, [\; U_1 > U_2 > ... > U_i \,] = \prod_{j=1}^{J} \{ exp(V_j) / [\; \sum_{k=j}^{J} exp(V_k)] \} \tag{6.18}$$

Assuming that the indirect utility function V is linear in parameters, a likelihood function is then derived defining the joint probabilities of the rank orderings as a function of the parameters of the indirect utility function. The method of maximum likelihood is then used to find the coefficients of the indirect utility function which maximise the probability that a given respondent ranks the alternatives in the order they were actually selected. While the estimated coefficients of V are constant across the sample, indirect utility varies because the parameters of the function (i.e. household socio-economic and demographic characteristics, attribute levels in the ranked choice set) vary across respondents.

4.3 Estimating Welfare Measures

The basic methodology used in early contingent ranking studies was extended by Lareau and Rae (1989) in their investigation of preferences for reductions in diesel odours and their ranked data model is now the most common approach to contingent ranking. Lareau and Rae used the estimators generated by the above procedure to derive expressions to demonstrate the trade-off between attribute levels and disposable income. They assumed an indirect utility function of the following form:

$$V = \alpha e + \mu c \qquad (6.19)$$

where c is a vector of the costs associated with given levels of environmental quality and e is a vector of the level of the environmental attributes used in the choice set. According to welfare economic theory a respondent's maximum WTP for the increase in environmental quality generated by a unit increase in e will be such that the respondent's overall level of utility remains constant, i.e. the increase in welfare brought about by a change in e *(Δe)* will be matched by the decrease in welfare represented by the change in cost of environmental quality *(Δc)*. The change in cost relative to the change in quality is the ratio $-\alpha/\mu$. In the case of an environmental improvement α is *a priori* assumed to be positive (an environmental improvement leads to increased amenity and therefore increased utility), while μ is assumed to be negative. Thus, the ratio of the two coefficients is expected to be negative and a more substantial environmental improvement should lead to a positive WTP.

Lareau and Rae introduced more complex specifications for the indirect utility function involving income and vectors of demographic and socio-economic variables S_i and S_j which interact respectively with e and c.

$$\text{e.g. } V = \alpha e + \mu c + \theta \, [c/I] + \sum \tau_i \, e \, S_i + \sum \tau_j \, e \, S_j \qquad (6.20)$$

where I is household income. The socio-economic and demographic variables must be entered interactively as they are specific to each respondent and invariant across the ranked alternatives. The WTP/income trade-off can be derived by taking first order partial derivatives of the indirect utility function with respect to e and c and is the following form:

$$\Delta c / \Delta e = - (\alpha + \sum \tau_i \, S_i) / (\mu + \theta/I + \sum \tau_j \, S_j) \qquad (6.21)$$

Where a unit increase in environmental quality is being measured (e.g. a one per cent reduction in the number of a particular type of service crossing) then this expression can be used directly to estimate the marginal WTP/income trade-off as a compensating surplus measure.

4.4 Experimental Design

The process of experimental design for contingent ranking applications is comparable with the design of choice experiments described earlier in this chapter. One additional consideration is the weight of the cognitive burden placed on respondents by the ranking exercise: this suggests that asking respondents to rank too many profiles would be unwise and could lead to unreliable responses (Desvouges *et al.*, 1983). Foster and Mourato (1997) provide a useful description of the experimental design of a contingent ranking application in their study of WTP to reduce the pollution effects of pesticides.

4.5 Problems with Contingent Ranking

While the contingent ranking model developed by Lareau and Rae (1989) is generally more efficient than other discrete choice models because of its exploitation of the full information on rankings, it does impose rather restrictive assumptions on the ranking behaviour. Typically, all rankings are assumed to be independent of each other and to follow a logistic distribution. It has been argued that only the first choices follow a logistic distribution and that only information on this ranking should be used in the modelling procedure. This would lead to a modelling procedure more akin to that used in stated preference choice experiments.

Ben-Akiva *et al.* (1992) found that response data from different ranking levels were not equally reliable and in some cases produced statistically significantly different estimates of welfare measures. This may be a reflection of the cognitive costs involved in the ranking exercise. Their investigation was based on the fact that if ranked data are to satisfy the properties of the MOL model, utilities based on different ranking levels (i.e. first, second, third, etc.) must be proportional. Based on a ranking of *N* profiles, *N-1* welfare estimates can be estimated by basing the estimation procedure on the *N-1* choice sets that can be created by omitting the first choice, second choice and so on down until the *(N-1)st* choice, e.g. a ranking of four profiles produces: (i) the first choice based on the full set of rankings; (ii) rankings with the first choice omitted, so the observed second choice is assumed to have been chosen; (iii) rankings with the second choice omitted, so the observed third choice is assumed to have been chosen. For their example, Ben-Akiva *et al.* found that welfare estimates based on the various ranking levels were not proportional, violating the MOL assumption. Ben-Akiva *et al.* suggested that respondents may use different criteria in making ranking decisions at different levels, i.e. the criteria for ranking the first and last choices may be different. Whether this is due to respondent fatigue or difficulty in discriminating between lower ranked alternatives is yet to be seen.

There is also some speculation as to whether the responses from contingent ranking experiments are consistent with the axioms of consumer theory. It is argued that the ranking task places a considerable cognitive burden on respondents and that the ranking may not be consistent across all alternatives. In some cases it would be relatively straightforward to empirically test whether or not the survey responses conform with the axioms of consumer theory. This would be possible, for example, if each choice set was to be based on an ordinal rating of the attribute sets offered. Foster and Mourato (1997) performed a variety of tests to evaluate the consistency of their ranking data with the axioms consumer theory, finding over 90% of their respondents failing one of these tests at least once but less than 30% failing one test on each occasion.

5 THE FUTURE FOR DISCRETE CHOICE METHODS

The econometric analysis of data with discrete or ordinal dependent variables has progressed considerably over the last few decades. In particular, work on random utility theory by McFadden (1974) has been particularly useful to practitioners. Recently, the more robust non-parametric approach to the estimation of welfare measures based on discrete choice expressed preference questions, as reported by Kriström (1990), has begun to attract attention. The continuing development of more powerful statistical methods and computational packages that can be used to estimate non-parametric models of consumer choice could encourage this trend as a new generation of practitioners attempt to improve the ways in which discrete choice data are generated and analysed.

Current trends in the literature concerning expressed preference techniques, suggest that the complexity of estimation techniques and experimental design will continue to increase over the coming years. This is partly a response to the particular problems of valuing environmental goods and partly a reflection of the market for papers in distinguished academic journals. At the same time more attention is being paid to the decision theoretic framework underlying expressed preferences in an attempt to better understand how preferences are formed and decisions reached with a view to informing the design of valuation methodologies. While both strands of development are crucial to the future of environmental valuation, the second will surely prove the more fruitful in the long term and play a more important role in establishing the credibility of these techniques across the broader academic, scientific and socio-political communities.

REFERENCES

Adamowicz, W.L., J.J. Louviere and M. Williams (1994), 'Combining revealed and stated preference methods for valuing environmental amenities', *Journal of Environmental Economics and Management,* **26**, 271-92.

Adamowicz, W.L., G.D. Garrod and K.G. Willis (1995), *Estimating the Passive Use Benefits of Britain's Inland Waterways,* Research Report, Centre for Rural Economy, Department of Agricultural Economics and Food Marketing, University of Newcastle upon Tyne, Newcastle upon Tyne.

Alberini, A. (1995), 'Optimal designs for discrete choice contingent valuation surveys: single-bound, double-bound and bivariate models', *Journal of Environmental Economics and Management,* **28**, 287-306.

Alberini, A., B. Kanninen and R.T. Carson (1997), 'Modelling response incentive effects in dichotomous choice contingent valuation data', *Land Economics* **73**, 309-24.

Arrow, K., R. Solow, E. Leamer, P. Portney, R. Radner and H. Schuman (1993), 'Report of the NOAA Panel on contingent valuation', *Federal Register,* **58**, 4601-14.

Batsell, R.R. and J.J. Louviere (1991), 'Experimental choice analysis', *Marketing Letters,* **2**, 199-214.

Beggs, S., S. Cardell and J. Hausman (1981), 'Assessing the potential demand for electric cars', *Journal of Econometrics,* **16**, 1-19.

Ben-Akiva, M., T. Morikawa and M. Shiroshi (1992), 'Analysis of the reliability of preference ranking data', *Journal of Business Research,* **24**, 149-64.

Bishop, R.C. and T.A.S. Heberlein (1979), 'Measuring values of extra-market goods: are indirect measures biased?', *American Journal of Agricultural Economics,* **61**, 926-30.

Bishop, R.C., T.A.S. Heberlein and M.J. Kealy (1983), 'Contingent valuation of environmental assets: comparison with a simulated market', *Natural Resources Journal,* **23**, 619-34.

Bowker, J.M. and J.R. Stoll (1988), 'Use of dichotomous choice nonmarket methods to value the whooping crane resource', *American Journal of Agricultural Economics* **70**, 372-81.

Boyle, K.L. (1990), 'Dichotomous choice, contingent valuation questions: functional form is important', *Northeastern Journal of Agricultural and Resource Economics,* **19**, 125-31.

Boyle, K.L., M.P. Welsh and R.C. Bishop (1988), 'Validation of empirical measures of welfare change', *Land Economics,* **64**, 94-8.

Cameron, T.A. (1988), 'A new paradigm for valuing non-market goods using referendum data: maximum likelihood estimation by censored logistic regression', *Journal of Environmental Economics and Management* **15**, 355-79.

Cameron, T.A. and M.D. James (1987), 'Efficient estimation methods for closed-ended contingent valuation survey data', *Review of Economics and Statistics.* **69**, 269-76.

Cameron, T.A. and J. Quiggin (1994), 'Estimation using contingent valuation data form a "dichotomous choice with follow-up" questionnaire', *Journal of Environmental Economics and Management,* **27**, 218-34.

Cattin, P. and D.R. Wittink (1982), 'Commercial use of conjoint analysis: a review', *Journal of Marketing*, **46**, 44-53.

Chapman R.G. and R. Staelin (1982), 'Exploiting ranked choice set data within the stochastic utility model', *Journal of Marketing Research*, **19**, 288-301.

Cooper, J.C. (1993), 'Optimal bid selection for dichotomous choice contingent valuation surveys', *Journal of Environmental Economics and Management*, **24**, 25-40.

Cooper, J.C. and J. Loomis (1992), 'Sensitivity of willingness-to-pay estimates to bid design in dichotomous choice contingent valuation models', *Land Economics*, **68**, 211-24.

Cosslett S. R. (1983), 'Distribution-free maximum likelihood estimator of the binary choice model', *Econometrica*, **51**, 765-82.

Cosslett S. R. (1987), 'Efficiency bounds for the distribution-free estimators of the binary choice mode and the censored regression model', *Econometrica*, **55**, 559-85.

Creel, M. and J. Loomis (1997), 'Semi-nonparametric distribution-free dichotomous choice CV', *Journal of Environmental Economics and Management*, **32**, 341-58.

Davis, D.D. and C.A. Holt (1993), *Experimental Economics,* Princeton University Press, Princeton, N.J.

Desvouges, W.H., V.K. Smith and M.P. McGivney (1983), *A Comparison of Alternative Approaches for Estimating Recreation and Related Benefits of Water Quality Improvements,* EPA 230-05-83-00, Environmental Protection Agency, Washington DC.

Desvouges, W.H., S.P. Hudson and M.C. Ruby (1996), 'Evaluating CV performance: separating the light from the heat', in D.J. Bjornstad and J.R. Kahn (eds), *The Contingent Valuation of Environmental Resources,* Edward Elgar, Cheltenham.

Duffield, J.W. and D.A. Patterson (1991), *Field Testing Existence Values: An Instream Flow Trust Fund for Montana Rivers,* Paper presented at the annual meeting of the American Economic Association, New Orleans.

Elnagheeb, A.H. and J.L. Jordan (1995), 'Comparing three approaches that generate bids for the referendum contingent valuation method', *Journal of Environmental Economics and Management*, **29**, 92-104.

Fisher, A.C. (1996), 'The conceptual underpinnings of the contingent valuation method', in D.J. Bjornstad and J.R. Kahn (eds), *The Contingent Valuation of Environmental Resources,* Edward Elgar, Cheltenham.

Foster, V. and S. Mourato (1997), 'Behavioural consistency, statistical specification and validity in the contingent ranking method: evidence from a survey on the impacts of pesticide use in the UK', *CSERGE Working Paper GEC 97-09,* University of East Anglia, Norwich.

Garrod, G.D. and K.G. Willis (1995), 'Valuing the benefits of the South Downs Environmentally Sensitive Area', *Journal of Agricultural Economics,* **46**, 160-73.

Garrod, G.D. and K.G. Willis (1997), 'The non-use benefits of enhancing forest biodiversity: a contingent ranking study', *Ecological Economics,* **21**, 45-61.

Green, P.E. and V. Srinivasen (1978), 'Conjoint analysis in consumer research: issues and outlook', *Journal of Consumer Research*, **5**, 103-212.

Greene, W.M. (1995), *LIMDEP Version 5.1,* Econometric Software Incorporated, New York.

Gurland, J., T. Lee and P. Dahm (1960), 'Polychotomous quantal response in biological assay', *Biometrics*, **16**, 382-98.

Haab, T.C and K.E, McConnell (1996), 'Referendum models and negative WTP: alternative solutions', *Journal of Environmental Economics and Management*, **32**, 251-70.

Hanemann, W.M. (1984), 'Welfare evaluations in contingent valuation experiments with discrete responses', *American Journal of Agricultural Economics*, **66**, 332-41.

Hanemann, W.M. and B.J. Kanninen (1998), 'The statistical analysis of discrete-response contingent valuation data', in I.J. Bateman and K.G. Willis (eds) *Contingent Valuation of Environmental Preferences: Assessing Theory and Practice in the USA, Europe and Developing Countries*, Oxford University Press, Oxford.

Hanemann, W.M., J.L. Loomis and B.J. Kanninen (1991), 'Estimation efficiency of double bounded dichotomous choice contingent valuation', *American Journal of Agricultural Economics*, **73**, 1255-63.

Herriges, J.A. and J.F. Shogrun (1996), 'Starting point bias in dichotomous choice valuation with follow-up questioning', *Journal of Environmental Economics and Management*, **30**, 112-31.

Holmes, T.P. and R.A. Kramer (1995), 'An independent sample test of yea-saying and starting point bias in dichotomous choice contingent valuation', *Journal of Environmental Economics and Management*, **29**, 121-32.

Horowitz J.L. (1992), 'A smoothed maximum score estimator for the binary response model', *Econometrica*, **60**, 505-31.

Horowitz J.L. (1993), 'Semiparametric estimation of a work-trip mode choice model', *Journal of Econometrics*, **58**, 49-70.

Kanninen, B.J. (1992), 'Optimal experimental design for double-bounded dichotomous choice contingent valuation', *Land Economics*, **69**, 138-46.

Kanninen, B.J. (1993), 'Design of sequential experiments for contingent valuation studies', *Journal of Environmental Economics and Management*, **25**, S-1-S-11.

Kealy, M.J. and R.W. Turner (1993), 'A test of the equality of close-ended and open-ended contingent valuations,' *American Journal of Agricultural Economics*, **75**, 321-31.

Kleppner, D. and N. Ramsay (1985), *Quick Calculus : A Self-Teaching Guide*, John Wiley, New York.

Kriström, B. (1990), 'A non-parametric approach to the estimation of welfare measures in discrete response valuation studies', *Land Economics*, **66**, 135-9.

Kroes, E.P. and R.J. Sheldon (1988), 'Stated preference methods: an introduction', *Journal of Transport Economics and Policy*, **22**, 11-25.

Lancaster, K. J. (1966), 'A new approach to consumer theory', *Journal of Political Economy*, **74**, 132-57.

Langford, I.H. (1994), 'Using a generalised linear mixed model to analyse dichotomous choice contingent valuation data', *Land Economics*, **70**, 507-14.

Langford, I.H., I.J. Bateman and H.D. Langford (1996), 'A multilevel modelling approach to triple-bounded dichotomous choice contingent valuation', *Environmental and Resource Economics*, **7**, 191-211.

Lareau, T.J. and D.A. Rae (1989) Valuing WTP for Diesel Odor Reductions: An Application of Contingent Ranking Technique. *Southern Economic Journal*, **55**, 728-42.

Li, C.-Z. (1996), 'Semiparametric estimation of the binary choice model for contingent valuation', *Land Economics*, **72**, 462-73.

Li, C.-Z., and L. Mattsson (1995), 'Discrete choice under preference uncertainty: an improved structural model for contingent valuation', *Journal of Environmental Economics and Management*, **28**, 256-69.

Louviere, J.J. (1988a), 'Conjoint analysis of stated preferences: a review of methods, recent developments and external validity', *Journal of Transport Economics and Policy*, **22**, 93-119.

Louviere, J.J. (1988b), 'Analyzing decision making: metric conjoint analysis', *Quantitative Applications in the Social Sciences Series No. 67*, Sage Publications Inc , Newbury Park, California.

Louviere, J.J. and G.G. Woodworth (1988), 'Design and analysis of simulated consumer choice or allocation experiments: an approach based on aggregate data,' *Journal of Marketing Research*, **20**, 350-67.

Louviere, J.J. (1996),'Relating stated preference measures and models to choices in real markets: calibration of CV responses', in D.J. Bjornstad and J.R. Kahn (eds), *The Contingent Valuation of Environmental Resources,* Edward Elgar, Cheltenham.

Luce, R.D. and P. Suppes (1965), 'Preference, utility and subjective probability', in R.D. Luce, R.R. Bush and E. Galanter (eds), *Handbook of Mathematical Psychology,* John Wiley, New York.

McCollum D. W., A. H. Gilbert and G. L. Peterson (1990), 'The net economic value of day use cross country skiing in Vermont: a dichotomous choice contingent valuation approach', *Journal of Leisure Research*, **22**, 341-52.

McFadden, D. (1974), 'On conditional logit model of qualitative choice behavior', in P. Zarembka (ed.) *Frontiers of Econometrics,* Academic Press, New York.

McFadden D. (1994), 'Contingent valuation and social choice', *American Journal of Agricultural Economics*, **76**, 689-708.

McFadden, D. and G.K. Leonard (1993), 'Issues in the contingent valuation of environmental goods: methodologies for data collection and analysis', in J.A. Hausman (ed.), *Contingent Valuation: A Critical Assessment,* Elsevier Science Publishers, Amsterdam.

McKelvey, R. and W. Zavoina (1975), 'A Statistical Model for the Analysis of Ordinal Level Dependent Variables', *Journal of Mathematical Sociology*, **4**, 103-20.

Maddala, G.M. (1983), *Limited Dependent and Qualitative Variables in Econometrics,* Cambridge University Press, New York.

Neill, H.R., R.C. Cummings, P.T. Ganderton, G.W. Harrison and T. McGuckin (1994), 'Hypothetical surveys and real economic commitments', *Land Economics*, **70**, 145-54.

Ouwersloot, H. and P. Rietveld (1996), 'Stated choice experiments with repeated observations', *Journal of Transport Economics and Policy*, **30**, 203-12.

Ozuna, T., K.Y. Jang and J.R. Stoll (1993), 'Testing for misspecification in the referendum contingent valuation approach', *American Journal of Agricultural Economics*, **75**, 332-8.

Rae, D.A. (1988), 'The value to visitors of improving visibility at Mesa Verde and Great Smoky National Parks', in R.D. Rowe and L.G. Chestnut (eds) *Managing Air Quality and Scenic Resources at National Parks and Wilderness Areas,* Westview Press, Boulder.

Ready, R.C., J.C. Whitehead and G.C. Blomquist (1995), 'Contingent valuation when respondents are ambivalent', *Journal of Environmental Economics and Management,* **29**, 181-96.

Roe, B., K.J. Boyle and M.F. Teisl (1996), 'Using conjoint analysis to derive estimates of compensating variation', *Journal of Environmental Economics and Management,* **31**, 145-59.

Scarpa, R., G. Sirchia and M. Bravi (1998), 'Kernal vs logit modelling of single bounded CV responses: valuing access to architectural and visual arts heritage in Italy', in R.C. Bishop and D. Romano (eds), *Contingent valuation in Italy, A Critical Assessment,* Kluwer, Amsterdam.

Schulze, W.D., G. McClelland and D. Waldman (1996), 'Sources of bias in contingent valuation', in D.J. Bjornstad and J.R. Kahn (eds), *The Contingent Valuation of Environmental Resources,* Edward Elgar, Cheltenham.

Schuman, H. (1996), 'The sensitivity of CV outcomes to CV survey methods', in D.J. Bjornstad and J.R. Kahn (eds), *The Contingent Valuation of Environmental Resources,* Edward Elgar, Cheltenham.

Seller C., J.R. Stoll and J-P. Chavas (1985), 'Validation of empirical measures of welfare change: a comparison of non-market techniques', *Land Economics,* **61**, 156-75.

Seller, C., J.P. Chavas and J.R. Stoll (1986), 'Specification of the logit model: the case of valuation of nonmarket goods', *Journal of Environmental Economics and Management* **13**, 382-90.

Thurstone, L.L. (1927), 'A law of comparative judgement', *Psychological Review,* **4**, 273-86.

Wardman, M. (1988), 'A comparison of revealed preference and stated preference models of travel behaviour', *Journal of Transport Economics and Policy,* **22**, 71-81.

PART FOUR

Case Examples

7. Recreation

No time to see, when woods we pass,
Where squirrels hide their nuts in grass.

A poor life this if, full of care,
We have no time to stand and stare.

William Henry Davies (1871–1940): *Leisure*

1 INTRODUCTION

The demand for outdoor recreation is growing as a consequence of increasing population, income, and holiday entitlements. Some outdoor recreational activities are available as open access, non-priced goods. Failure to charge a fee for the use of such a recreational resource may occur because (1) it is not feasible: e.g. if transactions costs are greater than income derived; (2) property rights cannot be exercised over the good: e.g. there is a legal right of way over the land, so visitors cannot be excluded; (3) the good is provided as a public service; (4) it is not optimal to charge because it is a 'public good': the marginal (opportunity) cost of admitting an additional user is zero, so any charge might deter a consumer with a positive marginal valuation whilst making no off setting cost saving. Whatever the reason for the open access, non-priced provision of the good, the problem still exists of evaluating whether or not the benefits provided by the good exceed the costs of its provision and maintenance.

This chapter illustrates the use of travel-cost models to assess the value of benefits of open access, non-priced recreation. Forests recreation areas (FRAs) in Malaysia are used as a case example; although the chapter concludes with an example of the use of contingent valuation methods to assess the additional value from on-site facilities, compared to natural amenities, of a forest recreation site in Italy. For the Malaysian case the

225

validity of the travel-cost model is investigated by comparing the results with those derived from a contingent valuation study of willingness-to-pay (WTP) to gain access to the same recreation area.

By 1994 there were 74 FRAs spread throughout the States of Peninsular Malaysia. FRAs are relative small areas of natural virgin forest which contain a variety of attractive landscape, fauna and flora, rivers and unique geological features making them attractive as sites for outdoor recreation. Activities pursued in FRAs range from hiking, camping, swimming, etc. to more passive pursuits such as picnics, walks, observing the ecology, and enjoying the scenic attractions of the forest. State governments incur costs for visitor facilities at FRAs: e.g. maintaining footpaths and toilets; collecting litter; providing information; and patrolling the site with park rangers.

2 TRAVEL-COST MODEL

Entry to FRAs is free, hence it is not possible to construct a conventional demand curve for forest recreation based on price and visit data. Moreover, one individual's visit to an FRA does not reduce its availability to others. A travel-cost method (TCM) can be used to estimate the recreation demand curve, and hence consumer surplus, by observing the number of visits to the FRA (quantity) in relation to price (i.e. the cost of a visit). The individual travel-cost method (ITCM) defines the dependent variable as the number of visits to an FRA made by each visitor over a specified period.

The individual travel-cost model was specified as:

$$V_{ij} = f(C_{ij}, E_{ij}, S_i, Y_i, A_i, H_i, N_i, M_i) \qquad (7.1)$$

where:

V_{ij} = number of visits made by individual i to site j
C_{ij} = individual i's total cost of visiting site j
E_{ij} = individual i's estimate of the proportion of the day's enjoyment which is attributable to the FRA
Y_i = income of individual i's household
A_i = age of individual i
H_i = size of individual i's household
N_i = size of individual i's party
M_i = dummy variable: whether individual i is a member of an outdoor organisation

Integrating over 7.1 permits consumer surplus per visit to be calculated.

A questionnaire survey at the FRA elicited information on: visits to the FRA; preferences and activities of visitors; and demographic details of visitors. The questionnaire was structured to allow respondents to think about their use of FRAs, and the availability and use of substitute recreational areas and activities. A random sample of visitors was obtained by interviewing on a next-to-pass basis. A sample size of 385 interviews was set at the Jeram Linang FRA to ensure a sample with sufficient variation in the number of visits to the FRA and to ensure that the contingent valuation question either: (a) estimated WTP deviated within 15% of the 'true' WTP 95% of the time, if the coefficient of variation was 1.5; or (b) estimated WTP deviated within 20% of the 'true' WTP 95% of the time, if the coefficient of variation was 2.0.

The dependent variable was specified as the number of visits made by a respondent to an FRA over the preceding six months. The cost or price of access to an FRA was measured by the amount that an individual paid on public transport, or incurred by using private transport[1] to visit the FRA. Since travel costs and travel time are correlated, to avoid multicollinearity, estimated time costs were monetarised and added to travel costs.

The opportunity cost of travel time is determined by an exceedingly complex array of institutional, social, and economic relationships, and yet its value is crucial in the choice of types and quantities of recreational experiences. As discussed in Chapter 3, the equilibrium labour market model only applies to groups such as the self-employed where individuals have discretionary work schedules and where earnings decline in proportion to absence from work. In the rest of the labour market some disequilibrium prevails, which severs the substitution between time and income at the margin, for groups such as students, retired and unemployed people, and also for employees on fixed hour employment contracts (unless unlimited voluntary overtime work is available) (McKean *et al.*, 1995). Therefore a value of time based on disequilibrium in the labour market was derived from Malaysian gross domestic product, hours worked, and labour market composition (to reflect employees, self-employed, and non-economically active individuals).

---

[1] The latest estimates of the unit running cost of an average car (RM/km in 1992 prices) were

cost element	financial cost	economic cost
fuel cost	0.110	0.060
lubricant oil	0.009	0.009
tyre cost	0.009	0.008
maintenance	0.053	0.045
depreciation	0.062	0.051
TOTAL	0.243	0.173

Source: Malaysian Government: Highway Planning Unit

In terms of the provision of recreational goods other recreation sites act as substitutes for FRAs. Greater distance from an FRA may mean greater proximity to a substitute site. Failure to include substitute sites in a travel-cost model constitutes an omitted variable problem, leading to an overestimation of visits to, and value of, an FRA. Where substitute sites are *imperfect* substitutes no problem arises. But a perfect substitute for an FRA should, in theory, result in recreationalists only visiting one site: the one with the lowest travel cost. However, in terms of outdoor recreation, perfect substitutes do not generally exist because all sites have different quality characteristics and no one site is a perfect substitute for another.[2] The importance of substitute sites and alternative recreational opportunities was assessed in two ways: first by asking respondents how many other FRAs they had visited apart from this one; and second by calculating trips to FRAs as a ratio of the individual's total annual number of recreational day trips to forests, countryside, mountains, and other sites.

There is no standard specification for the functional form of a TCM. Various criteria can be used to judge the appropriateness of a particular functional specification: (1) statistical fit; (2) conformity to economic theory; (3) predictive ability and (4) criterion and construct (convergence) validity (for the latter see Mitchell and Carson, 1989).

A linear specification implies an under-estimate of consumer surplus for those visitors who make only one trip to an FRA. In addition, for those individuals who visit the FRA more than once, the estimated consumer surplus of a single visit clearly under-estimates their total consumer surplus. Thus, in the case of FRAs, the use of single visit estimates to approximate total consumer surplus per visitor, regardless of the number of visits made, ensures that the linear functional form always gives lower bound estimates (Willis and Garrod, 1991a). The implication of this approach is that while any further visits after the first may possibly produce decreasing marginal consumer surplus, the overall total consumer surplus will increase.

Sampling on site at the FRA excluded any individuals who chose not to visit the site over that time period and consequently selects a sample based only on positive integer values of the dependent variable, thus altering the distribution the error term. Studies by Bockstael *et al.* (1984) and Balkan and Kahn, (1988) have shown that consumer surplus estimates derived from OLS

---

[2] A random utility model (RUM) may be used to deal with the problem of substitute sites with varying attributes. However, a RUM was not employed because (a) FRA sites are spatially dispersed and cannot be regarded as substitutes for each other; (b) the resources for the project did not permit other non-FRA local substitute sites to be included in the survey. Moreover, RUMs have a major shortcoming: they cannot explain, as a TCM does, the number of trips an individual makes to a site in a given season, nor the total number of visits a site attracts from the surrounding population.

models of such data produce over-estimates of the true magnitude of consumer surplus because of truncation bias. Hence a maximum likelihood (ML) estimator that took account of the truncated nature of the data was used to estimate the travel-cost model.

Table 7.1 Maximum likelihood estimates of visits to Jeram Linang FRA

variable	coefficient	std. error	T-ratio	Prob: t : > x	mean of x
ONE	-4.00525	1.25289	-3.197	0.00139	1.00000
X3	-0.64479	0.24658	-2.615	0.00893	2.34940
X10	-11.07460	1.64099	-6.749	0.00000	0.26216
X27	5.78721	1.09867	5.267	0.00000	0.18919
X29	6.04067	2.31138	2.613	0.00896	0.04594
X30	3.20342	1.17677	2.722	0.00648	0.13784
X4	0.48544	0.25220	1.925	0.05426	0.97297
X45	8.02514	3.22890	2.485	0.01294	0.00540
X51	-1.97990	1.10616	-1.790	0.07347	0.25135

Log-Likelihood = -605.22

X3 = combined time and travel cost (using standard hourly rate of 9.16 RM/hr as opportunity cost of time)
X10 = first visit
X27 = single: living with parents
X29 = educated to primary level
X30 = educated to secondary level
X4 = other FRAs visited in 6-month period
X45 = fished at this site
X51 = engaged in nature walking at this site

As an example, the linear truncated ML model for Jeram Linang FRA, in Kelantan, State, is presented in Table 7.1. Variables were included on the basis of *a priori* logic in economic theory, but the model reports only those variables which are significant at the 0.15 statistical significance level. The variables in this ML model make sense intuitively: visits to the FRA are negatively related to the time and travel cost of gaining access to the site. On the other hand, the number of visits an individual makes to Jeram Linang FRA is positively related to being single and living at home with parents; being educated only to a primary or secondary level (relative to a higher education level); having visited other FRAs in the previous six month period; and engaging in fishing at this site (Garrod and Willis, 1997).

Consumer surplus estimates for individual visits to the site were then calculated by substituting values from the linear equation and integrating over the demand function. These results are reported in Table 7.2, which documents the average economic benefit of the marginal visit for each visitor to FRAs. For comparability purposes, it is necessary to concentrate on the value of the marginal visit, rather than a value based on the average number of visits, since the CV estimates were also based on the value of the current (marginal) visit to each visitor.

Table 7.2: Comparison of CV and ITCM results (consumer surplus per visit per adult)

FRA	CV	ITCM
Jeram Linang (Kelantan)	1.05	0.78
Telok Bahang (Penang)	1.41	2.38
Gunung Pulai (Johor)	2.15	3.74

3 VALIDITY: CONVERGENT ASSESSMENT

The reliability of TCM and CV values can be assessed by the degree to which estimates converge when measuring the same theoretical construct (i.e. type of value of a specific good). CVM was used to determine maximum WTP to gain entry into Jeram Linang, and two other FRAs. The contingent valuation question was based on an open-ended format, in which respondents were asked the maximum sum that they would have been willing to pay to gain access to the FRA for their current visit. This simple approach was adopted in preference to the dichotomous choice question format recommended in the NOAA guidelines (see Arrow *et al.*, 1993) because the use values of the FRA were being estimated rather than non-use values. More importantly there are private sites similar to State FRAs where an entrance charge is made and most visitors to FRAs can be assumed to be aware of these charges and the competing facilities offered by these private sites. Thus, the majority of visitors can be expected to make rational comparisons between the sites that they visit, and their decision as to which site to visit should be based on a trade-off between their utility for the income lost to gain access and utility for the facilities available. This should mean that most visitors would be able to estimate the maximum amount that they would be willing to pay for access to the FRA, before deciding to visit another recreational site instead. Thus, the CV study estimated the same theoretical construct as the ITCM. Table 7.2 compares the ITCM and CV results for three FRAs. Clearly the CV and ITCM results are broadly similar. Both methods produce the same ordering of economic value for the marginal visit to the three FRAs surveyed: in all cases the value for the marginal visit to Jeram Linang is lowest, and that for Gunung Pulai is the highest. However, for two of the three sites the ITCM estimates are greater than the CV estimates.

The comparison of CVM with revealed preference (RP) estimates (such as TCM measures) has played a key role in assessing the validity of CVM. Of course RP estimates are themselves random variables which are sensitive to details of product definition, functional form of the RP methods (here ITCM), and other technique-specific assumptions such as the value of time and the definition of substitutes. Thus, both techniques measure the quantity demanded, and hence consumer surplus, with error. Consequently, neither of the measures can be assumed to be a *true* measure of the construct. Studies comparing CV and RP estimates (mainly TCM estimates) have generally found that CV estimates are smaller, but not grossly smaller than their RP counterparts. The overall CVM/TCM ratio in this study is 0.67. American studies have found the CVM/RP ratio (for trimmed or modified CVM WTP results) to average 0.77 (Carson *et al.*, 1996). Of course, correspondence between CV and TCM measures does not prove the accuracy of either, but rather contributes to the credibility of both. Cummings *et al.* (1986) point out that price elasticity can vary enormously for a specific good, and that the accuracy of values estimated by indirect market methods is likely to be no better than +/- 50%. However, using +/-50% for reference accuracy, the hypothesis that the CV and ITCM measures are the same cannot be rejected.

4 OTHER ISSUES IN RECREATIONAL SURVEYS

A survey of visits by recreationalists to a recreation site creates particular problems in data analysis. The survey based on visits may not be representative of visitors. The survey may result in an over-sample of 'avid' participants creating sampling bias. The fact that the survey is conducted 'on-site' also gives rise to a truncated sample. However, once these problems are recognised they can be controlled.

To illustrate this, assume a site has two types of visitor: frequent visitors and non-frequent visitors. Assume that there are 120 frequent visitors who visit five times per year; and 120 non-frequent visitors who visit only once a year. Assume visits are evenly distributed over the year: thus January has 50 visits from frequent visitors and 10 visits from non-frequent visitors, as have the months from February to December. A 10% sample of visits, randomly selected in any month, would consist of five frequent visitors and one non-frequent visitor. However, the true proportion of frequent to non-frequent visitors is 1:1. This type of site selection bias can be corrected by weighting the number in the visit sample by its reciprocal to derive the true proportion of visitors: in this case [(50 (1/5)) + (10 (1/1))].

Many on-site recreational surveys over-sample 'avid' participants. Mail surveys undertaken off-site, even those of the public in general, may also over-sample 'avid' participants because such individuals are more likely to respond to the survey, leading to estimates with sample selectivity bias.

Morey *et al.* (1991), in response to limited trip data and sample selectivity, developed a discrete choice random utility model of participation and site choice that corrects for the over-sampling of 'avid' participants, and that can be estimated with a data set that reports each individual's total number of trips but their actual destination for only one of those trips. Over-sampling of 'avid' participants was corrected by assuming that the probability of individual i being in the sample is a linear function of the total number of trips undertaken. Sample selectivity bias associated with over-sampling 'avid' participants can then be corrected by replacing the population distribution in the likelihood function with its sampling distribution.

Sampling procedure can give rise to apparent perverse results. For example Bell and Leeworthy (1990) noted that the recreation demand by tourists for beach days in Florida increased with distance travelled and with the total cost of the trip. In contrast economic theory, and travel-cost models, postulate that demand declines with increasing cost. Bell and Leeworthy modified theory to explain these supposed 'anomalies' by suggesting that tourists respond differently to on-site price (for beach access: a negative relationship with price) and travel cost per trip (a positive relationship with the number of beach days). However, their result is probably an artefact of sample selection bias induced by sampling tourists to Florida during one year, and regarding this as the relevant time period. Relating number of beach days in Florida over the life of a tourist in relation to cost would reveal fewer beach days in Florida, compared to those at a local beach at a lower cost. This is partly the point Shaw (1991) develops in suggesting a three-stage decision process to deal with this problem: stage 1 — households decide where to recreate out of their home state, and if yes; stage 2 — decide whether to recreate at Florida beaches versus other recreation sites, and if yes; stage 3 — decide to recreate *n* days on Florida beaches. Thus TCM should model the demand for beach days conditional on the decision to vacation in Florida. That is, demand for beach days in Florida equals beach days multiplied by the probability of taking a vacation in Florida. This clearly involves a time horizon of greater than one year. Other TCM studies of long-haul tourism, such as those by Tobias and Mendelsohn (1991) on ecotourism to a tropical rainforest in Costa Rica and Maille and Mendelsohn (1993) on tourism to a biological reserve in Madagascar, avoided these problems by using a simple model to determine consumer surplus per visitor for the whole recreational experience.

Where information is available on the choice of destination, random utility models have been used to describe this choice as a function of environmental attributes and quality differences between sites (Bockstael *et al.*, 1987;

Parsons and Kealy, 1992). Random utility models explain the probability of choosing a particular site, but are less able to explain intensity of participation. However, quality changes at a site induce two effects: substitution by existing recreationalists of higher quality sites for lower quality ones, and an increase in participation. Feather *et al.* (1995) neatly address these issues in an approach which:

1. uses a nested random utility model to estimate the probability of Minnesota anglers visiting remote northern lakes (pristine cold water fisheries: pike and walleye), compared to central and southern lakes (warmer game, with bass, bluegill, and other species) in the more populated part of the state; and within each of these two regions the probability of visiting the *jth* lake (most respondents expressed a preference to fish for cold water species found in the more remote northern lakes);

2. calculates the expected cost (based on probability) of visiting each lake on the basis of round distance transport costs and a shadow wage (opportunity) cost to reach the *jth* lake;

3. calculates expected quality (based on probability) and on various quality measures (such as lake size, depth, littoral acres, water quality and trophic status) observed at the *jth* lake;

4. estimates expected cost/quality, by regressing observed trips against expected cost, quality, and socio-economic variables using a count data model (e.g. a Poisson regression if the mean and variance of the dependent variable are equal; or negative binomial regression if the variance of the dependent variable exceeds the mean) to account for the fact that the dependent variable is a non-negative integer.

The above model was then used to predict participation and the welfare benefit changes that would accrue from improving lakes with below average clarity (due to stream run-off and pollution) up to average water clarity. Larger participation effects were predicted for improvements to lakes in the southern region (average +11.4%), where water quality is lower and more variable and where most of the population lives, than for lakes in the more remote northern region (average +1.6% increased participation). Similarly, welfare changes were predicted to be +$7.68 for the northern region and +$54.38 for the southern region from an average initial consumer surplus of $465. Benefits from improvements to southern lakes were low for residents in the northern region.

5 LINKING RECREATIONAL BENEFITS WITH ON-SITE AMENITIES

An increasing number of sites used for informal recreation benefit from the provision of various facilities, such as toilets, picnic areas or car parking, which may improve the recreational experience for the visitor. While these facilities provide benefits to visitors to the site they also incur a cost to the provider, often a local authority of state agency.

As demonstrated in the previous case studies, travel-cost methods are an effective tool for estimating the magnitude of the benefits generated by non-priced recreation. They will, however, prove a more blunt instrument when it comes to assessing the benefits provided by on-site amenities. For example, hedonic travel-cost methods (see Chapter 3) have been found to be a difficult instrument for the valuation of site attributes including facilities for visitors.

Contingent valuation techniques could prove a more effective means of addressing the question of value-added from amenities, provided that there was clear evidence that such amenities enhanced the utility which individuals gain from their recreation visits to a site. Such an approach could be conducted successfully within a context where respondents were familiar with the recreational experience and the potential benefits offered by improving facilities. A suitable payment vehicle that was within the experience of the visitor would also have to be available.

Jones (1998) examined the dual issues of visitor satisfaction and willingness to pay for improved on-site facilities at an open access recreational site in Cansiglio, a forested area 60 km north of Venice in northern Italy managed by Azienda Regionale delle Foreste Veneto (ARF Veneto). Her study first sought to investigate the determinants of visitor satisfaction at the site and then to link this with a contingent valuation exercise designed to estimate mean WTP for a clearly specified improvement in the facilities available to visitors.

Respondents' satisfaction with the recreational experience was measured using a five-point Likert scale which was used to rate the experience on a scale ranging from unacceptable to perfect. The responses from this exercise were treated as discrete, ordered data and modelled using an ordered probit model to investigate the relationship between satisfaction and a number of potential explanatory factors.

According to the ordered probit analysis, the most significant positive determinants of recreational satisfaction were the weather, peace and quiet and being in the company of friends and relatives. The only statistically significant negative determinant of satisfaction was lack of car parking facilities. Separate attitudinal data on satisfaction with service levels had suggested that provision of toilet facilities and presence of litter were things that might detract from the overall recreational experience but these things were not found to be significant in explaining variations in overall visitor satisfaction.

The contingent valuation question investigated maximum WTP for a hypothetical scenario where lack of funding for ARF Veneto meant that a parking charge had to be introduced on site in order to finance one of two specified levels of additional service provision. Having been taken through this scenario, respondents were asked an open-ended question to elicit the maximum parking charge that they would be willing to pay to obtain the specified increases in services.

The mean WTP for the first scenario was 414,300 Lira, and 507,900 for the second scenario that offered a higher level of services. Statistical tests showed that these two values were not significantly different, suggesting the presence of some form of embedding effect. This result did not seem unreasonable given the possible difficulty in framing answers dependent upon small increases in service levels, while other important determinants of visitor satisfaction remained constant across the two scenarios (e.g. weather, company, peace and quiet). The results could thus be interpreted as maximum WTP for a range of service standards symbolised by the scenarios offered.

The study demonstrated that while service levels do add to the utility of a non-priced recreational visit, they are not the most important determinants of visitor satisfaction. Even so, contingent valuation was shown to provide an effective means of determining public WTP for improvements in service levels which could subsequently be used in an *a priori* analysis to determine resource allocation decisions by the authorities responsible for recreational sites.

6 CONCLUSIONS

In the last decade approaches based on travel costs have attracted much less attention from researchers than contingent valuation methods and other expressed preference techniques. This is partly a reflection of the need to explore some of the more complex econometric problems that underlie expressed preference approaches and partly a recognition of the limited extent to which TCMs can be applied in policy appraisal. Such an attitude is unfortunate, given a presumption that techniques based on market data offer a fundamentally more reliable means of estimating welfare benefits based on use values than expressed preference techniques.

Travel-cost methodology requires researchers to make a number of difficult decisions relating to the assumptions that underpin their estimates. Issues such as the correct treatment of the opportunity cost of travel time and the appropriate estimation technique for travel-cost data continue to exercise the minds of practitioners and spark debate in the academic literature. These problems are reflected in the strong influence that the various assumptions, model specification, and estimation techniques have on the resulting consumer surplus estimates.

Until policy makers and practitioners reach a consensus on the most appropriate methods for dealing with travel-cost data the methodology will never have a significant role to play in the evaluation process. This would be a pity given that the technique is so well geared to estimating the benefits associated with non-priced recreation. Such recreation is becoming increasingly common throughout the world and is a key source of environmental benefits. Measurement of the magnitude of such benefits is important in determining resource allocation decisions whether at a policy level or at a simple site level and is a prerequisite if sustainable decisions are to be made regarding the environment.

As in the Cansiglio example, contingent valuation methods or choice experiments may have a role to play in investigating preferences for marginal changes in site attributes, but as an means of estimating the magnitude of welfare benefits from open-access non-priced recreation TCMs have a much stronger theoretical basis than any expressed preference technique.

REFERENCES

Arrow, Kenneth J., R. Solow, P.R. Portney, E.E. Leamer, R. Radner and H. Schuman (1993), 'Report of the National Oceanic and Atmospheric Administration (NOAA) Panel on Contingent Valuation', *Federal Register* **58** (10), 4016–614.

Balkan, E. and J.R. Kahn, (1988), 'The value of changes in deer hunting quality: a travel-cost approach', *Applied Economics* **20**, 533–9.

Bell, F.W. and V.R. Leeworthy (1990), 'Recreation demand by tourists for saltwater beach days', *Journal of Environmental Economics and Management* **18**, 189–205.

Bockstael, N.E., W.M. Hanemann and I.E. Strand (1984), *Measuring the Benefits of Water Quality Improvement Using Recreation Demand Models,* Environmental Protection Agency, Report CR-811043-01-1. U.S. Environmental Protection Agency, Washington DC.

Bockstael, Nancy, W. Michael Hanemann, and Catherine Kling (1987), 'Estimating the value of water quality improvements in a recreational demand framework', *Water Resources Research* **23**, 951–6.

Carson, Richard T., Nicholas E. Flores, Kerry M. Martin and Jennifer L. Wright (1996), 'Contingent valuation and revealed preference methodologies: comparing the estimates for quasi-public goods', *Land Economics* **72**, 80–99.

Cummings R.G., D.S. Brookshire and W.D. Schulze (eds) (1986), *Valuing Environmental Goods: An Assessment of the Contingent Valuation Method.* Rowman and Allenheld, Towowa, New Jersey.

Feather, Peter, Daniel Hellerstein and Theodore Tomasi (1995), 'A discrete count model of recreational demand', *Journal of Environmental Economics and Management* **29**, 214–27.

Garrod, G.D. and K.G. Willis (1997), 'The Recreational Value of Tropical Forests in Malaysia', *Journal of World Forestry Resource Management* **8** (2), 183–201.

Jones, Annali B. (1998), 'Consumer benefit and the determinants of visitor satisfaction in the forest of Cansiglio, Northern Italy', Paper presented at IUFRO Symposium on International Aspects of Managerial Economics and Accounting in Forestry, Rome, 15th–18th April 1998.

Maille, Peter and Robert Mendelsohn (1993), 'Valuing ecotourism in Madagascar', *Journal of Environmental Management* **38**, 213–8.

McKean, J.R., D.M. Johnson, and R.G. Walsh (1995), 'Valuing time in travel cost demand analysis: an empirical investigation'. *Land Economics* **71**, 96–105.

Mitchell, R.C. and R.T. Carson, (1989), *Using Surveys to Value Public Goods: The Contingent Valuation Method*, Resources for the Future, Washington DC.

Morey, E.R., W.D. Shaw, and R.D. Rowe, (1991), 'A discrete choice model of recreational participation, site choice, and activity valuation when complete trip data are not available', *Journal of Environmental Economics and Management* **20**, 181–201.

Parsons, George R. and Mary Jo Kealy (1992), 'Randomly drawn opportunity sets in a random utility model of lake recreation', *Land Economics* **68**, 93–106.

Shaw, W. Douglas (1991), 'Recreational demand by tourists for saltwater beach days: comment', *Journal of Environmental Economics and Management* **20**, 284–9.

Tobias, Dave and Robert Mendelsohn (1991), 'Valuing ecotourism a tropical rain-forest reserve', *Ambio* **20**, 91–3.

Willis, K.G. and G.D. Garrod, (1991a), 'Valuing open access recreation on inland waterways: on-site recreation surveys and selection effects', *Regional Studies* **25**, 511–24.

Willis, K.G. and G.D. Garrod, (1991b), 'An individual travel cost method of evaluating forest recreation', *Journal of Agricultural Economics* **42**, 33–42.

8. Landscape

That after many wanderings, many years
Of absence, these steep woods and lofty cliffs,
And this pastoral landscape, were to me
More dear, both for themselves and for thy sake!

William Wordsworth (1770–1850): *Lines Composed a Few Miles above Tintern Abbey, July 13, 1798*

1 INTRODUCTION

The landscape we experience today is the result of a long process of human intervention going back many hundreds of years and our present day enthusiasm for it is a relatively recent phenomenon. As well as interacting physically with the landscape, man responds emotionally and aesthetically to it and this response can be seen in the work of artists, musicians, writers and poets. Thus, while our new found enthusiasm for landscape stems in part from our desire to preserve what is natural, it has its roots in the past when an interest in art and culture first led to an appreciation of landscape and natural beauty. In Britain this interest was first manifested in the early eighteenth century in a developing taste for Italian art and in the study of classical antiquities and Renaissance architecture (Hale, 1993).

Until the 18th century the Italian Architectural Garden dominated ideas of garden design in Europe (e.g. Versailles); design was formal and symmetrical with house and garden in unity and plants treated as architectural features. This exemplified the ideals of balance and symmetry which existed at this time. The landscape movement wanted something more natural, and English landscapers - e.g. Sir John Vanburgh (1664-1726), William Kent (1684-1748) and Humphry Repton (1752-1818) - sought ways to replace formality with something more akin to the countryside or an idealised version of it. Rather than tame and formalise the existing landscape, the emphasis was on

239

enhancing the existing natural beauty, often by small alterations. Many of these changes were long-term in scope, e.g. tree planting, while others were more immediate, e.g. altering the flow or depth of a river. Ha-has replaced walls and fences, curves replaced straight lines, natural growth replaced controlled growth and so on.

These influences led to a new approach to the layout of the great estates in eighteenth century England, where 'parkland' views were created to please the eye without significantly reducing agricultural productivity. This work was exemplified in the activity of Lancelot 'Capability' Brown (1716-1783). Brown agreed with the artist Hogarth in feeling that serpentine lines created the feeling of beauty. Brown's landscapes are characterised by water, trees and lawns united by serpentine lines. Gently rolling contours were produced, covered in turf and studded with trees through which glimpses of a winding river can be seen (Turner, 1985).

Brown was responsible for many of the landscapes of the stately homes of England such as Blenheim, Wallington, Broadlands, Burghley, Longleat, Castle Ashby, Petworth and Stowe (Turner, 1985; Hinde, 1986). It has been estimated that, between 1763 and 1782, Brown was paid approximately £2,500 by Lord Dorchester for his work on the Milton Abbey estate alone (Turner, 1985). Other landowners spent considerable sums of money improving visual quality on their estates. For example, a former Duke of Devonshire relocated the village of Edensor behind a hill to prevent it being seen from Chatsworth House. The new church with its imposing spire was, however, considered to be a positive landscape feature and placed to form a focus for the new composition of grass, trees and water. The creation of landscaped gardens was not confined to Britain alone, and examples were common in Europe and subsequently in the United States.

The history of landscape appreciation in the UK can also be seen in contemporary society's reactions to landscape. Prior to the sixteenth century painters concentrated on religious subjects and little on landscape. Artists saw the countryside in idealistic terms, as beautiful and perfect: this notion of Arcadian landscapes, depicted in an unreal, stylised, artificial light persisted for some years. Attitudes gradually broadened as the gentry of lowland England enjoyed an era of unprecedented peace and prosperity (e.g. the Enclosure Acts, improvements in roads and communication, The Grand Tour, etc.).

Even so, natural landscapes were often regarded as barren, unproductive and unsightly, and of little value In 1753, John Brown described the Lake District town of Keswick as 'Beauty, horror and immensity united.' The picturesque style of writing embodied by William Gilpin (1724-1804) epitomised this attitude towards natural landscape and treated the countryside as a series of views to be enjoyed by the observer. The tradition of the picturesque was continued in the work of British painters such as Gainsborough (1727-1788).

Born in Suffolk and best known as a portrait painter, Gainsborough was nevertheless a pioneer in his depiction of nature in a romantic or poetic form. His trees have been described as 'bunches of parsley and celery stalks' and some landscapes are unrealistic or fanciful but often detail was well-observed and his later landscapes are often praised. His paintings may be described as looking forward to future trends but failing to capture the 'spirit of place' or *genius loci* that other writers and artists sought to define.

Genius loci is the special atmosphere that sets a place apart, and is felt especially by artists, musicians and poets, and is embodied in the natural beauty of landscape. This term was used by the poet William Wordsworth (1770-1850) in his famous 'Guide to the English Lakes'. Finding the picturesque unsatisfactory, Wordsworth articulated a desire for realism with regard to landscape, seeing it in naturalistic rather than in idealistic terms. In so doing, Wordsworth recognised the close relationship between man and nature, and the practical and the spiritual. An appreciation of the spirit of place and a less stylised response to natural beauty are the hallmarks of the works of a number of poets, writers, artists and composers. Attitudes from these sources pervade society and have influenced our cultural attitudes, values and preferences for landscape.

The main feature of the 20th century has not been to create the cherished landscapes so characteristic of the approach of the landed gentry of the 18th century, but to preserve landscapes that already exist, both natural and man-made. Environmental laws and land-use planning controls are the main regulatory mechanisms used to preserve landscapes. Creation of National Parks and legislation such as the Wilderness Act 1964 in the USA have defined and established regulatory instruments to preserve broad areas of the countryside deemed to be of outstanding natural beauty, of geomorpological interest, or of wilderness value. These environmental regulations are typically evaluated by an opportunity cost, or a preventative expenditure approach.

Opportunity costs arise because National Parks prohibit, or severely restrict, development (urban as well as mineral and timber production) to preserve the environmental character of the area. The cost of restricting development in a National Park can be viewed as a price differential between property or hotel accommodation inside the National Park compared to that outside the park[1] manifested as the additional cost of providing the output

---

[1] Between 1978 and 1986 the Lake District National Park in Britain would only grant planning permission for new homes on the condition they were occupied by someone who worked in the National Park, to prevent new houses being purchased by people outside the park and used for second homes and weekend cottages. This quickly led to a substantial price differential between homes built before 1978 without this occupancy condition, and those built after 1978 which could be purchased at a much lower price (see Shucksmith, 1981). In the USA, hotel room rates

elsewhere in the economy, e.g. by way of increased transport costs and travel time to commute into the park rather than to lodge within it.

Whilst planning is typically used to preserve the holistic landscape character of an area, individual attributes forming the landscape are often maintained or enhanced by preventative expenditure. The Environmentally Sensitive Area (ESA) programme in the European Union (EU) essentially involves paying farmers to farm in an environmentally friendly way which is consistent with maintaining the traditional agricultural landscape, wildlife, and historical interest of the area. However, opportunity cost and preventative expenditure approaches make explicit the cost to society of landscape preservation, but they do not estimate the benefits to society of this preservation.

Travel-cost methods (TCMs) and hedonic price methods (HPMs), only estimate use benefits, mainly with respect to the recreational value of the area. TCMs encounter problems of separability (people may derive utility from the trip to the landscape area as well as the area itself; and may participate in activities there (e.g. boating) which are enhanced by the landscape but are not a sufficient condition for participating in the activity itself). Unless an hedonic TCM is implemented, conventional TCMs cannot satisfactorily measure utility changes as a consequence of changes in landscape attributes. Attribute changes may evolve slowly over a number of years, and the net effect of this on visitor numbers and utility may be difficult to establish. Moreover, TCMs do not measure all use values nor do they measure non-use values. Indeed, the early debate about option values started in the USA with respect to the Sequoia National Park, where it was suggested that since park revenues failed to cover costs, conventional economics would suggest the closure of the park and an alternative land use such as forestry (felling the ancient redwoods and pines in the Sequoia National Park) or mining. Weisbrod (1964) argued that such a course of action might be socially unsound because it ignored the existence of people who anticipate visiting the park at some time in the future, but who, in fact, never visit it. Nevertheless, these consumers might be willing to pay something for the option to consume this good in the future.

Hedonic price models have been used to value landscape attributes (see for example, Garrod and Willis, 1992a, 1992b). However, doubt has been expressed as to whether HPMs can measure all the variations in the same attribute (e.g. different designs of electricity poles and pylons), all the different attributes comprising a landscape, and all the interactions between attributes, and still have sufficient degrees of freedom in the regression model. Aesthetic values in landscape are complex, based on a vast number of

---

are higher in National Parks than outside, e.g. at Yosemite National Park which only has one hotel.

visible features and qualities, as well as on the less tangible 'spirit of place'. The problems of valuing landscape features by HPMs are illustrated in Figure 8.1. Thus Price (1995) argues that the significance of some landscape features is a matter of judgement (Figure 8.1a); along with the problem of how to measure them (Figure 8.1b); whilst functional relationships in the hedonic price model are problematic (Figure 8.1c); with non-additive separability a problem, in that some independent variables cannot be expressed in a single dimension, but require a composite index of at least two factors such as geometry and topography (Figure 8.1d); whilst multicollinearity suggests that it is difficult to separate out the effect of two or more independent variables that vary systematically together (Figure 8.1e). Point (d) arises when two or more independent variables jointly affect a dependent variable; whilst point (e) arises when two or more independent variables vary systematically together. Point (e) also includes multicollinearity with socio-economic variables, such as high income people living in well-wooded, topographically varied, locations. Thus, in such complex landscape assemblages, HPMs may not be able to distinguish accurate values for attributes in a landscape. The values derived from such models may be context dependent in the sense that they measure the value of a landscape attribute in a particular landscape context.

Moreover, TCMs and HPMs can only value environmental goods which already exist, not those which may arise in the future. Landscapes are subject to change and policy appraisal may require an assessment of peoples' preferences for the different landscapes which may arise in the future, because of changing economic conditions, compared to the current landscape of the area. Thus whilst TCMs and HPMs can be employed in certain circumstances to value current landscape attributes, they are not able to value alternative future landscapes.

The limitations of using TCMs and HPMs to value the benefits of landscape protection have resulted in the application of various forms of contingent valuation methods (CVMs). This chapter illustrates the application of CVM and its use in cost-benefit analysis by reviewing several studies which have attempted to value the landscape of the Yorkshire Dales in Northern England.

2 YORKSHIRE DALES

The dales (or valleys) of the Pennines form a particular landscape in northern England. Their special character was recognised in 1954 when the area was designated as the Yorkshire Dales National Park, under the 1949 National Parks and Access to the Countryside Act. The area is an upland carboniferous limestone block, comprising of an escarpment in the west, with rivers flowing

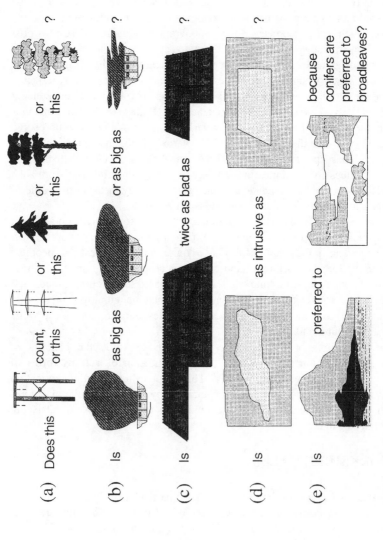

(a) Does this   count, or this   or this   or this   or this   ?

(b) Is   as big as   or as big as   or as big as   ?

(c) Is   twice as bad as   ?

(d) Is   as intrusive as   ?

(e) Is   preferred to   because conifers are preferred to broadleaves?

Figure 8.1 Problems with the hedonic price method.

east in long valleys or dales. The area exhibits all the geomorphological characteristics of a karst area: limestone caverns and caves, limestone pavements, sinks (where streams disappear underground), and fine waterfalls or 'forces' where rivers and streams encounter impervious geological strata.

The area was inhabited by Neolithic, bronze age, and iron age people, and important Roman routes passed through the area. Settlements in the lower dale areas date mainly from occupations by the Angles and Danes (7th to 9th centuries), and on the western fells and upper dales by Norsemen in the 10th century. Growing population in the 16th century led to farming extending up the valley sides, with common grazing on the moorland ridges and fells (hill and plateau tops). Common grazing still comprises 25% of all rough pasture, under which each village property owner has grazing rights or 'stints' entitling the grazing of a specified number of animals. The agricultural features of the Yorkshire Dales were established in the 17th and 18th centuries. The dales scenery became characterised by a seemingly endless network of dry-stone walls, enclosing a patchwork of meadows. Small stone barns are typically found in every field, or at least every two or three fields, and store hay for winter cattle feed. Small stone-built villages or hamlets occur every two or three miles along each valley. Archaeological remnants include medieval field terracing, monastic remains, and traces of 18th and 19th century lead mining. Meadows are cut for hay in summer and used for grazing in early spring and autumn. Because of this, where meadows are naturally fertilised and seeded, they are full of wild flowers and plants in late spring and early summer. The meadows, and small broad-leaved woodlands of ash and hazel, with oak and birch, form a habitat for many species of birds, butterflies and associated wild flowers; whilst the moorland is grazed by sheep, and forms an important area of grouse moor (for shooting).

3 YORKSHIRE DALES ESA

Many of the dales were designated in 1987 as the Pennine Dales Environmentally Sensitive Area.[2] ESAs are designed to safeguard areas of the countryside where landscape, wildlife or historic interest is of national importance recognising the major influence which agriculture can have on the maintenance and enhancement of these features. The ESA concept arose in Europe in the 1980s from concerns about the detrimental impact of more intensive agricultural practices in the countryside; and conversely the need to support the continuation of traditional farming practices in areas where these

---

[2] Namely Dentdale, Langstrothdale, Arkengarthdale, Wharfedale, Swaledale, and Waldendale. The ESA was reviewed and revised in 1992 with additional dales added to the ESA designation, namely Deepdale, Grisedale, Bishopdale, Littondale, Coverdale, Garsdale, Upper Wensleydale, Raydale and mid-Wensleydale, Teesdale; Mallerstang and the Upper Eden Valley, etc.

have contributed to a distinctive landscape, wildlife habitat, or to the preservation of archaeological and historic features.[3]

Preventative expenditure is incurred under the various Tiers of the Pennine Dales ESA programme in order to conserve the landscape. Four main categories of expenditure are specified.

1. Stone walls and stone field barns: 80% of the cost of conserving or repairing these features.[4]

2. Hay meadows: Tier 1 payments of £135 per hectare per year (1994 prices) to preserve traditional hay meadows by restrictions on stocking, use of artificial fertilisers and herbicides, cutting dates for hay, and improved drainage. Tier 2 payments of £210 per hectare per year, to increase the area and improve the nature conservation quality of hay meadows.

3. Woodland: the Forestry Authority's Woodland Grant Scheme offers grants for planting and maintenance of small woods on farms; and a supplementary ESA grant of £25 per hectare is payable for loss of grazing.

4. Public access for walking and other quiet recreation: £170 per kilometre per year for a 10-metre wide strip along the sides or across fields (existing rights of way are not eligible).

Such preventative expenditure to maintain a landscape can easily be quantified and aggregated, but this says little about people's preferences for that landscape, and its attributes, or preferences for alternative landscapes which might evolve in the future. Prior to the introduction of the ESA scheme, the current landscape (*today's agricultural landscape*) of the Yorkshire Dales was under threat. Financial profit-maximising motives and

---

[3] Other ESAs designated in 1987 were The Broads; Somerset Levels and Moors; South Downs; and West Penwith. Additional designations in 1988 comprised Breckland; North Peak; Shropshire Borders; Suffolk River Valleys; and Test Valley. Further designations in 1993 and 1994 included such areas as Exmoor; the Lake District; Wiltshire Downs; Blackdown Hills; Dartmoor; and Shropshire Hills.

[4] The Barns and Walls Conservation Scheme in Swaledale and Arkengarthdale was launched in 1989 English Heritage and the Yorkshire Dales National Park. Around one village, Muker, in upper Swaledale there are 100 barns within one square kilometre. Barns were built for storing hay in summer and sheltering cattle in winter. Changes in farming methods, with the centralisation of beef and dairy facilities on farmsteads, resulted in many barns being abandoned and allowed to fall into disrepair in the latter half of the 20th century. However, recent farming shifts to sheep are re-emphasising the importance of dispersed feed barns away from the farmstead. In 1997/98 the 250th barn restoration will be completed in Swaledale, and work continues on repairing the remaining 270 barns on the endangered list. Nearly half of the 1000 miles of dry stone walls in Swaledale and Arkengarthdale also require repairs.

increasing difficulties faced by hill sheep farmers resulted in some dry-stone walls and stone barns becoming derelict, in the growing use of artificial herbicides and fertilisers on meadowland (with consequential loss of wild flowers), the amalgamation of farms, and increasing numbers of hill sheep and ewes. O'Riordan *et al.* (1989, 1993) suggested seven alternative landscapes which might evolve in the Yorkshire Dales (Figure 8.2). Continued agricultural subsidies in the European Union prior to the MacSharry reforms of 1992 could have led to the agricultural landscape becoming a *semi-intensive agricultural landscape*, with increasing size and productivity of farms, and partial loss of some traditional landscape features such as dry-stone walls, heather moor and broad-leaved trees. By contrast, the withdrawal of upland subsidies could result in hill farmers having to compete with more fertile lowland farms, leading to either an uncontrolled, neglected and *abandoned agricultural landscape* where normal agricultural activity is discontinued; or an *intensive agricultural landscape* where profitability could be increased by buying out smaller farms to create livestock ranches, and by taking advantage or modern technology. Flower-filled meadows would be intensified for silage, outlying meadows and moorland would be abandoned for scrub, and stone walls and stone barns would become derelict. Alternatively, the withdrawal of agricultural subsidies and price support, and increasing time and resources for leisure in the future might result in opportunities for the creation of a *sporting landscape* by landowners, as tenant farms become unviable. Under this scenario, the land might be used like a series of large estates for grouse and pheasant shooting, deer hunting and outdoor recreation. Heather moor would increase to encourage grouse, new large mixed conifer and broad-leaved woodlands would be created for game cover, and some field barns might be converted to recreational uses. In the absence of agricultural subsidies, a *wild landscape* could be consciously created, with large areas of the Dales set aside for unmanaged wildlife. Without grazing, much of the land would eventually end up covered with natural broad-leaved woodland, with flowery glades replacing meadows, and heather moorland invaded by scrub and bog. Barns and stone walls would steadily become derelict. Conservation subsidies would, however, allow farmers to continue traditional farming practices, whilst simultaneously conserving the landscape to a greater degree than that undertaken prior to the 1987 ESA scheme. A *conserved agricultural landscape* under such a scheme, would have more traditional hay meadows than *today's* (i.e. pre-1987) *landscape* where some meadows had been re-seeded by higher yielding grasses and artificially fertilised, while broad-leaved woodlands, barns and dry-stone walls would be carefully maintained, and new broad-leaved woodlands planted. However, with limited conservation grants, a skeletal *planned agricultural landscape* could evolve, which enhances the best of the traditional landscape features, whilst derelict features are progressively removed. There would be more traditional hay meadows than in *today's landscape*, some new conifer and broad-leaved woods, but only some of the strategically placed field barns and dry-stone walls would remain.

4 HOLISTIC LANDSCAPE VALUES

The study by Willis and Garrod (1992) used these images (see Figure 8.2) of alternative future landscapes as depicted by O'Riordan (1993) to evaluate the preferences of residents and visitors, and their demand for various landscapes through their WTP for their creation. Respondents were presented with eight paintings of the landscape: one showing *today's* (pre-1987) *landscape* plus a painting of each of the other alternative future landscapes. Each painting was accompanied by a small literary description of its features and differences compared to *today's landscape*. To ensure standardisation, each picture was painted by the same artist and depicted the same dale and hill scene: the Dales National Park Authority validated the visual images and literary descriptions. To avoid any bias from titles, the paintings were labelled A, B, C, etc. After viewing the pictures and reading the descriptions, respondents were asked to rank their three most preferred landscapes and open-ended CV questions were directed at their WTP for their preferred landscape.

A random sample of 300 households in the 12 largest parishes in the Craven District, which covers most of the south-east area of the National Park, were selected and interviewed in 1990, representing 25% of households in the area. A random sample of 300 visitors were interviewed during the same period in the three main villages in the area.

Table 8.1 documents the preferences of visitors and residents for landscape in the Yorkshire Dales. The overwhelming preference of both groups was for *today's landscape*, perhaps an expected choice given known psychological bias for the *status quo* (Samuelson and Zeckhauser, 1988), and choice heuristics of individuals based on representativeness, availability, and anchoring (Tversky and Kahneman, 1974). The *conserved landscape*, which is very similar to *today's landscape*, was also a popular first choice. By comparison, other landscapes were rarely chosen as the most preferred landscape. For the second choice landscape, votes were fairly evenly split between the *planned landscape* and the *conserved landscape*, indeed more than half of those who voted for *today's landscape* as first choice, voted for the *conserved landscape* as second choice. As one moves away from the first choice (*today's landscape*), consensus about which landscape is the most desirable breaks down. For the third preference, whilst the planned landscape received most votes, there was considerable and evenly divided support for four other landscapes: *conserved*, *sporting*, *wild*, and *today's*. However, note that the *semi-intensive* and *intensive agricultural landscape* options remained the least preferred alternatives for residents and visitors.

Table 8.1: Landscape preferences for visitors and residents of the Yorkshire Dales (Percentage of respondents)

Landscapes

Choice	1 visitors	1 residents	2 visitors	2 residents	3 visitors	3 residents
Abandoned	2.6	3.1	5.6	4.1	5.3	5.2
Semi-intensive	0.3	0.3	0.7	0.3	0.7	1.0
Intensive	-	-	0.3	0.3	0.7	1.7
Planned	7.3	6.8	31.5	37.8	34.0	31.6
Conserved	28.7	29.5	38.4	36.1	17.3	19.1
Sporting	1.0	2.7	4.0	4.1	10.0	9.4
Wild	12.5	6.8	8.6	9.2	12.7	8.7
Today's	47.2	50.2	10.6	7.5	19.0	22.6

1. first choice or most preferred landscape; 2. second choice or preference; 3. third choice or preference

Consistency in landscape preferences was supported by the results of another series of questions asking respondents whether they would like to see less, the same, or more of certain attributes in the landscape: i.e. dry-stone walls, stone field barns, small fields of crops, wire fencing, wild flowers, broad-leaved woodland, hay meadows, heather moorland, grazing animals, coniferous woodland, modern sheds (Willis and Garrod, 1992).

Mean WTP to preserve the respondents' most preferred landscape varied from zero for *semi-intensive* and *intensive agricultural landscapes* to £18.18 per year for the *planned landscape,* to up to £34.96 for the *conserved landscape.* Standard deviations were large, and there was no significant difference between the landscape values where these were positive. Nevertheless, theoretical models were able to explain 25% of residents' and 18% of visitors' WTP for *today's landscape* (Willis and Garrod, 1992); a reasonable explanation for an open-ended WTP question. Moreover, there was a significant difference between the proportions of people who opted for different choices. When aggregated this resulted in significant differences in aggregate WTP for first preference landscapes: see Table 8.2. Table 8.2 also documents the costs to public sector agencies of maintaining these landscapes and simple benefit/cost (B/C) ratios. *Today's landscape* generates the highest B/C ratio: benefits are four times higher than the public sector costs of maintaining this landscape.

This study was limited in a number of ways. No information was available on respondents' ranking across all landscapes. The analysis of such a ranking using say a Borda count (Mueller, 1979; Willis, 1980) voting system might have revealed a different ranking of landscape types, especially if one landscape (e.g. *today's landscape*) was an irrelevant alternative in the sense it would not survive *ex ante* into the future anyway without a change in public support payments. Only a limited amount of information was available on respondents' utility differences between different landscapes. The ranking of landscape types could have usefully been analysed in a contingent ranking framework similar to that adopted by Lareau and Rae (1989).

Table 8.2: Aggregate WTP for first preference landscapes by visitors and residents and estimated public sector costs of each landscape (£, 1990 prices)

Landscape	Visitors	Residents	Public costs	benefit /cost ratio
Abandoned	2,470,000	2,164	2,800,000	0.88
Semi-intensive	0	0	6,000,000	-
Intensive	0	0	10,400,000	-
Planned	5,308,560	8,280	14,000,000	0.38
Conserved	40,134,080	73,663	19,000,000	2.12
Sporting	1,346,800	5,528	18,400,000	0.07
Wild	17,100,000	18,409	8,100,000	2.11
Today's	41,762,520	118,910	9,000,000	4.65

5 VALUING ESA ATTRIBUTES IN THE LANDSCAPE

Respondents can holistically rank different landscape representations relatively easily. Unfortunately, conventional pictorial representations of landscapes do not permit attributes to be varied within each landscape picture from respondent to respondent. Thus, unless pictorial representations are combined with a contingent ranking choice experiment in which attributes related to each picture are permitted to vary somewhat, and to overlap a little between pictures, it becomes much more difficult to assess the value of individual attributes within the landscape, and to assess the extent to which these are substitutes for one another, or the extent to which they are complements.

In a continuation of the work in the Yorkshire Dales National Park, Santos (1997) specifically addressed substitution relationships in people's valuation of three landscape attributes in the Pennine Dales ESA programme. This study used a dichotomous choice (DC) question to value the ESA scheme:

Suppose that your share of the scheme costs (comprising programme 1: stone walls and barns; programme 2: flower rich meadows; programme 3: broad-leaved woodlands) resulted in an increase in £ ____ in your household income tax. Would you be willing to pay £ ____ every year to ensure that the scheme can be carried out?

NO   YES   DON'T KNOW

The questionnaire also elicited discrete choices involving partial conservation schemes, such as:

Consider now a scheme only comprising programme 1: stone walls and barns: Would you be willing to pay £ ____ every year to ensure that the scheme can be carried out?

NO   YES   DON'T KNOW

In a series of such DC questions *the scheme* covered alternatively programme 1: stone walls and stone field barns; programme 2: flower rich hay meadows; programme 3: broad-leaved woodland; and also programmes 1 & 2; programmes 1 & 3; and programmes 2 & 3.

The presence of substitution and complementarity effects between elements of an environmental scheme, means that the benefits of any one policy can depend upon the sequence of policy (attribute) changes: i.e. benefits are path dependent. Substitution effects can arise because visitors to a landscape area such as the Yorkshire Dales perceive other landscape areas as substitutes (the Derbyshire Dales some 100 kms to the south of the Yorkshire Dales are geomorphologically similar and can be regarded as an imperfect substitute); and within a landscape they may perceive attributes comprising that landscape as substitutes for one another, at least over some variation in attribute levels. In addition, because of the budget constraint, having spent some money on the conservation of some landscapes or landscape attributes, the purchasing power of individuals for subsequent improvements is reduced: hence landscape attributes are substitutes when competing for the same fixed budget.

Substitution relationships between the three ESA programme elements (P1: stone walls and stone field barns; P2: flower rich hay meadows; P3: broad-leaved woodland), attributes which epitomise and characterise the Yorkshire Dales landscape, were estimated by Santos (1997) using a DC model following Cameron's (1988) censored logistic regression approach. The valuation function to be estimated was of the type $WTP_i = x_i \beta + \mu_i$, where : x_i is a vector of explanatory variables characterising the respondent and the programme content of the particular scheme valued by this respondent (including interaction terms); β is a vector of parameters to be estimated; and μ_i is a logistic random error term with zero mean and dispersion parameter κ. The estimation problem is how to estimate β from observations on x_i and I_i - a binary variable that is equal to one for 'yes' and 0 otherwise - and no direct observations on WTP. $I_i = 1$ implies that WTP_i should be larger than t_i, the bid amount presented to that particular respondent as the price to be paid for the particular scheme. Thus, it is possible to apply Cameron's log likelihood function:

$$log\ L = \Sigma (1 - I_i)\ [(t_i - x_i'\beta) / \kappa] - log\ \{1 + exp[(t_i - x_i'\beta) / \kappa]\} \quad (8.1)$$

which takes into account the fact that respondents are presented with a threshold value t_i. The presence of t_i allows κ to be identified, which then allows β to be isolated, and hence permits the underlying valuation function to be determined. When $t_i = 0$ for all i (that is: when t_i is included as an ordinary explanatory variable among the other x_i's), this equation collapses to the conventional logit likelihood function. Cameron shows that this function can be maximised either by (a) a general non-linear optimisation computer program in GAUSS or LIMDEP, or (b) including t_i among the explanatory variables in an ordinary maximum likelihood logit model and computing point estimates of β and κ from the logit parameter estimates. However, the latter approach requires the logit function to be linear in parameters; and further procedures are required to derive asymptotic standard errors.

Hoehn (1991) shows that using a second-order Taylor series approximation to specify the valuation function allows for either complementarity or substitution effects to be identified in the analysis. Complementarity or substitution effects are identified through the sign (+/-) of the parameter estimate of the particular pairwise interaction term. However, the second-order approach constrains each pairwise substitution relationship to be constant over the whole valuation sequence, although this is not a requirement in economic theory. Santos (1997) extended Hoehn's approach based upon a second-order Taylor series of constant curvature, with a third-order Taylor series, adding a third-order interaction term among the three programme elements (i.e. P1*P2*P3). This third-order interaction term increases the flexibility of the WTP model compared to the second-order approximation, in that it allows for pairwise substitution effects to change in size, and even to change in sign, along the valuation sequence. A change in sign implies that two attributes or programmes that were initially substitutes become complements later in the sequence, or *vice versa*.

Table 8.3: Estimated value function of ESA programme attributes in the Pennine Dales

Dependent variable: WTP for landscape conservation in Dales

Number of observations: 2295

Correct predictions: 84.0%

-2 Log-likelihood ratio: 1548.51

Degrees of freedom: 14

level of significance: P<0.0001

Prediction success %:

		actual		total
		will pay	will not	
Predicted	would pay	47.5	11.4	58.9
	would not	4.7	36.5	41.1
Total		52.1	47.9	100.0

Variables	Parameter estimates	t-ratios.	label
P1	18.52	3.395	Programme 1: stone walls and field barns
P2	19.07	3.651	Programme 2: flower rich hay meadows
P3	25.60	4.969	Programme 3: broad-leaved woodland
P1 * P2	-24.45	-4.084	Interaction between programmes 1 & 2
P1 * P3	-25.70	-4.286	Interaction between programmes 1 & 2
P2 * P3	-28.91	-4.819	Interaction between programmes 1 & 2
P1 * P2 * P3	22.59	2.322	Interaction among all three programmes
P1 * income	0.000771	4.616	Interaction between income and programme 1
P2 * income	0.000685	4.054	Interaction between income and programme 2
P3 * income	0.000535	3.235	Interaction between income and programme 3
P1 * firstP1	9.55	2.370	Programme 1 when first in programme ranking
P2 * firstP2	17.31	3.936	Programme 2 when first in programme ranking
P3 * firstP3	16.23	3.292	Programme 3 when first in programme ranking
κ	21.41	20.644	Dispersion parameter of the logistic distribution

Source: Santos (1997)

The constraints on the censored regression model were (1) a zero intercept and (2) that variables other than the programme (P1, P2, P3) dummy variables only entered the model as interactions with these dummies. Whilst a non-zero intercept specification of the model fitted the data better, a non-zero intercept is not consistent on theoretical grounds as it implies that individuals would be prepared to pay something for a null conservation scheme. Moreover the non-zero intercept specification resulted in negative regression coefficients for the individual ESA programme variables, which is inconsistent with the idea that the ESA programme attributes are economic goods, not bads. Besides, the zero-intercept third-order interaction model fitted the data as well as the non-zero-intercept second-order model.

Table 8.3 reports the results of the censored regression model with the third-order interaction term. The individual programme elements (P1, P2, and P3) are positive; the interaction between the attributes in the ESA scheme

(P1*P2; P1*P3; P2*P3) are negative, implying that they are substitutes for one another; whilst the third-order interaction is positive but smaller in absolute value than any of the three pairwise interactions between attributes, indicating a complement relationship between elements for the ESA programme as a whole.

Table 8.4 shows the mean WTP values for the different schemes. The narrow confidence intervals reveal a remarkable degree of precision in the estimates. WTP increases as the scheme becomes more comprehensive (P1, or P2, or P3 < P1+P2, or P1+P3, or P2+P3 < P1+P2+P3).

Table 8.4: Estimates of mean WTP for different landscape conservation schemes in the Pennine Dales ESA (£ per household per year, 1995 prices)

Scheme	E(WTP)	95% confidence interval
(1, 0, 0)	43.01	36.94 ; 49.07
(0, 1, 0)	42.62	36.52 ; 48.71
(0, 0, 1)	42.90	36.87 ; 48.93
(1, 1, 0)	61.17	52.75 ; 69.59
(1, 0, 1)	60.20	51.76 ; 68.65
(0, 1, 1)	56.61	48.28 ; 64.93
(1, 1, 1)	72.05	63.98 ; 80.12

Source: Santos (1997)

The value of each element of the ESA scheme when elements are added at different steps in the valuation sequence was also derived. These values were calculated as the difference in mean WTP for the two relevant schemes in Table 8.4. Thus, for example, the average value of programme 1 after valuing programme 2, is:

$$WTP[P1 \mid (0,1,0)] = WTP(1,1,0) - WTP(0,1,0) \qquad (8.2)$$

All possible sequence values of *WTP(P1)* conditional upon other programme elements (no programme; programme 2; programme 3; and programmes 2 & 3) also need to be determined. Differences between the sequential values of the same programme define the substitution effect between the programme and other programmes. Thus, for example, for P2:

$$WTP[P2 \mid (1,0,0)] - WTP[P2 \mid (0,0,0)] \qquad (8.3)$$

measures the substitution effect of P1 on the valuation of P2, with no previous programme elements in the sequence.

Table 8.5 presents the values for each programme when valued at different steps in the sequence. All programmes yield a similar value when they are the first in the sequence (P1 = 43.01; P2 = 42.62; P3 = 42.90). However, Table 8.5 shows that the sequential value of each programme in the Pennine Dales ESA depends upon the previous programmes in the sequence; a finding which is consistent with the sequence dependence of benefits demonstrated by Hoehn and Randall (1989). For all programmes sequential values decline with the number of programmes previously introduced into the sequence: this occurs because of substitution between programmes. ESA programmes are differentially substitutable. The decline in the sequential value of P1 (stone walls and barns) is smaller than the sequential decline in value experienced for P2 (flower rich hay meadows) and P3 (broad-leaved woodland). P1 and P3 appear to be more substitutable since the sequential value of P2 and P3 when added to each other is smaller than the sequential value of P1 when added to either P2 or P3. This conforms to the anecdotal evidence regarding general feelings visitors have for the Dales landscape: stone walls and barns provide the character of the Dales landscape, in which small broad-leaved woodlands are a noticeable feature to a lesser extent, and flower rich meadows even less so, except in late spring.

When there are significant substitution effects between attributes, the value of an environmental good or policy mechanism is not the sum of independently valued attributes changes. Independent valuation and summation (IVS) of attributes changes, with all other attributes held at their policy-off position, is prone to bias. The IVS bias is positive where attributes are substitute; and negative where attributes are complements (Hoehn and Randall, 1989). Santos (1997) demonstrates the effect of IVS bias in his data. The sequential value for the total ESA scheme programme attributes was £72.05 per household per year for visitor households. However, if each element of the scheme had been valued independently and summed (i.e. 43.01 + 42.62 + 42.90) (the IVS result: see Chapter 5), the total value for the complete scheme would have been estimated at £128.53 per household per year. This implies that an IVS procedure would have overestimated the value of the total ESA scheme by 78%, compared with its true value as estimated by Santos (1997) using Hoehn and Randall's (1989) model accounting for substitution effects in valuation. Clearly, such inappropriate aggregation under the IVS procedure can lead to extremely biased results, high B/C ratios, and too many schemes appearing to satisfy the cost benefit test. Only a small part of the work of Santos on the valuation of the Yorkshire Dales landscape is reported here. A comprehensive account can be found in Santos (1998).

Table 8.5: Estimates of the sequential value of each programme or group of programmes in the Pennine Dales ESA when added to different combinations of programmes (£ per household per year, 1995 prices)

Programme		Combinations of programmes already available (P1, P2, P3)					
		(1, 0, 0)	(0, 1, 0)	(0, 0, 1)	(1, 1, 0)	(1, 0, 1)	(0, 1, 1)
P1	43.01		18.55	17.31			15.44
P2	42.62	18.16		13.71		11.85	
P3	42.90	17.20	13.99		10.88		
P1 + P2				29.15			
P1 + P3			29.43				
P2 + P3		29.04					

Source: Santos (1997)

6 LANDSCAPES, VISIBILITY AND NATIONAL PARKS IN THE USA

A substantial part of research on the valuation of landscape in the USA has been concerned with people's WTP to view landscapes in terms of improving visibility through reductions in air pollution. Winger and McKean (1991) observed that visitors to the Mesa Verde National Park (MVNP) in Colorado altered their behaviour in a statistically significant way in response to environmental quality, particularly in relation to air pollution. Visibility is affected by copper smelting, coal-fired power plants and urban development upwind of the MVNP. Visit rates to the MVNP were observed to vary by 55% of the average visit rate according to visibility, with many more visitors being attracted when visibility was good.[5]

The analysis of the MVNP was based on an earlier survey in 1980 of people's WTP higher electricity bills for preserving the average current air quality and corresponding visibility in the Grand Canyon, MVNP, and Zion National Parks. The study surveyed over 600 households in Albuquerque, Chicago, Denver and Los Angeles. Respondents were shown sets of photographs of a particular National Park vista depicting five different levels of air quality. The five photographs were chosen so that perceptible differences existed between adjacent photographs, with each photograph linked to a regional emission level. Contingent valuation was used to elicit the amount respondents would be willing to pay for the visibility levels depicted

---

[5] By comparison the effect of temperature variation over the study period was less than half that of visibility (visits varied inversely with temperature); although variations in humidity had almost as great an effect on visitor numbers as visibility.

in the five photographs. In addition, participants were asked about their WTP to prevent a plume being seen from the Grand Canyon National Park (GCNP). The valuation scenario used two photographs of the same view towards Mt. Turnbull with the same lighting conditions and cirrus cloud cover, but with a narrow grey plume crossing the sky in one photograph. The study attempted to elicit both use values for visitors and option values and preservation or existence values for non-users. An entrance fee payment vehicle was used to elicit use value and electricity bill payments used to elicit existence value. (Schulze *et al.*, 1983).

A number of controversial conclusions emerged from this study. Contrary to economic theory respondents placed a higher value on enhancing visual quality compared to avoiding comparable decreases in visual quality. Second, use value was two orders of magnitude lower than preservation value. Third, the study was subject to embedding and substitution problems. This was demonstrated when Tolley and Randall (1985) replicated the 1980 survey of Chicago residents on their WTP to improve visibility at the Grand Canyon. The 1981 study by Tolley and Randall (1985), which is documented by Mitchell and Carson (1989), first elicited WTP for a reduction in air pollution which would improve visibility in Chicago (illustrated by sets of photographs from 9 to 18 miles visibility); then WTP for the same improvement in the rest of the USA east of the Mississippi. Finally, respondents were asked their WTP for improvements at the Grand Canyon, again illustrated with photographs. The WTP values for visibility improvement at the Grand Canyon differed significantly between the two surveys. The average Chicago resident was estimated to be willing to pay $90 per year in the 1980 survey, when the Grand Canyon visibility improvement was valued independently; and $16 in 1981 when the same visibility improvement was valued third in a three-part sequence.

In a subsequent econometric analysis of this data, Hoehn (1991) shows that as air quality increases at both sites, a respondent's valuation increases at a decreasing rate; however, the cross-quality interaction terms between Grand Canyon and Chicago air quality suggest that regional air quality conditions are substitutes in valuation. Thus Hoehn concludes that environmental values are contextual: i.e. conditional on the presence or absence of multidimensional resource flows. This illustrates the inappropriateness of transferring simple *IVS* values from parts to the whole, and from the whole to parts; the role and importance of substitutes in determining a WTP value; and the importance of *ceteris paribus* assumptions and the extent of the partial equilibrium assumptions framing the study. The aggregate valuation of a policy change is unique; whilst a theoretically consistent disaggregated valuation can only be obtained by valuing policy impacts along a path of valuation as Santos (1998) illustrates.

Rae (1983) used contingent ranking to test the importance of visibility to visitors to MVNP and Great Smoky National Park (GSNP). Each respondent was asked to rank in order eight MVNP alternatives on the assumption that the visibility, congestion, and price conditions specified on each card were known in advance of a visit. In another sample respondents were asked to rank the alternatives, but were also informed of the probability that the visibility conditions would occur. Data on visibility at the time of the study indicated that during daylight hours intense plumes occurred about 11% of the time, intense hazes 19%, moderate hazes 56%, and clear conditions 14%. The two approaches produced similar results. The probabilistic approach produced a value of $3.09 per vehicle for moving from the existing distribution of visibility to a guaranteed clear condition. The deterministic approach estimated values of $5.10 to ensure clear conditions over an intense plume; $4.57 to ensure clear conditions over intense haze; and $2.84 to ensure clear conditions over a moderate haze. This produces an expected value of $0.11(\$5.10) + 0.19(\$4.57) + 0.56(2.84) + 0.14(0) = \$3.02$ per vehicle. Similar results were reached for the GSNP, leading Rae (1983) to conclude that respondents were reasonably consistent when ranking alternatives both in a deterministic and probabilistic setting.

Crocker and Shogren (1991) argue for an *ex ante* valuation given that prospective visibility levels are inherently uncertain, implying that choice is based on the perceived probability of a visibility state for a landscape. Their CVM study, of a vista from the Central Oregon Cascades wilderness site and a vista from an urban park in Portland, Oregon, used photographs with haze levels superimposed to indicate four visibility ranges from each site related to distance. Respondents ranked each of the four vistas and indicated the probability, during a visit to the Cascades or the urban park, of encountering their most and least preferred vista. Respondents then stated their marginal WTP for the four vistas. A number of interesting conclusions emerged from this study. First, no preference reversals occurred between any respondents' rank ordering of vistas and marginal WTP estimates. Option price payments for improved visual range increased at a decreasing rate; with similar percentage rates of decrease at both the wilderness and urban sites. Second, respondents' value estimates for guaranteed provision of their most preferred vistas with respect to a change in the time of this provision produced discount rates between 10% to 49% depending on the site (Cascades or Portland), and the time period. The discount rates were inversely related to education. These high discount rates correspond to those derived in many studies of choice in consumer durable goods (see Loewenstein and Thaler, 1989). Third, since choice is *ex ante* this is the frame of reference that is most appropriate for valuation: it captures risk attitudes which are relevant when the exact environmental consequences of a policy choice are uncertain. Crocker and Shogren argue that, by allowing respondents to rank order preferred resource

Today's landscape

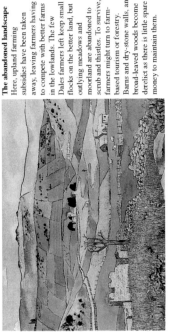

This typical Dales scene has much of the community earning a living from farming or tourism. Farm incomes are supported by government subsidies, some intended to increase production and maintain Dales farming. Some meadows are still cut for hay, others produce intensive silage. Most barns and dry-stone walls are well maintained, but some are derelict or replaced by fences and modern sheds. Broad-leaved woodland and heather moorland are starting to disappear because of over-grazing by sheep and cattle.

The abandoned landscape

Here, upland farming subsidies have been taken away, leaving farmers having to compete with better farms in the lowlands. The few Dales farmers left keep small flocks on the better land, but outlying meadows and moorland are abandoned to scrub and thistles. To survive, farmers might turn to farm-based tourism or forestry. Barns and dry-stone walls, and broad-leaved woods become derelict as there is little spare money to maintain them.

The planned landscape

Using their own finances, or by taking advantage of limited conservation grants, farmers in this future could enhance the best of their traditional landscape features, whilst tidying-up any dereliction. There would be a few more hay meadows, and more heather moorland managed for sheep, grouse and wildlife. A mix of new conifer and broad-leaved woodlands would be planted. Only some of the field barns and dry-stone walls would remain, but these would be well maintained.

The conserved landscape

Here, public money would be available to farmers who continue to produce livestock and show they are conserving the landscape at the same time. Conservation bodies, and a pool of labour, could provide extra help, but farmers could also supplement their income from farm-based tourism. There would be more heather moorland and many more hay meadows than today. Old broad-leaved woodlands would be well maintained, and new ones planted. Barns and dry-stone walls would be carefully looked after.

Figure 8.2 Future landscapes in the Yorkshire Dales

The intensive landscape

In this scene, little public money is available to subsidise the Dales farming. But agricultural business men could still make a profit by buying out the smaller farmers to create big livestock ranches, and taking advantage of modern technology. Flower-filled meadows would be intensified for silage. Large sheds and wire fences would replace most barns and dry-stone walls. Heather moorland would be lost through too much grazing, and broad-leaved woods would be left to die or be replaced by new conifer woodlands.

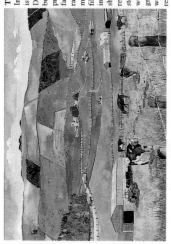

The semi-intensive landscape

In another 50 years or so the Dales might look like this if governments continue to subsidise livestock production. Some farmers would become very intensive, and others merely "tick over" with a few stock. Meadows would be intensified or abandoned to scrub and thistles; the moors would be a patchwork of over-grazed heather and grassland; old woodlands would die or be replaced by new conifer plantations; dry-stone walls and barns would be broken and collapsing.

The wild landscape

If large areas of the Dales were deliberately set-aside for wildlife, or if farm subsidies were stopped and the land was abandoned, this wilderness could develop. A few people could work in tourism. Without grazing, much of the land would eventually be covered by natural broad-leaved woodland. Flowery glades would replace meadows, and the heather moorland would be invaded by scrub and bog. Barns and dry-stone walls would have no further use so would collapse and become overgrown.

The sporting landscape

Here the land is run like big estates, for grouse and pheasant shooting, deer hunting and outdoor recreation. Many local people would work on the estates, and in tourism, but few would farm. There would be more heather moorland because it would be needed for grouse shooting. Large new mixed woodlands of conifers and broad-leaves would provide game cover and timber. Walls would be left to collapse or replaced by fences, and some barns would be converted to new uses.

Figure 8.2 Future landscapes in the Yorkshire Dales (continued)

levels, and to state their perceived likelihood of future provision of each level, as well as their WTP for an increase in the likelihood of provision, this approach captures the correct definition of *ex ante* value.

7 UTILITY SCALING

Although contingent valuation has been employed to assess landscape values, other techniques can be applied to value this complex good. Price (1993) argues that conventional methods are insensitive to subtle landscape changes. He suggests a standard reference gamble approach to establish the cardinal value of one landscape in relation to another. For example, individuals could be asked if they would prefer the certainty of valuing the *intensive agricultural landscape* in Figure 8.2; or a gamble, comprising a 40% probability of viewing the *conserved landscape* and a 60% probability of viewing nothing at all. Hence ordinal preferences can be mapped onto a cardinal utility scale in relation to best and worst landscape scenarios. The standard reference gamble (SG) approach has been used extensively in medicine to value different treatments in relation to best (utility = 1) and worst (utility = 0) outcomes (see Sox *et al.*, 1988). Price (1993) used the SG framework to measure the intrinsic value of preserving the landscape from pylons along two alternative routes through Glen Shiel around Kinloch Hourn in Scotland. The major problem with SG in medical decision-making is attaching a monetary value to the best (where this might be a normal life year) and worst outcomes (where this might be 'being in a permanent vegetative state' or even being dead). Invariably either contingent valuation or observing how much people actually spend in the private health care market (standardising for other attributes such as the quality of health care, ambience of hospital, and socio-economic characteristics of patients, etc.), is used to value one reference point on the standard reference gamble utility scale. Valuing landscape by SG methods involves similar problems.

8 RESEARCH ISSUES

Landscape is perhaps the most complex environmental good to value: it can be made up of an infinite number of configurations in terms of scale, shape, relief, vegetation cover, colour, and man-made features, all of which interact with each other in distinctive permutations. Landscapes also have seasonal effects which make them more attractive in some seasons than in others (e.g. New England in the fall).

Methods such as choice experiments, contingent ranking, standard reference gambles and utility scaling, which attempt to value the individual attributes characterising a landscape, their interactions with each other, or the relative value of landscape change, offer the most promising approaches to valuing multi-dimensional environmental landscape changes. However, many issues still remain to be resolved in applying these techniques. For example, in contingent ranking there are doubts about the cognitive ability of respondents to arrive at a complete ranking, which if confirmed would make the link between choice and ranking tenuous. Indeed, Foster and Mourato (1997) observed that significant proportions of respondents failed various tests of consistency. This observation may, of course, be an artefact of the particular way in which contingent ranking was applied in this study. In a theoretical review, Bergland (1994) suggested that the use of an incomplete ranking, with the few best and the few worst alternatives, was a feasible alternative avoiding some of these types of consistency problem in contingent ranking.

In the EU and the USA, considerable amounts of public money are now being devoted to removing land from agriculture and to compensating farmers for reducing agricultural intensity with the object of maintaining traditional landscape character. Such agri-environment schemes are likely to grow in importance in the future. Hence, it is vital that the value which the general public derives from these changes to landscape character is accurately valued, to ensure that efficiency and good value for money is attained in government expenditure.

REFERENCES

Bergland, Olvar (1994), 'Valuing multidimensional environmental changes with contingent ranking', *Discussion Paper D-15/1994*, Department of Economics and Social Sciences, Agricultural University of Norway, Ås, Norway.

Cameron, Trudy Ann (1988), 'A new paradigm for valuing non-market goods using referendum data: maximum likelihood estimation by censored logistic regression', *Journal of Environmental Economics and Management*, **15**, 355–79.

Crocker, Thomas D. and Jason F. Shogren (1991), '*Ex ante* valuation of atmospheric visibility', *Applied Economics*, **23**, 141–51.

Foster, Vivian and Susana Mourato (1997), 'Behavioural consistency, statistical specification and validity in the contingent ranking method: evidence from a survey on the impact of pesticide use in the UK', *CSERGE Working Paper GEC 97-09*, School of Environmental Sciences, University of East Anglia, Norwich.

Garrod, G.D. and K.G. Willis (1992a), 'Valuing goods' characteristics: an application of the hedonic price method to environmental attributes', *Journal of Environmental Management*, **34**, 59–76.

Garrod, G.D. and K.G. Willis (1992b), 'The environmental economic impact of woodland: a two-stage hedonic price model of the amenity value of forestry in Britain', *Applied Economics*, **24**, 715–28.

Hale, John (1993), *The Civilisation of Europe in the Renaissance*, Harper Collins, London.

Hinde, Roger (1986), *Capability Brown*, Hutchinson, London.

Hoehn, John P. and Alan Randall (1989), 'Too many proposals pass the cost-benefit test', *American Economic Review,* **79**, 544–51.

Hoehn, John P. (1991), 'Valuing the multidimensional impacts of environmental policy: theory and methods', *American Journal of Agricultural Economics,* **73**, 289–99.

Lareau, T.J. and D.A. Rae (1989), 'Valuing willingness-to-pay for diesel odor reductions: an application of the contingent ranking technique', *Southern Economic Journal,* **55**, 728–42.

Loewenstein, George and Richard H. Thaler (1989), 'Intertemporal choice', *Journal of Economic Perspectives,* **3** (4), 181–93.

Mitchell R.C. and R.T. Carson (1989), *Using Surveys to Value Public Goods: The Contingent Valuation Method*, Resources for the Future, Washington DC.

Mueller, Dennis C. (1979), *Public Choice*, Cambridge University Press, Cambridge.

O'Riordan, T., C. Wood and A. Shadrake (198) 'Interpreting Landscape Futures in the Yorkshire Dales National Park', School of Environmental Sciences, University of East Anglia, Norwich.

O'Riordan, Timothy, Christopher Wood, and Ann Shadrake (1993), 'Landscape for tomorrow', *Journal of Environmental Planning and Management,* **36** (2), 123–47.

Price, Colin (1993), 'Applied landscape economics: a personal journey of discovery', *Journal of Environmental Planning and Management,* **36**, 51–63.

Price, Colin (1995), 'The pros and cons of alternative valuation methods', in K.G. Willis and J.T. Corkindale (eds), *Environmental Valuation: new perspectives*, CAB International, Wallingford, Oxfordshire, (Chapter 10).

Rae, Douglas A. (1983), 'The value to visitors of improving visibility at Mesa Verde and Great Smoky National Parks', in Robert D. Row and Lauraine G. Chestnut (eds), *Managing Air Quality and Scenic Resources at National Parks and Wilderness Areas*, Westview Press, Boulder, Colorado.

Samuelson, W. and R. Zeckhauser (1988), 'Status quo bias in decision making', *Journal of Risk and Uncertainty,* **1**, 7–59.

Santos, José Manuel Lima e (1997), *Valuation and Cost Benefit Analysis of Multi-Attribute Environmental Changes: upland landscapes in England and Portugal,*.PhD thesis, University of Newcastle upon Tyne.

Santos, José Manuel Lima e (1998), *The Economic Valuation of Landscape Change*, Edward Elgar, Cheltenham.

Schulze, William D, David S. Brookshire, Eric G. Walther, Karen K. McFarland, Mark A. Thayer, Regan L. Whitworth, Shaul Ben-David, William Palm and John Molenar (1983), 'The economic benefits of preserving visibility in the national parklands of the south-west', *Natural Resources Journal,* **23**, 149–73.

Shucksmith, D.M. (1981), *No Homes for Locals?,* Gower, Aldershot.

Sox, Harold C., Marshal A. Blatt, Michael C. Higgins, and Keith I. Marton (1988), *Medical Decision Making*, Butterworths, Boston.

Tolley, George S. and Alan Randall, with G. Blomquist, M. Brian, R. Fabian, M. Grenchik, G. Fishelson, A. Franfel, J. Hoehn, A. Kelly, R. Krumm, E. Mensah, and T. Smith (1985), 'Establishing and Valuing the Effects of Improved Visibility in the Eastern United States', *Final Report to the US Environmental Protection Agency*, EPA, Washington DC.

Turner, Roger (1985), *Capability Brown and the Eighteenth Century English Landscape*, Rizzoli, New York.

Tversky, A. and D. Kahneman (1974), 'Judgement under uncertainty: heuristics and biases', *Science,* **185**, 1124–31.

Weisbrod, B.A. (1964), 'Collective consumption services for individual consumption goods', *Quarterly Journal of Economics* **78**, 471-7.

Willis, K.G. (1980), *The Economics of Town and Country Planning*, Granada (Collins), London.

Willis, K.G. and G.D. Garrod (1992), 'Assessing the value of future landscapes', *Landscape and Urban Planning,* **23**, 17–32.

Winger, Wendell D. and John R. McKean (1991), 'Visibility: a determinant of park visitor behaviour', *Geoforum,* **22** (4), 391–9.

9. Biodiversity

Thou wast not born for death, immortal bird,
No hungry generations tread thee down;

John Keats (1795–1821): *Ode to a Nightingale*

1 INTRODUCTION

The term biodiversity attempts to describe the innate variability that exists among living organisms, particularly the biological and genetic diversity that is observed both within and between ecosystems, habitats and species (Johnson, 1993). Weitzman (1992) attempts to quantify such diversity as the degree and distance of dissimilarity or difference between any pair of species.

The preservation of biodiversity has an opportunity cost. This may be in terms of human welfare forgone or it may mean that whilst there is a greater diversity of flora and fauna, the total number of individuals in the species represented is reduced. One definition of an optimal biodiversity policy is one which yields the highest present discounted expected value of diversity. A major problem for such a definition occurs in specifying the benefits of biodiversity. Levels of biodiversity influence vital ecosystem services and thus play an important role in the maintenance of many fundamental systems and processes. It is not clear, however, what levels of biodiversity are necessary to maintain these functions. Certain indications of the importance of biodiversity exist. For example, Watkinson (1997) describes some recent experimental studies suggesting that drought resistance and productivity increase with the number of species in a community. This seems to support the so-called rivet hypothesis, which states that as species are eliminated a threshold is reached at which a major ecosystem malfunction occurs, perhaps resulting in the lost of the ecosystem. However, he points out that there is considerable evidence supporting an alternative hypothesis: that there is considerable redundancy between species, and that some species are expendable within ecosystems. Watkinson suggests that it would be difficult to argue that the loss of most of the rare species and protected areas in the UK would have any impact on ecosystem function within the UK.

The immense diversity of biological organisms renders any objective measurement problematic: diversity is not merely a function of the ultrametric distance along some taxonomic evolutionary tree and number of bifurcation nodes back to a common ancestor. There is also the question of genetic diversity within species and the interaction and role of species in forming an ecosystem. Even if a measure of biodiversity could be produced which commanded consensus, lay people would have tremendous difficulty in understanding the measure, assessing its consequences for future productive and consumptives uses, and assessing just how much benefit they derived from biodiversity. This suggests that it may be easier for people to decide what is a reasonable cost for accepting various biodiversity measures, rather than trying to estimate what benefits biodiversity produces *per se*.

2 COST AND MARKET BASED APPROACHES

Biodiversity conservation costs arise primarily because of the opportunity costs of land-use: as the quantity of a habitat or species increases, it increasingly impinges on other production possibilities. However, at the same time, whilst the probability of species extinction is reduced, the marginal benefit of additional habitat or species numbers for biodiversity also declines. In addition to these direct marginal opportunity costs, Pearce and Moran (1994) have argued that the optimal amount of land use conversion to or from habitats depends upon the value of two externality components: (1) the externality or damage cost to biodiversity incurred by the nation from market failure through excessive agricultural subsidy and agricultural intensification; (2) the global externality, that is the cost borne by people outside the nation that owns the habitats. The externality cost through market failure and agricultural subsidies is relatively easy to quantify, as shown in Chapter 2. Global externalities, such as the value of carbon storage in tropical forests and the existence value attached to biodiversity, are more difficult to quantify and value. Some indication of the global externalities of biodiversity can be derived through debt-for-nature swaps (DFNs)[1] and the Global Environmental

---

[1] Debt-for nature swaps involve the purchase by international environmental organisations, governments, and others, of developing countries' debt (usually at a discount to reflect perception in the market on the probability of repayment) which is then written-off in exchange for an undertaking by the debtor country, or agency in the country, to protect a specified habitat or undertake other environmental protection work.

Facility (GEF).[2] Pearce and Warford (1993) detail examples of DFNs in Bolivia, Costa Rica, Ecuador, Madagascar, and Zambia, which have had significant local impacts on the preservation of biodiversity. The Gir National Park (NP) (259 sq. kms) and surrounding sanctuary area (SA) (1153 sq. kms) in Gujarat, India, provides an example of a GEF project. The Gir is the last remaining habitat of the Asiatic lion (estimated numbers 304 in 1995). The GEF project aimed to: (1) resettle 360 families from 54 villages in the SA to villages outside the SA, to reduce human pressure on the lions' habitat;[3] (2) improve pasture and soil, and develop non-conventional energy sources, employment, and community development in 58 other villages outside, but within two miles, of the SA to further reduce pressure within the SA and NP from illegal grazing, wood gathering, etc. (Singh and Kamboj, 1996).

However, DFNs and GEF almost certainly underestimate the extent of global externalities. DFNs and GEF may not create additional funds for conservation, but simply displace other conservation funds. Such initiatives may also suffer from free-rider and prisoner's dilemma problems. Even though biodiversity conservation may be in everyone's joint interest, any individual government and organisation has an incentive to free-ride off others' contributions and spend their potential contributions on social and environmental problems in their own countries. If too many take advantage of these individual incentives then too few resources will be devoted to global biodiversity conservation. Such an outcome seems evident in the distribution of resources to biodiversity conservation. The creation of international institutions capable of measuring, allocating, and regulating biodiversity is a prerequisite for efficient and optimal conservation (Swanson, 1994).

The number of species (e.g. Queen Alexandra's Birdwing (*Ornithoptera alexandrae*); Goliath Birdwing (*Ornithoptera goliath*); Cairn's Birdwing (*Ornithoptera euphorion*))[4] within any genus (e.g. birdwing butterflies

---

[2] The Global Environmental Facility was established in 1990 by the United Nations and the World Bank to provide assistance to developing countries for investments to reduce greenhouse gas emissions, protect the ozone layer, international water resources, and biodiversity.

[3] Initially there were 129 villages or 'nesses' with 845 families comprising some 4,802 people and 16,842 livestock in the NP and SA. A scheme was drawn up in 1972 to resettle the NP villagers (maldhais) outside the SA. Each maldhari (cattle grazing) family was given 3.2 ha. of agricultural land, and a 610 sq. m. plot for house construction free of cost. There are no nesses in the NP now.

[4] Queen Alexandra's Birdwing is the largest butterfly in the world, with a wing span >250 mm. It is an endangered species and restricted to south-east Papua New Guinea. Goliath birdwing is found in Indonesia and New Guinea; and Cairn's Birdwing in Queensland, Australia. The striking Rajah Brooke's Birdwing (*Trogonoptera brookiana*) belongs to another genus of birdwings.

(*Ornithoptera*)), family (e.g. swallowtail butterflies (*Papilionidae*)), and order (moths and butterflies (*Lepidoptera*)), tends to increase towards the equator (Collins and Morris, 1985; Cranbrook and Edwards, 1994), resulting in greater biodiversity in the equatorial compared to arctic areas. Hence, most biodiversity conservation should take place in tropical areas. However, richer western nations spend more on wildlife conservation in their own countries, conserving a few species, than in tropical areas with comparitively greater biodiversity.

Global biodiversity is maximised where there is a co-operative outcome and everyone is better off if conservation succeeds. But the structure of incentives is such that one country or organisation can minimise its vulnerability to the decisions of others by contributing to conservation in its own country. Other countries face similar incentives. In such situations free riding is the dominant strategy, with each nation investing in conservation in its own country, and with a very limited contribution to group co-operation and global conservation. Thus, a unique Nash equilibrium[5] occurs, which is Pareto dominant and which yields a lower payoff for all concerned with conservation.

Moreover, if the scale of DFNs, GEF, and other biodiversity conservation programmes is determined by the median voter, this too may result in a less than optimal amount of biodiversity conservation and environmental protection. Simple majority voting systems can devote too few resources to conservation, compared to a utilitarian Lindahl equilibrium, even where conservationists are in a majority (Willis, 1980). Hence basing the quantity of biodiversity conservation on the costs and expenditure actually incurred under conservation programmes may not be the most appropriate mechanism. Of course, non-additionality, free-riding, and prisoner's dilemma problems are always difficult to substantiate in practice, but the structure of incentives and outcomes in global biodiversity conservation suggest that they are present.

Biodiversity conservation also incurs direct costs. Expenditure under some environmental programmes actually entails paying farmers and other land users to manage their land more actively. Lowland heaths in Britain, for example, have developed principally on free draining, acidic, sandy or gravel soils, following the removal of natural woodland cover in ancient times, and are maintained by human management activities (grazing by livestock, cutting of vegetation, burning to improve grazing, etc.) that have prevented reversion to woodland. Changes in farming practices have led to the abandonment of traditional methods of heathland management and the need to subsidise the

---

[5] A Nash equilibrium is a strategy with the property that each player's equilibrium strategy is the best response to others' strategies. In many simple 'games' there is a unique Nash equilibrium that yields a lower payoff to participants, than some other more co-operative outcome.

reintroduction of these practices to maintain the habitat and prevent encroachment by scrub, bracken, or other trees and plants. Lowland heaths are recognised as an internationally important nature conservation resource (Wynne *et al.*, 1995; Webb, 1986), and a priority for nature conservation in Britain because it is such a rare and threatened habitat (Department of the Environment, 1995). Costs of heathland habitat maintenance are subsidised under various agri-environmental programs such as the Countryside Stewardship Scheme, and Wildlife Enhancement Schemes (Willis *et al.*, 1996).

Biodiversity conservation is characterised by risk and uncertainty. There is a risk in devoting resources to conserve a species: the species may still become extinct, or it may be uncertain whether or not its preservation has any benefit to an ecosystem or to mankind. Moreover, if ecosystems are non-linear, non-convex dissipative systems, with thresholds, a marginal change in the population of some species at a threshold level may cause a discontinuity in the ecosystem, and flip the system to another state. Threshold effects are one of the least tractable problems in biodiversity. Threshold levels are not known with certainty, and there is uncertainty as to the costs of exceeding thresholds. Hence, Perrings and Pearce (1994) argue that economic instruments (penalties) to account for the social costs of biological resource use, need to ensure a margin of safety above the threshold level to reflect society's degree of risk aversion to breaching the ecological threshold. Maintenance of safe minimum standards (SMSs) (i.e. the minimum stocks of biological resources consistent with the resilience of ecosystems of interest) may be a more effective conservation instrument to protect the total stock of a species (e.g. fish), in effect setting an aggregate reserve stock for species and habitats. The exploitation of stock in excess of the reserve can then be determined by the market, e.g. by auctioning quotas, thus combining greater efficiency in allocation with the safety of a reserve stock.

Some attempts have been made to evaluate biodiversity reserves and determine appropriate size in relation to risk and uncertainty. Montgomery *et al.* (1994) assessed the probability of species preservation, and conversely extinction, in relation to conservation cost in terms of the opportunity value of timber forgone in preserving the habitat of the northern spotted owl. Simpson *et al.* (1996) assessed the pharmaceutical value of biodiversity as a function of the probability that any species chosen at random will yield a commercially viable discovery.

The importance of biodiversity as a genetic and biochemical resource with potential commercial value is probably overestimated because of availability bias (cognitive misperception through recalling instances of the importance of natural organisms in medicines, and ignoring biological resources which contribute nothing to medicine),[6] and risk aversion (the thought that some species might exist which would be instrumental in discovering a cure for a currently incurable disease).

Simpson *et al.* (1996) value the marginal species on its incremental value to the probability of making a commercial discovery. Biological resources aid pharmaceutical research in identifying 'leads' or 'blueprints' to compounds, rather than providing pharmaceutical products that can be used in an unmodified form. There are estimated to be 10 million to 100 million living species, of which only 1.4 million have been described and of these only a small number have been subject to chemical and genetic analysis. Because there are so many species that can be used in biological prospecting, sources of useful products are either so common as to be redundant, or so rare as to make their discovery unlikely; hence losses in biological diversity have little bearing on when the next miracle drug is found (Simpson, 1997). Thus, since the set of organisms to be sampled is large, the value of the marginal species must be small. If all representatives of a species produce a compound, numbers in excess of a viable population are redundant. Moreover, there are many examples of identical drugs, or drugs with similar properties, being derived from different species, whilst non-organic sources also yield pharmaceutical compounds.

A new pharmaceutical product earns a revenue R, net of advertising and marketing costs, but gross of research and development (R&D) costs c. If p is the probability that a new species sampled at random (assuming independent Bernoulli trials) yields a commercial product, then following Simpson *et al.* (1996), the value of n samples is:

$$V(n) = pR - c + (1-p)(pR - c) + (1-p)^2 (pR - c) + \ldots + (1-p)^{n-1} (pR - c) \quad (9.1)$$

The value of the marginal species is then:

$$V(n + 1) - V(n) = [(pR - c)/p][1 - (1 - p)^{n+1}] - [(pR - c)/p][1 - (1 - p)^n] = (pR - c)(1 - p)^n \quad (9.2)$$

---

[6] In the USA nearly 25% of prescription medicines contain active ingredients from plants, whilst many others are synthesised to replicate or improve naturally produced molecules. Leukaemia is treated with medicines derived from the rosy periwinkle of Madagascar, and ovarian cancer with taxol from the bark of the Pacific yew (Simpson, 1997). Such discoveries have attracted widespread press reports (see *The Economist* February 9th 1991, p. 51). Here cognitive misperception stems from an inability to 'think Bayesian': recent events (topical information on the value of some biological resources) are given undue prominence in assessment, and baseline information (the thousands of non-events) is ignored.

This is the expected return in the event that the species is sampled, $pR - c$, multiplied by the probability with which the search is unsuccessful in the set of n other species, $(1 - p)^n$.

Differentiating 9.2 with respect to p:

$$\delta(v)/\delta p = - n\,(pR - c)\,(1 - p)^{n-1} + R(1 - p)^n \qquad (9.3)$$

yields the value of p which maximises $V(n)$. In this function the value of the marginal species declines relatively rapidly with respect to probability after having reached a maximum. If future returns are discounted over t years at discount rate r, the expected value of the marginal species is:

$$\sum_{t=0}^{\infty} \lambda(1 + r)^t\,(pR - c)\,(1 - p)^n = \lambda/r\,(pR - c)\,(1 - p)^n \qquad (9.4)$$

where λ is the expected number of new potential products identied. Favourable assumptions are used by Simpson *et al.* (1996) to derive values for the marginal species. For example, it is unlikely that all biological resources have an equal probability of yielding a new product, so the range is restricted to the 250,000 species of higher plants[7]. Despite the use of favourable assumptions Simpson *et al.* calculated that the value of the marginal species for pharmaceutical research was relatively small at \$9,431. This figure was highly sensitive to the specification of p and the revenue to cost ratio.

The value of habitats for pharmaceutical research is also small, even for biodiversity hotspots. The estimate of \$9,431 for the marginal species of higher plant translates, for various biodiversity hotspots, to a maximum value of \$21 per hectare in western Ecuador, \$17 in south-west Sri Lanka, \$12 in New Caledonia, \$7 in Madagascar, down to \$1 in North Borneo.

Of course biodiversity could be conserved for other reasons: e.g. existence value, bequest value and other non-use motives. Indeed, an analysis of preservation decisions and conservation spending in the USA indicates the importance of existence value relative to scientific values. Metrick and Weitzman (1994) undertook a series of regression analyses of factors in: (1) listing decisions under the Endangered Species Act 1973; (2) spending decisions; and (3) the US Fish and Wildlife Service priority system for the preservation of endangered animals and plants. They included proxies in the

---

[7] Compounds produced by higher plants have much greater pharmaceutical potential. Asprin, quinine, and the anti-cancer drugs taxol, vinblastine, and vincristine are all derived from higher plants.

regression models for 'scientific' species' characteristics, such as 'degree of endangerment' and 'taxonomic uniqueness'; as well as 'visceral' characteristics, such as physical size, and the extent to which a species is considered a 'higher form of life'. Both kinds of characteristics, but especially 'visceral' characteristics, influenced decisions on whether to protect a species under the Endangered Species Act; and 'visceral' characteristics were especially important in explaining how much was spent on an endangered species. Spending was biased towards large well-known birds and mammals: 'charismatic megafauna' such as the bald eagle and grizzly bear, which are less endangered than many species with less charisma. Other fauna, such as eels and toads, and all flora, received relatively little by comparison.

One charismatic species which has incurred considerable resource costs in its preservation is the northern spotted owl in the old growth redwood forests in the north-west United States, and south-western British Columbia. The cost of preserving this species was modelled by Montgomery *et al.* (1994) in terms of a probabilistic supply model which took the form:

$$S(C) = Prob[Y(T_0) > Y_{min} \mid C] \qquad (9.5)$$

where C = quantity of protected habitat, in terms of species numbers; $Y(T)$ = population size at T the chosen time horizon; Y_{min} = a chosen minimum population size. The estimated cost of biodiversity or species protection is thus dependent upon the choice of T and Y_{min}. Biologists may be uncertain, about the likelihood of survival, and hence the magnitude of Y_{min}. Each habitat area is characterised by its potential contribution to species habitat capacity, c_i, and by its potential contribution to an annual public timber stumpage supply, q_i. The ratio q_i/c_i gives the physical price per 'owl' (or per other species) associated with that habitat tract. Ranking the tracts by price and summing across them gives habitat capacity as a function of the total area allocated to habitat protection and also the marginal cost of habitat supply. Y_{min} was assumed to be 500 pairs (biologists believed the survival rate would be zero for less than 500 birds over 150 years, after which habitat capacity would have substantially increased to reduce the chance of extinction). One pair of spotted owls requires at least 3,000 acres of old growth forest. Survival probability simulation models and stumpage supply reduction in critical habitat areas indicated that for the US Department of Interior recovery plan of 1,600 owl pairs, (designed to ensure an estimated 82% chance of survival), the welfare loss in foregone timber products would be $21 billion, with a marginal cost per unit of probability of $0.6 billion. Increasing habitat capacity to 1,900 pairs increased the chance of survival to 91%, at a cost of $33 billion, and a marginal cost of $1.4 billion per unit of probability; whilst increasing numbers to 2,400 pairs increased survival probability to 0.95, at a cost of $46 billion, and a marginal cost of $3.8 billion per unit of probability (e.g. to increase the chance of survival from 94% to 95%). A decision could then be taken about whether it is worth $12 billion to increase the chance of the owl's survival from 82% to 91% and whether it is worth an additional $13 billion to increase the chance of its survival from 91% to 95%.

Costs of conservation vary enormously for different species. Moreover, as Simpson (1997) shows, the value of the marginal hectare for biological prospecting varies enormously between countries. Whilst individual countries have established priorities for biodiversity, global prioritisation remains an issue. Moran *et al.* (1996) propose a cost-effective priority investment index (CEPII) which attenuates cost ranking of biodiversity conservation with information on threat and probability of successful intervention. Their index is:

$$E = [(A_{pt} / A_t) (1 - k)^n \Delta B] / C \qquad (9.6)$$

where A_{pt} = area protected at time t; A_t = total protectable area at time t; k = rate of growth of selected threat, given by the rate of land conversion (estimated using either the deforestation rate or the population growth rate); B = biodiversity measure; and C = cost measure. CEPII emphasises cost-effectiveness consistent with maximisation of conservation within a limited budget, and seems a feasible approach at the international scale given the problems of establishing 'true' cross-national WTP for biodiversity. However, priorities for biodiversity conservation within a nation might be informed by an assessment of the benefits, including non-use benefits, of biodiversity conservation.

3 BENEFIT MEASURES OF BIODIVERSITY IN CONIFEROUS FORESTS

Biodiversity priorities within a country are often set by an amalgam of expert opinion and the activities of environmental pressure groups. WTP of conservationists for additional habitats may conform to perceptions of different types of habitat which are threatened (Garrod and Willis, 1994). However, it is also important that conservation priorities take account of the preferences of the general public and their WTP, through the taxation system, for biodiversity conservation. The following case study illustrates how contingent ranking can be used inform biodiversity priorities in forestry.

The area of woodland in the UK has doubled over the last 70 years, but the majority of new forests have been planted with non-native coniferous trees with the aim of maximising timber production. In addition, some existing ancient woodlands (which constitute 13% of the total forest area) have been replanted with coniferous species, though the most important ancient and semi-natural woodlands have been given some measure of protection by being designated as Sites of Special Scientific Interest (SSSI). Many exotic coniferous species planted for commerical timber production have low biodiversity values when compared with native species such as the English Oak.[8] 20th century forests in the UK also lack the structure and diversity of ancient woodland. Levels of biodiversity in coniferous plantations can be increased by investment in diversification and restructuring. Diversification involves planting additional, but less commercially productive, tree species, and creating more open areas within plantations. Restructuring entails staggering the rotation period between areas of the forest in order to permit species which inhabit the forest at different stages of its development to move to new locations as the forest evolves over its rotation period and as it is felled and replanted.

Progress has been made in identifying methods for improving biodiversity in forests, and in determining the biodiversity standards that need to be achieved in forests (Ratcliffe, 1993) as part of the UK government's obligation under the Rio Convention (Department of the Environment, 1994). However, at the time of the study the Forestry Commission had little knowledge of the general public's preferences for forest management with respect to biodiversity, and the overall level of resources it should devote to biodiversity conservation. Forest management decisions involve a trade-off between biodiversity and commercial timber production. Curtailing timber production in the interests of biodiversity, and accepting lower commercial rates of return on forest investment, would only be acceptable if the benefits society derived from greater biodiversity in forests exceeded this loss.

The Forestry Commission suggested that biodiversity could be improved in 300,00 hectares of their remote coniferous forest. This forest is located in areas that very few people ever visit. Thus, any value that individuals might hold for improving biodiversity in these forests comprises mainly non-use value. The Forestry Commission identified four different forest management standards for achieving different levels of biodiversity in this remote forest:

(1) 'do nothing', and maximise timber production   [Standard 0]
(2) a 'basic' standard of biodiversity conservation   [Standard A]
(3) the 'desired' standard of biodiversity conservation [Standard B]

---

[8] Exotic trees, such as the sitka spruce, are hosts to fewer species of insects (e.g. plane, 0; horse chestnut, 4; fir, 16; larch, 17; sycamore, 43; Norway spruce, 70) compared to native trees (e.g. willow, 450; oak, 423; birch, 334; Scots pine, 172; beech, 98); but are comparable with native evergreens (e.g. holly, 10; yew, 1) (Kennedy and Southwood, 1984). Some insects associated with sitka spruce are dependent on nectar and pollen from flowers in rides (open land) between forest blocks whilst blanket plantation sitka spruce is home to relatively few birds and mammals.

(4) conversion to native woodland. [Standard C]

These forest management standards are described in more detail in Appendix 9.1. The Forestry Commission has for some years been moving towards the 'basic' biodiversity management standard (Standard A) in certain areas. Felling plans now encompass the whole pattern of felling coupes, with an eight to 15 years gap between felling adjacent coupes and a landscape plan for felling and new planting, requiring that between 10% and 20% of land is maintained as open space within forests. The 'desired' management standard (Standard B) would meet UK biodiversity obligations for managed forests, whilst still permitting some timber production. Conversion to native woodland (Standard C) is the most far-reaching option for biodiversity conservation, but only a small proportion of the forest area would remain viable for timber production.

3.1 Contingent Ranking

Public preferences for enhancing biodiversity in forests was assessed through contingent ranking of different biodiversity standards, and estimating willingness to pay for forest management standards that would improve the quantity and diversity of plants and animals in large areas of remote forests which are currently managed on a commercial basis. Where there are a number of alternative biodiversity standards that have to be compared and valued, each with different combinations and quantities of flora and fauna, a ranking experiment offers advantages over a series of contingent valuation questions.

Contingent ranking (CR) is an ordered choice experiment that can be used to assess preferences for different forestry management standards and the levels of biodiversity. In CR a sample of individuals is required to rank a discrete set of alternatives from their most to their least preferred (Beggs *et al.*, 1981). Each alternative in the choice set differs from the others in the levels of its component attributes, and the cost which the respondent would incur as a result of the choice. The attribute levels of each alternative are used along with the observed rankings to estimate a discrete-choice, utility-maximising model for the sample data. Assuming an indirect utility function of the form

$$V = ae + \mu c \qquad (9.7)$$

where e = vector of level of biodiversity attributes used in the choice set; c = vector of costs associated with these levels of attributes; the estimated coefficients are then used to determine the trade-off which respondents make between disposable income and an improvement in the provision of attribute levels in the choice sets. The change in cost relative to the change in biodiversity is Δc / Δe, which is the ratio $-a/\mu$. In this study a is assumed to be positive (more biodiversity), whilst μ is assumed to be negative; hence the ratio of the two coefficients is negative: a percentage increase in land under various management standards should lead to a positive WTP.

The marginal WTP/income trade-off, as a compensating surplus measure, can be derived from the first order partial derivatives of the indirect utility function with respect to e and c as shown in Chapter 6.

3.2 Focus Groups

A series of eight focus group meetings were held to inform the design of the CR study. The meetings were conducted by a professional firm, specialising in focus group work, with the groups selected from a stratified sample of the general public, designed to include a quota of environmentalists and outdoor enthusiasts. The main objectives of the focus group meetings were to examine public awareness of, and interest in, biodiversity both in general and in relation to forests, and to explore what biodiversity was worth to individuals, and to test comprehension of the four forest management standards.

A great deal of consistency was exhibited across the groups: criticism of conifer plantations; desire to see more deciduous trees; and confusion about the precise meaning of the word biodiversity. Participants felt constrained by an ignorance of the economics of forestry but assumed that there was a trade-off between the interests of wildlife and production of timber and pursuit of profit. There were questions about whether a greater abundance of wildlife was good for biodiversity *per se* and whether or not economic imperatives should be ignored. Participants understood the different management standards defined by the Forestry Commission, but had more difficulty understanding that different areas of forest could simultaneously be maintained under different forest management standards. In all groups most respondents seemed preoccupied with the need to be realistic, and were attracted by a compromise between wildlife conservation and timber production.

3.3 Pilot Survey

The pilot survey comprised 121 interviews conducted over four locations. It revealed that CR could be applied successfully to sample the general public, including respondents with different abilities, given a satisfactory explanation of the choice alternatives from the interviewer. Respondents were given realistic alternatives to rank which rendered the exercise less abstract and engendered more pragmatic decision-making, thus reducing the potential for hypothetical bias.

3.4 Questionnaire Design

The CR experiment was used to investigate public WTP for the levels of biodiversity offered by the forest management standards described in Appendix 9.1. Respondents were shown a simple diagram highlighting the differences between the four forest management standards. This was used by the interviewer to explain the different effects that each management standard would have on the 'variety of plants and animals found in the forests' (this latter phrase was used in the questionnaire as a proxy for 'biodiversity'). Respondents were told that the Forestry Commission could manage all 300,000 ha of remote forest in the way shown in the diagram as Standard 0 (plantation forest used for commercial timber production); alternatively they could use some combination of the other forest management standards depicted in the diagram. It was made clear that any changes in forest management would have to be paid for by the general public through increases in general taxation since the Forestry Commission is subsidised by the government, and that most respondents would never visit these remote forests. To motivate participation, respondents were informed that the results of the survey would be used to help decide on changes in forest management that could increase the variety of animals and plants found in forests in the UK. Respondents were, however, reminded that there were other nature conservation schemes which they might like to support, and that paying to help enhance biodiversity in remote forests might mean that they could not contribute towards other worthwhile schemes.

Respondents compared and ranked four different combinations of forest management standards, any of which could be used to manage the 300,000 ha of remote Forestry Commission forest. Each combination was made up of a list of the percentages of forest that would be managed under the various forest management standards (i.e. % Standard 0, % Standard A, % Standard B, and % Standard C), along with the additional taxes that an average household would have to pay to fund that particular combination.

Respondents were hypothesised to rank the four combinations on the basis of their respective utilities for the improvements in biodiversity brought about by the forest management standards; trading-off any increase in utility that would result from that increase in biodiversity, against any disutility that would arise from the consequent decrease in their disposable income through subsidising the resulting reduction in timber production. These trade-offs revealed respondents' relative preferences for the various forest management standards in terms of their willingness to pay additional taxes for them. The combinations given to respondents comprised one card drawn from four classes: no increase in biodiversity; low/medium increase in biodiversity; medium/high increase in biodiversity; and high increase in biodiversity.

COMBINATION 1	
STANDARD A	0%
STANDARD B	0%
STANDARD C	0%
STANDARD 0	100%
Cost = £0 in tax, per year, to average household (or 0p per week)	

COMBINATION 2	
STANDARD A	90%
STANDARD B	0%
STANDARD C	10%
STANDARD 0	0%
Cost = £1 in tax, per year, to average household (or 2p per week)	

COMBINATION 3	
STANDARD A	20%
STANDARD B	70%
STANDARD C	10%
STANDARD 0	0%
Cost = £6 in tax, per year, to average household (or 12p per week)	

COMBINATION 4	
STANDARD A	30%
STANDARD B	50%
STANDARD C	20%
STANDARD 0	0%
Cost = £15 in tax, per year, to average household (or 29p per week)	

Figure 9.1: Example of combinations used in the contingent ranking exercise

By managing only a certain proportion of forest under each of the four management standards, each combination was able to offer a particular level of biodiversity. Furthermore, in each set of combinations presented to respondents, those combinations offering higher increases in biodiversity always cost more than combinations offering lower increases.

The actual per household costs required to pay for each combination were very small and the focus group results suggested there was little realistic prospect of respondents bothering to make such a cost/quality trade-off. Thus, in order to assess consumer surplus for the improvement in biodiversity achieved by each combination of forest management standards, a range of higher tax costs were used in the ranking experiment. One design limitation inherent in the study was that each combination of management standards (the percentage of Standard 0, Standard A, Standard B and Standard C forest) had to sum to 100. In addition, the percentage of Standard C forest used in any combination could not exceed 30%: the maximum percentage of that standard envisaged under Forestry Commission plans. Combination 1 is the state where all forests are managed for maximum revenue at no additional cost to the taxpayer: this acts as the base case in terms of analysis and was fixed for all respondents. An orthogonal experimental design generated 64 sets of combinations for use in the ranking experiment.

The main survey was carried out by a professional survey firm among a nationally representative stratified random sample of over 650 households. Fieldwork was undertaken during September 1995 over 146 sampling points throughout Britain, and was carried out face-to-face in respondents' homes. Within each sampling point, interviewers worked to strict quotas according to sex, age, work and social status, to reflect the national population profile.

3.5 Empirical Results

A total of 648 individuals gave usable responses to the CR experiment. Table 9.1 summarises the responses for each category of woodland. The first choice for the vast majority of respondents was a combination giving an improved level of biodiversity. Most first choices came from Combination Class 3, giving a medium to high level of improvement in forest biodiversity; with the least popular options from Combination Class 1. When first and second choices were taken into account, Combination Class 4 was found to be only the third most popular; this was in spite of the fact that it was the only class to provide more than 10% coverage with Standard C forest. This suggested that the majority of respondents did not have a particularly high preference for that Standard.

Respondents indicated that the most common reason for choosing a first-choice combination was that it gave the best balance between financial factors and conservation (i.e. led to an improvement in levels of biodiversity whilst still permitting some commercial forestry). This was consistent with the findings of the pre-survey focus groups. However, 70 respondents based their first choice primarily on their willingness-to-pay for the opportunity of visiting these forests in the future. This option value perspective contradicted the valuation scenario which stated that respondents were unlikely to ever to visit the forests in question. Hence, these observations were excluded from subsequent analysis. (In practice the estimated coefficients were almost identical whether option value observations were included or excluded).

Table 9.1: Results of the contingent ranking experiment

Combination Class	First Choice (%)	Second Choice (%)	Third Choice (%)	Fourth Choice (%)
Class 1 (null)	10.0	5.6	17.7	66.7
Class 2 (low/med)	22.7	39.5	35.8	2.0
Class 3 (med/high)	41.4	34.4	22.8	1.4
Class 4 (high)	25.9	20.5	23.6	29.9

The ordinally-ranked responses were used to estimate a discrete-choice probability model in LIMDEP (Greene, 1989). In its basic form this model estimated the probability that a respondent ranked the set of combinations in a particular order, based on the percentage values of the forest management standards and the cost of each option. A positive sign on a variable coefficient indicates that an increase in the level of the factor in question increases the probability of a high ranking; while, conversely, a negative sign indicates that an increase in the level of that factor reduces the likelihood of a high ranking.

The results of the model in Table 9.2 seem quite plausible. Many respondents considered that a compromise between conservation and commercial timber production was necessary when selecting their first choice combination. Standard B woodland offered improved forest biodiversity, while still retaining some commercial timber production. Thus, it may seem preferable to Standard A which had commercial timber production as its priority, and Standard C which offered little in the way of commercial timber production. Standard C is the most expensive of the forest management standards, and respondents seemed unwilling to pay higher taxes merely to turn a lot of commercial woodland into a wildlife sanctuary that they would never visit. Thus, the results suggested that respondents were willing to pay most to achieve the more commercially oriented Standards A and B. A CR model based only on those respondents who gave data on their household income levels revealed only small differences between mean WTP estimated with and without these responses.

Table 9.2: CR model of forest biodiversity standards

Variable	All CR Responses Minus Observations Demonstrating Option Values (n=578)		CR Responses where Household Income Known Minus Observations Demonstrating Option Values (n=404)	
	Coefficient Value	WTP (£,1995) [d]	Coefficient Value	WTP (£,1995)
Constant	-0.9821 (-12.48)[a]	-	-1.0854 (-11.04)	-
Area under Management Standard A (%)	0.01568 (13.91)	0.265	0.01554 (11.22)	0.301
Area under Management Standard B (%)	0.02559 (18.06)	0.433	0.02705 (15.84)	0.523
Area under Management Standard C (%)	0.006103 (1.14)	0.103	0.008516 (1.36)	
Cost (£, 1995)	-0.05915 (-5.11)	-	-0.05168 (-3.84)	-
Unrestricted log-likelihood	1527.1	-	1047.3	-
Restricted log-likelihood	1836.9	-	1283.9	-
Likelihood ratio test stat [b]	619.6	-	473.2	-
Pseudo R-squared[c]	0.1687	-	0.1843	-

a. T-values are shown in parentheses.

b. The likelihood ratio test statistic is computed as twice the difference between the initial and maximum log-likelihood values: asymptotically this statistic has a chi-squared distribution with n degrees of freedom (see Gujarati, 1995). At the 95% confidence level the critical value of the chi-squared distribution is 7.81 with 3 df.

c. Pseudo R-squared is computed as 1-(restricted log-likelihood/unrestricted log-likelihood) and is according to McFadden (1974) an alternate measure of goodness-of-fit for probabilistic choice models.

d. WTP measured for a 1% increase in area.

More complex specifications of the CR choice model can be used incorporating variables such as household spending and environmental activism,[9] interactively with cost. The addition of these variables as cost

---

[9] Variables such as SOCIETIES reflected household membership of environmental and conservation groups by recording how many societies from a given list had members in the

interaction terms marginally improved the explanatory power of the model; however, WTP remained fairly constant (Garrod and Willis, 1997). The inclusion of the income interaction term only raised estimated marginal WTP slightly (Table 9.3). At the estimated sample mean income of £17,896, the income elasticity of WTP for each forest management standard was about 0.15. This income inelasticity level suggests that respondents judged that a certain quantity of forest biodiversity was a necessity and that they were willing to pay for that level regardless of their incomes. Furthermore, this expenditure would not be expected to change dramatically with changes in the economy, highlighting that such long-term projects require steady state rather than increasing funding.

The results suggest substantial non-use values would be generated if the UK Forestry Commission continued its efforts to develop management practices that promoted an increase in biodiversity across a large area of its commercial holdings. Estimated WTP for an additional unit of Standard A (basic standard of biodiversity conservation) forest varied between 30.1p and 33.4p per household per year; while for Standard B (desired standard of biodiversity conservation) forest it varied between 52.3 and 56.2p per year. WTP was lowest for Standard C (conversion to native woodland) forest, varying between 16.5p and 19.9p per year.

Mean WTP for Standard C forest was relatively low. There are a number of possible explanations for this. For example, respondents may have believed that the low levels of Standard C forest offered in the choice sets represented poor value for money compared with the alternatives that offered high proportions of Standard B forest and provided substantial timber and biodiversity benefits. Alternatively, some form of *status quo* bias may have been present with respondents reluctant to make choices that implied very large changes compared with the current situation. Clearly, Standard C forest represents a dramatic change in approach by the Forestry Commission, and this may have discouraged some individuals from choosing alternatives with a high Standard C content. Standard A and Standard B both offer more familiar management styles and may thus be preferred by more conservative or cautious respondents.

---

respondent's household (mean = 0.33); ACTIVITIES (mean = 2.98) indicated how many of the seven specified environmentally related activities were undertaken by members of the respondent's household in the last two years; SPEND (mean=0.075) indicated whether or not a respondent's household spent more than £50 a year on environmental and wildlife causes; and RETIRED (mean=0.174) whether or not the respondent was retired and thus might be expected to have less disposable income to contribute towards forest management. For example, if the respondent was retired then the variable RETIRED took the value 1 (rather than 0): Since the estimated coefficient on RETIRED was negative, this decreased estimated WTP. Similarly, respondents with higher values for the variables SOCIETIES and ACTIVITIES had a greater WTP than those with lower values. (See Garrod and Willis, 1997).

Table 9.3: Further specifications of the CR choice model

Variable	Coefficient Value	WTP (£,1995)	Coefficient Value	WTP (£,1995)
Constant	-1.09546	-	-1.09101	-
	(-11.75)		(-11.69)	
Area under Management	0.01585	0.334	0.01576	0.315
Standard A (%)	(12.05)		(11.39)	
Area under Management	0.02668	0.562	0.2786	0.535
Standard B (%)	(16.39)		(16.43)	
Area under Management	0.008959	0.189	0.01370	0.199
Standard C (%)	(1.51)		(2.23)	
Cost (£, 1995)	-0.08422	-	-0.04750	-
	(-4.64)		(-3.44)	
Cost/Income (£ / £10^3)	-0.06048	-	-0.04210	-
	(-1.01)		(-0.69)	
Cost*SPEND	0.07718	-	-	-
	(3.72)			
Cost*ACTIVITIES	0.01153	-	-	-
	(3.08)			
Area under Management	-		-0.0004585	-
Standard A (%) * RETIRED			(-0.91)	
Area under Management	-		-0.006669	-
Standard B (%) * RETIRED			(-2.49)	
Area under Management	-		-0.02163	-
Standard C (%) * RETIRED			(-2.24)	
Unrestricted log-likelihood	1167.1	-	1171.8	-
Restricted log-likelihood	1439.7	-	1439.7	-
Likelihood ratio test stat [a]	545.2	-	535.8	-
Pseudo R-squared	0.189	-	0.186	-

a. At the 95% confidence level the critical values of the chi-square distribution with 5df and 8df respectively, are 11.07 and 15.51.

The values for the WTP trade-offs are dependent upon the specification of the indirect utility function and the design of the ranking exercise. Different specifications may lead to somewhat different estimates, as might alternative experimental designs. Nevertheless, contingent ranking provides a reasonable means of investigating public preferences and valuations for biodiversity forest management standards.

The Forestry Commission estimated the additional cost of different biodiversity standards compared to the Standard 0 ('do nothing') as £5, £15, and £45 per ha. per year for Standards A, B, and C, respectively. Thus the cost of managing the 300,000 ha of forest in the following combination of forest management standards: 70% Standard A, 20% Standard B, 10% Standard C, would cost an additional £3.3 million per annum (1995 prices). However, total benefits from even modest increases in biodiversity when aggregated across the 23.09 million households in Britain in 1995, exceed biodiversity costs. Thus, as far as the general public in the UK is concerned, the benefits of changing forest management to enhance biodiversity far outweigh the financial costs involved.

4 CONCLUSIONS

Expressed preference methods such as contingent valuation have tended to be used to value endangered species (see for example, Jakobsson and Dragun, 1996) rather than biodiversity *per se*. Nevertheless, as illustrated above, these methods can be used to estimate the value of some local biodiversity issues. However, where more than one habitat or species is involved, these benefit estimation approaches, and cost-effectiveness approaches such as that of Moran *et al.* (1996), tend to be used to produce rankings of habitats for conservation in strict lexicographic order, as in a conventional cost-benefit analysis.

Global biodiversity conservation, the dependence of some species on different habitats, and the interdependence of the value of biodiversity on the preservation of a spatial distribution of ecosystems and habitats, presents additional problems for biodiversity conservation and valuation techniques. The value of any one site for biodiversity is contingent on the conservation and spatial distribution of other sites, and this can create problems when simultaneously evaluating large numbers of specific sites with different combinations of biodiversity attributes. Such problems might be more easily handled by other decision-making tools. Techniques such as multi-criteria analysis (MCA), pioneered by Nijkamp (1979) and Nijkamp *et al.* (1990), can be seen as complementing monetary evaluation methods (Munda, *et al.*, 1995). In cases where it is difficult to optimise all criteria simultaneously, where there are multiple objectives and a need to incorporate qualitative as well as quantitative information, and to search for compromise solutions, MCA may offer additional insights.

Faith (1995) illustrates the use of MCA to estimate the most efficient set of areas for biodiversity protection, where the value of a set of biodiversity areas to be protected is not simply the sum of the biodiversity (i.e. number of different species) contained within each member of the set. Since different areas in the set will have overlapping or common species, the contribution of any one area to total biodiversity depends upon which other areas are protected. For example, the greater the habitat differences between two areas, the greater might be the degree to which their member species complement one another, providing a rationale for evaluating the different sets of areas chosen for protection. Conservation may also have a number of objectives, not all of which can be achieved in specific cases. The relative importance of these different objectives or criteria must be taken into account in MCA. One of the main problems in MCA is the choice of the relative weightings to be attached to the different objectives or criteria. Weights attached to different criteria are instrumental in determining outcomes and trade-offs between different species quantities conserved and the amount of development or production foregone.

Some biodiversity problems do not have clear or easily agreed solutions. Environmental valuation may not produce straightforward or unambiguous results in all cases whilst biodiversity policy and practice is often characterised by the search for acceptable or compromise solutions. In such cases MCA can complement environmental valuation methods, by making options and alternatives more transparent and explicit, and thus contributing to more informed decision-making on biodiversity issues.

REFERENCES

Collins, N. Mark and Michael G. Morris (1985*), Threatened Swallowtail Butterflies of the World: the International Union for Conservation of Nature and Natural Resources Red Data Book*, IUCN, Glad, Switzerland and Cambridge, UK.

Cranbrook, The Earl of, and David S. Edwards (1994*), Belalong: A Tropical Rainforest*, The Royal Geographical Society, London.

Department of the Environment (1994), *Sustainable Forestry: The UK Programme*, HMSO, London.

Department of the Environment (1995), *Biodiversity: the UK Steering Group Report*, Volume 2: Actions Plans, HMSO, London.

Faith, Daniel P. (1995), *Biodiversity and Regional Sustainability Analysis*, CSIRO Division of Wildlife and Ecology, ACT, Australia.

Garrod, G.D. and K.G. Willis (1994), 'Valuing biodiversity and nature conservation at a local level', *Biodiversity and Conservation, 3*, 555–65.

Garrod, G.D. and K.G. Willis. (1997). 'The non-use benefits of enhancing forest biodiversity: a contingent ranking study', *Ecological Economics, 21*, 45–61.

Greene, W.M. (1989), *LIMDEP Version 5.1*, Econometric Software Incorporated, New York.

Gujarati, D.N., (1995), *Basic Econometrics*, McGraw-Hill, New York.

Jakobsson, Kristin M. and Andrew K. Dragun (1996), *Contingent Valuation of Endangered Species: Methodological Issues and Applications*, Edward Elgar, Cheltenham.

Johnson, S.P. (1993), *The Earth Summit: the United Nations Conference on Environment and Development (UNCED),* Graham and Trotman, London.

Kennedy, C.E.J. and T.R.E Southwood (1984) 'The number of species of insect associated with British trees: a re-analysis', *Journal of Animal Ecology, 53*, 455–78.

McFadden, D. (1974), 'On conditional logit model of qualitative choice behaviour', in P. Zarembka (ed) *Frontiers of Econometrics*, Academic Press, New York.

Metrick, Andrew and Martin L. Weitzman (1994), *Patterns of Behavior in Biodiversity Preservation*, Policy and Research Working Paper 1358, Environment Infrastructure and Agriculture Division, Policy Research Department, The World Bank, Washington DC.

Montgomery, Claire A., Gardner M. Brown and Darius M. Adams (1994), 'The marginal cost of species preservation: the northern spotted owl', *Journal of Environmental Economics and Management*, **26**, 111–28.

Moran, Dominic, David Pearce and Anouk Wendelaar (1996), 'Global biodiversity priorities: a cost effectiveness index for investments', *Global Environmental Change*, **6**, 103–19.

Munda, G., P. Nijkamp and P. Rietveld (1995), 'Monetary and Non-Monetary Evaluation Methods in Sustainable Development Planning', *Economie Appliquée*, **48** (2), 143–60.

Nijkamp, Peter (1979*), Multidimensional Spatial Data and Decision Analysis*, Wiley, New York.

Nijkamp, Peter, Piet Rietveld and H. Voogd (1990), *Multicriteria Analysis in Physical Planning*, North-Holland, Amsterdam.

Pearce, David W. and Jeremy J. Warford (1993), *World Without End*, Oxford University Press, Oxford.

Pearce, David W. and Dominic Moran (1994), *The Economic Value of Biodiversity*, Earthscan, London.

Perrings, Charles and David Pearce (1994), 'Threshold effects and incentives for the conservation of biodiversity', *Environmental and Resource Economics*, **4**, 13–28.

Ratcliffe, Philip R. (1993), *Biodiversity: Britain's Forests*, Forestry Commission, Edinburgh.

Simpson, R. David, Roger A. Sedjo, and John W. Reid (1996), 'Valuing biodiversity for use in pharmaceutical research', *Journal of Political Economy*, **104**, 163–85.

Simpson, R. David (1997), 'Biodiversity Prospecting: shopping the wilds is not the key to conservation', *Resources Issue,* **126**, 12–15. Resources For the Future, Washington DC.

Singh, H.S. and R.D. Kamboj (1996), *Biodiversity Conservation Plan for Gir: a management plan for Gir Sanctuary and National Park*, Forestry Department, Gujarat State, Ghandinagar.

Swanson, Timothy M. (1994), *The International Regulation of Extinction*, Macmillan, London.

Watkinson, Andrew R. (1997), 'Biodiversity: an ecological perspective', in Tim O'Riordan (ed.*), Economics of Biological Resources and Biodiversity: summary of a seminar*, CSERGE, School of Environmental Sciences, University of East Anglia.

Webb, N.R. (1986), *Heathlands: A Natural History of Britain's Lowland Heaths*, Collins, London.

Weitzman, Martin L. (1992), 'On diversity', *Quarterly Journal of Economics,* **107**, 363–405.

Willis, K.G. (1980), *The Economics of Town and Country Planning*, Collins (Granada), London.

Willis, K.G., G.D. Garrod and Peter Shepherd (1996), *Towards a Methodology for Costing Biodiversity Targets in the UK*, HMSO, London.

Wynne, G, M. Avery, L. Campbell, S. Gubbay, S. Hawkswell, T. Juniper, M. King, P. Newbery, J. Smart, C. Steel, T. Stones, A. Stubbs, J. Taylor, C. Tydeman and R. Wynde (1995), *Biodiversity Challenger*, 2nd edition, Royal Society for Protection of Birds, Sandy, England.

APPENDIX 9.1

Forestry Commission Biodiversity Standards

These descriptions relate to different standards that could be achieved in a typical mature remote forest planted with sitka spruce. Open ground currently comprises 10% of this forest and consists of narrow shaded forester's paths with little current wildlife value. There are no broadleaved trees. A typical example of 'blanket conifer forest'.

Standard 0: Do nothing

Continue with blanket conifer forest. All trees would be felled at their age of maximum discounted revenue: between 45 and 60 years depending on local conditions determining yield and windthrow. There is no additional cost under this option: it is the benchmark against which other management standards are judged.

Standard A: Basic Standard

The main purpose of this standard of forestry is to produce as much timber as possible (85% of the forest is made up of sitka spruce), whilst meeting the following minimum standards for nature conservation:

- Instead of a blanket of trees of uniform age and size, the forest is made up of patches of young saplings, bushy young trees and dense thickets of taller trees about 30 feet high.
- 1% of the forest will never be cut down, encouraging large, old trees, dead and dying wood and a shrub and grassy layer.
- 10% of the area will be left unplanted after the sitka has been felled for timber, creating open areas of grass, bog, heath, or rock.
- 5% will be replanted with native broad-leaved (i.e. woodland) trees and shrubs.
- The rest will be progressively replanted with sitka spruce.

This helps to significantly increase the variety of wildlife compared to a blanket conifer forest:

- The sapling areas encourage tall grasses, ferns, heather, rushes, self-sown birches or willow, and flowering herbaceous plants such as foxgloves and tormentil. There are dense populations of field voles and a wide range of predators such as weasel, stoat, fox, kestrel, hen harrier and tawny, short-eared and long-eared owls.

- Moorland moths and butterflies are common in the sapling areas and on the larger areas uncommon moorland birds, e.g. curlew, snipe, short-eared owl and hen harrier sometimes breed.
- The bushy areas and dense thickets support several species of songbird, e.g. goldcrest, coal tit, willow warbler, robin, wren and chaffinch. Deer shelter in dense cover and feed in the areas of young trees.
- The older, taller sitka spruce trees support seed-eating animals such as red squirrel, field mice and birds such as siskin and crossbill, and encourage breeding birds such as goshawks, redstarts, spotted flycatchers, warblers and other songbirds. As the retained trees eventually die and decay, they attract bats, woodpeckers, beetles, fungi, moss and lichens. Plants may include specialist orchids such as the creeping lady's tresses.
- The open areas create patches of heather with moorland moths, butterflies, adders and lizards; wet grassy glades whose rich insect life is vital food for young chicks of birds like black grouse and woodcock; and bogs with rare plants like sundew and rosemary.
- The broad-leaved trees and shrubs attract hundreds of species of insects and several bird species such as garden warbler, grasshopper warbler and redwing. Mammals include bats, badger, bank vole, hedgehog and wood mouse. The woodland floor may eventually be colonised by violets, wood anemone, stitchwort and bluebell.

Standard B: Enhanced Standard

As with Standard A, the main purpose is to make a profit from the sale of timber from sitka spruce. However, in forests managed to this standard, sitka spruce makes up only 55% of the forest area. The minimum requirements for nature conservation are enhanced to provide a greater variety of tree sizes and species, and of other forest habitats than in Standard A:

- Four stages will be present: young saplings, bushy young trees and dense thickets as in Standard A, plus patches of older trees about 40 feet high.
- The proportion of forest which will never be cut down is increased from 1% to 3%.
- The proportion of open area is increased from 10% to 20%.
- The proportion of native broad-leaved trees and shrubs is increased from 5% to 10%.
- Other conifers (e.g. Scots pine) will be used instead of sitka over 15% of the forest.

Compared to Standard A, Standard B helps to support larger populations of the same plant and animal species. It also increases variety by encouraging new species (some rare) to colonise the forest, and helps wildlife to develop faster:

- The wider spread of sitka spruce age groups further increase the variety of wildlife.
- Wider corridors of open space and smaller, more numerous patches of different habitat make it easier for plants and animals to spread throughout the forest.
- Larger open areas sustain more species adapted for grassland, moorland, bog and wetland habitat, e.g. birds such as snipe, curlew, common sandpiper, oyster-catcher on grassland and red and black grouse and merlin using tracts of heather.
- Larger areas of forest where trees are allowed to mature and die can encourage rarer species of ferns, mosses, liverworts, fungi and beetles than the smaller areas in Standard A.
- Larger areas of native broad-leaved trees also encourage uncommon species with special needs, e.g. wood ants, and act as both a refuge and a source for the onward spread of slower moving species. The numbers of woodland plants like wood sorrel, insects such as carabid beetles and animals like frogs and toads will increase.
- The planting of conifers other than sitka spruce increases the variety of plant and animal wildlife. Their cones provide a valuable food source for the red squirrel and other seed-eating birds and mammals, which also encourages rare predators such as the pine marten. It also encourages rare species of pinewood birds such as crested tit, Scottish crossbill and capercaillie.

Standard C: Conversion To Native Woodland

Unlike A and B, nature conservation is the main purpose of this standard of forestry. As areas of the blanket conifer forest are felled, they are re-planted with local native species instead of exotic introduced conifers. In this way the forest is gradually converted to native woodland which is used for limited timber production.

The species used for re-planting are birch, Scots pine, rowan, willow, oak, alder, aspen, holly, ash, hazel, hawthorn, bird cherry and wild cherry, juniper and blackthorn. They are planted in patches of the same age group to create a patchwork of young and old woodland. Within each even-aged patch, there will be a number of different tree and shrub species, with varied spacing between trees and small glades around wet hollows or rocky knolls. The woodland canopy which results will be patchy, creating vigorous ground vegetation in open areas interspersed with stands of dense tree cover. There will be open spaces of varying size within the woodland.

The structure of the new native forest has a similar effect on wildlife as Standard B and this greatly increases the richness of the forest for wildlife.

- Native trees and shrubs will provide a habitat for hundreds of insects which are not found on spruce or other introduced conifers. Lichens, fungi and mosses will also be more varied than in Standard A or B. Plants will be more varied and woodland rarities will appear which need substantial areas or special conditions to maintain themselves, e.g. globeflower, beech fern, pale sedge and enchanter's nightshade.
- There will be more species of animals, especially mammals and birds, than in Standard A or B. The only exceptions which may be less common are goshawk, crossbill, coal tit, goldcrest, siskin, and perhaps red squirrel and pine marten, all species which do better in conifer forest.
- The soil improving effect of many broad-leaved trees will increase fertility and overall amounts of wildlife in the soil and vegetation and therefore animals too.

10. Water Quality

Here lie I and my four daughters
Killed by drinking Cheltenham waters
Had we but stuck to Epsom salts
We wouldn't have been in these here vaults.

Anon: *Cheltenham Waters*

1 INTRODUCTION

A combination of circumstances has meant that the issue of water quality has become increasingly important over recent years. Good water quality is important for a variety of reasons, not only for the provision of water to households and industry, but for recreational purposes as the growth in the use of freshwater sites for angling, bathing and a variety of water-borne pursuits increases. At the same time, freshwater habitats are an important ecological resource and any threat to them constitutes a severe problem for a number of important species.

As public awareness of the need for high quality water has increased so has the perception that much water, both freshwater and sea water, has suffered a decline in quality owing to the detrimental effects of human activities. In the UK, this problem was highlighted by a 1985 survey of river water quality which revealed the first fall in quality since the surveys began in 1958 (Department of the Environment and Welsh Office, 1986). Internationally, a number of influential pressure groups including Greenpeace and Friends of the Earth campaign vigorously about water quality issues, highlighting problems of industrial and agricultural pollution.

A number of studies have applied environmental valuation methods to investigate a range of water quality issues, focusing on public willingness to pay for improvements in water quality. These studies have often been associated with recreational activities, such as fishing and swimming, that depend on good quality water.

Many early studies investigating water quality issues utilised some form of contingent valuation method. Subsequently, researchers turned towards other more sophisticated expressed preference techniques to estimate willingness to pay for water quality improvements. The bulk of this chapter is devoted to reporting one such study in detail and another more briefly.

The first study focuses on one particular aspect of water quality, that of river flows. Low flows in rivers result in a shortening of the angling season and have a detrimental effect on wildlife. The ecological balance of plant communities changes, excessive growth of some weeds occurs, and there is reduced growth of others. In UK rivers there is a change from perennial stream flora to winterbourne flora, with an increase in terrestrial plants in the stream channel. Some species of wildlife may even disappear. Increased siltation in the channel also occurs on low flow rivers, reducing the areas of gravel in which salmon, trout, and other fish spawn. The second study looks at broader amenity and recreational issues surrounding water quality in a North American context.

2. CASE 1: THE ENVIRONMENTAL COSTS OF LOW RIVER FLOWS

2.1 Background

River flows may be reduced to sub-optimal levels by natural phenomenon such as low rainfall, or may be caused by the abstraction of water either from the river itself or from the underlying aquifer. In the UK when river flows are seriously low, the Environment Agency (EA) is responsible for the design and implementation of schemes to alleviate this problem. A number of options are available to the EA to alleviate low flows in these rivers.

All of the available options involve a cost, and before any decisions are made regarding which particular solutions to the low flow problem are adopted, careful consideration has to be given to the question of whether or not the additional benefits from increasing the flow to some environmentally acceptable flow regime (EAFR) outweigh the costs involved. Under the UK Environment Act 1995, the EA is obliged to undertake a cost-benefit analysis to consider this problem.

The case study focuses on the south west of England, an area encompassing an unusually large number of beaches (176 beaches were designated as Euro-beaches by the European Community, though other smaller beaches and coves also exist) and approximately 4,000 miles of rivers. The particular focus was on seven rivers that were identified as being seriously affected by low flows at certain times of the year. These problems were caused by a number of factors.

On one river, the Tavy, water was abstracted for use in a small hydro-electric power station, while the River Meavy, which is a salmon spawning river, has water imponded by a reservoir. Porous chalk rock underlies parts of all the other rivers in the south west suffering from low flows. Abstractions were made by water companies either from the rivers themselves, or from the underlying aquifer. On some rivers, for example the Allen, flows were augmented at various points in order to compensate for abstraction, but over the course of the year the augmentation proved inadequate.

Given that the benefits of increasing river flows were likely to comprise both use values and non-use values, it was decided that some form of expressed preference method would be most appropriate to elicit willingness to pay. The issue of non-use values was an important consideration, and any survey of the general public was likely to result in a high proportion of non-users being sampled. This would include individuals who do not visit rivers at all and, more commonly, individuals who do not visit any of the designated low-flow rivers in the south west of England. This lack of familiarity would have made it difficult for respondents to give meaningful answers to an open-ended WTP question or to a bidding game relating to EA activities. This consideration led to the concentration on the choice experiment approach with the aim of estimating the marginal WTP of the general public for unit improvements in low flow alleviation in rivers in the south west of England. The choice experiment would also be used to estimate the public's marginal WTP for unit improvements in the numbers of clean beaches and miles of unpolluted rivers in the area.

This concentration on marginal WTP confronts the issue of scale and should provide more robust welfare estimates for decision making. Furthermore, the more holistic choice experiment approach is less vulnerable to other sequencing effects such as embedding.

2.2 The Benefits of Low Flow Alleviation

The total economic value of low flow alleviation in a given river is the sum of all use values derived from it, plus any non-use values which this activity may generate. Use values are benefits arising either directly or indirectly from the improvement in flows, while non-use values are generated by the consumption of the flow of information about the good which is consumed as a preservation benefit, i.e. a value arising from the knowledge that the river remains healthy and viable and will persist.

A survey of the general public survey in the south west of England was carried out in the summer of 1996, including both users and non-users. Non-users were identified as those respondents who did not visit any of the low flow rivers in the south west specified in this project.

2.3 Questionnaire Design

A series of focus groups was undertaken prior to the design of the questionnaire with the intention of informing the design process and suggesting the levels of information that respondents would require. The focus groups suggested that the public considered problems of coastal and river pollution to be the most pressing water quality issues in the south west; however, when shown a portfolio of photographs illustrating the varying effects of low flows most participants agreed that this issue was also important (though not as pressing as pollution, to which it was seen as a contributory factor).

The design of the questionnaire was intended to provoke respondents into thinking more deeply about the consequences of their responses to the choice experiments and to make those responses as realistic as possible given the artificial context. The effect of the questionnaire design on welfare estimates in this case should have been to limit them rather than inflate them, thus leading to conservative welfare estimates that can be interpreted as lower-bound figures. The magnitude of welfare estimates was limited by using a sequence of questions and statements designed to remind respondents of other environmental quality issues that they might wish to support, rather than allowing them to focus on the water quality issues with which this study was concerned.

The notion of a multi-good environment was introduced early in the questionnaire, when respondents were asked questions regarding their donations to good causes and their willingness and ability to contribute more to such causes in the future. This helped to establish a context within which respondents could begin to determine how much they would be willing to pay towards water quality improvements. This approach was tested and refined over two separate pilot surveys.

Respondents were then presented with a brochure describing the EA's activities under three headings: reducing river pollution; monitoring marine pollution in coastal waters; and improving flows in low flow rivers. Text was kept to a minimum and illustrations were used wherever possible. Information was limited to bullet points describing the problem being tackled, its causes and consequences and what the EA was doing to tackle the problem across the south-west (including details of spending brought down to an average per household per year basis). Rather than just emphasise the scale of the problem the brochure also attempted to show how much had in fact been achieved in tackling these problems. This had the twin effects of demonstrating that additional spending could bring about further positive environmental benefits but that current levels of spending (£90 million per year in 1996) were already achieving significant improvements in each of the categories shown in the brochure.

The focus on activities in the south west was thought most appropriate in a survey that would cover a wide variety of households in that region. Specifically, it was felt that respondents would relate better to more familiar local issues than to national ones and this would promote more considered responses to the choice experiment questions.

Following the methodology used by Adamowicz *et al.* (1996), this survey used both a stated preference choice experiment and a dichotomous choice contingent valuation question (discussed in Chapter 6). Both approaches used a similar valuation scenario: that is, whether or not respondents were willing to pay a specified amount to increase the overall levels of environmental quality along rivers and beaches in the south west. Environmental quality was expressed as the level of three attributes shown in the left hand column of Figure 10.1.

In the choice experiments respondents were given a sheet similar to that shown in Figure 10.1 and asked to choose one of the three choices. Having made their choice respondents were shown three more cards and asked to choose their preferred choice from each. Cards were chosen at random from an orthogonal set of 64 choice cards.

In the choice experiments the issue of low flows is embedded in a broader set of water quality goods discouraging a single focus on the issue of low flows. This confronts the issue of embedding by ensuring that respondents act consistently and make choices based on the same set of related goods. Thus, in both of the approaches used in this study it is made clear to respondents that low flow alleviation is embedded within a more holistic set of EA water quality objectives.

2.4 River Usage by the General Public

Nearly half of the households interviewed claimed to live one mile or less from a river; and more than two-thirds lived within two miles of a river. Most households regularly undertook recreational activities along rivers, with only 23% claiming not to undertake some form of regular recreation along rivers.

Around 88% of households had visited more than one river over the 12 months preceding the survey, but only 45% had visited one of the low flow rivers in the south west. The frequency of visits to beaches over the summer months had much the same distribution as visits to rivers, though greater differences began to emerge during the winter.

CARD 06

Please choose one column

	CHOICE 1 (Current Situation)	CHOICE 2	CHOICE 3
Increase in water charges needed to achieve targets	No increase	£5 increase	£10 increase
Beaches in the South West NOT MEETING European standards on cleanliness	9 beaches	5 beaches	3 beaches
Rivers in the South West WITHOUT good quality water	990 miles	350 miles	350 miles
Rivers in the South West WITHOUT acceptable flow levels	130 miles	80 miles	60 miles

Figure 10.1: An example of a choice experiment card

2.5 Empirical Results

Preliminary questions demonstrated public perceptions of the abstraction problem. Nearly three-quarters of respondents thought that rivers were an important source of water; but just over half thought too much water was being abstracted from rivers by water companies and other users.

Investigations into the public's WTP for good causes showed that 80% of respondents would prefer to see additional public expenditure on the natural environment (a lower rate than for health or education). However, only 40% of respondents indicated that they would be willing to contribute more than they currently contribute towards what they considered 'good causes'.

Following the preliminary questions respondents were shown a set of four choice experiment cards selected at random without replacement from the set of 64. For each card, respondents were asked to select one of the three alternatives depicted thereon. Alternatives on each choice card could be distinguished by the level of environmental improvement that they offered across three areas regulated by the EA (river pollution, beach pollution and low flows in rivers) and by the amount that each alternative would cost respondents annually.

As expected, the randomisation of choice experiment cards throughout the survey meant that the proportion of respondents selecting each of the three choices did not vary with the order in which the cards were presented. This indicated that respondent fatigue did not set in and that responses were consistent throughout the sequence of four choice experiments. The fact that in over 40% the experiments respondents selected Choice 1, the current situation at no extra charge, tallies with responses to the referendum CVM question where nearly two-thirds of respondents stated they did not wish to pay more for water quality improvements.

Potential advantages of the choice experiment approach when compared to the referendum CVM format were suggested by the observation that around a third of those respondents who had stated that they would not be willing to pay prior to the referendum CVM question were tempted to make a choice that would, in fact, mean paying an additional sum each year. The choice experiment format allowed these respondents to compare possible outcomes and costs and, in the light of the additional information provided by the choice card, change their minds and opt for a choice that offered them acceptable value for money in terms of pound for pound environmental improvement. This ability to provoke a greater proportion of respondents into making reasoned trade-offs between money and environmental improvement should, on the whole, lead to more robust responses and prevent the type of knee-jerk answer that can be engendered by referendum-type questions. Similarly, the additional information and thinking time provided by the choice experiments can lead to a more positive decision in risk averse respondents than the simple referendum choice: an earlier question asking respondents whether or not they would pay more for water quality improvements revealed that over half of the responses (both negative and positive) to the question were prefaced by the word 'probably.'

Following Adamowicz *et al.* 1996 the responses from choice experiments were used to estimate a discrete choice model of the probability $Pr(i)$ of choosing a given alternative i, i.e.:

$$Pr(i) = exp\ (sV_i) / \sum_{j\ \varepsilon C} exp\ (sV_j) \qquad (10.1)$$

where C is the choice set and s is a scale parameter. This assumes a Type I extreme value distribution for the error terms and that there is independence between different individuals and choices.

Models were estimated using linear and quadratic functional forms. Under the quadratic specification some attribute coefficients were not statistically significant, therefore the linear functional form was used for benefit estimation. Table 10.1 presents the results of the basic model incorporating only attribute values. Note the highly significant coefficient values on CHARGES and BEACHES and the lower significance of those coefficients associated with variables measuring some aspect of river water quality.

The alternative specific constants associated with selecting Choice 2 or Choice 3, were negative and statistically significant. This demonstrates that there is a negative utility associated with changing from the current situation (Choice 1) to one of the other alternatives — this is regardless of any utility respondents may have for the attributes of these choices or any disutility arising from the increased water charges. A similar result was observed by Adamowicz *et al.* (1996) in their study and was interpreted as a form of endowment effect.

This term describes situations where respondents have a utility for remaining in the current situation rather than moving to an alternative. There could be a number of reasons for this effect. In contingent valuation, respondents have been observed to prefer the *status quo* above options based on other criteria that would seem to provide them with greater utility (e.g. Willis and Garrod, 1992). This has been interpreted as a psychological bias associated with a preference for the *status quo*. Alternatively, respondents may mistrust the ability of the EA to make the improvements in water quality specified on the choice cards. It is also possible that respondents chose the current situation as a form of protest, or that the selection was a response to confusion over the choice experiment (though piloting suggested that this was not the case).

The discrete choice probabilities are homogenous of degree zero in the parameters, implying that any attributes which are the same for all outcomes will drop out of the probability model. Thus, individual characteristics, such as income, cannot be treated as standard explanatory variables. Such individual specific variables can only be entered into the model interactively by using the equivalent of dummy variable interaction terms. Individual specific variables are incorporated in the model as *(n-1)* alternative specific variables, where n is the number of choices in each choice card. The coefficient values and t-statistics associated with the dummy variables are reported in Table 10.3, and represent the set of individual specific characteristics which best explain observed choices.

Table 10.1:Attribute coefficients in basic choice experiment model

Variable	Coefficient	t-statistic
ASC-CHOICE2	-0.57574	-4.46
(Alternative specific constant for choice 2)		
ASC-CHOICE3	-0.27078	-2.80
(Alternative specific constant for choice 3)		
CHARGES	-0.02727	-7.44
(Increase in water charges)		
BEACHES	-0.03564	-4.33
(No. of beaches below EC standards in south west)		
POLLUTE	-0.00047426	-2.87
(Miles of polluted rivers in south west)		
LOWFLOW	-0.0014250	-2.01
(Miles of low flow rivers in south west)		

Number of observations = 2676
Log likelihood function = -2775.20
Log L: Constants only = -2817.85
Log L: No coefficients = -2939.89
Chi-squared (4df) =85.30

Table 10.2: Attribute coefficients in extended choice experiment model

Variable	Coefficient	t-statistic
ASC-CHOICE2	-1.3871	-8.15
(Alternative specific constant for choice 2)		
ASC-CHOICE3	-1.0414	-7.88
(Alternative specific constant for choice 3)		
CHARGES	-0.027644	-7.19
(Increase in water charges)		
BEACHES	-0.039563	-4.66
(No. of beaches below EC standards in south west)		
POLLUTE	-0.0005139	-3.00
(Miles of polluted rivers in south west)		
LOWFLOW	-0.0016081	-2.22
(Miles of low flow rivers in south west)		

Number of observations = 2676
Log likelihood function = -2601.96
Log L: Constants only = -2817.85
Log L: No coefficients = -2939.89
Chi-squared(26df) = 431.79

Case Examples

Tables 10.2 and 10.3 report the coefficients of the discrete choice model estimated incorporating a variety of alternative specific variables (two for each individual specific variable specified). These coefficients are all significant at the 10% significance level. The signs on the coefficients must be interpreted in terms of their effect on the estimated utility from choosing any given alternative.

For example, respondents with high incomes gain more utility from their choices than those on the lowest incomes. Respondents who do not visit rivers have a lower utility for their choice than river visitors (see Table 10.3).

Table 10.3: Coefficients of alternative specific variables in extended choice experiment model

Variable	Coefficient	t-statistic
CHOICE2*HIGHINC	0.70583	5.079
(dummy variable: respondent household income > £26,000 per year)		
CHOICE3*HIGHINC	0.25712	2.015
CHOICE2*LOWINC	-0.60245	-2.055
(dummy variable: respondent household income < £4,000 per year)		
CHOICE3*LOWINC	-1.0460	-4.018
CHOICE2*U36	0.90659	7.170
(dummy variable: respondent is aged 35 years or under)		
CHOICE3*U36	0.83685	7.706
CHOICE2*EDUC18	0.36182	2.373
(dummy variable: respondent continued education after age 18)		
CHOICE3*EDUC18	0.38382	2.858
CHOICE2*NONRIVER	-0.71055	-4.871
(dummy variable: respondent did not visit any rivers in last year)		
CHOICE3*NONRIVER	-0.32243	-2.870
CHOICE2*AVON	0.48284	3.557
(dummy variable: respondent lives in county of Avon)		
CHOICE3*AVON	0.39384	3.377
CHOICE2*DORSET	0.41598	2.661
(dummy variable: respondent lives in county of Dorset)		

Variable	Coefficient	t-statistic
CHOICE3*DORSET	0.40795	3.072
CHOICE2*HEALTHY	0.47268	3.960
(dummy variable: respondent strongly agrees rivers will be healthy as today in 50 years' time)		
CHOICE3*HEALTHY	0.41163	4.071
CHOICE2*SATISFIED	0.30713	2.725
(dummy variable: respondent strongly agrees rivers are well looked after)		
CHOICE3*SATISFIED	0.52057	5.477
CHOICE2*LOWGIVE	-1.7314	-4.246
(dummy variable: respondent spends < £1 a year supporting good causes)		
CHOICE3*LOWGIVE	-1.1333	-4.414
CHOICE2*HIGHEXTRA	1.1482	5.419
(dummy variable: respondent willing to spend >£100 a year supporting other good causes)		
CHOICE3*HIGHEXTRA	0.76433	3.740

Table 10.4: Willingness to pay for marginal improvement in water quality

Reduction	Basic specification	Extended specification
1 polluted beach	£1.307	£1.431
1 mile of polluted river	£0.017	£0.019
1 mile of low flow river	£0.052	£0.058

Table 10.4 reports WTP for the marginal improvements in water quality defined by unit reductions in the number of polluted beaches and the lengths of river affected by low flows and poor water quality. Respondents were willing to pay between £1.31 and £1.43 to ensure that one additional beach meets EC standards on cleanliness and £0.02 to clean up a mile of polluted river. Similarly, respondents were willing to pay up to £0.06 per mile to improve conditions on low flow rivers. These estimates were used for the purposes of aggregation, but this relies on the presumption that it is reasonable to assume constant marginal WTP for water quality improvement measures across the south west. This may be the case for beaches but it is possible that following substantial reductions in the length of rivers affected by low flows and pollution that WTP for additional lengths to be improved

could change. Economic theory suggests that marginal WTP should decrease as the provision of the environmental good increases. This should be kept in mind when using aggregate estimates for appraisal purposes.

Table 10.5: Median welfare estimates for CVM scenario

Model	Annual Welfare Measure
Basic specification	£12.80
Extended specification	£15.36

Median welfare measures for non-marginal water quality improvements can also be estimated following the method of Hanemann (1984). This requires an examination of how utility levels change as a result of a specified improvement and then calculating the magnitude of the associated increase in water charges (decrease in income) that would be required to make utility the same before and after the improvements. As Adamowicz *et al.* (1996) point out, the resulting welfare measures are multi-attribute versions of Hanemann's median WTP estimate for contingent valuation. The models in Tables 10.2 and 10.3 were used to calculate the welfare estimates reported in Table 10.5, which relate to the water quality improvement scenario used in the referendum CVM question applied in a parallel study (i.e. a reduction in the number of polluted beaches from 9 to 0; a reduction in the length of polluted rivers from 990 miles to 750 miles; and a reduction from 130 miles to 0 miles in the length of low flow rivers).

These median annual welfare measures apply across the whole population of respondents. These are very close to the estimates of population mean annual maximum WTP for the same scenario that were estimated using referendum CVM (i.e. £17.24 per household).

2.6 Estimating the Number of Users and Non-users

The population of users for this study was defined to encompass all households who had visited a given low flow river in the two-year period immediately preceding the survey. Respondents were shown a list of the seven low flow rivers that were the main focus of this study and asked whether or not they had visited these rivers at any time during the last two years. This data can be used to estimate the number of households that visit each low flow river. Nearly 45% of households in the south-west had visited at least one of the low flow rivers during the last two years. Table 10.6 reports aggregated results for each river to give an estimate of the bi-annual number of visitors to each river.

Table 10.6: Estimated number of visitors to low flow rivers from the south west

River	Estimated Number of Households*	Percentage of South West Households
Allen	85,897	5.21
Upper Avon	230,717	14.00
Meavy	166,760	10.12
Otter	157,982	9.58
Piddle	157,854	9.58
Tavy	240,155	14.57
Wylye	162,481	9.86
One or more of the above	734,161	44.54
None	914,269	55.46

* Some households visit more than one low flow river, so these figures should not be aggregated.

Although quite high, these estimates seemed reasonable. Rivers are linear features and instead of offering a single point of access provide many and varied opportunities for individuals to encounter them. Added to this is the fact that all of the rivers are located in areas with considerable scenic attractions where local people as well as those from further afield would be expected to enjoy the considerable recreational opportunities on offer.

Table 10.7 divides the population of the south west into user and non-user households for each of the seven low flow rivers. It also reports the length of each river affected by low flows. This latter figure is important in the estimation of the aggregate benefits of low flow alleviation.

2.7 Aggregate Benefit Estimates

The choice experiments reported in the previous section can be used to derive random utility models based on the subsets of users and non-users defined previously. These models yield estimates of the marginal WTP for a unit decrease in the length of rivers affected by low flows (see Table 10.8).

The estimate for users will comprise a combination of use values and non-use values, while for non-users the estimate is made up entirely of non-use values. The validity of this latter estimate is highly suspect because the coefficient on the LOWFLOW variable in the non-users' model was not statistically significant at any reasonable level. This implies that when selecting their preferred card in the choice experiments, the non-user population did not give much weight to improvements in low flow rivers. Rather, their choices were based upon cost and the improvements that could be made to polluted rivers and beaches. Given that these respondents had not visited any rivers in the south west that had been seriously affected by low flows in the last two years this does not seem an altogether surprising result.

Table 10.7: User and non-user populations for low flow rivers from the south west

River	User Households	Non-User Households	Miles Affected by Low Flows
Allen	85,897	1,562,533	20
Upper Avon	230,717	1,417,713	35
Meavy	166,760	1,481,670	7
Otter	157,982	1,490,448	5
Piddle	157,854	1,490,576	16
Tavy	240,155	1,408,275	16
Wylye	162,481	1,485,949	30

Table 10.8: Marginal WTP for unit reduction in length of low flow rivers in south west by user and non-user populations

	Number of Respondents	Marginal WTP
Users	290	£0.0760
Non-Users	379	£0.0435*

* this estimate is based on a coefficient value that was not statistically significant at any reasonable level.

The population of low flow river users was estimated at 734,161. For each low flow river the maximum aggregate annual benefit for user households is calculated by multiplying this figure first by the length of river affected by low flows, and then by £0.076 per mile (see Table 10.9). The proportion of this amount contributed by visitors can also be calculated using the same procedure and substituting the estimated number of visitors for the user population. The aggregate benefits for non-user households is calculated in a similar fashion, using the marginal value of £0.0435.

Table 10.9: Approximate aggregate annual benefits for improving low flows across the entire length of all low flow rivers in the south west

River	Aggregate Benefits for User Households	Aggregate Benefits for Visitor Households	Aggregate Benefits for Non-User Households*
Allen	£1,115,925	£130,563	£795,414
Upper Avon	£1,952,868	£613,707	£1,391,975
Meavy	£390,574	£88,716	£278,395
Otter	£278,981	£60,033	£198,854
Piddle	£892,740	£191,950	£636,331
Tavy	£892,740	£292,028	£636,331
Wylye	£1,673,887	£370,457	£1,193,121

* these estimates are based on a coefficient value that was not statistically significant at any reasonable level.

2.8 The Costs of Low Flow Alleviation

The costs of various options to alleviate low flows on rivers in the south west were calculated by Environmental Resources Management (ERM) (see ERM and University of Newcastle, 1997). Table 10.10 summarises the present values of the costs of the cheapest available option for low flow alleviation on six of the seven rivers: no solution has yet been put forward for low flow alleviation on the Tavy.

Table 10.10 also reports the present value of the benefits of low flow alleviation for the user sub-sample: present values were calculated by assuming a constant flow of benefits across the period 1997 to 2017 and discounting at 6%). Net benefits and benefit cost ratios were calculated using these figures and the results also reported in Table 10.10. These figures can be used to carry out partial benefit-cost analysis in order to identify which options require further investigation before they can be implemented.

Benefits exceed costs by a wide margin for the rivers Avon, Meavy and Wylye, and to a lesser extent for the Piddle. Costs are prohibitive only on the Otter, while the benefit-cost ratio for the Allen suggests that while benefits probably exceed costs there is relatively little difference between them. As benefits are based only on the user sample, these benefit-cost ratios ignore any benefits that might accrue to non-users but include non-use benefits for low flow river visitors who do not visit the river in question.

If only the present value of the aggregate benefits accruing to visitors is considered then the least cost solutions for the Piddle and Allen fall to levels substantially below that of the associated costs, while the benefits for the Avon, Meavy and Wylye still outstrip costs by a ratio of at least 10 to 1.

Table 10.10: Net present value of aggregate benefits for improving low flows across the entire length of all low flow rivers in the south west

River	Present Value of Costs*	Present Value of Aggregate User Benefits*	Net Present Value	Benefit-Cost Ratio
Allen	11,867,000	13,915,000	2,048,000	1.17
Upper Avon	763,000	24,352,000	23,589,000	31.92
Meavy	80,000	4,870,000	4,790,000	60.88
Otter	34,430,000	3,480,000	-30,950,000	0.10
Piddle	5,471,000	11,132,000	5,661,000	2.03
Tavy	Unknown	11,132,000	-	-
Wylye	224,000	20,873,000	20,649,000	93.18

* Annual stream of costs and benefits discounted at 6% between 1997 and 2017.

2.9 Discussion

The estimates in Table 10.9 should be interpreted with caution. Most importantly, the estimated aggregate benefits for households who do not visit any low flow rivers should not be included in benefit-cost analysis as they are based on a coefficient that is not statistically different from zero. The other estimates are based on more reliable coefficient values, but still require some sort of 'health warning'. Firstly, the use of marginal WTP estimates that are identical across all seven low flow rivers in the south west means that the aggregate user benefits are related to length of river rather than visitor numbers (e.g. low visit rates to the Allen are not reflected in aggregate user WTP). Respondents who do not visit the river in question, but visit other low flow rivers, are assumed to have the same marginal WTP for a unit reduction in the length affected by low flows as those respondents who visit the river. Secondly, the use of constant marginal WTP across the whole length affected by low flows would be expected to generate an estimate of maximum WTP.

The difference between the aggregate WTP for the user population and the visitor population must be interpreted as a non-use value. Respondent's decisions in the choice experiment could not reflect their preferences for individual low flow rivers, only their desire to see the problem reduced throughout the south west. If such preferences could be incorporated into the estimates then aggregate WTP for visitors would be expected to be higher than they are in Table 10.9, i.e. there would be a smaller proportion of non-use values in the user population aggregates.

The results of the study strongly suggest that there are considerable welfare gains to be made from implementing the least cost low flow alleviation options on the Rivers Wylye, Meavy and Upper Avon. Similarly, there is strong evidence to suggest that only a low flow alleviation option costing considerably less than the one costed in this study would be justified on the Otter. The benefits of the least-cost low flow alleviation options for the Piddle and Allen can only be justified on the basis of non-use values, and then only tentatively. In these cases we would recommend that investigation of the non-recreational benefits of low flow alleviation be carried out to provide a clearer picture in a fuller benefit-cost analysis.

3 CASE STUDY 2: RECREATIONAL CHOICE AND WATER QUALITY

3.1 Background and Data

This study was carried out by Adamowicz *et al.* (1994) using a combination of stated preference choice experiments and a revealed preference approach based on actual behaviour. In the stated preference application respondents were faced with choosing one of three options presented on a choice card. These options related to choice of recreational activities, with the first based on recreation at a standing-water site, the second on recreation at a running-water site and the third being to participate in some non-water based recreational activity or alternatively to stay at home. The stated preference analysis was used to explain choice of recreational sites and this was compared with actual recreational choice as modelled in the revealed preference element of the study.

The two water-based recreational alternatives were described by a variety of site attributes including the distance that respondents would have to travel to reach the site, water quality, terrain, camping facilities, the presence of a beach and various attributes relating to fishing and other recreational activities.

Water quality was presented as either good or bad and recreational quality was characterised by the attribute descriptions reported in Table 10.11. The levels of the various attributes offered to respondents in the choice experiment were based on a factorial statistical design that provided orthogonal attribute data. Individual attribute levels were based on observed ranges of values and characteristics of sites and site visits in south-western Alberta where the study was being carried out.

Table 10.11: Recreational attributes offered in stated preference choice cards

Attribute	Description	
Fish Size	Large	
	Small	
Fish Catch rate	1 fish per 4 hours	
	1 fish per 80 minutes	
	1 fish per 45 minutes	
	1 fish per 35 minutes	
Terrain	Flat prairie	
	Rolling prairie	
	Foothills	
	Mountains	
Facilities	None	
	Day-use only	
	Limited facilities campsite	
	Fully serviced campsite	
Swimming	Yes	
	No	
Water Feature	Still:	Natural lake
		Reservoir
	Running	River
		Stream
Fish Species	Still:	Pike & Perch
		Pickerel, Pike & Perch
	Running	Mountain Whitefish
		Rainbow Trout & Mountain Whitefish
		Rainbow Trout, Mtn Whitefish & Brown Trout
		Cutthroat Trout, Mtn. Whitefish & Bull Trout
Distance to Site	25 km	
	50 km	
	100 km	
	150 km	
Boating	Still:	None
		Small crafts
		Power boats (limited)
		Unrestricted
	Running	None

The attributes of the standing and running water alternatives were treated as a collective factorial and an orthogonal main effects design was chosen which would vary all attribute levels simultaneously. This permitted the attributes of the choice alternatives to be orthogonal within and between alternatives which would allow the IIA property to be tested.

Data were collected using a telephone survey conducted by Alberta Environment. Within this survey respondents were asked to participate in the choice experiment and to provide information that could be used in the revealed preference model. This information included the number and destination of recreation trips carried out in August 1991.

Table 10.12: Selected attribute coefficient values from choice experiment model

Attribute	Standing Water	Running Water
Distance	-0.007	-0.007
(km)	(0.0004)	(0.0004)
Catch rate	0.062	0.105
(fish per unit time)	(0.028)	(0.026)
Fish size	0.058	0.090
(large =1 vs. small =-1)	(0.028)	(0.025)
Water quality	0.394	0.321
(good =1 vs. bad =-1)	(0.027)	(0.025)
Swimming	0.274	0.158
(yes =1 vs. no =-1)	(0.026)	(0.025)
Beach	0.198	0.123
(yes =1 vs. no =-1)	(0.026)	(0.024)
Boating	N/A	N/A

3.2 Empirical Results: Choice Experiment

Following the survey, a multinomial logit discrete choice model was estimated based on the choice experiment data. All parameters, with the exception of distance, were estimated as interaction terms associated with standing or running water. Table 10.12 reports coefficient values for standing and running water options for selected recreational attributes: coefficient values are reported fully in Adamowicz *et al.* (1994).

The model was found to fit the observed data well and to have parameters with coefficients consistent with the authors' expectations. Factors which were found to have a positive influence on utility included: larger fish; good water quality; increased catch rates; the availability of swimming; and the presence of beaches. Respondents were also found to prefer upland topography rather than prairie and to prefer a higher diversity of fish species rather than fewer species. The most popular package of species was a combination of rainbow trout, mountain whitefish and brown trout. As might be expected fully-serviced campsites were preferred by respondents, who also had a higher utility for not having to travel so far to the site. There were also differences between the estimated coefficient values for parameters between running water and standing water sites, for example, increased fish size and catch rates offer more utility at running water sites compared with standing water sites.

Table 10.13: Selected attribute coefficient values from revealed preference model

Attribute	Standing Water	Running Water
Distance	-0.0282	-0.0282
(km)	(0.001)	(0.001)
Catch rate	2.0338	2.0338
(fish per unit time)	(0.237)	(0.237)
Fish Size	N/A	N/A
Water quality	-0.8197	-3.129
(poor = 1 vs. good = 0)	(0.494)	(0.3749)
Swimming	2.7477	0.9148
(yes = 1 vs. no = 0)	(0.290)	(0.251)
Beach	0.9918	-1.955
(yes = 1 vs. no = 0)	(0.302)	(0.369)
Boating	6.6620	1.7335
(unrestricted = 1	(1.024)	(0.289)
vs. none = 0)		

3.3 Empirical Results: Revealed Preference Analysis

The telephone survey provided information on 730 separate recreational trips during August 1991. The destination for each trip was characterised by the actual levels of the recreational attributes described in Table 10.11.

This characterisation of sites by their constituent attributes allowed the authors to estimate a model of recreational choice, where travel costs and site attributes were used to explain site choices; however, as the authors point out, such choices will be influenced by many factors unavailable to the model and any model will of necessity be a much simplified version of reality. Furthermore, not all factors could be entered into the model due to similarity across sites, so the revealed preference model is based on a subset of the attributes used in the choice experiment analysis.

A multinomial discrete choice model was estimated for the site choice decision. Table 10.13 reports coefficient values for standing and running water sites for selected recreational attributes: coefficient values are reported fully in Adamowicz *et al.* (1994).

The model suggested that a number of factors were significant in explaining site choice including distance to be travelled to gain access to the site, water quality, catch rates and the availability of swimming, fishing and boating.

3.4 Comparison of Approaches

Adamowicz *et al.* go on to estimate a joint version of the choice experiment and revealed preference models by combining the data and jointly estimating a new model where all parameters are estimated using information from both the choice experiments and the revealed preference data. Such joint estimation was possible because the survey was designed to ensure that the choice experiments and revealed preference questions conformed to a common random utility formulation.

The authors suggest that this approach allows them to improve the quality of the estimates based on the revealed preference model. In particular they argue that the joint estimation reduces the collinearity present in that model.

Both individual and jointly estimated models were used to investigate the welfare implications, in terms of altered levels of utility, from changes in water quality attribute levels at recreational sites. This type of estimation has particular importance for site management, indicating the welfare implications of various management and resource allocation decisions.

Overall, they argue that while the choice experiment approach is attractive because of its flexibility, its usefulness is further enhanced by the fact that both this approach and the revealed preference approach produce similar models.

4 CONCLUSIONS

The choice experiment approach offers considerable advantages when examining water quality issues. The multiple attribute nature of water quality is a particular problem for management decisions requiring trade-offs to be made between them. The first case study examined a range of broad water quality attributes within a wider policy context, while the second case illustrates how choice experiments can be applied at a site level and used to discover how the utility of individuals is affected by changes in the levels of various recreational and water quality attributes.

Both case studies suggest that choice experiments offer at least as fruitful an avenue of research as conventional contingent valuation methods. As Adamowicz *et al.* (1994) argue, the approach also offers considerable promise for the estimation of non-use values as demonstrated in the first case study.

REFERENCES

Adamowicz, W.L., J.J. Louviere and M. Williams (1994), 'Combining revealed and stated preference methods for valuing environmental amenities', *Journal of Environmental Economics and Management* **26**, 271–92.

Adamowicz, W.L., P. Boxall, M. Williams, and J.J. Louviere (1996), 'Stated preference approaches for measuring passive use values choice experiments versus contingent valuation', Paper presented at the *4th Annual Canadian Resource and Environmental Economics Workshop*.

Department of the Environment/Welsh Office (1986), *River Quality in England and Wales - 1985*, HMSO, London.

ERM/University of Newcastle upon Tyne (1997), *Economic Appraisal of the Environmental Costs and Benefits of Potential Solutions to Alleviate Low Flows in Rivers*, Report to the Environment Agency South West Region, ERM Economics, London.

Hanemann, W.M. (1984), 'Welfare evaluations in contingent valuation experiments with discrete responses', *American Journal Of Agricultural Economics*, **66**, 332–41.

Willis, K.G. and G.D. Garrod (1992), 'Assessing the value of future landscapes', *Landscape and Urban Planning*, **23**, 17–32.

11. Amenity Values

The beauty of the morning: silent, bare,
Ships, towers, domes, theatres and temples lie
Open unto the fields, and to the sky,
All bright and glittering in the smokeless air.

William Wordsworth (1770-1850): *Upon Westminster Bridge*

1 INTRODUCTION

In an earlier chapter, the concept of recreational value was discussed in relation to a number of case studies, where the recreational benefits offered to visitors to various sites were measured. Many recreational sites offer benefits both to visitors and to people who live nearby. In some cases it may be useful to be able to estimate the benefits which these local users obtain from the site. Benefits, however, may be the result of both the active enjoyment of the site, i.e. recreation, and of more passive enjoyment, such as the utility obtained from a pleasant view or from the sound of running water.

The sum of these benefits to local people may be termed the amenity value of the site and this should be separated from any recreational benefits that accrue to visitors. Thus, a particular feature or facility can be said to generate an amenity value if proximity to that feature or facility is in some way pleasing, or useful, to an individual or group of individuals.

2 MEASURING AMENITY VALUES

In terms of the measurement of amenity value, the travel-cost method is clearly unsuitable as the costs incurred by local people enjoying a site will be negligible. Expressed preference methods may prove more suitable, and have been used in a number of cases to measure the willingness-to-pay of local people to maintain or enhance the landscapes within which they live (e.g. Willis and Garrod, 1992 in the Pennine Dales).

This chapter, however, will concentrate on the use of the hedonic price method to measure the amenity value offered by environmental features. Hedonic pricing offers the useful facility of allowing researchers to estimate the marginal contribution that a change in particular type of feature makes to the price of a good. For example, in order to measure the amenity value offered by a particular landscape feature, the task becomes one of estimating the premium which that feature adds to the price of those houses in close proximity to it.

Several problems are associated with this. Landscape features vary both in quality and quantity and proximity to different examples of a particular landscape feature may offer different benefits. This may require some acknowledgement in the model, for instance by the use of variables that incorporate some measure of quantity. Quality is harder to measure objectively, and a common approach is to assume that individuals have equal utility for particular landscape features regardless of quality. Similarly, proximity may be hard to define and perceptions of what is near enough to provide a residential amenity may differ across individuals. Such problems are best dealt with on a case-by-case basis.

Another potential problem is the argument that the benefits offered by landscape features may depend on other aspects of the landscape. This argument has been made by Price (1995) who has argued that, while the approach may be suitable for the estimation of the premiums that certain clearly defined housing attributes add to house prices, aesthetic preferences for landscape features tend to be too complex to be modelled in this fashion. The basis of this argument is the notion that the aesthetic value of landscape is based on a range of visible features and qualities some of which cannot be measured objectively. In Price's view, any attempt to separate out the effects of different landscape features, such as trees or woodland, and model their effect on house prices is problematic because of the interdependence of a much larger set of features in creating an aesthetically pleasing landscape.

In terms of estimating the hedonic price model, this is a similar problem to that of the multicollinearity often present in data measuring the levels of the various elements which make up a landscape. When various physical features integrate to give an overall aesthetic effect upon which house buyers base their premium for landscape, then it may be very difficult for them to separate the influence of one feature from another. Price's argument suggests that isolating one particular landscape feature and investigating its effect on amenity value will at best produce an estimate which describes the effect of the total landscape on house price rather than the effect of that feature. The logical extension of this argument is that hedonic pricing may only be able to value the effect of different levels of landscape quality, and that these levels would have to be determined holistically for each property in the sample using the aesthetic judgement of the researcher or an expert in landscape design.

This chapter will document a number of case studies which approach the problem from different angles. The first case study examines the amenity value of water frontage, a single discrete feature which is widely acknowledged to increase property values. The second case ignores the arguments of Price and attempts to value individual landscape features and local services. The final case attempts to alleviate the problem by measuring the amenity values associated with access to a particular element of landscape, woodland.

3. CASE 1: THE AMENITY VALUE OF WATER FRONTAGE

3.1 Background

It has been observed that properties located in close proximity to water, and especially those commanding a water frontage, often command a price premium over and above that of equivalent properties located elsewhere. A reliable estimate of the magnitude of this premium is important to any developers interested in exploiting the potential of a waterside lot for property development and to landowners hoping to realise the value of their waterside land.

One such landowner is British Waterways, a public body responsible for the upkeep and development of canals and inland waterways in the UK. With the decline in freight traffic British Waterways generates an increasing proportion of its income through recreational activities on waterways such as fishing and pleasure cruising. In addition, they have sought to justify their grant-in-aid from the UK Government by demonstrating the magnitude of the non-priced recreational benefits provided by inland waterways in the UK (e.g. Willis and Garrod, 1991). It is not surprising, in the light of this, to discover that by the early 1990s British Waterways were keen to exploit the development potential of land under their ownership that was situated alongside canals.

In the past, British Waterways' interest in property development was mainly restricted to properties close to, or integrated with, waterways and where such development did not clash with the waterways environment, e.g. through the conversion of existing buildings into residential or commercial premises. A more proactive approach to property development along canals and inland waterways could permit British Waterways to realise a considerable return on their land which could be used to re-develop or preserve other aspects of the inland waterway network.

3.2 Case Study and Data

The study reported here was commissioned by British Waterways to investigate some of the issues detailed above, with the main objective being to quantify the premium on house prices generated by their location on the waterfront or their proximity to waterways. This was to be achieved in two ways: first, through an hedonic price model, and second through a contingent valuation question eliciting expert judgement on the house price premiums offered by proximity to waterways. The results from the latter will only be presented briefly to provide an interesting comparison with the hedonic price estimates.

Two case study areas were used, the main one concentrating on properties close to the Regents Canal in London, the other focusing on properties in close proximity to any of a group of canals located in the English West Midlands. There are substantial differences between the housing markets in these two areas, particularly in relation to price, with houses close to the capital attracting a substantial premium, so the two data sets were treated separately.

Three categories of properties were identified as having special interest to this study; they were properties with:

i   a canal-side location;
ii   a location adjacent to a canal but with no water frontage;
iii no proximity to a canal.

British Waterways identified postcodes for each of these three categories which provided locational indicators down to a street level. These postcodes were then compared with the records from a major mortgage lender to identify properties sold in each category during the five-year period 1985 to 1989. These records could then be used as the raw material for the hedonic study, providing details of sale price plus structural and other details that are relevant in determining house price.

This process yielded over 2,000 usable records, 1,787 for the London area and 275 for the West Midlands. Additional data on the socio-economic characteristics of the areas surrounding the properties in the data set were obtained from the 1981 population census and NOMIS (see Chapter 4).

3.3 Empirical Study

The house price opportunity locus was specified empirically as:

$$P_{ho} = P_{ho}(ENV_i, Q_i, S_i, SE_i) \tag{11.1}$$

where P_{ho} is the selling price, ENV_i is a vector of the environmental characteristics in the neighbourhood of the ith property, Q_i is the quarter of the year in which the house was sold, S_i is a vector of the structural characteristics of the house and SE_i is a vector of variables describing the social economic characteristics in the district containing the house.

In this study the only variables used to define ENV_i were indicator (0–1) variables denoting, respectively, whether the ith property was situated either on the waterfront (WSIDE) or adjacent to the canal (ADJ).

A restricted version of the linear Box-Cox functional form used in Cassel and Mendelsohn (1985) and Dinan and Miranowski (1989) was used to estimate the model. The form of the model used for estimation was:

$$P(\theta) = \infty_0 + \Sigma \infty_j x_j(\pi) \tag{11.2}$$

where:

$$P(\theta) = \begin{cases} (P^\theta - 1)/\theta & \text{when } \theta \neq 0 \\ ln(P) & \text{when } \theta = 0 \end{cases}$$

and:

$$x_j(\pi) = \begin{cases} (x_j{}^\pi - 1)/\pi & \text{when } \pi \neq 0 \\ ln(x_j) & \text{when } \pi = 0 \end{cases}$$

Here ∞_j is the coefficient value of the explanatory variable x_j and π and θ are the parameters of the Box-Cox model across which the grid search is carried out to determine the best-fitting functional form.

3.4 Results

The results of these studies are reported fully in Willis and Garrod (1993) but are summarised for the variables of interest in Table 11.1. Over 75% of the variation in the dependent variable was explained in each of the two models, which seemed acceptable given the nature of the data and the assumptions underlying the analysis.

Table 11.1: Premium added to house prices by proximity to canals based on an hedonic price study

	Midlands	London
Waterside Frontage	5.18%	2.92%
Adjacent to Canal	-	1.46%

In both models the variable WSIDE had a positive, statistically significant coefficient indicating that water frontage does indeed add a premium to house prices. The variable ADJ had a statistically significant coefficient value only for the London data set, this was again positive but less than the coefficient value for WSIDE indicating that properties adjacent to the Regents Canal but with no water frontage commanded a smaller premium than those houses with a water frontage.

The calculation of the implicit prices for these variables is complicated by the functional form of the hedonic price model (see Willis and Garrod, 1993) but revealed that in London a waterside frontage offered a price premium of £1,909 or nearly 3% of the sample average house price for the London data set. In the Midlands a similar frontage offered a premium of £1,598 which was just over 5% of the average price of properties in the data set. Location adjacent to a canal but without a water frontage did not command a premium in the Midlands but added about 1.5% to house prices in the London case.

3.5 Comparison with the Contingent Valuation Study

These premiums were considerably lower than those estimated in the contingent valuation survey of estate agents. In this survey members of the Royal Institute of Chartered Surveyors (RICS) were sent a brief questionnaire accompanied by the specifications for the same new four-bedroomed house. Respondents were asked to estimate market price if an identical house with the given specifications were to be situated in each of following three locations:

i   a waterside location overlooking a river, waterway or well-tended canal, with a private garden and landscaped public area in-between the house and the water. The water space has pleasure boat traffic but no moorings or waterside facilities;

ii   a location on the same development with no view over water. The house is located 20 metres away from the water but enjoys the same level of landscaping and design ambience and reflects the overall scheme's waterfront location;

iii   a location some miles away from a river or waterway but on a development of similar quality and size as that envisaged in the above descriptions.

Given that all other attributes were held constant, any differences in market price across the three locations could reasonably be held to reflect the premium added by proximity to the waterfront. Table 11.2 reports the mean percentage premiums based on the 59 responses to the 200 questionnaires that were mailed to RICS members.

Table 11.2: Premium added to house prices by proximity to canals based on a contingent valuation study of estate agents

	Midlands	London	All
Waterside Frontage	9.3%	24.3%	16.4%
Adjacent to Canal	4.9%	12.4%	8.1%

The results for London and the Midlands are based on small samples and could be inflated by sampling error. The 16.4% premium reflects the responses of all 59 estate agents who returned completed questionnaires and this is still three times greater than the highest premium reported in the HPM study.

One worry about the results of the contingent valuation survey was the wide variation in responses. In a number of cases two or more respondents in the same town estimated widely different values for identical houses in identical locations in their towns. This suggested a degree of uncertainty even in the responses of individuals whose job it is to value properties. Such uncertainty may have been the result of inexperience in valuation of waterside property or to different perceptions about the material presented in the survey. In some towns different respondents gave reassuringly similar valuations, suggesting that consistency was possible (for further details see Willis and Garrod, 1993).

3.6 Discussion

The wide variation between the premiums estimated by the hedonic price model and the contingent valuation survey of estate agents requires explanation. Apart from problems caused by the small sample size in the contingent valuation survey, another possibility is that the variety of housing covered in the hedonic price survey was far wider than that used in the estate-agent survey. Premiums may be linked to other housing characteristics: for example, houses with certain other desirable characteristics (e.g. detached houses) might attract a proportionately higher premium than properties without these characteristics. If this was the case it would suggest a degree of multicollinearity not accounted for in the hedonic price model. Alternatively, the quality of the waterside environments offered by the majority of houses in the hedonic price survey may have been well below the quality portrayed in the contingent valuation specification. Indeed, many of the areas covered in the hedonic price data set were located in older, more run-down areas.

Even if the hedonic price models suffered from problems with multicollinearity, comparison of results suggests that the hedonic price estimates could at least be treated as lower-bound estimates of the potential benefits of waterside developments in the areas specified in the study. Prestige developments could be judged to attract higher premiums, possibly more in line with those suggested in the contingent valuation survey. Thus, while no firm conclusions can be drawn regarding the exact premium offered by waterside amenity, this study does confirm the observation that a waterside location does generate an amenity value which is reflected in the public being willing to pay more for properties with a waterfront location.

4 CASE 2: VALUING LANDSCAPE AND AMENITY ATTRIBUTES

4.1 Background and Data

This study was based on an area of some 4,800 square kilometres in Central England offering a considerable variety of landscape form and feature. The chief focus was the county of Gloucestershire but the study also encompassed large areas of Hereford and Worcester, plus smaller areas of Gwent, Wiltshire, Oxfordshire and Avon. The variety offered by the landscape coupled with the area's relatively large rural populations was thought to provide a good opportunity to investigate the impact which individual landscape and amenity features have on house prices.

The first task undertaken after the choice of study region was the identification of house sale transactions within the area from the data set of a large mortgage lender. Following this, postcode data was used to identify any transactions that had occurred within urban areas. These records were then removed from the data set to leave only transactions that had occurred in rural or semi-rural areas. Local knowledge was used to define these areas rather than some more systematic data-based approach.

Over the five-year period from 1985 to 1989 it was found that nearly 2,000 mortgages were processed by the lender to fund the purchase of properties within the non-urban part of the study region. These formed the core data for the study, and as in the previous case provided a wealth of information on the structure and condition of the properties in question. There remained the question of how to obtain relevant socio-economic data about the areas in question and how to define and measure proximity to various landscape attributes.

Socio-economic data was obtained from the 1981 census and from various other sources suggested in the chapter on hedonic pricing. The main sources of data on landscape features were Ordnance Survey (OS) 1:50,000 map sheets. Over 50 variables which could influence house prices were found to be available from OS maps. Obtaining these variables for each of the properties in the house sale data base required considerable time and patience. The use of Geographic Information Systems was not feasible owing to copyright restrictions on OS maps, so all data had to be derived by hand. This led to a concentration on simple 0–1 variables which simply identified whether the 1 km OS map square containing the property of interest contained a particular landscape feature. Landscape features measured in this way included rivers, wetlands and overhead cables. Other amenity features identified using this convention were post offices, public houses and country parks. Other 0–1 variables identified the presence of features such as golf courses and large industrial facilities within the eight 1-km squares surrounding the square containing a property of interest.

In addition, a number of variables were defined based on continuous rather than discrete data. These measured attributes such as approximate land cover from forestry, buildings, open water, etc. in the 1-km square and approximate distance in kilometres to the nearest urban centre, settlement, school, etc. Similarly, lengths of roads and rail track were measured. In addition, the predominant aspect of the 1-km square was noted as was its average height above sea level and the approximate degree of slope.

Particular problems were found in defining the proximity of a property to forestry. Wooded areas are noted on OS maps but owing to the dynamic nature of the industry these areas may change in size over relatively short periods of time. As noted above, the area of land covered by woodland in the 1-km grid square was measured. This was used in its own right in the modelling procedure but was also used as the basis of defining a number of 0–1 variables indicating whether or not the 1-km square had greater than a given percentage of woodland cover.

The precise relationship between these variables and the houses incorporated in the data set was somewhat ill-defined. Without breaking agreements on data protection, there was no means of identifying the exact location of a property within a 1-km OS square. Thus, the variables defined using OS maps would only provide an approximation of a given property's proximity to particular landscape attributes. Despite this, it was felt that such an approximation would be sufficient to reveal any significant relationships between landscape features and house price.

The use of data from a five-year period meant that the effects of market fluctuations and inflation had to be accounted for. This was accomplished using a series of dummy variables reflecting the year and quarter of sale. Although the study area was reasonably small and could be argued to represent a contiguous housing market area, socio-economic dummies and dummies reflecting local authority areas were used to model differences across the study region, e.g. caused by localised supply problems or planning policies.

4.2 Empirical Results

A semi-log functional form was used to model the data described above. This was chosen as a result of a grid search across the parameters of a linear Box-Cox function similar to that described in the previous case. In terms of modelling the data, special consideration was given to the variables measuring proximity to landscape and amenity attributes. These were subjected to rigorous examination with respect to their statistical significance and freedom from the effects of multicollinearity and omitted variable bias.

Variables measuring structural attributes of the model and socio-economic characteristics of the study area were permitted to enter the model even if they displayed some degree of collinearity. Such relationships are almost certain to occur in data on the structural attributes of housing and the socio-economic characteristics of the areas within which they are found. Affluent areas contain a greater proportion of larger houses and these houses have more bedrooms, bathrooms and double garages than the smaller houses found more commonly in less affluent areas. This meant that while the coefficient values revealing the contribution of structural and other attributes to house price could be biased, those coefficients relating to landscape and amenity variables were reliable and robust indicators of the contribution that those features made to house prices.

Many of the variables relating to landscape and other amenity features were found not to have a significant effect on house price or to suffer from some degree of multicollinearity. Even so, the nine variables shown in Table 11.3 were found to be both statistically significant but robust in terms of estimation.

Table 11.3: Statistically significant landscape and amenity variables

Variable	Definition
FOR20	0–1 variable: over 20% woodland in same 1-km square as property
RIVER	0–1 variable: river or canal in same 1-km square as property
SETTLEMENT	0–1 variable: rural settlement in same 1-km square as property
WETLAND	0–1 variable: area of wetland in same 1-km square as property
WOODVIEW	0–1 variable: probable woodland view in same 1-km square as property
URBANVIEW	0–1 variable: probable urban view in same 1-km square as property
SLOPE	Predominant gradient of slope in same 1-km square as property
ROAD	Kilometres of road in same 1-km square as property
RAIL	Kilometres of rail track in same 1-km square as property

Overall, the model explained nearly 77% of variation in the data, which was acceptable given the limitations of the data set and also reflected the absence of certain variables from the data set which could conceivably have a significant effect on house values. Table 11.4 reports the coefficient values of the amenity variables and the marginal implicit price which can be inferred directly from the coefficient values of the semi-log model as the percentage increase in average house values brought about by a unit change in the value of the amenity variable. For 0–1 variables this translates directly into the percentage increase in average house prices offered by proximity to the amenity variable in question.

Proximity to rivers and other waterways, and to land with reasonably high woodland cover, both yield a premium to house prices. Similarly, a premium was offered for houses within good reach of local amenities and communications as shown by the positive coefficient values on the variables denoting proximity to settlements and roads. While there may be some argument over the magnitude of these premiums, it seems reasonable to conclude that improved access to these features does inflate rather than depress house prices.

Locating houses close to areas of wetland or to rail lines depresses house prices as does the possibility of a view over an urban area or a wooded area. The latter result is perhaps the most curious of those reported in the Table above. It may be that most of the houses thought to command such a view either failed to do so, or had a view over a forestry plantation, many of which are rather unattractive areas of uniform monoculture of non-native species.

Table 11.4: Premium offered by proximity to landscape and other amenities

Variable	Coefficient (t-value)	Marginal Implicit Price (% of sample average house values)
FOR20	0.0710 (2.53)	7.10
RIVER	0.0490 (2.74)	4.90
SETTLEMENT	0.0834 (5.34)	8.34
WETLAND	-0.1800 (-1.75)	18.00
WOODVIEW	-0.0735 (-3.10)	7.35
URBANVIEW	-0.0580 (-3.55)	5.80
SLOPE	-0.0030 (-2.50)	0.30
ROAD	0.0279 (3.66)	2.79
RAIL	-0.0543 (-2.77)	5.43

4.3 Discussion

This study failed to produce any comprehensive estimates of the marginal value of landscape and other amenity attributes but it does suggest that a number of amenity features have a significant effect on house price. Limitations in terms of the data used and potential inaccuracies in linking the properties used as a basis for the data set with amenity variables means that the estimates of marginal implicit price documented above have to be treated with some caution.

Subsequent studies may improve on the one reported here by linking individual properties with amenity attributes much more accurately through the use of Geographical Information Systems and OS map data. This is, however, a problem with data rather than methodology and this study amply demonstrates the potential of hedonic pricing for estimating amenity values of amenity attributes, which include both willingness to pay for the recreational opportunities offered by that attribute and the direct utility arising from the amenity of living in close proximity to that attribute.

Lack of amenity value should not detract from the possibility that particular attributes do not have a substantial non-market value. In this example, the data suggested that houses located close to wetland areas would be valued less than identical properties in drier areas. This is plausible given potential problems with damp and flooding and the possibility of increased insurance and maintenance costs. However, wetlands offer a valuable habitat for a number of important species and are becoming increasing scarce in both the UK and Europe. Thus, they offer society other benefits in terms of their contribution to biodiversity and species preservation and these should not be forgotten in the focus on just one aspect of their value.

5 CASE 3: THE BENEFITS OF WOODLAND ACCESS

5.1 Background and Data

As mentioned in the introduction to this section, a number of authors, most notably Price (1995), have argued that hedonic pricing is not an appropriate means of measuring the benefits produced by various landscape attributes such as woodland and water. In response to this argument, Powe *et al.* (1997) moved the focus away from the contribution of a particular feature or set of features to landscape amenity towards the premium respondents are willing to pay for increased access to that feature. This reflects a subtle difference in approach and moves the welfare measure to be estimated away from amenity values towards recreational values similar to those estimated in travel-cost models. Even so, it can be argued that the amenity aspect of a feature may be subsumed within these estimates provided that it is significant in its own right as well as forming an integral part of the wider landscape.

For the purposes of this study, Powe *et al.* focused on access to areas of woodland. Woodland forms an important feature within a landscape but as Price argues the benefits it provides may be influenced by the levels of other features (the type of relationship which could perhaps be modelled in a basic way through multi-level modelling techniques). It may be that close proximity to woodland offers its own benefits in terms of potential for quiet recreation and in terms of general amenity. If some objective measure of woodland access could be obtained for particular properties then it would be possible to use an hedonic pricing approach to investigate the magnitude of the benefits offered by that access.

One area of England that is particularly renowned for the quality of its woodland is the New Forest, a large area of native and exotic planting with important historical associations. The abundance of wooded areas in this region constitutes an important local amenity and is probably an important factor in the decision of many people to move to the area. Every house in the vicinity of the New Forest will have access to a certain quantity of woodland

and the extent of this access could be hypothesised to influence the magnitude of house prices. As the area is relatively flat with few interesting views, it is fair to say that the New Forest offers what is probably the most significant local contribution to environmental amenity.

The main data source for the hedonic price study was the same mortgage data set utilised in the previous two cases. In this case 872 properties were identified as having been sold in the New Forest area over the period 1990 to 1992. Socio-economic data was obtained on a ward basis for each property using the 1991 population census.

Data on access to woodland and other significant landscape and amenity features was obtained using a Geographical Information System (GIS) and map data digitised from Bartholomew maps. GIS provided clear advantages over the manual method of data collection described in the last case. While also involving a considerable investment in time, the GIS approach is more flexible in that new variables based on digitised data can be constructed relatively easily and because it allows measurement of distance and area to be carried out in a straightforward manner. The additional accuracy and speed of calculation provided by GIS software is also an advantage over manual methods.

Access to woodland was measured both in terms of proximity to woodland and the area of that woodland. In order to provide a consistent measure of access Powe *et al.* constructed a forest access index for each property in the sample. This index took into account the distance from the property to each sector of amenity woodland (defined as having either a car park or a picnic area) in the district, the most significant of which was the New Forest Park. For a particular property the access index was constructed as shown below:

$$Forest\ access\ index = \sum_i (area_i/distance_i^2)$$

where $area_i$ is the area of forest sector i and $distance_i$ is the distance from forest sector i to the property in question. Thus, the access index becomes smaller the greater the distance between the property and the sector of forest but increases with the area of woodland. Details of woodland composition or quality were not incorporated in the index; however, it can be argued that as the mix of species and ages does not vary substantially across the area the index should still be useful for measuring the benefits that the majority of amenity woodlands offer to local people.

Other variables estimated using the GIS included: distance from the sea; location within 200m of a river; location within a large urban area (e.g. Southampton); location within 100m of a motorway or main road; and location within 100m of a rail line.

5.2 Empirical Results

A search across the parameters of a linear Box-Cox function revealed that the best fit was obtained from taking the log of both the dependent variable (house price) and the forest access index. Table 11.5 below shows the coefficient values and implicit prices associated with this model.

The variables relating to the proportion of children in the population of the ward containing the house and situation in a large urban area seem to act as proxies for social factors that indicate the presence of lower-cost housing. The significant negative coefficient on the variable denoting a 1990 house sale reflects the drop in market prices observed between 1990 and 1991.

A number of tests were carried out to investigate the robustness of this model. These were principally concerned with investigating changes in the coefficient of the forest access index variable caused by changes in specification. The reliability of this coefficient was important if any weight was to be given to the estimation of the benefits of woodland access. Omitted variable bias was tested by omitting significant variables in sequence and examining the effects on the implicit price of access. Multicollinearity was investigated by using principal component analysis to look for independent sources of variation within the data and potential heteroscedasticity was investigated using residual analysis and a Park Test (Maddala, 1992).

Table 11.5: Estimated coefficient values and implicit prices from hedonic price model

	Coefficient	t-ratio	Implicit Price (£1991)
Intercept	10.27	330.3	N/A
log(forest access index)	0.0461	7.8	N/A
Proportion of children in ward population	-0.0076	-7.3	-482
Location within large urban area (0-1)	-0.0736	-4.9	-4,672
Floor area (square metres)	0.0057	30.0	362
Detached house (0-1)	0.3307	18.4	20,993
Semi-detached house (0-1)	0.1115	7.0	7,078
Age of property	-0.0004	-2.4	-25
Full central heating (0-1)	0.1003	6.6	6,367
House purchased in 1990 (0-1)	0.1073	3.3	6,812
House has garage (0-1)	0.0736	5.1	4,672

The non-linear functional form of the hedonic price model meant the marginal price of any characteristic was dependent upon the level to which that characteristic was present. With the exception of the woodland access index the model has a log-linear (semi-log) functional form. The marginal or implicit price of a given attribute under this specification can be calculated straightforwardly as the product of the regression coefficient and the sample mean house price.

The log-log functional relationship between house price and the forest access index in the hedonic price model is reflected in the calculation of marginal price, i.e.

$$\text{marginal price of woodland access} = (\text{regression coefficient/access index})*\text{house price}$$

For the model as a whole if average values for house price are applied then marginal values for specific changes in the forest access index can be calculated. The mean value of the index across the sample is 54, with a mean value of 5.4 emphasising the effect of a number of extreme values where properties are located in close proximity to large areas of woodland (e.g. location within the New Forest Park). To put these figures in perspective it can easily be demonstrated that planting an additional hectare of woodland within 100 metres of a particular house will raise the access index by only one unit. For a house of sample average price with a sample average forest access index of 54 such an increase would be translated into a £543 increase in house price.

5.3 Discussion

The study goes on to use the approach outlined above to examine the effects that various planting and felling strategies would have on the overall amenity benefits provided to local residents by the New Forest. These were then compared with the opportunity costs of felling and planting. What this comparison showed was that, depending upon the location of forested areas in relation to centres of population, large net benefits could be gained by new planting or preserved by preventing clear felling. The magnitude of these benefits depends, like the access index, on the area of woodland involved and the magnitude of the population living in close proximity to the wooded areas.

Most importantly, this study demonstrated the large net benefits that would accrue from planting new areas of woodland in close proximity to substantial areas of population that were currently poorly served with woodland amenity. Such an analysis gives a clear pointer to decision makers involved in forest planting (which could represent a significant growth sector if the recommendations of the 1995 Rural White Paper for England for significant expansion in planting are implemented). Of course, such an analysis is only applicable to the study region which, as mentioned earlier, is uncommonly well-served with high quality woodland.

6 CONCLUSIONS

The effects of context on the benefits estimated in hedonic pricing and other environmental valuation studies are a common theme running through the case studies presented in this chapter. Hedonic pricing does not offer an effective means of separating out the individual contributions of landscape attributes in cases where those attributes combine to form an overall effect that is different from the impacts of the individual attributes. Thus, it may prove unwise to attempt to value the contribution of individual landscape attributes when it is thought that their contribution is dependent upon the levels of other landscape amenities rather than independent of them. The first case study takes the example of the amenity benefits of a waterside location as reflected in the premium which they offer to house price. This premium could be argued to be independent of other features but as the parallel contingent valuation study of estate agents revealed, individual perceptions of quality may differ widely. Thus, if individuals perceived that one waterside location was more run down or less scenic than another, then the premium which they would pay for that location might be lower, thus suggesting an interdependence between waterfront location and general environmental quality.

Such problems are better illustrated in the second case where a number of individual landscape and amenity characteristics were valued using an hedonic price approach. Again, the context in which these features were found could influence the premium which they offer. In addition, this study highlighted the problems of accurately linking individual properties with the environmental attributes which the study sets out to value. Even so, the results do give very positive indications of the usefulness of these techniques for measuring the magnitude of residential amenity values.

The final case study attempted to circumvent the problems of measurement by using a Geographic Information System and avoided the problems of interdependence of landscape features by concentrating on the premiums offered by additional access to substantial landscape features, i.e. woods and forests. This study was relatively successful in achieving its main aims and provides further pointers towards the practical application of hedonic pricing in valuing residential amenity.

This study also illustrated the dangers of transferring amenity benefits across widely different study regions. It may be tempting to infer that the results shown for the New Forest could be applied to other regions; however, the special features of the New Forest in terms of quantity and quality of woodland suggest that such an extrapolation would be foolhardy without further research. For further discussion on this topic, the reader is referred to the chapter on benefit transfer.

REFERENCES

Cassel, E. and R. Mendelsohn (1985), 'The choice of functional forms for hedonic price equations: comment', *Journal of Urban Economics,* **18**, 135–42.

Dinan, T.M. and J.A. Miranowski (1989), 'Estimating the implicit price of energy efficiency improvements in the residential housing market: a hedonic approach', *Journal of Urban Economics,* **25**, 52–67.

Garrod, G.D. and K.G. Willis (1992), 'Valuing goods' characteristics: an application of the hedonic price method to environmental attributes', *Journal of Environmental Management,* **34**, 59–76.

Maddala, G.S. (1992), *Introduction to Econometrics,* Second Edition, Macmillan Publishing Company, New York.

Powe, N.A., G.D. Garrod, C.F. Brunsdon and K.G. Willis (1997), 'Using a geographic information system to estimate an hedonic price model of the benefits of woodland access', *Forestry,* **70**, 139–49.

Price, C. (1995), 'The pros and cons of alternative valuation methods', in K.G. Willis and J.T. Corkindale (eds) *Environmental Valuation New Perspectives,* CAB International, Wallingford.

Willis, K.G. and G.D. Garrod (1991), 'Valuing open access recreation on inland waterways: on-site recreation surveys and selection effects', *Regional Studies* **25**, 511–24.

Willis, K.G. and G.D. Garrod (1992), 'Assessing the value of future landscapes', *Landscape and Urban Planning,* **23**, 17–32.

Willis, K.G. and G.D. Garrod (1993), 'Not from experience: a comparison of experts' opinions and hedonic price estimates of the incremental value of property attributable to an environmental feature', *Journal of Property Research,* **10**, 193–216.

PART FIVE

Policy Use and Decision Making

12. Benefit Transfer

It is enjoyable to taste
These items ere they go to waste,
But how annoying when one finds
That other mice with pagan minds
Come into church my food to share
Who have no proper business there.

John Betjeman (1906–84): *Diary of a Church Mouse*

1 INTRODUCTION

Benefit transfer refers to the process by which a demand function or value, estimated for one environmental attribute or group of attributes at a site, is applied to assess the benefits attributable to a similar attribute or site.

Benefit transfer is generally advocated on the grounds of resource constraints: it is less costly to engage in benefit transfer than to commission new research projects to analyse the benefits of every new project, policy, or regulatory change. Before such procedures become widespread it is important to investigate the extent to which the benefits estimated by travel-cost methods (TCMs), hedonic price methods (HPMs), contingent valuation methods (CVMs), or other benefit estimation techniques, in one specific policy context or location, can be transferred to other situations. The problem becomes one of assessing whether estimates of the value of an environmental good can be transferred to another situation rather than letting them 'go to waste' and ensuring that existing values are not used inappropriately in benefit transfer (BT) situations by policy and decision-makers with 'pagan minds' and little knowledge of the issues involved.

The UK government's 'Green Book' on investment appraisal explicitly recognises that:

Approaches to valuation can sometimes be borrowed from other contexts or from similar programmes, but that the values derived are often quite specific to a particular area of application. For example, (i) the characteristics of the consumers or client group may differ (ii) the demand for units of output will depend in part on relative prices of other goods and services. These may vary. Such factors limit the extent to which values can be generalised (H.M. Treasury, 1991).

The Asian Development Bank (1996) suggests that BT is likely to be a feasible approach for many applications. However, it advocates caution in the use of such transfers, especially where cultural differences exist and where projects have large environmental impacts. It also stresses the need to assess the technical quality of the original study from which benefits are being transferred.

BT is used by the US National Oceanic and Atmospheric Administration (NOAA) to assess damages resulting from small 'Type A' spills or accidents in marine or coastal environments under the Comprehensive Environmental Response, Compensation and Liability Act (CERCLA) (1980), and subsequent regulations. BT is based on the Natural Resource Damage Assessment Model for Coastal and Marine Environments (NRDAM/CME) which is a computer model. BT is used in 'Type A' assessments since the effects of minor oils spills are often transitory and thus difficult to establish with a full CV study to estimate lost consumer surplus and passive use values. For example, Grigalunas and Opaluch (1988) point to the Arco Anchorage crude oil spill in December 1985, in which assessment costs were $245,000, but detectable damages only $32,930.

Thus BT can be both pragmatic and cost-effective. Biological damage can be difficult to detect, not because there are no injuries, but because injuries are unobservable, e.g. if the spill occurred during a storm, several days might pass before a study team could visit the site, by which time dead organisms would have dispersed. Economic damages under 'Type A' assessments are measured to account for injuries to commercial and recreational fisheries; waterfowl, shorebirds, and sea birds; fur seals; and public beaches (Ward and Duffield, 1992). The reduction in use value is measured by the change in the value of harvesting or the cost of harvesting; or from any change in the value of viewing or visiting the resource. Damages to waterfowl, shore and sea birds are assessed from use values for hunting and viewing, based on previous studies of waterfowl hunting and the change in visitor days at wildfowl refuges as a function of changes in bird populations.

In some contexts, such as the appraisal of transport, health, and safety regulations, the 'value of a small change in risk' (VSCR) is readily transferred between activities and policies to value lives saved. This standard value of life is usually applied in valuing changes in safety across policies and any individuals affected. In this way the transfer of a statistical average benefit estimate is routinely undertaken[1]. This benefit transfer procedure rarely accounts for differences in age, income, and other characteristics of individuals, where fatilities are rare. Moreover, research has shown that different individuals attach different values to safety, and have different attitudes towards risk;[2] whilst psychologists have revealed that individuals do not view different causes of death with equal equanimity, and have different values for avoiding death according to the particular context.[3]

Whilst the validity and accuracy of BT is hotly debated in environmental economics, it is ironic that BT is the normal procedure adopted in regulatory command and control mechanisms in which common standards are applied. The European Union (EU) assumes that the benefits of environmental improvements are of equal value in different areas of the EU (e.g. bathing water quality) and enforces common standards throughout the EU (although the probability, and hence the health risk, of any one bathing in the bitterly

---

[1] However, variations in the value of life abound as revealed in the implicit decisions of environmental and safety regulators. Recently van Houtven and Cropper (1996) have pointed out for the EPA in the US, which administers the Clean Air Act; Clean Water Act; Federal Insecticide, Fungicide, and Rodenticide Act; and the Toxic Substances Control Act; that:
(i) regulations under different Acts imply different values of life for cancer cases avoided, from $52 million for cancer cases avoided amongst pesticide applicators; and $49 million per case for asbestos regulations;
(ii) for air pollution regulations to reduce carcinogens risks from vinyl chloride, benzene, inorganic arsenic, and radionuclides, $15 million per cancer case avoided if the risk was less than 1 in 10,000, both before and after the vinyl chloride decision of the US Court of Appeals for the District of Columbia in 1987, but for risks greater than 1 in 10,000 an infinite value of life;
(iii) these values were much higher than the value of life implicit in workers' occupational choices of about $5 million.
Viscusi (1993) also documents the tremendous range of values of life from different studies using various methodologies to assess the value of avoiding risks.

[2] Jones-Lee and Loomes (1994) have pointed out that because of preferences and attitudes to risk, there is no reason to suppose that WTP to prevent a fatality on the London Underground need be the same as on roads. They suggest that WTP is 1.75 times greater for the Underground than for roads.

[3] Similar arguments about individual values and average values occur in other professions. British medicine operates on reasonable doctor and patient standards which preclude strict liability for damages to remote chances (1% to 2%) of serious unintended consequences of operations (Brahams, 1985), although allowing negligence. American clinical-legal practice is patient orientated, based on the patient's need to know. For example, the American rule would have found in favour of the plaintiff in the Sidaway case; whereas under British law Mrs Sidaway lost her case for compensation when the court ruled that although the surgeon had not told her about the 1% to 2% chance of becoming paralysed as result of a laminectomy to relieve back pain, negligence had not occurred, and a reasonable patient might well have accepted such a risk (Schwartz and Grubb, 1985).

cold North Sea is quite different from the Mediteranean).[4] Nevertheless, in
environmental regulation, physical standards apply in air and water pollution
which are also assumed to be readily transferable between different locations.
Moreover, in evaluating policy many environmentalists make comparisons
between different countries and policies. So to some extent the concept of
transferability is implicitly accepted. Brookshire and Neill (1992) argued that
'benefit transfers are valid under well defined conditions', and that no-one
appears to suggest that BT is impossible. Thus, the debate becomes one of
limits of use and the protocol associated with BT.

This chapter explores how different approaches have been used to
implement BT of environmental values, and assesses the validity and
accuracy of these attempts. It first explores transferability of environmental
values from experts' opinions, intuition, and unit day values; before moving
on to review transferability through travel-cost models, contingent valuation,
and meta-analysis.

2 EXPERT JUDGEMENT AND UNIT DAY VALUES

The use of expert judgement and intuition is perhaps the most ubiquitous
form by which BT is accomplished. An early application was the 'unit day
value' method widely used by the US. Forest Service in the 1970s and 1980s.
The approach relies on expert judgement to estimate average WTP,
considered to be equivalent to consumer surplus, for recreation use. Federal
guidelines in 1982 recommended a value in the range of \$6.10 to \$17.90 per
day for specialised recreation (wilderness use, trout fishing, big-game
hunting, white water boating, etc.) and \$1.50 to \$4.50 per day for general
recreation (picnicking, swimming, small game hunting, camping, boating,
etc.) (Walsh, 1986; Loomis and Walsh, 1997). When applied to a new site
these unit day values are adjusted on the basis more of the demand functions
of site visitors. Demand depends upon site attributes such as: (1) congestion;
(2) accessibility and parking conditions; (3) environmental quality: scenery,
pests, water, air, climate, etc.; as well as the (4) socio-economic

---

[4] Applying benefit transfer to determine bathing water quality standards is problematic.
Sampling pollution levels is an inexact science: bacteria are not evenly distributed throughout
the water, and bacteria counts can vary by depth of sampling point, marine currents, tides, time
of day, water temperature, wind direction, rainfall, underlying sea bed and shore (mud and sand
reduce transparency) whilst high turbidity leads to less UV penetration and slower bacterial
death rates (Fleisher, 1990). Sampling points may not be where the average density of bathers is
highest; and bathing and swimming habits can vary between sites and countries, making it
inappropriate to transfer estimates of water-associated illness and hence bathing water quality
standards between countries (Cheung *et al.*, 1990; Kay *et al.*, 1994). Non-marine related factors
also compound the relationship between exposure to marine water pollution and gastro-enteritis
(Fleisher *et al.*, 1993, 1996).

characteristics of the recreationalists; (5) their preferences; and the (6) price; and (7) availability of substitute sites. None of these factors will be identical across different sites, so expert judgement is required to assess what the benefits of a new site might be from a range of possible values. Unit day values can be updated to account for inflation and observed changes in the price and income elasticities for recreation over time.

Real estate agents' judgements were employed by the Roskill Commission (Commission on the Third London Airport, 1970) to estimate the utility loss (cost) of environmental externalities associated with noise from the site of the proposed Third London Airport, based on knowledge of the effect of noise on house prices around Heathrow and Gatwick airports. Environmental externalities (bads) were valued at the minimum households would be willing to accept (WTA) as just compensation for their loss, in terms of: (1) depreciation in house prices as a result of the increase in noise (based on estate agents' intuitive judgements); (2) transactions costs for those households indicating that they would move house to avoid the increase in noise (which could have been estimated from the market prices of legal, removal, and other associated costs); (3) loss of consumer surplus over and above the market price of the house (from a CV survey of households).[5]

The argument for using expert opinions was that:

> The professional valuer is constantly in touch with the prices at which houses change hands and with the valuations made for other purposes (e.g. estate duty). His professional skill lies largely in making suitable allowance for the multitude of factors entering into the valuation of any particular house i.e. that part of the problem which causes difficulty for the statistician (Commission on the Third London Airport, 1970).

While some research has suggested a close correlation between estate agents' estimates of total house price and estimates derived from an hedonic price model (Dodgson and Topham, 1990); other research has revealed discrepancies between different estate agents in their valuations of the same property. Greater discrepancies (up to 100%) were found in their assessment of the effect of an environmental attribute even when all other variables were held constant, (see Chapter 10, Section 2). Moreover, a large number of

---

[5] The consumer surplus and removal expenses were elicited by the following CVM question: 'Suppose your house was wanted to form part of a large development scheme and the developer offered to buy it from you, what price would be just enough to compensate you for leaving this house (flat) and moving to another area?' (Commission on the Third London Airport, 1970).

empirical studies in the clinical field have revealed that intuitive judgements are subject to considerable biases and errors.[6]

In the environment field, intuitive, measures employed in assessing benefits arising from water supply projects frequently turn out to be inaccurate. Pearce and Warford (1993), for example, report a CV study by Whittington *et al.* (1990) in Haiti which estimated an average WTP of 1.7% of household income for stand-pipes and 2.1% for private connections, both significantly lower than the assumed WTP of 3% to 5% of household income used by the World Bank in appraising the feasibility of water supply projects.

People, including experts, have limited information processing abilities, and this bounded rationality affects how people interpret values and make choices.[7] Tversky and Kahneman (1974) point to representativeness, availability, and anchoring as heuristics employed by people when making judgements under uncertainty. These heuristics, lead to systematic and predictable errors. This suggests that in some situations it may be preferable to use more objective techniques to implement BT.

3 BENEFIT TRANSFER VIA TRAVEL-COST MODELS

The earliest examples of systematic BT applications occur in recreational demand studies employing travel-cost models. Early zonal travel-cost models (ZTCMs), developed by Clawson and Knetsch (1966), related the quantity of participation (demand), expressed as visits per unit of population per zone of origin, to the price of access, and the characteristics (income, and so on) of residents in each zone:

$$V_{ij}/N_i = f(TC_{ij}, T_{ij}, Y_i, S_i, A_k) \qquad (12.1)$$

---

[6] For example, McGoogan (1984) revealed that 39% of main clinical diagnoses were not confirmed at autopsy, and even in cases where physicians were reasonably confident of their diagnosis, their main diagnosis was not confirmed in 25% of cases. de Dombal (1984) found that the accuracy of diagnosis of cases in an accident and emergency department of a hospital varied from 42% for admitting doctors; to 71% for house surgeons; 79% for registrars; 82% for senior clinicians; but was 91% for a computer aided bootstrapping system, in which clinicians were out-performed by the systematic application of their own judgements! Renwick *et al.* (1991) found that radiographers disagreed with radiologists in 9.4% of examinations: there were 7% false positives and 14% false negatives. (A false positive occurs where a patient is diagnosed as having a disease, but doesn't actually have it. A false negative occurs where a patient is diagnosed as not having a disease, whilst he or she actually has the disease).

[7] Indeed, a linear model of the decision-maker's own judgements invariably outperforms the intuitive predictions of the expert himself (see Dawes and Corrigan, 1974; Dawes, *et al.*, 1989). By estimating the implicit weights used by the human judge, and eliminating any noise or inconsistencies, such bootstrapping models (so called because an individual can improve his judgement or pull himself up by his own mental bootstraps) typically outperform individual judgement.

where V_{ij} = trips from zone i to site j
N_i = population of zone i
TC_{ij} = travel costs from zone i to K sites,
T_{ij} = travel time from zone i to site j
Y_i = average income in zone i
S_i = socio-economic characteristics of zone i
Q_j = recreation quality at site j
A_k = measure of the cost and quality of substitute site k.

The benefits to consumers from proposed facilities were estimated by transferring the demand functions from existing facilities, where the prospective facility closely resembled the existing facility in the type of recreation it would provide. If the catchment areas of the two sites are mutually exclusive, then multiplying the existing site coefficients by the values of the independent variables for the new site should give reasonable estimates of both the number of visits and benefits attributable to the new site. Thus only by chance would the same social valuation be placed on the new facility as the old, despite the fact that the same basic relationship is assumed. Loomis (1992) argued that this approach is likely to yield a more accurate estimate of the benefits of a new site than simply applying an average value of benefit per visitor day to the site, since benefits are a complex function of site characteristics, user characteristics, and the spatial characteristics of the site relative to visitors' residences (i.e. each site has a unique matrix of own price and substitute prices).

Problems arise where a proposed facility is situated within the catchment area of an existing facility: transferring the demand function to the proposed site as if this site were the only one, without any substitutes, will grossly over-estimate the benefits of the new site. A solution to this problem is to apply the existing demand function to the new site as if it were unique, and then, if consumer surplus from the proposed facility exceeds that of the existing one, the net gain from having the proposed facility is calculated as the difference between the two consumer surplus values, summed over all zones. Often the proposed site does not exactly resemble any existing site, due to differences between the mix of recreation facilities offered, or differences in the scenic backdrop. The lack of homogeneity in product mix may be remedied by valuing the different recreational activities separately and then aggregating, rather than developing a demand curve for the site as a whole (see for example, Lewis and Whitby, 1972). In theory, if sites are perfectly homogeneous, then all visits should be diverted to the site with the lowest cost of access. This problem can be eliminated by assuming degrees of diversion depending upon the price reduction, according to some formula, e.g. (PL - PB) / 0.5(PL + PB), where PL = price of visiting site L, and PB =

price of visiting site B. The formula indicates an increasing willingness to substitute one site for the another as the price differentials grow. Thus when PB falls to 0.333(PL), complete diversion occurs (see Mansfield, 1971). With the development of multi-site or regional TCMs incorporating variations in site quality (e.g. reservoir size, water quality, fish catches, etc.) it is no longer necessary to find a similar site: a new site could be represented by any linear combination of site characteristics from existing sites (see Dwyer *et al.*, 1977). The multi-equation approach treats alternative sites that are either imperfect substitutes or complements as different products. Theoretically demand for different products is expressed in different demand functions, with substitutability and complementarity reflected in cross-price terms (see Anderson and Bishop, 1986). This has obvious implications for BT when attributes vary across sites.

BT problems in both ZTCMs and individual travel cost models (ITCMs) stem from the many potential errors in estimating recreational demand functions and the calculation of implied benefits. McConnell (1992) lists errors in the demand function as:

1. choosing the wrong functional form. Different functions produce very different estimates of consumer surplus[8], the number of visitors[9], and the extent of the market area;
2. selecting an incomplete or inappropriate set of arguments, e.g. ignoring some of the q values. Thus, truncated maximum likelihood estimates are significantly lower than ordinary least squares estimates;
3. measuring arguments incorrectly, as frequently occurs with income, the value of time, cost of access (price per mile for car usage);[10]
4. measuring the dependent variable with error: the frequency of visits is especially important for the ITCM.[11]

---

[8] Smith (1988) calculated that consumer surplus increased by 50% with a semi-log function rather than a linear model; while in Kling's (1988) study it doubled. Larger variations were observed by Willis and Garrod (1991).

[9] Gibson (1974) showed that the semi-log and double log models produced substantial differences in the estimated numbers of participants from changes in admission prices; whilst each of these models fitted the data equally well, so that it was difficult to choose between them. Willis and Garrod (1991) showed that linear, semi-log and double log models varied significantly in their prediction of visits compared to actual visits to sites, and in the correlation between predicted and actual visit numbers across distance zones.

[10] Estimates of consumer surplus vary depending upon whether access costs are based on petrol costs only, or include depreciation and services costs associated with car usage. Adding in time costs of travel similarly increases consumer surplus associated with recreational facilities (Willis and Garrod, 1991).

The presence of substitute sites in TCMs is also important, usually deflating the travel-cost model's expected consumer surplus. However, Donnelly and Price (1984) have shown, though a simulation model, that if sites are randomly distributed, substitution effects cancel out and a ZTCM correctly estimates the contribution of the site to the value of a recreation system. In theory, clustered sites should be over-valued by a simple ZTCM which ignores substitutes, and sites which are systematically spaced should be under-valued.

Loomis (1992) assessed the validity of the transferability of TCM benefit estimates by comparing site specific benefit estimates with those derived from transferring TCM equations: a multi-site TCM demand equation for steelhead fishing in Oregon was estimated for *n-1* of the Oregon steelhead rivers and then the equation used to predict the *nth* or missing, river. The percentage difference between total recreation benefits estimated from the full multi-site TCM and from the transferred model (omitting the specified river) ranged from a few percentage points to 17.5%. Transferring the equation to that unstudied site rather than simply using the benefits per trip average over all *n* rivers from the full model, provided a better indicator of benefits for the site: the transferred equation benefit per trip only once differed from the actual site-specific estimate by more than 10%. Loomis (1992) did note, however, that cross-state benefit transfers, even for identically defined activities were more inaccurate, and suggested further investigation of factors affecting transferability between states to ensure that future models were more transferable.

BT using an amalgam of CV and TCM estimates has also been adopted. For example, Bateman *et al.* (1995) derived a function for the number of visits to a forest in East Anglia based on travel time along the actual road network. This simple model was then applied to predict the number of visits on a zonal travel time basis to areas in Wales. Predicted visits were compared to actual visits recorded at two forest recreation sites in Wales. This revealed high correlations between predicted and actual visits across zones from each site ($R^2 > 0.83$), although the difference between actual and predicted visitor totals for the two sites as a whole were not reported. Meta-analysis was then used to derive a CV value for forest recreation to transfer to the sites in Wales. The accuracy of this approach is unknown, since the hypothesis that there is no difference between the BT values and actual site values in Wales was not tested.

---

[11] McConnell (1992) reported a study which found that the estimated number of annual fishing trips was 27% higher with an annual recall period, than with a six-month period, with the annual mean from an annual recall of an in-person interview being almost twice the annual mean from a two-month recall in a telephone interview.

4 BENEFIT TRANSFER VIA CONTINGENT VALUATION

A systematic, conceptual foundation for conducting benefit transfer studies was suggested by Boyle and Bergstrom (1992). This involved defining the relevant Hicksian measure of utility for the good or policy change being measured; in their case the recreational value to white water rafters of the various water flow levels in the Kennebec River, Maine, which might arise through hydro-electric power generation, i.e.:

$$V(P_w, P, Y - WTP_{f*}; A_f, S) = V(P^x_w, P, Y; A_{f*}, S) \qquad (12.2)$$

where P_w is the cost of a white water raft trip; P is a vector of other goods and services; Y is income; WTP_{f*} is the value to be estimated for the fixed water flow $f*$; A is a vector of exogenous attributes of a trip for various flow levels; S is a vector of the socio-economic characteristics of the participants including flow level; P^x_w is the choke price where the individual would not make any further trips.

This formulation allows key aspects of BT to be identified. Particularly important are the vectors of attributes and socio-economic characteristics that determine the similarities and differences which exist between the policy site and the study sites from which values are to be transferred. Where differences exist, but their magnitude is known, it may be possible to manipulate the values to provide valid BT estimates. Boyle and Bergstrom also set out technical criteria for the selection of potential study sites from which benefits could be transferred, namely that:

1. the non-market good to be valued at the policy site must be identical to that already valued at the study site;
2. the populations affected by the non-market good must be identical at each site;
3. the same welfare measure should be theoretically appropriate at each site, e.g. property rights existing at each site should imply the use of either WTP or WTA measures.

Such a rigorous criteria means that study sites may be difficult to find from which benefit estimates can be transferred to the policy site. Indeed, Boyle and Bergstrom rejected all five of their potential study sites on the basis of their own criteria.

Whilst Boyle and Bergstrom outlined some of the issues in BT, there are additional problems which can lead to biased BT estimates. The *ex ante-ex post* valuation perspective; scale or quantity value; sequential position of the supply of the good; differences in attributes; and compositional effects can all affect the applicability of BT values.

Some CV estimates elicited at the study site, e.g. recreational use values of visitors, are *ex post* values derived after the uncertainty about the good has been removed. Employing these *ex post* values in an *ex ante* project appraisal of a new scheme may lead to biased estimates: existing utility for a good is not the same as expected utility for another good or more of the same good. Individuals may be uncertain about the probability of success of the new scheme (and hence be willing to pay an amount below *ex post* study site BT value); or because of risk aversion they may be willing to pay a premium for the increased probability of the supply of a good over and above expected consumer surplus.

BT also needs to address the problem of scale. If the new good or policy site is identical to the old, and lies within the same market area, then it represents an additional quantity of the good which, in theory, ought to be valued less than the existing good at the study site. However, Hanemann (1994) has argued that more empirical information is required on scale or scope effects: for example how much should people value preventing additional bird deaths in the central flyway of the USA? If q_0 is the number of birds in the population; q_r the number of birds at risk from dying; and q_s the number of those saved; are q_0, q_r, and q_s perfect substitutes? Hanemann argues that economic theory is silent on this issue and that further empirical tests are required to trace out these types of relationships.

Where goods are substitutes or complements, the sequence in which a particular good is provided in relation to others determines its value. Thus, for example, because the interaction of landscape attributes affects valuation, the value of a particular conservation scheme is not the sum of the individual attribute changes, unless these are being evaluated along a sequential path. If attributes are independently valued (i.e. all other attributes are maintained at their policy-off level), and then summed, the result is an independent valuation and summation (IVS) estimate of benefits. This will be larger than the actual value of the complete scheme if attributes are compensated substitutes; whilst the IVS result will be smaller than the actual value of the scheme if attributes are compensated complements (Santos, 1997).

BT based on CV estimates also suffers from the compositional problem for some goods. This occurs when respondents have difficulty in disentangling the structure of the substitution and complementary interrelationships among attributes within the same holistic set. Compositional problems beset landscape valuation, and also the valuation of recreational goods which have a landscape backdrop. Landscapes are a complex blend of natural and man-made features and our aesthetic response to them depends upon the composition and configuration of these features. Particular features complement one another and some attributes may be substitutes for others. Any respondent viewing a landscape would probably find it extremely difficult to disentangle these relationships, giving the landscape a unique, rather than a transferable, benefit value. Hanemann (1994) points out that demand is context specific, i.e. people will perceive broad-leaved trees, for example, differently in different landscapes. The more that is known about the influence of these contexts, the greater the confidence that can be placed in benefit transfers.

Whether CV estimates are transferable or not depends upon their accuracy, and whether the good to be valued is sufficiently similar to the existing good for which CV estimates are available. CV estimates have been shown to roughly match market values when the methodology has been applied experimentally to situations in which these exist (see Bishop and Heberlein, 1986; Dickie *et al.*, 1987). This criterion validity of CV estimates suggests that they are transferable in some circumstances. For specific goods, different assessment methods have sometimes been shown to produce convergent results (see Smith *et al.*, 1986). Cummings *et al.* (1986) report reasonably strong convergent validity for CVM, with the studies that they reviewed producing estimates within a +/- 50% range: an error which may not affect a cost-benefit analysis outcome, but which might worry a polluter faced with a bill for damages under CERCLA.

Downing and Ozuna (1996) tested the reliability of referendum CVM BT value functions for angling in eight contiguous Texas Gulf coast regions. They used a dummy variable model, with pooled observations from two time periods, within and across bay regions, to estimate the function:

$$Y_i = \beta_0 + \beta_1 \ln(A_i) + \beta_2 D_i + \beta_{33}(D_{ii} * \ln(A_i)) + e_i \qquad (12.3)$$

where $i = 1, 2,...,n$ individuals, Y_i represents a dichotomous 'Yes/No' response to the natural logarithm of the offer amount, A_i , by the *ith* individual, and e_i is a logistic error term. Equation 12.3 can be re-written, given $E(e_i) = 0$, as

$$E(Y_i \mid D_i = 1, \ln A_i)) = (\beta_0 + \beta_2) + (\beta_1 + \beta_3) \ln(A_i) \qquad (12.4)$$

which is the mean response function for the given time period. In equation 12.4, β_2 is an intercept shifter, and β_3 a slope shifter. Benefit function transfers (BFTs) were deemed:

1. permissible, when the estimated coefficients β_2 and β_3 are statistically insignificant;
2. questionable, when coefficient β_2 is significant and coefficient β_3 insignificant, and *vice versa*;
3. not transferable, when coefficients β_2 and β_3 are significant.

Downing and Ozuna found that of eight potential within-bay BFTs between 1987 and 1988 , five were transferable, two questionable, and one was not transferable. For across-bay transfers, of 56 potential BFTs, 50% were transferable, 36% were questionable, and 14% were not transferable. Transfers over a two-year period, between 1987 and 1989, had slightly lower proportions of transferable, and higher proportions of questionable and non-transferable cases. Nevertheless, in general, the results indicated that many benefit transfer functions are transferable. The crucial question, however, is whether BFTs yield statistically similar welfare measures. Downing and Ozuna discovered, based upon median WTP measures,[12] and using 95% confidence intervals, that the welfare measures were statistically different in over 90% of the cases. This arose because of the non-linearity of the logit model used to estimate benefit functions, and the non-linearity of the benefit function estimates themselves. Downing and Ozuna therefore concluded that transferring benefits from a study site to a policy site using the BFT approach could be misleading or inaccurate.

Kirchhoff *et al.* (1997) assessed BT in terms of:

1. convergent validity of benefit function transfer: $H_0: CV_{p/s} = CV_{p/p}$ which tests whether the compensating variation estimate for the policy site obtained by transferring the function from the study site is statistically different from the original estimate for the policy site by testing: (a) $CV_{p/s} \in CV_{p/p}$, i.e. whether the estimate from the BT function lies within the confidence interval of the original the policy site estimate; and (b) $CV_{p/p} \in CI_{p/s}$, i.e. whether the original estimate lies within the confidence interval of the BT estimate;

2. comparison of actual sample means: actual mean compensating variation for the policy site (CV_p) was also compared to the BT estimates by testing whether the mean policy site value was located within the confidence limits of the BT function estimates: $H_0: CV_p \in CI_{p/s}$; and, for convergent validity, whether the mean policy site value were within the confidence limits of the compensating variation mean value for the study site itself: $H_0: CV_p \in CI_{s/s}$;

3. percentage error resulting from the BT function: (a) between the compensating variation estimate from the BT function and the predicted site-specific estimate $(CV_{p/s} - CV_{p/p}) * 100 / CV_{p/p}$; (b) between the WTP estimate from the BT function and the actual sample mean for the policy site $(CV_{p/s} - CV_p) * 100 / CV_p$; (c) between the site-specific predicted WTP estimates from the study site and policy site respective demand functions $(CV_{s/s} - CV_{p/p}) *$

---

[12] Median WTP measures were computed as WTP = $-\exp(\beta_0/\beta_1)$ where β_0 and β_1 are the estimated coefficients from the discrete choice function $Y_i = \beta_0 + \beta_1 \ln (A_i) + e_i$, where Y_i represents a dichotomous 'Yes/No' response to the natural logarithm of the offer amount, A_i, by the *i*th individual, and e_{ij} is a logistic error term (see Hanemann, 1984).

100 / CV$_{p/p}$); and (d) between the actual sample means for the study site and the policy site *(CV$_s$ - CV$_p$) * 100 CV$_p$)*.

These tests led to the rejection of convergent validity in nearly all cases for the New Mexico policy and study sites and for most cases at the Arizona sites. Of the 24 comparisons of BT measures, only two involved errors in excess of 100%; and in 16 out of 24 cases errors were less than 50%. Hence some BT measures may provide useful information to decision-makers. Kirchhoff *et al.* (1997) ascribed the more questionable results to a number of factors. First, whilst minor differences in the description of the resource to be valued did not necessarily cause significant differences in benefit estimates, changes in the recreational focus of sites increased percentage errors in BT. Second, measurement of a dominant indicator of site quality, in their case stream flows for rafting, was not sufficient to assure convergent validity in BT because other differences in site characteristics, that may be harder to quantify, can influence the quality of recreational experiences and can thus cause substantial biases in BT estimates. Third, differences in the market for the good, e.g. availability and price of substitutes, can lead to biases in BT estimates.

Kirchhoff *et al.'s* analysis led to the rejection of the transfer of a simple mean site-benefit estimate, since it led to large percentage errors. Benefit function transfer performed better in nearly all cases; a finding consistent with that observed by Loomis (1992) for BT using travel-cost models.

Whilst CVM is perhaps the most widely employed technique for valuing environmental assets, it is commonly applied to environmental, natural and wildlife, resources which are:

1. unique or have unique combinations of attributes;
2. less than perfectly described in the CV survey;
3. measured in relation to an incomplete substitute set;
4. measured in an IVS framework with a single focus CV question rather than as part of a sequential or simultaneous method based on a more inclusive set;
5. valued as an intra-marginal unit rather than a marginal unit of the resource.

All of these factors detract from the transferability potential of benefit functions and benefit values.

Future research into BT might usefully address whether the process could be improved by:

1. more carefully specifying the good, being valued; including the context (e.g. site characteristics within which the good is set); and improving the methodology, perhaps by developing benefit function transfers through choice

experiment or contingent ranking techniques which permit the attributes of the good to be valued in a BT application;

2. further investigating the psychological process by which respondents arrive at a value for the good.

CV estimates for private goods are generally readily transferable to other private goods, where homogeneity prevails, with the same protocols as those applying to travel-cost estimates. In public good situations recommendations for improving both the definition of the good and the methodology used have been advocated by the Arrow-Solow (1993) Panel and by Gregory *et al.* (1993). These recommendations involve greater concentration on valuing the attributes of the good, tighter definitions of the description of the good and substitute set, improving the focus of WTP questions, and more consideration of embedding and scoping effects.

Stated preference choice experiments might further unpack the contribution of attributes to the value of a specific good or site, thus aiding the transferability of values by addressing the issue of the effect of different combinations of attributes associated with a resource. Adamowicz *et al.* (1994) have shown that stated preference (SP) and revealed preference (RP) methods can yield similar results for water based recreation use values, whilst SP improves on the quality of estimates of an RP model by avoiding collinearity which is so often a feature of RP models.

The transferability of non-use values remains more problematic since, for example, in biodiversity conservation it involves attribute concepts such as size, naturalness, rarity, fragility, recorded history, location, potential value, and intrinsic appeal. But evaluating these attributes is not necessarily an intractable problem. Gregory *et al.* (1993) argue that such an exercise requires a Multi-Attribute Utility Theory (MAUT) approach since open-ended holistic responses perform poorly in terms of construct validity for goods with several value-relevant attributes.[13] MAUT also tackles the embedding problem because it focuses responses to the specific issue rather than to general 'moral satisfaction' and because responses are found to be more sensitive to specification.

Psychologists use 'verbal protocols' to gain insight into how respondents arrive at particular answers. Verbal protocols can provide an indication of respondents' thought processes whilst answering a CV question. This is

---

[13] Studies have found that when people are asked to make holistic judgements about multidimensional stimuli, they typically make use of fewer cues than they say they do (see Willis and Hardy, 1995). Faced with complexity people resort to simplifying strategies. The more complex the decision problem the more likely that expressions of value will be constructed based only on a subset of the available information. Thus accurate and transferable values are more likely to be obtained from decompositional procedures than from holistic ones.

important since research suggests that CV responses can be sensitive to
certain irrelevant factors[14] and insensitive to some relevant ones.[15] Verbal
protocols might be able to establish under what conditions CV estimates for
one good, or site, can be applied to others. Conditions under which values
might be transferred, because they derive from common processes in
formulating values, are where:

1. *respondents have well-formed and articulated values which can be
retrieved through an appropriate CV elicitation question.* WTP responses
constructed during an elicitation process are more sensitive to the task and
context of a particular CV survey, and hence are less likely to be readily
transferable;

2. *respondents adopt the same rational economic model.* Even though values
may differ across individuals (because they have different utility functions),
or across situations (because some things are worth more than others), the
process by which values are calculated should be the same in all cases
(whether the maximisation of expected utility, minimisation of regret, or
whatever). If different people use different strategies, or the same person uses
different strategies in similar situations, then values will not be transferable.
Similarly, transferability should be enhanced where people adopt the same
strategy with regard to the ambient tendencies in the environment (base rate
information) and relevant features of the current situation (case-specific
information).[16]

3. *expressed values are not highly labile* (liable to change). However, in
practice many expressed values do appear to be highly labile: subtle aspects
of how problems are posed, questions are phrased, and responses are elicited
can have a substantial impact on judgements that supposedly express people's
'true values'. If values for particular goods are labile, then the transferability
of such values will pose problems. Fischhoff *et al.* (1980) argued that in
tackling this problem there may be no substitute for an interactive, dialectical

---

[14] For example, the payment vehicle, gain/loss framing, sunk costs, etc.

[15] For example, embedding, the question of capital versus annual payments and intertemporal
choice (see Loewenstein and Thaler, 1989), dichotomous choice versus open-ended question
formats (Viscusi *et al.*, 1986).

[16] Bayesian statistical analysis reveals that people typically ignore base rates and over-
emphasize case-specific information in decisions (Fischhoff and Beyth-Maron, 1983). For an
accurate estimate of WTP for a good this is important; but it is not important for the
transferability of values, since all values will be equally biased.

elicitation procedure that acknowledges the elicitor's role in helping the respondent to create and enunciate values. Such help might include a conceptual analysis of the problem, and of the personal, social and ethical issues to which the respondent might wish to relate, and also the provision of tools (including education in economics) and training to aid decision-making.

4. *procedural invariance does not exist.* Equivalent procedures should result in the same order of preference for a set of objects. Preference reversals, where A is preferred to B under one method of measurement while B is preferred to A under a different but equivalent measurement procedure[17] violate procedural invariance. Procedure invariance is likely to hold if people have well-established preferences or have an algorithm for computing the answer.[18]

5 META-ANALYSIS

CV estimates of annual WTP by individuals or households for an environmental good, such as landscape or nature conservation, vary enormously between studies. However, many of the differences between estimates from various studies can often be accounted for, or explained, by: (1) differences in populations of reference; (2) different values held by users compared to non-users; (3) the different number of benefit issues estimated by the study; (4) whether a marginal change in quantity is being valued or the value of the good in total is being assessed; (5) whether the change is irreversible or not; (6) the elicitation format employed by the CVM study; (7) the extent to which embedding is a problem in the valuation of the good; the framing of the study and the questions; (8) the uniqueness of the good; and

---

[17] For example, most subjects choose an H bet (8/9 odds to win $4) over an L bet (1/9 odds to win $40). When asked to state the minimum price they would sell each gamble if they owned it, most subjects put a higher price on the L bet. Preference reversals have been observed in a range of situations (see Slovic and Lichtenstein, 1983; Irwin *et al.*, 1993).

[18] Consider two traffic safety improvement proposals. Programme A saves 30 lives each year at an annual cost of $12 million. Programme B saves 100 lives each year at an annual cost of $55 million. When a sample of people are asked which program they prefer, a substantial majority indicate a preference for Programme B. A second sample are asked to state the cost that would make the programmes equally attractive, and an even greater majority gave figures smaller than $55 million. Tversky and Thaler (1990) quote this as an example of preference reversal. Jones-Lee (1990) argues that two meanings can be placed on 'equally attractive': (1) equal value for money, i.e. equal B/C ratios; (2) that one would be indifferent between the two programmes. Respondents who adopt (1) as a decision criterion for computing an answer, requiring *equality in cost per life saved*, would logically quote a value less than $55 million, i.e. $40 million to be exact.

(9) whether substitutes are available and considered in the valuation of the good. This list is not exhaustive, but provides some flavour of the factors which can give rise to different CV benefit estimates for, say, nature conservation objectives, which conserve a number of different goods.

In a similar comparison, but across a range of landscape and nature conservation goods in Britain, Bateman *et al.* (1994) have argued, by intuitive inspection, that:

1. where many substitutes exist in a local area then low WTP valuations are elicited;
2. as the number of substitutes falls, then WTP valuations rise significantly;
3. where there are no local substitutes, and where the landscape would change in a significant way, then WTP valuations rise further still (e.g. for the Yorkshire Dales);
4. where the good is a truly unique resource for which there is no substitute, and for which the change would be irreversible (e.g. flooding of the Norfolk Broads), then WTP rises still further;
5. household WTP values for large areas such as Environmentally Sensitive Areas (ESAs) are much greater than WTP estimates for smaller Sites of Special Scientific Interest (SSSIs), and for less well-known sites.

Meta-analysis improves upon this type of intuitive judgement by using data-based aids to explain variations in estimated benefits across different studies. Meta-analysis attempts to assess environmental values by investigating the relationship between benefit estimates (e.g. WTP), the features of the goods, and the assumptions of the models, with the explicit aim of applying past results to future resource policy decisions. Meta-analysis thus entails the systematic application of statistical methods to assess common features and variations across a wide range of prior studies.

The study by Walsh *et al.* (1989) of 287 benefit estimates (156 based on TCMs, 129 on CVMs, and two on HPMs) sought to explain variations in net economic benefits per activity day in terms of site, location, and methodological variables. Three models of recreational benefits were reported: one for all observations; and one each for TCM and CVM studies. Around two-thirds of the explanatory variables were significant at the 0.01 level, with the models explaining between 36% and 44% of the total variation in reported values. Their principle findings were that:

1. omitting travel time in TCM studies reduced benefit estimates by 34%;
2. ITCM estimates were about 46% greater than ZTCM estimates using the same functional form;
3. omitting an effective cross-price term for substitution raised TCM values by about 30%;

4. if TCM was accepted as the standard for benefit estimation, then CV estimates needed to be adjusted upwards by 20% to 30%, but that referendum CVM estimates were closer to TCM values;
5. significant spatial variations in recreation values existed, along with significantly different values for different activities, e.g. various kinds of fishing and hunting.

Smith and Kaoru (1990) found both the type of recreation site involved, and the assumptions implicit in the TCMs, to be instrumental in explaining TCM results. Specifically that:

1. site usage measurement in terms of days produced smaller values than for trips;
2. truncated maximum likelihood estimators reduced consumer surplus estimates substantially;
3. trips to National Parks were worth $20 more than trips of comparable length to coastal areas;
4. inclusion of substitute sites and exclusion of the value of time decreased consumer surplus estimates.

Walsh *et al.* (1989) suggested that controlling for the effects of payment vehicle, functional form, question format, information, uncertainty, and substitutes might permit the transferability of benefit estimates; while Smith and Kaoru (1990) believed that meta-analysis could best serve as a consistency check to the processes used in benefit transfer analysis for policy.

A meta-analysis of marginal WTP estimates from hedonic price models of particulate matter in air pollution was reported by Smith and Huang (1995). Results, based on 86 observations from 37 different studies, suggested that market conditions reveal a consistent relationship between estimates of the incremental value of reducing air pollution, the level of air pollution in each city, and the average income of its residents, as well as a number of other variables in the specification of the models. These latter included model estimation procedures, data, and data sources, functional specification, year of study, and whether or not the study had been published. Many of these variables were highly significant in explaining marginal WTP estimates.

Smith and Huang (1995) suggest that selecting a best point estimate from other studies and applying this to areas expected to achieve a reduction in air pollution could lead to serious errors. Variations due to local conditions can be substantial: local economic and air quality conditions are important in HPM estimates. By contrast, meta-summaries reduce sensitivity to extreme results and offer a systematic way of adjusting for local conditions found important to benefit estimates. Meta-analysis is thus important in improving the adjustment practices applied to empirical estimates used in policy analysis.

Air pollution and global warming are intimately linked with energy use and transportation demand. The prediction of future energy use and transport trends is thus important in assessing future levels of these environmental externalities. Meta-analysis has been used extensively in transport studies to determine factors which systematically affect price and income elasticity estimates in studies of gasoline demand (Espey, 1996), and in explaining variations in public transport demand elasticities (Nijkamp and Pepping, 1998).

Espey (1996) found that price elasticity estimates for the demand for gasoline in the USA ranged from -0.2 to -1.59, averaging -0.53, based on 70 estimates from 41 separate studies over the period 1936 to 1986. The basic hypothesis of Espey's study was that price elasticity estimates varied because of differences in (a) demand specification and model structure, e.g. the inclusion or exclusion of explanatory variables such as automobile ownership, vehicle characteristics, population density, functional form, and lag structure; (b) data characteristics, e.g. gasoline consumption per capita, per vehicle, or per household; (c) environmental characteristics, geographical area and time span covered; and (d) estimation method. Investigation of these issues led to a number of interesting findings. Inclusion of vehicle ownership was found to result in lower estimates of income elasticity; pooled US and foreign data sets positively biased income and negatively biased price elasticity, suggesting account should be taken of cross-national studies; small differences between static and dynamic models suggested that lagged responses to price or income changes were relatively short; and elasticity estimates appeared to be relatively robust across estimation techniques.

Meta-analysis can be undertaken using a variety of techniques, encompassing both qualitative and quantitative econometric methods. Nijkamp and Pepping (1998) use rough set analysis to estimate key factors influencing the sensitivity of public transport consumers to transport costs across EU states. Rough set analysis is a nonparametric statistical method which can handle a diverse and less immediately tangible set of factors, transforming a data set, such as a collection of past examples or a record of experience, into structured knowledge, classifying objects having a distinctive pattern of attributes. Using 12 studies on demand elasticities across EU states, it was found that country, number of competitive modes, and type of data collected (time series and survey (cross-section or panel)), had the strongest explanatory influence on elasticity. Again this implies that elasticities cannot be generalised across different EU countries, even when estimation methods are the same. In a more theoretical investigation, based on set theory, Bal and Nijkamp (1997) concluded that the larger the set of characteristics which span the constellation in which a particular good is categorised, the smaller is the set of common characteristics across all goods in the constellation. This inverse relationship implies that only parts of cumulated knowledge can be transferred to valuing other goods in the constellation. Thus, where research findings are not context free, the generalisation possibilities of cumulated knowledge, via benefit or value transfer, is limited. In essence, as the collective set of goods increases in number, and with it the variance in their characteristics, the less likely is it that the *ceteris paribus* condition will be met in any benefit or value transfer.

Meta analysis is a relatively underdeveloped field of enquiry in the assessment of the transferability of benefit estimates. Meta-analysis should not be seen merely as modifying existing estimates to produce a value for a new policy situation; but also as a means of investigating the factors and issues involved in the derivation and construction of values.

6 CONCLUSION

Whilst broad similarities and trends in environmental values are discernible, past applications of environmental valuation techniques do not bode well for benefit transfer studies. Valuation exercises tend not to be designed with future benefit transfers in mind, but rather to explore new methodologies, survey designs, and modelling techniques, or to test specific hypotheses. So whither benefit transfer? Progress can be made on a number of fronts.

First, it would be useful to investigate the theoretical conditions under which benefit transfers are possible. For example, the value of statistical life and values for morbidity avoided, are readily transferred between geographical areas. What other values fall into this category? What types of environmental value are most difficult to transfer? More research should address how independent valuation and summation, compared to sequential and simultaneous approaches affects transferability; how utility functions vary between different types of environmental goods with differing scope effects, and what implications this has for BT.

Second, more empirical studies specifically designed to test the feasibility of benefit transfer, along the lines of those conducted by Downing and Ozuna (1996) and Kirchhoff *et al.* (1997), could be undertaken. Such studies might seek to address the issues raised by Kirchhoff *et al.*, namely, how can qualitative differences in site characteristics be standardised to aid BT?

Third, more meta-analytical studies could be undertaken to draw additional insights and information to help highlight those areas where further detailed studies may prove to be worthwhile. Santos (1997) has shown, in a meta-analysis, that values for some types of landscape good are readily transferable, even across countries. Meta-analysis might reveal other areas where BT is reasonably reliable and robust. For better or for worse, implicit BT will be made in policy decisions. Button and Nijkamp (1997) have argued that meta-analysis, by synthesising a range of forecasts and seeking moderator variables, can provide a useful basis for improving the forecasts of the direct physical implications of decisions that may then be fed into the more explicit environmental assessment process.

However, caution must be exercised in applying meta-analysis results, since meta analysis may be subject to publication bias, which reduces its credibility for informing policy. In theory, meta analysis should review all studies, statistically significant or insignificant, to provide a total perspective on a particular issue. But since insignificant studies are published less frequently, if at all, a meta analysis is inherently subject to bias from being based on only part of the real population.[19] Publication bias may be partly remedied by searching for unpublished negative studies to include in the meta analysis data set. Givens *et al.* (1997) suggest an alternative Bayesian approach which adjusts for publication bias. Applying this technique to studies of non-smoking women exposed to spousal environmental tobacco smoke (ETS), they suggested that the US Environmental Protection Agency's (EPA) assessment of relative risk (RR)[20] of ETS, at 1.19, was over-estimated.[21] Accounting for publication bias reduced the RR to 1.10, with a confidence interval which now included the null value.

Finally, whilst research documenting the value of environmental outcomes and goods needs to continue in order to build a more comprehensive picture of values in different contexts, the process whereby outcomes are generated should also be explicitly incorporated into the analysis, since people patently care about how this happens.[22] Simultaneously assessing the extent to which

---

[19] Meta analysis is probably additionally biased because most studies set out to prove positive relationships between variables (i.e. they are hypothesis driven) and most actually find a positive relationship. Few studies set out to disprove hypotheses. Hence, the studies available for publication are themselves a biased sample of all possible procedurally neutral studies which could be undertaken.

[20] Relative risk is the ratio: Prob[contracting disease I exposure] / Prob[contracting disease I no exposure]. Estimates of RR permit 'excess risk' to be calculated: excess risk = RR - 1, and is used as a measure of the impact of exposure on disease incidence. Hence a decrease in RR from 1.19 to 1.10 effectively halves the number of cases attributable to ETS exposure

[21] The EPA report, based on a meta analysis of published studies, classifying ETS, or passive smoking, as a human carcinogen was subsequently challenged by several tobacco companies in a law suit against the EPA, claiming that various sources of bias including publication bias could explain any association claimed by the EPA between ETS and lung cancer.

[22] The death of an estimated 70,000 sea birds, washed up on shores around the North Sea in the winter of 1994, from starvation through severe weather, was newsworthy. But imagine the outcry which would have occurred if they had been killed through industrial pollution.

benefits can be transferred also requires the factual assumptions implicit in CV studies to be tested,[23] and psychological techniques to be applied to help understand the contexts in which individuals express rational choices and values and those in which expressed preferences are subject to biases.

Until a research agenda is developed and undertaken to establish the conditions under which credible benefit transfers can be made, only pragmatism remains: decision-makers are left arguing whether a benefit value is 'tenable', whether they 'feel comfortable' with that value, and whether the value is 'close enough'.

REFERENCES

Adamowicz, W., J. Louviere, and M. Williams (1994), 'Combining revealed and stated preference methods for valuing environmental amenities', *Journal of Environmental Economics and Management* **26**, 271–92.

Anderson, Glen D. and Richard C. Bishop (1986), 'The valuation problem', in Daniel W. Bromley (ed.) *Natural Resource Economics: policy problems and contemporary analysis*, Kluwer, Boston, pp. 89–137.

Arrow, K., R. Solow, P.R. Portney, E.E. Leamer, R. Radner, and H. Schuman (1993), 'Report of the NOAA Panel on contingent valuation', Report to the National Oceanic and Atmospheric Administration. *Federal Register,* **58**, *No. 10* Friday 15th January 1993.

Asian Development Bank (1996), 'Economic evaluation of environmental impacts. a workbook. Parts I and II', Chapter 4: Secondary Valuation Methods: Benefit Transfer; and Appendix 1: 'Using per-capita GDP to adjust values', Asian Development Bank, Manila.

Bal, Frans and Peter Nijkamp (1997), 'In Search of Valid Results in a Complex Economic Environment: The Potential of Meta-Analysis and Value Transfer', Working Paper, Department of Spatial Economics, Vrije Universiteit, Amsterdam, The Netherlands.

Bateman, Ian J., K.G. Willis, G.D. Garrod (1994), 'Consistency between contingent valuation estimates: a comparison of two studies of UK National Parks', *Regional Studies* **28**, 457–74.

Bateman, Ian J., Julii S. Brainard and Andrew A. Lovett (1995), 'Modelling woodland recreation demand using geographical information systems: a benefit transfer study', CSERGE Working Paper GEC 95-06, CSERGE, University of East Anglia, Norwich.

Bishop, R.C. and T.A. Heberlein (1986), 'Does contingent valuation work?' in R.G. Cummings, D.S. Brookshire and W.D. Schulze (eds) *Valuing Environmental Goods: A State of the Arts Assessment of the Contingent Valuation Method*, Rowman and Allanheld, Totowa, N.J. Ch. 9 123–47.

---

[23] For example, the extent to which individuals care only about the size of a wildlife population, rather than how many were in the original population, at risk, or saved.

Boyle, Kevin J. and John C. Bergstrom (1992), 'Benefit transfer studies: myths, pragmatism, and idealism', *Water Resources Research* **28** (3), 657–63.

Brahams, D. (1985), 'Doctor's duty to inform patient of substantial or special risks when offering treatment', *The Lancet*, March 2nd, 528–30.

Brookshire, D.S. and H.R. Neill (1992), 'Benefit transfers: conceptual and empirical issues, *Water Resources Research* **28**, 651–55.

Button, Kenneth and Peter Nijkamp (1997), 'Environmental policy assessment and the usefulness of meta-analysis, *Socio-Economic Planning Sciences* **31** (3), 231–40.

Cheung, W.H.S., K.C.K. Chang, R.P.S. Hung and J.W.L. Kleevens (1990), 'Health effects of beach water pollution in Hong Kong', *Epidemiological Infection* **105**, 139–62.

Clawson, M. and J. Knetsch (1966), *Economics of Outdoor Recreation*, John Hopkins Press for Resources for the Future, Baltimore.

Commission on the Third London Airport (1970), *Papers and Proceedings Vol. 111 (Parts 1 and 2) — Stage 111 Research and Investigation — Assessment of Short-Listed Sites*, HMSO, London.

Cummings R.G., D.S. Brookshire. and W.D. Schulze (eds) (1986*), Valuing Environmental Goods: An Assessment of the Contingent Valuation Method*, Rowman and Allanhed, Totowa, NJ.

Dawes, R.M. and B. Corrigan (1974), 'Linear models in decision making', *Psychological Bulletin* **81**, 95–106.

Dawes, R.M., D. Faust, and P. Meehl (1989), 'Clinical vs. actuarial judgement', *Science* **243**, 1668–73.

de Dombal, F.T. (1984), 'Computer-aided diagnosis of acute abdominal pain: the British experience', *Revue d'Épidémiologie et de Santé Publique* **32**, 50–56.

Dickie, Mark, Ann Fisher and Shelby Gerking (1987) 'Market transactions and hypothetical demand data: a comparative study', *Journal of the American Statistical Association* **82**, 69-75.

Dodgson, J.S. and N. Topham (1990), 'Valuing residential properties with a hedonic price method: a comparison with results of professional valuations', *Housing Studies* **5**, 209–13.

Donnelly, D.S. and C. Price (1984), *The Clawson Method and Site Substitution: Hypothesis and Model*, Department of Forestry, University College of North Wales, Bangor.

Downing, Mark and Teofilo Ozuna (1996), 'Testing the reliability of the benefit function transfer approach', *Journal of Environmental Economics and Management* **30**, 316–22.

Dwyer, J.F., J.R. Kelly, and M.D. Bowes (1977), *Improved Procedures for Valuation of the Contribution of Recreation to National Economic Development*, Report UILU-WRC-77-0128, Water Resource Centre, University of Illinois at Urbana-Champaign.

Espey, Molly (1996), 'Explaining the variation in elasticity estimates of gasoline demand in the United States: A Meta-Analysis', *The Energy Journal* **17** (3), 49–60.

Fischhoff, B., P. Slovic and S. Lichtenstein (1980), 'Knowing what you want: measuring labile values', in David E. Bell, Howard Raiffa and Amos Tversky (eds) (1988), *Decision Making: descriptive, normative, and prescriptive interactions*, Cambridge University Press, Cambridge, pp. 398–421.

Fischhoff, Baruch and Ruth Beyth-Marom (1983), 'Hypothesis evaluation from a Bayesian perspective', *Psychological Review* **90**, 239–60.

Fleisher, Jay M. (1990), 'The effects of measurement error on previously reported mathematical relationships between indicator organism density and swimming associated illness: a quantitative estimate of the resulting bias', *International Journal of Epidemiology* **19**, 1100–6.

Fleisher, J.M., F. Jones, D. Kay, R. Stanwell-Smith, M. Wyer, and R. Morano (1993), 'Water and non-water related risk factors for gastro-enteritis among bathers exposed to sewage contaminated marine waters', *International Journal of Epidemiology* **22**, 698–708.

Gibson, J.G. (1974), 'Recreation cost-benefit analysis: a review of English case studies', *Planning Outlook, Special Issue Panning for Recreation 1974*, pp. 28–46.

Givens, G.H., D.D. Smith and R.L. Tweedie (1997), 'Publication bias in meta analysis: a Bayesian data-augmentation approach to account for issues exemplified in the passive smoking debate', *Statistical Science* 12 (4), 221-50.

Gregory, R., S. Lichtenstein and P. Slovic (1993), 'Valuing environmental resources: a constructive approach', *Journal of Risk and Uncertainty* **7**, 177–97.

Grigalunas, T.A. and J.J. Opaluch (1988), 'Assessing liability for damages under CERCLA: a new approach for providing incentives for pollution avoidance', *Natural Resources Journal* **28**, 509–33.

Hanemann, W. Michael (1984), 'Welfare evaluations in contingent valuation experiments with discrete responses', *American Journal of Agricultural Economics* **66**, 332–41.

Hanemann, W.M. (1994), *Contingent Valuation in Economics*, Draft paper, Department of Agricultural and Resource Economics, University of California, Berkeley, CA.

H.M. Treasury (1991), *Economic Appraisal in Central Government: a technical guide for government departments*, HMSO, London. (see Annex B, page 48).

Irwin, Julie R., Paul Slovic, Sarah Lichtenstein and Gary H. McClelland (1993), 'Preference reversals and the measurement of environmental values', *Journal of Risk and* Uncertainty **6**, 5–18.

Jones-Lee, M.W. (1990), 'Preference Reversals: A Comment', Personal communication.

Jones-Lee, M.W. and G. Loomes (1994), 'Towards a willingness-to-pay based value of underground safety', *Journal of Transport Economics and Policy* **28**, 83–98.

Kay, D., J.M. Fleisher, R.L. Salmon, F. Jones, M.D. Wyer, A.F. Godfree, Z. Zelenauch-Jacquotte and R. Shore (1994), 'Predicting likelihood of gastro-enteritis from sea bathing: results from randomised exposure', *The Lancet* **344**, 905–9.

Kirchhoff, Stefanie, Bonnie G. Colby and Jeffrey T. LaFrance (1997), 'Evaluating the performance of benefit transfer: a empirical inquiry', *Journal of Environmental Economics and Management* **33**, 75–93.

Kling, C.L. (1988), 'The reliability of estimates of environmental benefits from recreation demand models', *American Journal of Agricultural Economics* **70**, 892–901.

Lewis, R.C. and M.C. Whitby (1972), 'Recreation Benefits from a Reservoir', *Research Monograph No. 2*, Agricultural Adjustment Unit, Department of Agricultural Economics, University of Newcastle upon Tyne.

Loewenstein, George, and Richard H. Thaler (1989), 'Intertemporal choice', *Journal of Economic Perspectives* **3** (4), 181–93.

Loomis, J.B. (1992), 'The evaluation of a more rigorous approach to benefit transfer: benefit function transfer', *Water Resources Research* **28**, 701–5.

Loomis, John B. and Richard G. Walsh (1997), *Recreation Economic Decisions: Comparing Benefits and Costs*, Venture Publishing Inc., State College, Pennsylvania.

McConnell, K.E. (1992), 'Model building and judgement: implications for benefit transfers with travel cost models', *Water Resources Research* **28**, 695–700.

McGoogan, E. (1984), 'The autopsy and clinical diagnosis', *Journal of the Royal College of Physicians of London* **18**, 240–43.

Mansfield, N.W. (1971), 'The estimation of benefits from recreation sites and the provision of a new recreation facility', *Regional Studies* **5**, 55–69.

Nijkamp, Peter and Gerard Pepping (1998), 'Meta-analysis for explaining the variance in public transport demand elasticities in Europe', *Journal of Transportation and Statistics* **1**, 1–14.

Pearce, D.W. and J.J. Warford (1993), *World Without End*, Oxford University Press, Oxford.

Renwick, I.G.H., W.P. Butt and B. Steel (1991), 'How well can radiographers triage X-ray films in accident and emergency departments', *The Radiographer* **38** (3), 112–14.

Santos, José (1997), *Valuation and Cost-Benefit Analysis of Multi-attribute Environmental Changes: Upland Agricultural Landscapes in England and Portugal*, PhD thesis, Department of Town and Country Planning, University of Newcastle, Newcastle upon Tyne.

Schwartz, R. and A. Grubb (1985), 'Why Britain can't afford informed consent', *Hasting Centre Report* **15**, 19–25.

Slovic, P. and S. Lichtenstein (1983), 'Preference reversals: a broader perspective', *American Economic Review* **73**, 596–605.

Smith, V.K. (1988), 'Selection and recreation demand', *American Journal of Agricultural Economics* **70**, 29–36.

Smith, V. K., W.D. Desvouges, and A. Fisher (1986), 'A comparison of direct and indirect methods for estimating environmental benefits', *American Journal of Agricultural Economics* **68**, 280–90.

Smith, V.K. and Y. Kaoru (1990), 'Signals or noise? Explaining the variation in recreation benefit estimates', *American Journal of Agricultural Economics* **72**, 419–41.

Smith, V. Kerry and Ju-Chin Huang (1995), 'Can markets value air quality?: a meta-analysis of hedonic price models', *Journal of Political Economy* **103**, 209–27.

Tversky, A. and D. Kahneman (1974), 'Judgement under uncertainty: heuristics and biases', *Science* **185**, 1124–31.

Tversky, Amos, and Richard H. Thaler (1990), 'Anomalies: preference reversals', *Journal of Economic Perspectives* **4** (2), 201–11.

Van Houtven, George and Maureen L. Cropper (1996), 'When is a life too costly to save? the evidence for U.S. government environmental regulations', *Journal of Environmental Economics and Management* **30**, 348–68.

Viscusi, W.K., W.A. Magat and J. Huber (1986), 'Information regulation of consumer health risks: an empirical evaluation of hazard warnings', *Rand Journal of Economics* **17**, 351–65.

Viscusi, W. Kip (1993), 'The value of risks to life and health', *Journal of Economic Literature* **31**, 1912–46.

Walsh, Richard.G. (1986), *Recreation Economic Decisions: Comparing Benefits and Costs*, Venture Publishing Inc., State College, Pennsylvania.

Walsh, R.G., D.M. Johnson and J.R. McKean (1989), 'Issues in nonmarket valuation and policy application: a retrospective glance', *Western Journal of Agricultural Economics* **14**, 178–88.

Ward, Kevin M. and John W. Duffield (1992), *Natural Resource Damages: Law and Economics*, J. Wiley, New York.

Whittington, D., J. Briscoe, X. Mu and W. Barron (1990), 'Estimating the willingness to pay for water services in developing countries: a case study of the use of contingent valuation surveys in Southern Haiti', *Economic Development and Cultural Change* **38**, 293–312.

Willis, K.G. and G.D. Garrod (1991), 'An individual travel-cost method of evaluating forest recreation', *Journal of Agricultural Economics* **42**, 33–42.

Willis, K.G. and Richard K. Hardy (1995), 'Environmental management decisions: a paramorphic analysis of planning permission for mineral development', *Journal of Environmental Management* **43**, 249–64.

13. Policy Implications and Conclusions

The World is not Conclusion
A species stands beyond —
Invisible, as Music —
But positive, as Sound —
It beckons, and it baffles —
Philosophy — don't know —
And through a Riddle, at the last —
Sagacity, must go —

Emily Dickinson (1830–86): *The World is not Conclusion*

1 INTRODUCTION

Environmental values are used in policy and project appraisal in a variety of ways. The explicit valuation of a statistical life saved has been an integral part of economic appraisal of road transport projects for many years. But environmental values are less routinely incorporated into policy and project appraisal in a systematic way. Environmental changes tend to be assessed through Environmental Impact Assessment in the USA and the European Union (since these are statutory requirements for land-use planning decisions on major projects); rather than through the estimation of changes in environmental values and cost-benefit analysis (CBA). Environmental valuation of use and non-use values is explicitly and systematically employed by the Environmental Protection Agency (EPA) in the USA, under CERCLA, 1980, and various other Acts. It is also used on occasion by The World Bank, and various other development organisations, and a number of European Union governments. Applications range from an often superficial use of valuation techniques (as, for example, in the case studies of developing country projects reviewed by Abelson, 1996); to extremely detailed applications and methodological developments of techniques (see for example, Choe *et al.*, 1996 and Lauria *et al.*, 1998).

2 INTUITIVE VALUES

There are many instances where the environmental impacts of projects are only described or enumerated in physical terms, with no monetary values being attached to them. This leaves the decision-maker with the unenviable task of trying to judge whether the welfare gains from the project will outweigh the ensuing environmental degradation. Clearly it is important that environmental impacts are valued in monetary terms in order that they are given due and proper weight in the decision-making process.

An example of the intuitive assessment of environmental values occurs in the CBA procedure adopted in assessing new road schemes by the Department of Environment, Transport and the Regions in the UK. Their CBA procedure is merely a costs and operational benefits assessment (COBA) and falls short of a full CBA. Table 13.1 documents the different ways in which costs and benefits are assessed in a COBA analysis. Operating costs and benefits are monetarised, but environmental impacts are either quantified in physical terms, or merely documented descriptively. The non-monetarisation of such environmental impacts may mean that they are either under-valued or over-valued in the intuitive decision-making process. Under-valuation will occur in a COBA appraisal when environmental benefits are not given due weight in the decision-making process because they are not expressed in monetary terms. Conversely, environmental benefits may be over-valued if environmental and ecological considerations are given too much weight by decision-makers when balancing the unquantified or intangible disbenefits caused by a road scheme against the quantified net benefits (time savings plus fuel and non-fuel vehicle operating costs, plus accident savings minus construction costs) estimated in a COBA. With the advances in the development and application of contingent valuation and stated preference techniques documented in earlier chapters of this book, there is no reason why the environmental impact (in terms of noise, visual impact, air pollution, recreation, heritage, wildlife, landscape preservation, severance, etc.) of road schemes, cannot be valued in monetary terms. The application of such techniques would also permit a variety of traffic management proposals to be valued for the purposes of comparison (Willis *et al.,* 1998). These techniques can be applied to both users and to non-users to obtain both use and non-use values for the amenity attributes of each alternative traffic management option in an area.

Table 13.1: Enumeration and method of evaluation of items in COBA

Items which are monetarised		Items which are not monetarised		Items which are omitted
item	*method*	*item*	*method*	*item*
capital	market prices	noise	quantified (distance or dBA bands)	planning blight
land	market prices*	visual obstruction	quantified (expert analysis)	night time noise
compensation	market prices*	visual intrusion	descriptive	climate change impacts
maintenance	market prices	air pollution	quantified or unassessed	
vehicle operating	market prices	recreation	quantified (area, quality)	
time savings	RP and EP WTP+	built heritage	descriptive	
accident reductions	CV and SG WTP+	severance	descriptive / qualitative	
		ecology	descriptive / qualitative	
		pedestrian/ cyclists	descriptive	
		disruption during construction	descriptive / qualitative	

Note: COBA uses a 'resource cost' basis for its calculations. Resource costs are obtained by adjusting market prices to exclude indirect taxation and transfers.
* Debate regarding the appropriateness of market prices for this item.
+ Large variance relative to mean value from case studies/data; and or variance in value estimate depending on technique used.
RP = revealed preference; EP = expressed preference; CV = contingent valuation; SG = standard gamble; WTP = willingness to pay.

Source: Bateman, *et al.* (1993)

Many studies have revealed the inconsistency of intuitive decision-making, compared with a more structured approach (see, for example, Sox *et al.*, 1988 and de Dombal, 1984 in medicine; Dawes, 1980 for university admissions; and Meehl, 1986 in clinical psychology). Although on occasion policy-capturing studies have also revealed non-discrimination in human judgement (see Maniscalo *et al.*, 1980). *Ex post* assessments of the implementation of water resource projects in the USA have also revealed distributions of benefits between income and ethnic groups inconsistent with *ex ante* government policy (Weisbrod, 1968). Hence the study of *ex post* decisions may neither be very useful in guiding decisions on future environmental policies and projects; nor in revealing anything about *ex ante* intentions. The numerous cognitive psychological biases in intuitive decisions render rational choice problematic. As President John F. Kennedy once observed 'The essence of ultimate decisions remains impenetrable to the observer — often, indeed to the decider himself...There will always be dark and tangled stretches in the decision making process — mysterious even to those who may be most intimately involved'.

3 INFORMAL, AD HOC INCLUSION

A review of environmental valuation studies in different European countries revealed that studies were undertaken spasmodically, with varying degrees of influence on decisions, and with marked variation between countries (Navrud, 1992). Despite its small size, Switzerland has produced a number of studies of academic and scientific note; with travel-cost methods (TCMs), hedonic price methods (HPMs) and contingent valuation methods (CVMs) all being applied, and researchers receiving funds from a variety of institutions (Römer and Pommerehne, 1992). Studies in Germany have been proportionately fewer and more policy orientated. In the UK a switch of emphasis occurred in the 1990s away from TCMs, to HPMs and CVMs. However, this was largely a product of the type of environmental goods being valued.[1] In the Netherlands, whilst academic interest in environmental economics is strong, valuation only forms a small fraction of this research, and demand for valuation studies by government and other organisations is low (Hoevenagel *et al.*, 1992). In Norway benefit estimation studies have provided support for environmental decision-making, but have not played a crucial role in the process. Nevertheless, there is increasing interest in benefit estimation within the Norwegian government as a means of developing practical tools for evaluating environmental effects (Navrud and Strand, 1992).

In the UK, the Department of the Environment (1991) advocated the systematic application of benefit estimation techniques in economic appraisal. Following this, many studies were commissioned by the UK government on a range of topics (including the externalities of fuel cycles, radon emissions,

---

[1] TCMs were used in the 1970s and 1980s to value recreation facilities by various organisations including the Forestry Commission (see Grayson *et al.*, 1975; and Willis and Benson, 1989). In the late 1980s and 1990s, an emerging interest in valuing other environmental goods, not amenable to TCM measurement, led to more HPM and particularly more CVM studies.

landfill and incineration waste disposal sites, and the benefits of biodiversity, forest recreation and amenity). Most of these studies have been publicly documented (Department of the Environment, 1994). However, no indication is provided about how these studies have been used in decision-making.

It is clear that benefit estimation techniques are not applied to every project or policy in the UK. Evidence suggests that even when environmental valuation is applied it is applied in an *ad hoc* and unsystematic manner often a procedure not conducive to consistent decision-making and economic efficiency. Nevertheless, environmental valuation studies have shaped the outcome of some projects in the UK.

One example was a study of low flow alleviation (LFA) along the River Darent in Kent. A CVM study estimated the use benefits to residents and visitors (recreationalists) of both maintaining existing flow levels and improving flows to an environmentally acceptable flow regime (EAFR). The study also estimated the non-use value of LFA to the rest of the general public. Estimates of the benefits and costs of LFA were forwarded by the National Rivers Authority (NRA), who wished to undertake low flow remedial measures, to the Department of the Environment (DoE) and to H.M. Treasury for financial authorisation to undertake the engineering works required. The public exchequer cost of the project, i.e. NRA expenditure, was £5 million for a pipeline to pump water into the Darent from disused mineral workings some 20 miles away, and an additional £1 million for drilling boreholes to pump water into the Darent from the underlying aquifer and for remedial work to the river bed to prevent leakage back into the underlying chalk. Use values to residents and visitors clearly justified maintaining existing flows rather than allowing further reductions through increased water abstraction. However, use values gave a B/C ratio close to 1.0 for increasing the flow to an EAFR, which would be achieved by the construction of a pipeline. The inclusion of non-use values would have resulted in benefits exceeding costs by a whole order of magnitude for the EAFR option. However, DoE did not sanction capital expenditure of £5 million on the pipeline for the EAFR, but did authorise the other remedial works (boreholes and bed lining). One can only speculate on the reasons for this decision. Anecdotal evidence suggests DoE and H.M. Treasury are sceptical about non-use values, and the entire engineering works could only be justified with confidence if non-use values were included (Garrod and Willis, 1996). Thus, DoE seems to have accepted the findings of the study, but to have based its decision on minimising public expenditure (a government policy at the time), and ignoring benefits to non-users.

The existing limited use of environmental values in decision-making derives from a number of factors: scepticism towards environmental valuation methods; lack of environmental economists within government agencies; absence of a formal legal requirement to undertake a CBA of projects or policies;[2] uncritical acceptance of other methods such as effect on production, dose response, and opportunity cost approaches; suspicion of non-use values; distorted perceptions of the valuation methods by non-economists; and the large variance associated with mean WTP and WTA values. This last phenomenon leads to suspicions that CVMs are unreliable, rather than the acceptance that differences in people's incomes, preferences, and availability of substitutes will result in large variances, especially for goods which are relatively unimportant in Maslow's hierarchy of needs (see Kleindorfer *et al.*, 1993), and whose consumption is not systematic and occupies only a tiny fraction of most people's expenditure.

Both the Asian Development Bank and The World Bank advocate the use of valuation methods to estimate the welfare effects of environmental changes. Indeed, significant methodological improvements to contingent valuation methods have been made by World Bank staff whilst appraising particular projects and policies with these techniques (see for example, Whittington *et al.*, 1992; Choe *et al.*, 1998). However, it is difficult to gauge to what extent environmental valuation methods have become formally institutionalised into the decision-making processes of these organisations.

4 FORMAL INSTITUTIONAL INCLUSION

In some cases the environmental valuation process is formalised and fairly explicit, and institutionally incorporated into the decision-making process. Thus, for example, the explicit inclusion of environmental values occurs in US Forest Service applications of unit day values of recreational opportunities and resources. Environmental values are also explicitly included in Type A assessments of natural resource damages from pollution spills under CERCLA legislation. Economic damages are calculated from an economic data base in which injuries and losses to particular species of fish, water fowl, etc. are measured as reductions in harvesting or in recreational use values. For major pollution incidents a Type B assessment under CERCLA requires a site-specific investigation. US Department of Interior (DOI) regulations provide a range of authorised methods for estimating lost use and non-use values. Where a reasonably competitive market exists for a resource, market price is used to estimate economic damages. If market prices are not appropriate, appraisal can be based on Uniform Appraisal Standards for Federal Land Acquisition. Where neither of these approaches is appropriate, environmental valuation methodologies are adopted. Specific methodologies listed comprise TCM, HPM, unit values, CVM, and stated

---

[2] Although the Environment Act, 1995 (section 39) in the UK, states that the Environment Agency will 'take into account the likely costs and benefits of the exercise or non-exercise of (any) power', this need not necessarily be a formal nor rigorous exercise.

preference (SP) techniques. All techniques can be employed to estimate use values, but only expressed preference techniques such as CVM and SP can be used to measure non-use values. DOI generally assume that market based and revealed preference methodologies are more reliable for use values than expressed preferences methods and also that use values can be more reliably measured by CVMs than non-use values.

In Britain several manuals have been produced by government to provide technical guidance and detail on how to value various environmental benefits, in terms of both 'desk-top valuation' and by fieldwork and surveys. The Foundation for Water Research (1994) manual on assessing the benefits of river water quality improvements is lengthy and highly specific in terms of methodology and the procedures it recommends. It also details the questionnaires to be used in estimating the benefits of water quality improvements in rivers to the various user groups and in terms of informal recreation, drinking water, general environmental value, and replacement cost. In contrast the MAFF (1993) manual on project appraisal guidance for flood and coastal defence is much more concise and readable. It outlines the principles by which various environmental gains and losses can be valued, and stresses the need to account for the probability of floods and also the importance of undertaking sensitivity analysis. Anecdotal evidence suggests that the MAFF manual is regularly used to appraise investment in defences against coastal erosion and flooding. The value of water quality improvements seems to be assessed on a more *ad hoc* basis, with the UK Environment Agency seeking to meet specified targets for improving bathing water quality, river water quality, and low flows in rivers, rather than using environmental valuation or other systematic approaches to judge the efficiency of investment in these activities.

The desire to establish formal benefit transfer values by various governments and agencies, and the advocacy of the use of benefit transfer by organisations such as the Asian Development Bank (1996) suggests that, in time, environmental valuation methods may become more institutionalised, and environmental values more routinely included in the cost-benefit analysis of projects.

5 CLARITY AND COMPLEXITY

Environmental impact assessment (EIA), which simply quantifies and describes the physical impact of projects and policies, is institutionalised in law in the European Union (EU) and the USA as the method for appraising the environmental consequences of major projects. EIA documents the complexity of environmental issues, but does not add much clarity in the sense that the decision-maker has little knowledge of how these environmental changes affect the utility of individuals. Decision-making involves weighing up the probability that an environmental loss will occur, or be averted, if some action is taken; against the likely utility changes to individuals in society. By contrast environmental valuation attempts to determine the 'true' value of environmental resources to society, and hence to assess whether or not they should be preserved. Environmental decision-making by government seeks to produce an authoritative finality by inducing the public to defer to its verdict or that of a public inquiry. In other words, one of the main aims of this type of decision-making is not only to take the 'correct' decision in terms of economic efficiency, but also the legitimisation of the resolution of the environmental dispute. A precise estimate of the value of natural resource damage might destroy the basis for deference and legitimisation of a particular decision. In the legal system, it is argued, people defer to the court's decision because of the existence of evidence which introduces complexity and ambiguity, thereby preventing the adoption of mechanistic Bayesian statistical rules for guilty or innocent verdicts.

'so long as evidence prevents specific quantification of the degree of that uncertainty, an outside observer has no reasonable choice but to defer to the jury's verdict' (Nesson, 1979).

Thus an absence of monetary values for the environment and the resulting uncertainty can function as social lubricants: society can accept the decision so long as it doesn't know what values are placed on the different aspects of the case. It also leaves developers free to apply for planning permission again, if the initial decision is not in their favour, on the grounds that some condition has changed. Environmental pressure groups can continue campaigning too, on the grounds that not all relevant values were included in the original study. The partial or non-monetary assessment of environmental values also leaves the decision-maker with more discretion and power as to what to do about the problem than would occur with environmental valuation. Thus a cynical view would be that environmental valuation does not have a formal role in the decision process precisely on the grounds that it would remove vagueness and ambiguity!

6 INSTITUTIONAL CAPTURE

Environmental values can justifiably be estimated for use in the *ex ante* appraisals of projects and policies and also estimated *ex post* to evaluate existing environmental policies. However, as with the application of any technique, environmental valuation methods can be applied in particular ways to an environmental issue so as to produce the values and answers that politicians and decision-makers require in playing various strategic games.

This practice was noted by Bowers (1988) in a review of the application of CBA to appraise the feasibility of land drainage projects. Agricultural outputs from drained land were based upon theoretically possible 'best practice' yields, and valued at market prices without modification to these prices to account for subsidies from the European Common Agricultural Policy (CAP). The result was too much land being drained; greatly reducing the supply of wetland habitats. This inadequate CBA procedure could be seen as an attempt by an EU national government to exploit the provisions of the CAP for its own advantage, with the Ministry of Agriculture, Fisheries and Food (MAFF) attempting to shift the balance between expenditure and receipts under the CAP in Britain's favour by promoting the growth of agricultural output, in this instance through land drainage. Such a common agricultural policy, with decisions on structural adjustments left to national discretion, is a classic prisoner's dilemma problem. Institutional capture has also been noted in EIA, where firms apply these techniques in a manner most conducive to producing a favourable outcome to themselves in a planning application for a land-use change or for development permission.

Environmental valuation methods have been employed *ex post* to evaluate policies already in existence; and, in a less scientifically objective way, to justify the continuance of existing policies. Of course, justifiable *ex post* applications of environmental valuation occur under CERCLA legislation, to assess natural resource damages due to pollution incidents, where techniques are applied objectively and using best practice. What should not be acceptable is the application of environmental valuation methods in such a way as to maximise benefits in order to justify a policy;[3] or to minimise the estimated externality values of a project in order to secure its approval.[4]

Many environmental valuation studies are commissioned by organisations seeking to promote a particular cause. Researchers are subject to pressures to produce environmental values which are favourable, or at least not detrimental to the organisation. This is a perennial problem with contract research and consultancy activities, and is not likely to enhance environmental valuation and environmental economics as a discipline. It may also be one reason why some environmental values are inapplicable for benefit transfer, and why meta-analysis fails to explain some of the variance in environmental values between studies.

---

[3] E.g. by deliberately using DC instead of open-ended CV questions; ignoring embedding problems etc. to maximise benefits.

[4] E.g. by using WTP instead of WTA, ignoring non-use values, adopting a low starting point in a bidding game, assuming a general equilibrium framework where the respondent is required to simultaneously pay to preserve everything he cares about from his fixed budget by using a top down method to disaggregate a total WTP amount (see Kemp and Maxwell, 1993), etc.

7 PROSPECTIVE ISSUES

Most applications of environmental valuation methods, have employed parametric approaches to parameter estimation. The formulation of these models has usually involved an additive linear structure, with a restrictive assumption about the distribution of the error term or unobservable element in the random utility model. However, the increasingly ubiquitous application of CVM and probabilistic choice models in the last two decades of the 20th century has been paralleled by an econometric search for more robust estimators of indirect utility functions, with less restrictive and simpler assumptions than those of conventional parametric models. The next two decades will see an increasing use of these semi- and non-parametric methods in parameter estimation, and the use of more flexible functional forms, which are more robust to distributional mis-specifications. Since estimated welfare changes depend on assumptions about individual preferences and the shape of the utility function; as well as on the goodness of fit of the econometric model, with even minor distributional mis-specifications causing variations in WTP estimates, these issues in utility maximisation are likely to continue to command the attention of environmental economists.

Eliciting accurate observations on people's values of environmental attributes through contingent valuation and choice experiments underpins the subsequent econometric analysis. Psychologists have made a substantial contribution to identifying the need to correctly define the good to be valued; the importance of framing and context in decisions and values; and the difficulty of making coherent trade-offs between objectives and goods with a multi-dimensional nature. Psychologists have also pointed out that differences (aleatory and epistemic) between experimenters' and respondents' interpretations and assumptions about which strategies are appropriate for choice experiments, and differences between the motivational aspects of experimental and applied settings affect the performance and generalisability of results. Thus Beach *et al.* (1986) argued that both experimenters' and respondents' repertories, task interpretations, and motivation to be accurate must be taken into account in interpreting the results of choice studies. Economists typically observe and analyse outcomes of choice experiments, and try to infer processes from these outcomes on the basis of assumptions. However, it is seldom possible to infer process, repertories, interpretations and motivations, from *ex post* analyses of outcomes. Much more research effort needs to be devoted to systematising experimenters' and respondents' repertory, selection, motivation, and implementation strategies as an integral part of choice experiments. Failure to do so will mean that research results remain equivocal that conflicting results will continue to fuel controversy and inhibit real understanding in environmental valuation. Insights from behavioural decision theory and decision pathway surveys (see Gregory *et al.*, 1997) might then reveal how values are determined and the reasoning process behind the construction of expressed preferences.

Environmental values vary in space, but environmental valuation research tends to be aspatial in character: independent studies determine values of a good at different points in space, with meta-analysis seeking to determine why these WTP values vary and benefit transfer assessing whether the value from one area can be transferred to another. There is scope in environmental valuation for research into spatial variations in value estimates, as distinct from merely replicating valuation studies at different points in space. For example, HPMs traditionally estimate the value of environmental attributes across space, ignoring the fact that environmental attributes, and other housing characteristics, vary between neighbourhoods, within landscape types, and within housing-market areas. Cross-sectional regression models, ignoring this hierarchy in the data and its effect on error terms, can produce inaccurate coefficient estimates. By focusing attention on levels in the hierarchy, a greater understanding might be achieved of how, where and why environmental values vary. Spatial statisticians have also developed other new and innovative techniques to analyse variations in geographical data. These geographically-weighted regression models are also likely to be increasingly applied to investigate the extent to which coefficients and values attached to environmental characteristics are non-stationary over space.

There is a danger that research in environmental valuation will seek to improve accuracy and robustness in explanations of phenomena only by making its existing methodologies more sophisticated and esoteric. Whilst the increasing sophistication of environmental valuation techniques is to be welcomed, this does not obviate the requirement to search for other appropriate techniques to analyse environmental values. There are other perspectives in the economic literature which might be applied to environmental problems. For example, the area of interactive epistemology, asymmetric information, and the influence of common knowledge in determining preferences, outcomes, and values (see Geanakoplos, 1992) for particular environmental goods. Bayesian perspectives and game theory might also be used to account for whether, and to what extent, the actions of others are instrumental in the decision-making of individuals in respect different environmental problems. For example, to what extent do respondents regard an initial bid as a piece of information to update their priors, and by how much; and to what extent does pooling of knowledge and new information affect respondent's values pre-and post-focus group events? Multiattribute utility theory (MAUT) might also be helpful in specifying the conditions under which numbers can be attached to values and provide an easier set of cognitive demands than the holistic measures of monetary values elicited in most CV studies (Gregory *et al.*, 1993). Experimental economics (see Smith,

1994) could also provide a useful research tool to investigate a number of environmental economic issues. There are many such challenging new areas waiting to be developed in environmental valuation.

Such new developments in environmental valuation — the search for more accurate and robust semi- and non-parametric estimators, improved understanding of the psychology by which environmental values are formulated and decisions made, the analysis of the non-stationarity of environmental values, and the application of additional theories and techniques from other branches of economics — will not only provide a rich research vein, but also appeal to policy-makers searching for some 'holy grail' out of which to take appropriate values to assign to non-market goods in cost-benefit analyses of environmental projects and policies.

REFERENCES

Abelson, Peter (1996), *Project Appraisal and Valuation of the Environment: general principles and six case studies in developing countries*, Macmillan, London.

Asian Development Bank (1996), *Economic Evaluation of Environmental Impacts: a work book: parts 1 and 2*, Asian Development Bank, Manila.

Bateman, Ian J., R. Kerry Turner and Seeseana Bateman (1993), *Extending cost-benefit analysis of UK highway proposals: environmental evaluation and equity*, CSERGE Working Paper PA 93-05, Centre for Social and Economic Research on the Global Environment, University of East Anglia, Norwich.

Beach, Lee Roy, Valerie E. Barnes, and Jay J.J. Christensen-Szalanski (1986), 'Beyond heuristics and biases: a contingency model of judgmental forecasting', *Journal of Forecasting*, **5**, 143–57.

Bowers, John K. (1988), 'Cost-benefit analysis in theory and practice: agricultural land drainage projects', in R. Kerry Turner (ed.), *Sustainable Environmental Management: principles and practice*, Belhaven, London.

Choe, Kyeong A., Dale Whittington and Donald T. Lauria (1996), 'The economic benefits of surface water quality benefits in developing countries: a case of Davao, Philippines', *Land Economics* **72**, 519-37.

Choe, Kyeong A., William R. Park and Dale Whittington (1998), 'A Monte Carlo comparison of OLS estimation errors and design efficiencies in a two-stage stratified random sampling procedure for contingent valuation studies', in I.J. Bateman and K.G. Willis (eds), *Contingent Valuation and Environmental Preferences*, Oxford University Press, Oxford.

Dawes, Robyn M. (1980), 'You can't systematise human judgement: dyslexia', *New Directions for Methodology of Social and Behavioural Science*, **4**, 67–87.

Department of the Environment (1991), *Policy Appraisal and the Environment:A Guide for Government Departments*, HMSO, London.

Department of the Environment (1994), *Environmental Appraisal in Government Departments*, HMSO, London.

de Dombal, F.T. (1984), 'Computer-aided diagnosis of acute abdominal pain: the British experience', *Revue d' Épidémiologie et de Santé Publique*, **32**, 50–56.

Foundation for Water Research (1994*), Assessing the Benefits of River Water Quality Improvements: Manual*, FWR, Marlow, Buckinghamshire.

Garrod, G.D. and K.G. Willis (1996), 'Estimating the benefits of environmental enhancement: a case study of the River Darent', *Journal of Environmental Planning and Management,* **39**, 189–203.

Geanakoplos, John (1992), 'Common Knowledge', *Journal of Economic Perspectives,* **6 (4)**, 53–82.

Grayson, Arnold J., R.M. Siddaway and F.P. Thompson (1975), 'Some aspects of recreation planning in the Forestry Commission', in G.A.C. Searle (ed.), *Recreational Economics and Analysis*, Longman, London.

Gregory, Robin, Sarah Lichtenstein and Paul Slovic (1993), 'Valuing environmental resources: a constructive approach', *Journal of Risk and Uncertainty,* **7**, 177–97.

Gregory, Robin, James Flynn, Stephen M. Johnson, Theresa A. Satterfield, Paul Slovic and Robert Wagner (1997), 'Decision pathway surveys: a tool for resource managers', *Land Economics,* **73 (2)**, 240–54.

Hoevenagel, Ruud, Onno Kuik, and Frans Oosterhuis (1992), 'The Netherlands', in Ståle Navrud (ed.), *Pricing the European Environment*, Scandinavian University Press, Oslo.

Kemp, Michael A. and Christopher Maxwell (1993), 'Exploring a budget context for contingent valuation estimates', in J.A. Hausman (ed.*), Contingent Valuation: a critical assessment*, North-Holland, Amsterdam.

Kleindorfer, Paul R., Howard C. Kunreuther and Paul J.H. Schoemaker (1993), *Decision Sciences: an integrative perspective*, Cambridge University Press, Cambridge.

Lauria, Donald T., Dale Whittington, Kyeonge A. Choe, Cynthia Turigan and Virginia Abiad (1998) Household demand for improved sanitation services: a case study of of Calamba, the Philippines, in I.J. Bateman and K.G. Willis (eds) *Contingent Valuation and Environmental Preferences: assessing theory and practice in the USA, Europe, and Developing Countries.*

Maniscalo, Charles I., Michael E. Doherty and Douglas G. Ullman (1980), 'Assessing discrimination: an application of social judgement technology', *Journal of Applied Psychology,* **65 (3)**, 284–8.

Meehl, Paul E. (1986), 'Causes and effects of my disturbing little book', *Journal of Personality Assessment,* **50 (3)**, 370–5.

Ministry of Agriculture, Fisheries and Food (MAFF) (1993), *Flood and Coastal Defence: Project Appraisal Guidance Notes*, MAFF, London.

Navrud, Ståle (1992), *Pricing the European Environment*, Scandinavian University Press, Oslo.

Navrud, Ståle and Jon Strand (1992), 'Norway', in Ståle Navrud (ed.*), Pricing the European Environment*, Scandinavian University Press, Oslo.

Nesson, C.R. (1979), 'Reasonable doubt and permissive inferences: the value of complexity', *Harvard Law Review,* **92**, 1187–225.

Römer, Anselm U. and Werner W. Pommerehne (1992), 'Germany and Switzerland', in Ståle Navrud (ed.), *Pricing the European Environment*, Scandinavian University Press, Oslo.

Smith, Vernon L. (1994) 'Economics in the laboratory', *Journal of Economic Perspectives* **8** (1), 113-31.

Sox, Harold C., Marshal A. Blatt, Michael C. Higgins, and Keith I. Marton (1988), *Medical Decision Making*, Butterworths, Boston.

Weisbrod, B. (1968), 'Income redistribution effects and benefit-cost analysis', in S.B. Chase (ed.), *Problems in Public Expenditure Analysis*, Brookings Institution, Washington DC and Allen and Unwin, London.

Whittington, D., V.K. Smith, A. Okorafor, A. Okore, J.L. Liu and A. McPhail (1992), 'Giving respondents time to think in contingent valuation studies: a developing country application', *Journal of Environmental Economics and Management*, 22, 205–25.

Willis, K.G. and J.F. Benson (1989), 'Recreational values of forests', *Forestry*, 62 (2), 93–110.

Willis, K.G., G.D. Garrod, and D.R. Harvey (1998), 'A review of cost-benefit analysis as Applied to the evaluation of new road proposals in the UK', *Transportation Research Part D: Transport and Environment* 3, 141-56.

Index

Abelson, P. 32, 91, 359
ACORN 104
Adamowicz, W.L. 65, 127, 130, 203-204, 207, 209, 211, 293, 295-296, 300, 305-310, 345
Adams, R.M. 24, 25
Agriculture Act (1986) 22
air pollution 5, 25-27, 34-38, 43, 256-258, 333, 349-350
aircraft noise 100
Alaska 8, 141
Alberini, A. 190, 201-202
Alberta 306-309
Alonso, W. 87
ambivalence 198
Anderson, G.D. 338
Anderson, L.M. 96
angling 305-309
Arizona 344
Arkes, H.R. 161-162
Arrow, K.J. 134, 137, 150, 164, 188, 197, 230, 345
Asian Development Bank 332, 365
Australia 168, 265
averting behaviour 7, 42-46, 91
Aylen, J. 73

Balkan, E. 60, 228
Banford, N. 127
Barnet, A.H. 154, 183
barns 245-246, 251-255
Bartik, T.J. 47, 88
Bateman, I.J. 57, 59, 71-72, 135, 144, 152, 157, 339, 348, 361
Batsell, R.R. 206
Bayes theorem 160-161, 346, 352, 366

Beach, L.R. 368
Beggs, S. 212-213, 273
Bell, F.W. 232
Ben-Akiva, M. 215
benefit transfer 12, 331-353
Benson, J.F. 43, 70-71, 362
bequest value 10
Bergland, O. 156-157, 260
Bergstrom, J.C. 132, 340-341
Beyth-Marom, R. 346
bias
    availability 162-163, 336, 339
    embedding 163-166, 235, 257, 345-346,
    strategic 127-128, 153-154, 185
    design 153-159
    endowment effect 127
    starting point 155, 336
    framing 156-157
    payment vehicle 157
    information 159-160
    representativeness 160-162, 336
biodiversity 142, 263-288
pharmaceutical values of 267-269
Bishop, R.C. 72, 74-75, 127, 143, 145, 188, 195, 200, 338, 342
Bockstael, N.E. 67, 72, 228, 232
Bohm, P. 144
Bojo, J. 71, 77
Bolivia 265
bootstrapping 336
Bowers, J.K. 367
Bowes, M. 58, 79
Bowker, J.M. 188, 194-195
Box, G. 111-112, 315
Box-Cox functions 111-112, 315
Boyle, K.J. 155, 190-191, 194, 340-341

Brahms, D. 333
Brewer, D. 69, 77-78
British Columbia 270
British Waterways 312-318
Brookshire, D.S. 96, 127, 143, 334
Brown, D. 25
Brown, G.M. 79, 97, 127
Brown, H. 107
Brown, J.N. 93
Brown, Lancelot 'Capability' 240
Brown, R.L. 116
Brown, W.G. 63, 78
Browning, E.K. 32
Burt, O.R. 96-98
Butler, R. 105
Button, K. 41, 352

California 10, 25, 45 242, 256
Cameron, T.A. 72, 197, 201, 251
Canada 44-45, 59, 100-101, 163-165
canals 41, 65-66, 173, 312-318
card sorts 204
Carolina 132
Carrier, J.G. 24
Carson, R.T. 9, 68, 138-139, 143, 151-152, 169, 189, 228, 231, 257
Cassel, R. 112-113, 315
castles 149-150
Cattin, P. 204
Caulkins, P.P. 77
CERCLA 7, 12, 27, 39, 41, 45, 50-54, 141, 332, 342, 364, 367
Cesario, F.J. 72
Chapman, R.G. 212
Cheshire, P.C. 33, 69
Chestnut, L.G. 25
Cheung, W.H.S. 334
Choe, K.A. 360, 364

choice experiments 8-9, 203-211, 295-309, 345, 368
    analysis 208-210
    attribute screening 206-207
    experimental design 207-208
    history 204
    independence of irrelevant alternatives property 209
    profiles 204-205
    welfare measures 210-211
Christensen, J.B. 70, 77
Cicchetti, C.J. 69, 77
Clanton, C.H. 161
Clark, D.E. 101
Clawson, M. 55, 56
Clean Air Act (1970) 37
Coase, R.H. 19, 36
COBA 360-361
Cobb, S. 105
Collins, N.M. 266
Colorado 39, 99, 256, 258
command-and-control mechanisms 4
Common Agricultural Policy 30, 32, 367
common knowledge 369
Common, M. 65, 70, 72
commons 18, 20, 245
compensation 23-24, 126
compulsory purchase 22, 127-128
congestion 17-18, 21, 78
conjoint analysis 204
Conservation Reserve Programme (US) 28-29
consumer theory 87-88, 204, 216
contingent ranking 211-216, 250, 260, 273-282
contingent valuation (see also bias, referendum CVM and validity of CVM) 8, 74, 152-182, 291, 314-318, 340-347, 348-349, 364

aggregating bids 141
closed-ended format 134
context effects 158-160
elicitation formats 134-136
hypothetical markets 132, 143
iterative bidding 135
means bids 139-140
median bids 139-140
modified estimators 140
open-ended format 134
payment card 136
scale effects 158
scope effects 158-159
trimmed estimators 140
convergence 130-131
Cooper, J.C. 189-191
Cordell, H.K. 96
Correll, M.R. 99
Corrigan, B. 336
Cortens, I. 33
Cosslett, S.R. 195
cost-benefit analysis 360, 363, 367
cost-effective priority investment index 271
Costa Rica 232, 265
count data models 233
Countryside Stewardship Scheme 267
Coursey, D.L. 127, 130
Cox, C. 111-112, 315
Cranbrook, Earl of 266
Creel, M. 195
Crocker, T.D. 26, 258
Cropper, M.L. 37-38, 95, 102, 113-114, 333
Crowards, T. 34
Cummings, R.G. 146, 163, 231, 342

Danielson, L.E. 99
Darling, A.H. 98

David, E.L. 68
Davis, D.D. 198
Davis, R.K. 74,
Dawes, R.M. 161, 336, 361
de Dombal, F.T. 336, 361
debt-for-nature swaps 264-266
decision making 361-366
deer hunting 147
Deming, W.E. 153
Department of Environment 41, 360, 362-363
Department of the Interior (US) 41, 364
depletable externalities 20-21
Desvouges, W.H. 61, 71, 74-78, 158, 195, 197, 212, 215
developing countries 118
dichotomous choice questions 188-189, 250-251, 343
Dickie, M. 146, 342
Dillman, B.L. 132
Dinan, T.M. 112, 315
discount rate 28, 258
discrete choice contingent valuation 188-203
disequilibrium labour market model 72-73
Dixon, J.A. 32
Dobbs, I.M. 62
Dodgeson, J.S. 103, 335
dose response approach 5, 22, 25, 33-38
double-bounded referendum contingent valuation 201-203
Downing, M. 342-343, 351
Dragun, A.K. 282
Drake, L. 168
Dubin, R.A. 107
Duffield, J.W. 27, 196-197
Dwyer, J.F. 338

ecological doom 3
economic efficiency 40-41, 225
Ecuador 265, 269
Eddy, D.M. 161-162
Edwards, D.S. 266
effect on production approach 5, 21-27, 37
effective protection rates 29-31
Einhorn, H.J. 161
electro-magnetic fields 44-45
Elnagheeb, A.H. 190-191
embedding effects 163-166, 235, 257, 345-346
eminent domain 22, 127-128
Endangered Species Act 1973 (USA) 18, 269-270
England 5, 43-44, 67, 70-71, 96, 98, 100, 239-241, 243-256, 318, 323, 348, 362
Englin, J. 72, 79
Environment Agency 105, 290-305, 364
Environmental Impact Assessment 12-13, 365
Environmental Protection Agency (USA) 37-38, 115-116, 352, 359
Environmental Resources management 303
Environmentally Sensitive Areas Scheme 5, 22-24, 167, 245-246, 250-256, 348
epidemiology 44
Epple, D. 94
Ervin, D.E. 99
Espey, M. 350
Ethiopia 166
Evans, A. 103
ex ante 258, 341, 362
ex post 341, 362, 367
existence values 10, 291
expert judgement 314-318, 334-336

Faith, D.P. 282
false positives 148, 161, 336
Farber, S. 24, 57, 75
Feather, P. 233
Feitelson, E. 108-109
Fischhoff, B. 346-347
Fishbein, M. 143
Fisher, A.C. 28, 78, 158, 197
fishing 52, 54, 233, 339, 349
fishing quotas 267
Fleischer, J.M. 334
flood defence 365
Flores, N.E. 169
Florida 26, 232
Flowerdew, A.D.J. 126
focus groups 133-134, 274, 292
foliar injury models 25
Follain, J.R. 94, 105
forest access index 324-326
forest design 272-273, 285-289
forestry 10, 24, 63-65, 70-71, 96-97, 157, 225-226, 234-235, 242, 271, 323-325, 334, 339, 362, 364
Forestry Commission (UK) 70, 105, 272-282
Forrest, D. 101
Foster, V. 212, 215-216, 260
Foundation for Water Research 365
France 78
Frech, H.E. 98
free market 31
Freeman, A.M. 56, 73, 78, 88, 90, 91, 95, 102, 108
Frey, B.S. 131
Friedman, M. 141
Friends of the Earth 289

Gainsborough, Thomas 241
garden design 239-240

Garrod, G.D. 63, 65, 70, 72, 76-77, 96-98, 105, 116, 133, 137-138, 152, 168, 200, 212, 229, 242, 248, 271-282, 296, 312-327, 338, 363
gasoline 350
GAUSS 252
Geanakoplos, J. 369
genius loci 241
Geographic information systems 57-59, 71, 80, 104-105, 322, 324-327
Georgia 96
Germany 362
Ghana 118
Gibson, J.G. 76, 338
Gillingham, R. 105
Givens, G.H. 352
Global Environmental Facility 264-266
Goodman, A.C. 112
goose hunting 72, 74, 145
Grand Canyon 256-257
Graves, P. 113-114
Grayson, A.J. 362
grazing livestock units 23
green belt 33, 98-99, 174-175
Green, P.E. 204
Greene, W.M. 209, 278
Greenpeace 289
Gregory, R. 45, 345, 369
Grigalunas, T.A. 332
Griliches, Z. 91
Grubb, A. 332
Gujarati, D.N. 279
Gum, R.L. 78
Gurland, J. 212

Haab, T.C. 196
Haiti 336
Hale, J. 239
Hall, J. 32

Halvorsen, R. 98
Hammack, J. 127
Hammes, B.D. 99
Hanemann, W.M. 68, 128-129, 158, 191-192, 194-195, 197, 210-211, 300, 341-343
Hanley, N.D. 28, 57, 64-65, 70, 79, 131, 159
Hardy, R. 345
Harrison, D. 88,
Harrison, G.W. 146
Harvey, D.R. 32, 169
health effects 34-38, 44-45
Heberlein, T. 72, 74-75, 127, 147, 188, 195, 342
hedonic price method 7-8, 87-118, 150, 242-243, 312-328, 348-349, 364
   agricultural land values 99
   air pollution 99-100, 108
   choice of functional form 110-114, 315-316
   data requirements 102-105
   environmental protection 98
   environmental risk 96
   estimation 115-117
   first-stage model 91-93
   landscape 96-98, 318-323
   measurement error 106-107
   multicollinearity 107-109
   noise 100-101
   second-stage model 93-95
   simultaneity problem 94
   social factors 101
   submarkets 109-110
   urban amenity 98
   water frontage 313-318
   water quality 96-98
   woodland access 323-327
hedonic travel-cost method 79
hedonic wage method 8, 101-102
Hellerstein, D. 72-73

Herriges, J. 135, 202
heuristics 336
Hicksian surplus 46, 128-130, 140, 166, 343
HM Treasury 332
Hoehn, J.P. 12, 164-167, 252, 255, 257
Hoevenagel, R. 159, 362
Hoffman, J.V. 101
Holmes, T.P. 189, 202
Holt, C.A. 137, 198
Horowitz, J.L. 91, 195
Hotelling, H. 55
household production functions 55
Huang, J-C. 349
Hufschmidt, M.M. 58
human capital approach 33-38
hunting 145, 349

income effect 128
income elasticity 128-130, 169-173
independence of alternative attributes property 68, 306
independent valuation and summation 166-167, 255, 257, 341, 344
India 265
individual travel-cost method 59-66, 79, 226-232, 338-339, 348-349
compared with zonal method 63-64
functional specification 61-62, 64-66
interpretation 62
sample selection effects 79-80
truncation problem 61-62, 79
information effects 159-160
institutional capture 366
Irwin, J.R. 347
Italy 234-235, 239

Jakobsson, K.M. 157, 282
James, M.D. 201
Jimenez, E. 94
Johannson, P-O. 73, 78
Johnson, R. 103, 111
Johnson, S.P. 263
Johnson, W.R. 32
Jones, A.B. 234
Jones-Lee, M.W. 36, 155, 158, 333, 347
Jordan, J.L. 190-191
Jud, G.D. 93, 101, 103, 107

Kahn, J.R. 60, 101, 228
Kahneman, D. 127-128, 155-156, 160, 163, 165, 248, 336
Kamboj, R.D. 265
Kanninen, B.J. 191-192, 194-195, 201
Kaoru, R.J. 79
Kasserman, D.L. 103, 111
Kawai, M. 112
Kay, D. 334
Kealy, M.J. 200, 233
Kemp, M.A. 163, 367
Kennedy, C.E.J. 272
Kenya 32, 133
Kerala State 146-148
Kirchhoff, S. 343-344, 351
Kirschner, D. 97
Kleindorfer, P.R. 364
Klepper, S. 108
Kleppner, D. 197
Kling, C.L. 61, 78, 338
Knetsch, J.L. 55, 56, 72, 74, 127, 163, 165, 336
Knowles, S. 33
Kohlhase, J.E. 115-116
Kopp, R.J. 58
Kramer, R.A. 189, 202
Kripple, J. 24
Kriström, B. 195, 216

Kroes, E.P. 204
Krutilla, J.V. 24, 28, 78-79

labile responses 346
laboratory experiment 128
Lafferty, R.N. 98
Lancaster, K.J. 7, 87, 160, 204
Land Compensation Act (1961) 22
Land Compensation Act (1973) 22
land-use planning 33, 241-242
Langford, I.H. 195, 201
Lareau, T.J. 213-215, 250
Larsen, O.I. 101
Lauria, D.T. 360
Leamer, E.E. 108
Leeworthy, V.R. 232
legal decisions 366
Leonard, G.K. 190
Lewington, P. 138
Lewis, R.C. 337
Li, C-Z. 195, 198, 202
Li, M. 107
liability 27, 39
Lichtenstein, S. 162, 347
lighthouses 19
LIMDEP 209, 252, 268
Lindahl equilibrium 154, 183, 266
linear programming 25
Linneman, P. 94, 105
Lockwood, M. 72
Loewenstein, G. 258
logit models 153, 193-195, 208-209, 212, 215, 251-252
London Underground 158
Loomes, G. 333
Loomis, J.B. 58, 170-172, 189, 195, 334, 337, 339
Louisiana 57, 75
Louviere, J.J. 203-204, 206-207
low flow alleviation 363

Luce, R.D. 212
LULU 131

MacLennan, D. 91
Madagascar 232, 265, 268-269
Maddala, G.S. 61, 65, 107, 325
Magnussen, K. 168
Maine 74, 340
Majid, I. 164, 168
Malaysia 226-231
Maniscalo, C.I. 362
Mansfield, N.W. 338
Markandya, A. 88-91, 99, 106, 127
market failure 264
Martin, W.E. 78
Maryland 109
Massachusetts 67, 96, 101, 110
Mattsson, L. 198, 202
Maxwell, C. 163
McConnell, K.E. 72-73, 87, 196, 338-339
McDonald, J. 105
McFadden, D. 68, 188, 190, 193, 195, 208, 216, 279
McGoogan, E. 336
McInernry, J. 29
McKean, J.R. 72-73, 75-76, 227, 256
McKelvey, R. 212
Meehl, P.E. 361
Mendelsohn, R. 50, 72-73, 79, 112-113, 232, 315
meta analysis 151, 347-351, 369
Metrick, A. 269
Michaels, R.G. 103, 109-100, 116-117
Mieszkowski, P. 101
Mill, John Stuart 19
Mill, J.W. 99
Miller, R. 113
Minnesota 78, 233

Miranowski, J.A. 99, 112, 315
Missouri 69
Mitchell, R.C. 129, 138-139, 143,
    152, 228, 257
mitigating expenditure 42-47
Montana 78, 158
Monte Carlo simulations 191
Montgomery, C.A. 267, 270
Moore, D. 97
Morales, D.J. 96
Moran, D. 264, 271, 282
Morey, E.R. 232
Morris, M.G. 266
Mosteller, F. 65, 116
Mourato, S. 212, 215-216, 260
Mueller, D.C. 33, 40, 140, 249
multi-attribute utility theory 345,
    369
multi-criteria analysis 282-283
Munch, P. 22
Munda, G. 282
Munroe, A. 159

Nash equilibrium 266
National Parks and Access to the
    Countryside Act (1949) 243
National Rivers Authority 363
natural resource damage 39, 50-54
Navrud, S. 362
Nawas, F. 78
negligence 333
Neill, H.R. 148, 200, 334
Nelson, J.P. 72, 93, 100, 106
Nesson, C.R. 366
Netherlands 362
New Caledonia 270
New Jersey 127
New Mexico 75, 344
New York 45
Newfoundland 20
Nicholson, W. 154
Nijkamp, P. 282, 350-352

Nitrogen Sensitive Areas 22
NOAA 134, 137, 150, 164, 188,
    230, 332
NOMIS 104, 314
non-use values 10-11, 32, 271,
    291, 347, 363
Nonneman, W. 1997
North Borneo 271
North Carolina 99, 103
North Dakota 158
Norway 101, 168, 362

O'Riordan, T. 247-248
Ohio 100
Oil Pollution Act (1990) (US) 46
Ontario 163-166
Opaluch, J.J 332
opportunity cost method 5, 9, 17-
    21, 225, 241-242, 246
option values 10, 27-33
ordered probit 212
Oregon 156, 258, 339
Ouwersloot, H. 204, 210
Ozuna, T. 195, 343, 351

Palmquist, R.B. 99, 115
Pareto criterion 18, 23
parks 164
Parks, P.J. 29
Parliamentary constituency class
    104
Parsons, G.R. 76
path dependency 165, 167-168,
    255, 341
Patterson, D.R. 196-197
Pearce, D.W. 34, 41, 88-90, 99,
    106, 127, 264-265, 267, 336
Pearse, P.H. 59
Peltzman, S. 43
Pennsylvania 75, 127
Pepping, G. 350
Perrings, C. 267

policy capturing 336, 361
Polinsky, A.M. 95
Pollakowski, H.O. 98
Porter, P. 28
Portugal 168
posted-offer markets 198, 200
Poulton, E.C. 156
Powe, N.A. 106, 108, 149, 150, 323-325
predictive value positive 148, 161
preference uncertainty 197-200
preventative expenditure approach 7, 246
Prewitt, R.A. 55
price elasticity 170-173, 350
price flexibility of income 128-130, 169-170
Price, C. 65, 77, 243, 259, 312, 323, 339
prisoner's dilemma 265
probit analysis 38, 146, 153, 234
procedural invariance 347
producer subsidy equivalents 29-31
property rights 3, 5, 17, 21, 26, 126-127, 175, 225, 241, 246
prospect theory 128-129
public goods 9, 18-21, 225

Quiggin, J. 201
Quigley, J.M. 88, 94

Rae, D.A. 212-215, 250, 258
Ramsey, N. 197
Randall, A. 128, 159, 164-166, 255, 257
random utility theory 66-68, 77, 188, 204, 213, 216, 228, 233
Rao, P. 113
Rasmussen, D.W. 112
Ratcliffe, P.R. 272
Ready, R.C. 136, 199-200, 202

real economic commitments 148-150
real estate agents 102-103, 316-318, 335
referendum contingent valuation method 9, 130, 135, 152, 187-203, 300, 250-251, 295, 342
    anchoring bias 190
    bid design 189-192
    comparison with open-ended format 200
    estimating WTP from referendum CVM data 196-197
    follow-up questions 201-203
    modelling referendum CVM data 192-196
    non-parametric estimators 195-196
    preference uncertainty 197-200
    question format 188-189
    semi-parametric estimators 195
Renwick, I.G.H. 336
repeat sales model 50-51
replacement cost technique 7, 39-42, 52
Rietveld, P. 204, 210
risk 162-163, 333
river flows 290-305
rivers 168, 363
rivet hypothesis 263
road traffic noise 101
Rodriguez, F. 126
Roe, B. 203
Römer, A.U. 362
Rosen, H. 93
Rosen, S. 88, 91-92, 110, 112
Rosenthal, L. 103
rough set analysis 350
Rowe, R.D. 155
Royal Society for the Protection of Birds (UK) 43-44

Rubinfield, D.L. 88
Ruffell, R. 79

Sadler, H. 28
safe minimum standards 267
sample selection bias 138, 228-229, 231-232
sample size 138-139, 227
Samples, K.C. 159
Samuelson, W. 128, 248
Santos, J.M.L. 167-168, 250-256-257, 341, 351
Saper, A.M. 101
SAS 208
Saunders, C.M. 31
Scarpa, R. 195
Schafer, R. 101
Schnare, A.B. 109
Schorr, J.P. 29
Schulze, W.D. 198, 200-201, 257
Schuman, H. 190, 198
Schwartz, J. 34
Schwartz, R. 333
Scotland 10-11, 65, 172, 259
Sellar, C. 151, 188, 200
sequential valuation 167-168, 255, 341
Shavell, S. 95
Shaw, T. 127
Shaw, W.D. 73, 232
Sheldon, R.J. 204
Sheppard, S. 33
Sherman, P.B. 32
Shogren, J.F. 135, 202, 258
Shonkwiler, R. 72,
Shucksmith, D.M 241
Simpson, R. 267-271
simultaneous valuation 167-168
Sinden, J.A. 58, 127
Singh, H.S. 265
Sites of Special Scientific Interest 32, 42, 271, 348

Slovic, P. 163, 347
Smith, M. 25
Smith, V.K. 58, 61, 65-66, 71, 77-79, 103, 109-110, 116-117, 163-164, 338, 342, 349
Smith, V.L. 153, 370
social opportunity cost 29-32
South Carolina 132
Southwood, T.R.E. 272
Sox, H.C. 261, 361
Spash, C.L. 26, 131
spatial equilibrium model of the city 87
SPSS 208
Sri Lanka 269
Srinivasen, V. 204
Stabler, M.J. 69
Staelin, R. 212
standard reference gamble 259
Stankey, G.H. 78
stated preference (see choice experiments)
status quo bias 296
Stevenson, G.G. 18
Stoll, J.R. 128-129, 188, 194-195
stone walls 245, 251-255
Strand, I. 72, 362
Strong, E. 58
Struyk, R.J. 109
substitutes 228, 338-339, 341, 344
substitution effect 128-130, 251
Sung, C-H. 107
Suppes, P. 212
Swanson, T.M. 265
Sweden 168, 202
Switzerland 18, 131, 362

Tennessee 103
Texas 45, 158, 342
Thaler, R.H. 260, 346-347
Thayer, M.A. 75
Thurstone, L.L. 188, 204, 208

Tobias, D. 232
Tolley, G.S. 257
Topham, N. 103
Tracy, K. 72
trade-off matrices 204
transfer-price method 204
travel cost methods (see also individual travel-cost methods, validity of travel-cost methods, and zonal-travel cost methods) 7, 55-81, 138, 150, 151, 173, 225-246, 348-349, 364
    applications 73-76
    car running costs 70-71
    central assumptions 76
    functional form 64-66
    historical sites 73
    hunting 74-75
    landscape value 75-76
    multi-purpose trips 68-70
    National Parks 75-76
    opportunity cost of time 70-73
    sample selection effects 79-80
    separabilty 68-70
    treatment of substitute sites 77-78
        wetlands 75
Trice, A.H. 55
true positive rate 148, 161
Tukey, J.W. 65, 116
Turner R. 240
Turner R.K. 5,
Turner, R.W. 200
Tversky A. 127, 155-156, 160, 248, 336, 347
Type A assessment 332

undepletable externalities 21
unit day values 52, 334-335
United Kingdom 30, 103, 135, 200, 264, 272-282, 289, 312, 348, 365

United States of America 12-13, 28, 35, 44, 66-67, 69, 74, 115-116, 141, 148, 164, 212, 241-242, 260, 268, 364
US Fish and Wildlife Service 271
Utah 78
utility scaling 259

validity of contingent valuation 141-153
    construct 150-153
    content 142-143
    convergent 150-151, 342
    criterion 143-150, 342
    theoretical 152-153
validity of the travel-cost method
    statistical 228
    convergent 230-231
value of a statistical life 35-38, 158, 333, 347
value of small change in risk 155, 332
value of travel time 227, 338
van der Linden, J.W. 159
van Houtven, G. 37-38, 333
verbal protocols 346
Vickrey auctions 130, 148-149, 200
Viscusi, W.K. 38, 333, 346
visibility 75-76, 258
von Winterfeld, D. 44

Wabe, J.S. 98
Wales 67, 339
Walsh, R.G. 137, 170, 172, 334, 348
Ward, F.A. 72-73
Ward, K.M. 27, 332
Wardman, M. 204
Warford, J.J. 267, 336
Washington DC 100

water quality 26, 154, 157, 183-185, 233, 333-334, 365
water supply 337
waterfowl 43, 158, 332, 341
Watkinson, A.R. 263-264
Watts, J.M. 93, 101, 103, 107
Webb, N.R. 267
Weisbrod, B.A. 242, 362
Weitzman, M.L. 263, 269
wetlands 43-44, 75
Whitby, M.C. 33, 174, 337
Whitehead J.C. 136
Whittington D. 32, 135, 336, 364
Wilderness Act (1964) (US) 241
Wildlife and Countryside Act (1981) 5, 18, 22, 24
Wildlife Enhancement Scheme 267
Willig, R.G. 128, 150
Willis, K.G. 23, 24, 28, 31 33, 41, 57, 63, 65, 70-72, 76-77, 96-98, 105, 116, 138, 149, 152, 168, 173-174, 200, 212, 228, 248, 249, 266-267, 271-282, 296, 312-327, 338, 345, 360, 362
Wilman, E.A. 71
Wilson, R.A. 33
Winch, D.M. 17
Winger, D. 75-76

Winpenny, J.T. 32
Wisconsin 145-147
Wittink, D.R. 204
Wolfe, F.M. 162
Wood, S.E. 55
Woodland Grant Scheme 246
Woodworth, G.G. 207
World Bank 146-148, 336, 359, 364
Worrell, A.C. 58
WTA 126-131, 174, 335
WTP 125-174
Wynne, G.M. 267
Wyoming 78

Yandle, B. 154

Zambia 265
Zavoina, W. 212
Zeckhauser, R. 128, 248
Ziemer, R. 65
zonal travel-cost method 56-59, 63-64, 77, 336-337, 349
    comparison with ITCM 63-64
    functional specification 64-66
    zonal choice 58-59
Zuehlke, T.W. 112